Microsoft® Azure™ SQL Database Step by Step

Leonard G. Lobel
Eric D. Boyd

PUBLISHED BY
Microsoft Press
A Division of Microsoft Corporation
One Microsoft Way
Redmond, Washington 98052-6399

Library of Congress Control Number: 2014940679
ISBN: 978-0-7356-7942-9

Printed and bound in the United States of America.

First Printing

Microsoft Press books are available through booksellers and distributors worldwide. If you need support related to this book, email Microsoft Press Book Support at mspinput@microsoft.com. Please tell us what you think of this book at http://aka.ms/tellpress.

Acquisitions Editor: Devon Musgrave
Project Editor: Rosemary Caperton
Editorial Production: Waypoint Press, www.waypointpress.com
Technical Reviewer: Scott Klein; Technical Review services provided by Content Master, a member of CM Group, Ltd.
Copyeditor: Roger LeBlanc
Indexer: Christina Yeager
Cover: Twist Creative • Seattle and Joel Panchot

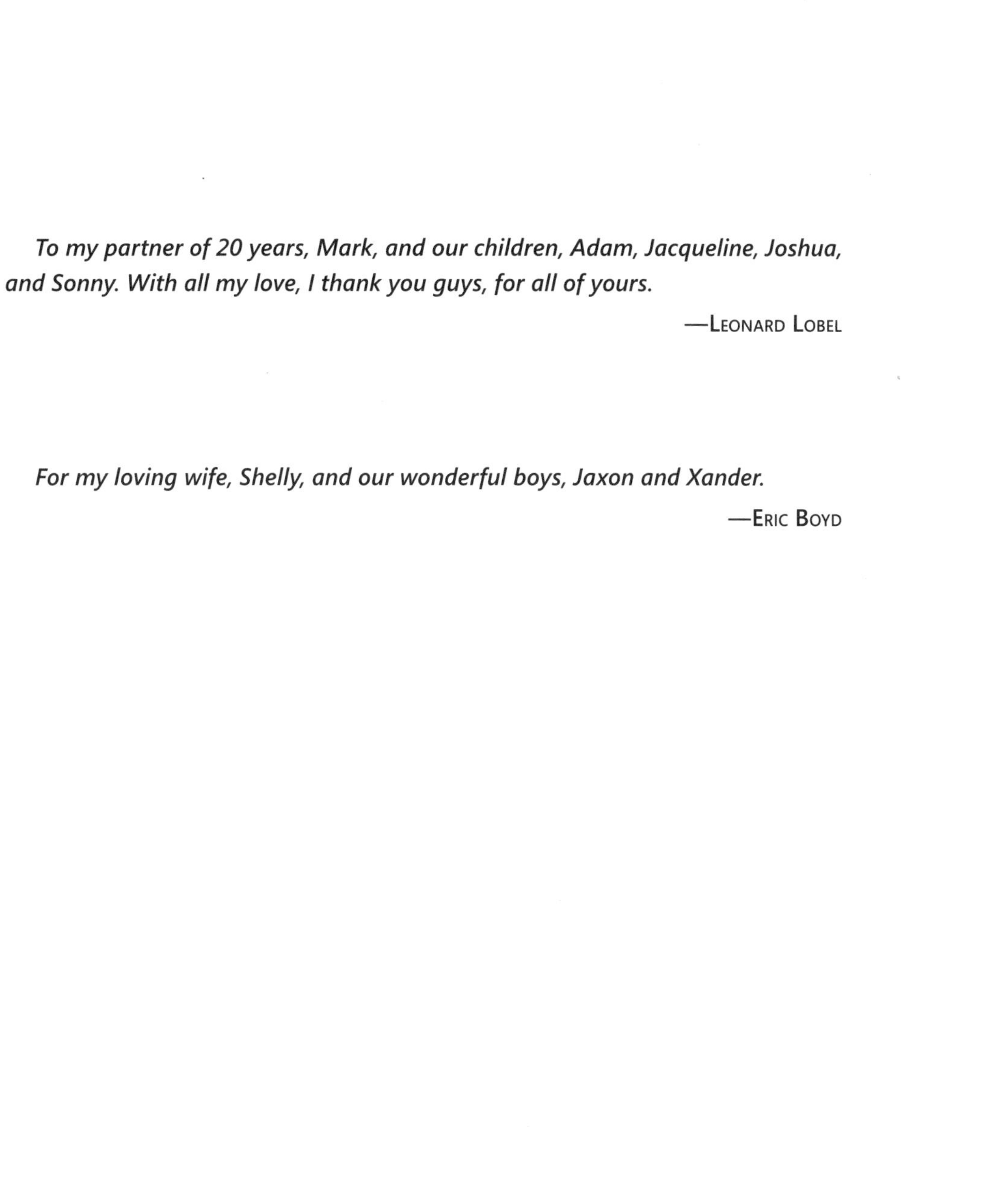

To my partner of 20 years, Mark, and our children, Adam, Jacqueline, Joshua, and Sonny. With all my love, I thank you guys, for all of yours.

—Leonard Lobel

For my loving wife, Shelly, and our wonderful boys, Jaxon and Xander.

—Eric Boyd

Contents at a glance

	Introduction	*xiii*
CHAPTER 1	Getting started with Microsoft Azure SQL Database	1
CHAPTER 2	Configuration and pricing	31
CHAPTER 3	Differences between SQL Server and Microsoft Azure SQL Database	57
CHAPTER 4	Migrating databases	63
CHAPTER 5	Security and backup	97
CHAPTER 6	Cloud reporting	123
CHAPTER 7	Microsoft Azure SQL Data Sync	173
CHAPTER 8	Designing and tuning for scalability and high performance	217
CHAPTER 9	Monitoring and management	261
CHAPTER 10	Building cloud solutions	289
	Index	*357*

Contents

Introduction . . . . *xiii*

Chapter 1 Getting started with Microsoft Azure SQL Database 1

Cloud computing: The concept 1

Instant dynamic provisioning. 2

The Microsoft Azure cloud. 2

Getting signed up for SQL Database. 5

Creating a Microsoft account. 5

Creating a Microsoft Azure subscription 7

Creating a server. 8

Creating a SQL Database instance. 13

Using the SQL Database management portal 15

Designing tables and relationships. 17

Inserting data 21

Querying the database 24

Exploring additional portal capabilities. 27

Summary. 30

Chapter 2 Configuration and pricing 31

Using the Microsoft Azure platform management portal. 31

Creating a new database 31

Setting firewall rules 35

Obtaining connection strings 38

Deleting a database. 40

Using SQL Server Management Studio. 40

Connecting to SQL Database. 41

Creating a new database 43

Changing the database edition and maximum size. 44
Deleting a database. 44
Using PowerShell. 44
Installing the Microsoft Azure PowerShell cmdlets 44
Using the PowerShell Integrated Scripting Environment 46
Configuring PowerShell for your Microsoft account 46
Creating a new server 47
Creating a new database 48
Deleting a database. 50
Budgeting for SQL Database. 50
SQL storage. 50
Client bandwidth 51
Backup storage space 51
Backup storage bandwidth. 52
Support 53
Optimizing your costs 54
Configuring the database edition and size .55
Summary. 56

Chapter 3 Differences between SQL Server and Microsoft Azure SQL Database 57

Size limitations. 58
Connection limitations. 58
Unsupported features 59
Summary. 62

Chapter 4 Migrating databases 63

Making the case for data migration 63
Migrating data using Transact-SQL scripts. 64
Setting up a local SQL Server database 64
Creating the T-SQL scripts 67
Generating T-SQL scripts 68
SQL Data-Tier Applications. 70
Creating a Microsoft Azure Storage account 71
Exporting a BACPAC to Microsoft Azure Storage 74
Importing a BACPAC to Microsoft Azure SQL Database. 77

SQL Server Bulk Copy (bcp). 80
Migrating Schema 81
Exporting data 83
Importing data 84
SQL Database Migration Wizard 86
Downloading the tool 87
Migrating a database 88
Summary. 95

Chapter 5 Security and backup 97

Addressing major cloud concerns 97
Security responsibilities of the public cloud vendor 98
Shared security responsibilities 98
Security in Microsoft Azure 99
Securing SQL Database 100
Creating a SQL Database 100
Configuring SQL Database Firewall. 101
Authenticating and authorizing users 105
Backing up SQL Database 112
Copying a database. 112
Monitoring the progress of a database copy operation. 113
Exporting a BACPAC 115
Importing a BACPAC 117
Scheduling BACPAC exports. 120
Summary. 122

Chapter 6 Cloud reporting 123

Creating a SQL Server Reporting services virtual machine 125
Creating the virtual machine from the image gallery 126
Configuring SSRS in the virtual machine 128
Opening firewall access to the report server 130
Creating the sample database 132
Using Report Builder 135
Installing Report Builder 135
Creating a report using Report Builder 137

Using Visual Studio Report Server projects 150
Installing AdventureWorks2012 for SQL Database 152
Installing SSDT Business Intelligence for Visual Studio 2012 154
Creating a report using Visual Studio. 156
Implementing report security. 170
Shutting down the SSRS virtual machine 171
Summary. 171

Chapter 7 Microsoft Azure SQL Data Sync 173

Getting to know SQL Data Sync. 173
Exporting data from SQL Server to SQL Database. 175
Importing data from SQL Database to SQL Server 175
Sharing data between multiple locations 176
Scaling out. 178
Creating the SQL Database 180
Working with SQL Data Sync 182
Creating a sync group 182
Creating sync rules. 188
Running a manual sync. 191
Establishing conflict resolution 196
Creating an automated sync schedule. 200
Creating a local SQL Server database. 202
Creating a sync agent 204
Pitfalls and best practices 215
Summary. 216

Chapter 8 Designing and tuning for scalability and high performance 217

Achieving high performance in the cloud 218
Creating a RESTful web API. 218
Creating the sample database 219
Creating a new solution 221
Creating an ASP.NET Web API project 222
Adding an Entity Framework Code First Web API controller 223
Testing the Wine Web API 228

Adding an ADO.NET Web API controller 230
Testing the Customer Web API 233
Managing SQL Database connections 234
Opening late, closing early 234
Pooling connections 234
Recovering from connection faults 234
Adding the Transient Fault Handling Application Block 235
Using the Transient Fault Handling Application Block with ADO.NET 237
Using the Transient Fault Handling Application Block with Entity Framework 239
Reducing network latency 243
Keeping services close 243
Minimizing round trips 243
Effectively using SQL Database 244
Using the best storage service 244
Optimizing queries 245
Scaling up SQL Database 245
Partitioning data 250
Scaling out with functional partitions 250
Scaling out with shards 251
Summary 260

Chapter 9 Monitoring and management 261

Creating the sample database 261
Monitoring 263
Using the management portal 264
Microsoft Azure Service Dashboard 269
SQL Database management portal 270
Dynamic management views and functions 275
Programming the Service Management REST API 281
Summary 288

Chapter 10 Building cloud solutions **289**

Creating the SQL Database 292
Extending the SQL Database 294
Creating a new solution 294
Creating a SQL Server Database project 295
Setting the target platform 296
Importing from SQL Database into the project 297
Adding a new column to the *Wine* table 300
Deploying the project to Microsoft Azure SQL Database 301
Creating the *Order* table 305
Creating stored procedures for the *Order* table 307
Creating the data access layer 312
Introducing the Entity Data Model 313
Creating the Data Access Layer project 314
Creating an Entity Data Model 315
Creating the website 321
Creating an ASP.NET web application project 321
Referencing the data access layer 323
Creating the user interface 324
Testing the website locally 328
Deploying the website to Microsoft Azure .331
Creating the ASP.NET Web API services 336
Adding a Web API controller 337
Testing the Web API 339
Deploying the Web API 340
Creating the Windows Phone application 341
Installing the Windows Phone SDK 8.0 341
Creating the Windows Phone Project 343
Adding Json.NET 343
Creating the App's main page 344
Testing the Windows Phone application 353

Index *357*

Introduction

Microsoft Azure SQL Database is the cloud version of Microsoft SQL Server, which is Microsoft's well-established on-premises relational database engine platform. Despite some noteworthy differences, SQL Database (the short name for Microsoft Azure SQL Database) is largely compatible with SQL Server, so for the most part, any experience you have working with SQL Server can be directly and immediately applied to SQL Database. If you are a software professional looking to consider the cloud as a platform for the database in your next application, SQL Database can be just the right tool for you. And if you want to get up to speed quickly with this emerging platform, with or without SQL Server experience, this is just the right book for you.

Microsoft Azure SQL Database Step by Step provides an organized walkthrough of the SQL Database platform. Our goal was to produce an end-to-end treatment of SQL Database that balances coverage and depth. In the first chapter, you will quickly create your first SQL Database on Microsoft Azure. By the last chapter, you will create a full multitiered solution in the cloud—including a website and a Windows Phone 8 app—all layered on top of SQL Database. And in every chapter in between, you will explore other facets of SQL Database and many of its orbiting technologies. SQL Database is a huge topic, but we carefully crafted each chapter to tackle one piece at a time, with easy-to-follow procedures that put digestible concepts to immediate applied use. Your knowledge will build in each chapter, as you learn about configuration, migration, security, backup, reporting, and more.

One big difference between on-premises software and cloud services is that the latter can be updated and enhanced much more frequently than the former, given that no installation or customer infrastructure is required in the cloud case. Cloud services are subject to frequent changes in pricing as well. As such, features, limitations, costs, the tooling user interface, or even the branding of Microsoft Azure SQL Database, as described in this book, may have evolved by the time you read it. For example, shortly before going to press, the platform formerly branded as Windows Azure was changed to Microsoft Azure. (Although the book title and textual references were updated accordingly, many screen shots still show the older name, *Windows Azure*.) Regardless of the potential for such changes, the principles and techniques covered throughout this book will help you achieve comfort with and mastery of Microsoft Azure SQL Database.

Note As Azure evolves, we evolve with it. Even as this first edition goes to press, we are busy planning the next edition with expanded coverage of the recently announced Basic, Standard, and Premium editions. These new service tiers (which have limited preview availability at the time of this writing) can support larger and more scalable databases than the current Web and Business editions offer. Our next edition will also be revised for the upcoming release of a new management portal currently being developed by Microsoft.

Who should read this book

This book exists to help software developers and database professionals understand the core concepts of Microsoft Azure SQL Database and its related technologies. Many readers will have little or no prior experience with either SQL Database or SQL Server, and that's perfectly fine. This book starts with square one, and gets you off to a good start even if you have no prior knowledge of SQL Server or relational database concepts.

The book is also useful for those familiar with on-premises SQL Server and are interested in creating new applications to work with SQL Database, or those who would like to migrate existing applications that currently work with on-premises SQL Server to work with SQL Database as well.

Assumptions

No prior knowledge or experience with Microsoft Azure and cloud computing is assumed or required. Furthermore, although experience with Microsoft SQL Server is certainly useful, that too is not required.

Several chapters involve .NET programming. Here, too, prior experience with Microsoft Visual Studio and C# is helpful but not required. The procedures in these chapters include complete code listings, and clear explanations of the code are provided.

This book might not be for you if...

This book might not be for you if you already have extensive knowledge and experience with SQL Database, and are seeking to delve deeper into internals or other specialized focus areas not covered in this book. Still, this book contains useful information even for experienced users. Therefore, we recommend that you take a quick glance at the chapter descriptions in the next section. Doing so should help you quickly determine if there are specific areas of interest we cover that you would like to learn more about.

Organization of this book

This book is composed of ten chapters, each of which focuses on a different aspect of Microsoft Azure SQL Database. Most readers will probably benefit by starting with Chapter 1, but by no means does this book need to be read in any particular order. Read it from start to finish if you want, or jump right in to just those chapters that suit your needs or pique your interests. Either way, you'll find practical guidance and walkthroughs to help get your job done with SQL Database.

- **Chapter 1—Getting started with Microsoft Azure SQL Database** The opening chapter gets you acquainted with the SQL Database platform. After a brief overview of cloud computing with SQL Database, you'll create a Microsoft account (if you don't already have one) and a Microsoft Azure subscription. Then you will learn how to use the Microsoft Azure management portal to create servers and databases. You'll move on to use the SQL Database management portal, where you'll design tables, views, and stored procedures, and then populate and query tables in the database. Absolutely no local tools are required to follow along with the procedures in this chapter; all you need is a web browser and Internet access.

- **Chapter 2—Configuration and pricing** With the basics covered, this chapter explains additional options for configuring SQL Database, beyond the browser-based portals introduced in Chapter 1. You will learn how to connect to SQL Database using familiar local tools, such as SQL Server Management Studio (SSMS) and SQL Server Data Tools (SSDT) inside Visual Studio. You will also learn how to configure and manage SQL Database using PowerShell, by downloading the Microsoft Azure PowerShell cmdlets. The chapter concludes with an explanation of how SQL Database pricing is structured on Microsoft Azure, and it provides tips to help you budget for a SQL Database solution.

- **Chapter 3—Differences between SQL Server and Microsoft Azure SQL Database** Readers with prior SQL Server experience will want to know about the important differences between the on-premises relational engine they are familiar with and the SQL Database implementation on Microsoft Azure. This brief chapter enumerates these differences and explains the rationale behind them. Where possible, we suggest workarounds for SQL Server features that are not supported in SQL Database.
- **Chapter 4—Migrating databases** When building systems on Microsoft Azure, there is often a need to migrate databases from existing on-premises SQL Servers to SQL Database. There are numerous techniques and tools you can use to migrate databases and data to SQL Database. In this chapter, you will learn about and use Transact-SQL scripts, SQL Data-Tier Applications, bulk copy, and the SQL Database Migration Wizard to migrate databases to SQL Database.
- **Chapter 5—Security and backup** Security, availability, and disaster recovery top the list of concerns when customers consider new data centers and public cloud providers. In this chapter, you will learn about security in Microsoft Azure and how to secure your SQL Database with firewall rules, as well as users and permissions. In addition to gaining knowledge about security, you will learn how to handle disaster recovery with SQL Database backup techniques.
- **Chapter 6—Cloud reporting** When you have data in a database, it's only a matter of time before you also have reporting requirements related to that data. And when that database is hosted in the cloud on Microsoft Azure, it's only natural to consider using the Azure cloud to host a reporting solution as well. In this chapter, you will learn how to create an Azure virtual machine (VM) to host SQL Server Reporting Services (SSRS) in the cloud. (No prior SSRS experience is needed.) Once the VM is configured, you will learn how to build SSRS reports using two report authoring tools: Report Builder and SSDT Business Intelligence for Visual Studio. After building and previewing reports locally, you will learn how to deploy them to the VM for a complete reporting solution in the cloud.
- **Chapter 7—Microsoft Azure SQL Data Sync** In this chapter, you will learn how to use the SQL Data Sync service available on Microsoft Azure to replicate data between multiple databases. You will learn about the hub-and-spoke architecture upon which the service is based, and see how SQL Data Sync can be used to implement solutions for a variety of scenarios, including one-way or bi-directional replication across a set of databases in multiple locations. The procedures in this chapter walk you through the process of configuring the SQL Data Sync service and creating sync groups that replicate between multiple databases

hosted both in the cloud (on Microsoft Azure SQL Database) and on-premises (using SQL Server). You will also learn how to establish a conflict-resolution strategy and set up an automated synchronization schedule.

- **Chapter 8—Designing and tuning for scalability and high performance** Applications and systems intended for real production use need to provide responsive experiences and good performance. In this chapter, you will optimize and tune database performance for SQL Database. Next, you will improve application reliability by managing database connections and connection errors using both ADO.NET and Entity Framework. Finally, you will explore how to scale databases in SQL Database using a special partitioning technique known as *sharding*.
- **Chapter 9—Monitoring and management** Services used by production applications must provide monitoring and management capabilities. In this chapter, you will learn how to monitor the health of SQL Database using the management portal, the Service Dashboard, and dynamic management views and functions. You will also learn how to automate SQL Database operations programmatically, using the REST-based Service Management API.
- **Chapter 10—Building cloud solutions** In the book's closing chapter, you will learn how to build a complete solution in the cloud on top of Microsoft Azure SQL Database. Specifically, you will create a Visual Studio solution that includes a SQL Server Database project, an Entity Framework data-access layer, ASP.NET MVC, and ASP.NET Web API. The solution provides a website, web services, and a Windows Phone 8 app with functionality for users to retrieve and update data stored in SQL Database.

Conventions and features in this book

This book presents information using conventions designed to make the information readable and easy to follow:

- Each procedure consists of a series of tasks, presented as numbered steps (1, 2, and so on) listing each action you must take to complete the exercise.
- Boxed elements with labels such as "Note" provide additional information or alternative methods for completing a step successfully.
- Text that you type (apart from code blocks) appears in bold.

- A plus sign (+) between two key names means that you must press those keys at the same time. For example, "Press Alt+Tab" means that you hold down the Alt key while you press the Tab key.
- A vertical bar between two or more menu items (for example, File | Close) means that you should select the first menu or menu item, then the next, and so on.

System requirements

At a minimum, there are no special system requirements for working with SQL Database. The Microsoft Azure management portal requires only a web browser and Internet access. Similarly, the SQL Database management portal requires only a browser with the Silverlight plug-in.

Some chapters walk you through procedures that use local tools—typically, SQL Server Management Studio (SSMS) and Visual Studio 2013. To complete these procedures, you will need to have those tools installed as well, which requires the following:

- One of Windows 7, Windows 8, Windows Server 2008 with Service Pack 2, Windows Server 2008 R2, or Windows Server 2012.
- Visual Studio 2013, any edition. (Multiple downloads may be required if using Express Edition products.)
- SQL Server 2012 Express Edition or higher, with SQL Server Management Studio 2012 Express or higher. (Included with Visual Studio, Express Editions require separate download.)

Depending on your Windows configuration, you might require Local Administrator rights to install or configure Visual Studio 2013 and SQL Server 2012 products.

Chapter 4, "Migrating databases," and Chapter 7, "Microsoft Azure SQL Data Sync," include procedures that require a local SQL Server instance on which you have permissions to create a database. If you don't have access to a local SQL Server instance, you can install SQL Server Express Edition (the free version of SQL Server) by following the instructions shown in the next section.

Finally, several individual chapters work with additional software that gets installed locally. These chapters include detailed procedures for downloading and installing the necessary software so that you can follow along with the rest of the chapter.

Downloads: SQL Server Express Edition

There are several SQL Server Express Edition downloads available on the Microsoft site, and they are available in both 32-bit and 64-bit versions. You can choose to install just the SQL Server Express database engine (and nothing else), or you can choose one of two other (larger) downloads: Express With Tools (which includes SQL Server Management Studio [SSMS]) or Express With Advanced Services (which includes SSMS, Full Text Search, and Reporting Services). There are also separate downloads for SSMS and LocalDB, but these do not include the SQL Server Express database engine needed to host local databases.

To install the SQL Server Express Edition database engine, follow these steps:

1. Open Internet Explorer, and navigate to *http://www.microsoft.com/en-us/download/details.aspx?id=29062*.
2. Click the large orange Download button.
3. Select the appropriate download for your system, as shown in Figure I-1:
   a. For 64-bit systems, choose *ENU\x64\SQLEXPR_x64_ENU.exe*.
   b. For 32-bit or 64-bit WoW systems, choose *ENU\x86\SQLEXPR32_x86_ENU.exe*.
   c. For 32-bit systems, choose *ENU\x86\SQLEXPR_x86_ENU.exe*.

Note If you need to download SQL Server Management Studio (SSMS) as well, choose the Express With Tools file instead, which is the one that includes *WT* in the filename.

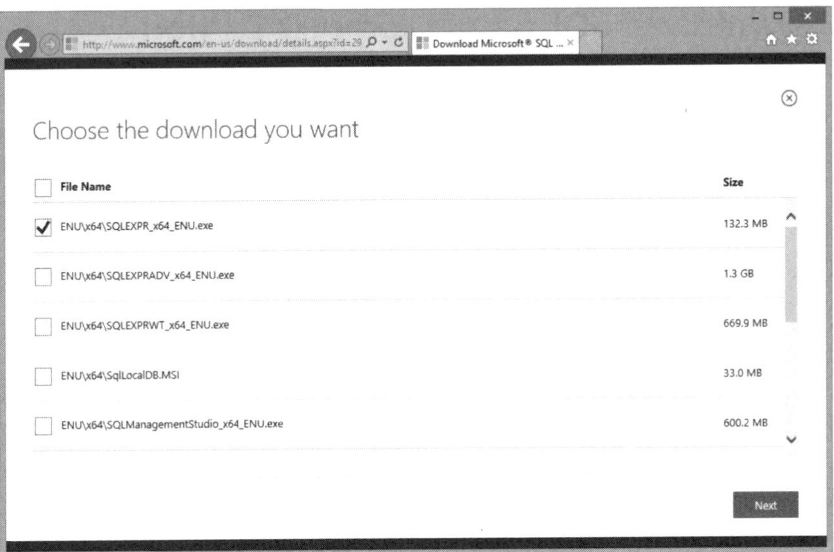

FIGURE I-1 Downloading SQL Server 2012 Express Edition (64-bit version)

4. Click Next.
5. If you receive a pop-up warning, click Allow Once, as shown in Figure I-2.

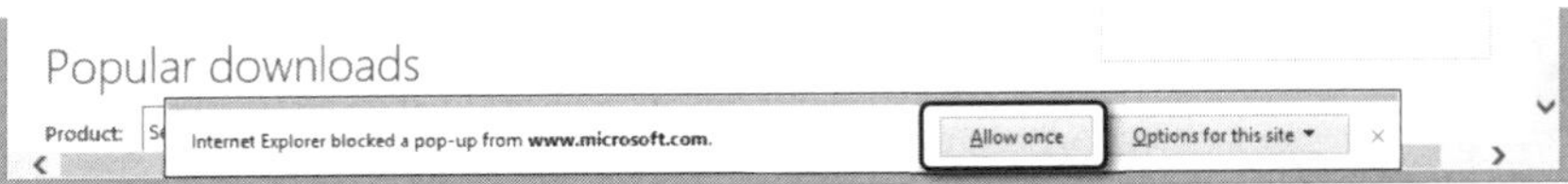

FIGURE I-2 Temporarily allowing pop-ups to enable the download, if necessary

6. When prompted to run or save the file, choose Run. This starts and runs the download.
7. If the User Account Control dialog appears after the download files are extracted, click Yes.
8. In the SQL Server Installation Center, click New SQL Server Stand-Alone Installation, as shown in Figure I-3.

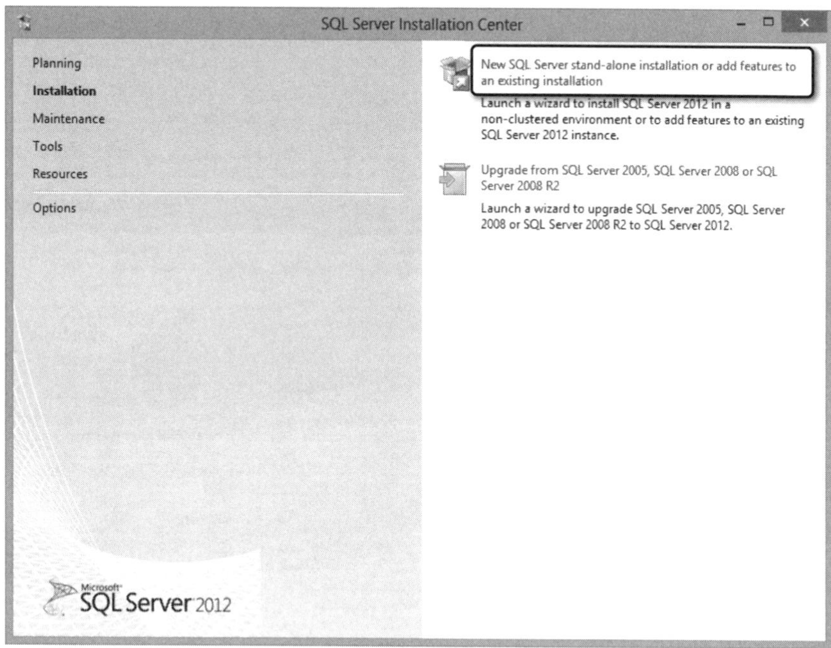

FIGURE I-3 Choosing a new SQL Server installation

9. In the SQL Server 2012 Setup wizard, do the following:

   a. On the License Terms page, select I Accept The License Terms and click Next.

   b. On the Product Updates page, allow the wizard to scan for updates, and then click Next.

   c. On the Install Setup Files page, wait for the installation to proceed.

   d. On the Feature Selection page, Click Next.

   e. Continue clicking Next through all the remaining pages until the Installation Progress page, and wait for the installation to proceed.

   f. On the Complete page indicating a successful setup (shown in Figure I-4), click Close.

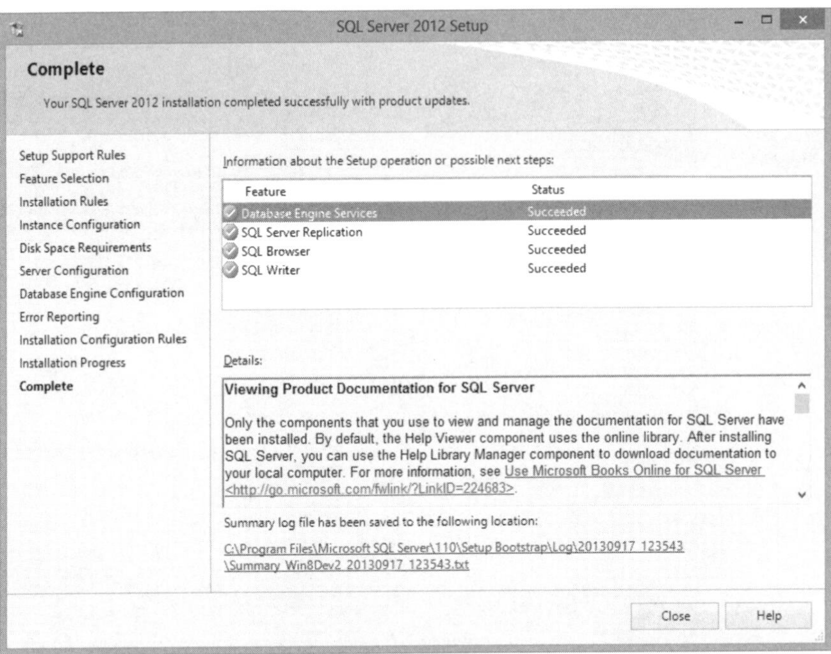

FIGURE I-4 SQL Server Express installation in progress

Downloads: Code samples on the book's companion website

Many chapters have procedures in which you will write actual code. In most cases, there is only a small amount of code, but you may still find it helpful to download the completed code listings from the book's companion website. Doing so can help you work through the procedures, particularly those few procedures that have a bit more code than others. All the code found in this book can be downloaded at the following page:

http://aka.ms/AzureSQLDB_SBS

Installing and using the code samples

Simply download the zip file to your local machine and extract it. You will find one folder for the code in each chapter, although note that there is no code for Chapters 2 and 3. The code folders contain listing files that correspond to the listing numbers found in each of the chapters. Finally, the code folders for Chapters 6, 8, and 10 also include the completed Visual Studio solutions for the exercises found in those chapters.

Acknowledgments

I was first asked to write a book on SQL Azure—back when it was still *called* SQL Azure—nearly two years ago. It's been a long road since then, and despite seismic shifts both in the Azure product platform and in the book publishing ecosystem (not to mention an unexpected curve ball or two), I am extremely delighted to finally publish!

This is my third technical book, and although each experience has been unique, I've learned the same lesson in each case: I could not have even contemplated the challenge without the aid of numerous other talented and caring individuals. These are folks who deserve special recognition—people who lent their generous support out in so many different ways that it's impossible to mention names in any prescribed order.

So I'll start with Andrew Brust. If not for Andrew (who himself is a well-established leader in the software industry), I would never have started down the book-writing path in the first place. I am grateful for our personal friendship, as well as our working relationship writing books and presenting workshops together. These experiences truly help me thrive and grow.

I'm also fortunate to have teamed up with my colleague and co-author Eric Boyd, who produced four excellent chapters on several advanced topics. Eric is an extremely talented software professional, whose expertise and passion for technology comes through clearly in his writing.

Russell Jones, my pal at O'Reilly Media, gets special mention of course, because he's the one who asked me to write this book in the first place. I thank Russell, not only for offering me the opportunity, but for his expert guidance and assistance during the transition to Microsoft Press. More thanks go out to Roger LeBlanc for his copyediting review, and to Scott Klein for his technical review. Special thanks as well to Devon Musgrave and Rosemary Caperton at Microsoft Press, and Steve Sagman of Waypoint Press. Their guidance has been vital to the successful production of this book, and it has been an absolute pleasure working with each one of them.

I would like to give special mention to the Microsoft MVP program, which was an indispensable resource during the writing of this book. So thank you Microsoft, and to my MVP lead Simon Tien as well, for his constant encouragement.

This book could not have been written, of course, without the love and support of my family. I owe an enormous debt of gratitude to my wonderful partner Mark, and our awesome kids Adam, Jacqueline, Josh, and Sonny, for being so patient and tolerant with me throughout this project.

And greatest thanks of all go out to my dear Mom, bless her soul, for always encouraging me to write with "expression."

—Leonard Lobel

I have been developing software professionally for almost 20 years and I am grateful for being blessed with deep interest and excitement for this industry, the ability learn and understand what are sometimes very complex concepts, and the support of my family, friends, mentors and peers throughout my career. Writing a book like this requires lots of guidance and help from many people, and I have many people to thank.

First and foremost, I want to thank God for everything: for life, salvation, family, friends, talents, abilities and everything.

Working on this project over the past year has been a lot of fun, but it has also been a lot of work. My family has been extremely supportive, even when I had to block off nights and weekends to write. I owe so much to my wife, Shelly, for everything that she does for our family. And I'm so thankful for our two wonderful boys who enjoy sitting next to me in my office and cuddling up next to me with my laptop in the living room, when my evenings and weekends get occupied with writing.

In addition to family, I want to thank friends and co-workers who have also been very supportive during this project, even when I bring my laptop to their living rooms, kitchens and dining rooms so that I can write a few more words, paragraphs and pages.

I want to thank Lenni Lobel who invited me to join him on this project. Lenni has been a fantastic co-author and has done a great job leading this project and driving it to completion. His guidance, editing and feedback has been extremely valuable for me personally and for the project. I'm also very appreciative of his patience throughout this project.

Last, but certainly not least, thank you to everyone at Microsoft and Microsoft Press who have helped with this project both directly and indirectly, this list includes Scott Klein, Dora Chan, Mark Brown, Devon Musgrave, Rosemary Caperton, Steve Sagman, Conor Cunningham, the Azure CAT team, and so many more.

—Eric Boyd

Errata, updates, & book support

We've made every effort to ensure the accuracy of this book and its companion content. You can access updates to this book—in the form of a list of submitted errata and their related corrections—at:

http://aka.ms/AzureSQLDB_SBS

If you discover an error that is not already listed, please submit it to us at the same page.

If you need additional support, email Microsoft Press Book Support at mspinput@microsoft.com.

Please note that product support for Microsoft software and hardware is not offered through the previous addresses. For help with Microsoft software or hardware, go to *http://support.microsoft.com.*

We want to hear from you

At Microsoft Press, your satisfaction is our top priority, and your feedback our most valuable asset. Please tell us what you think of this book at:

http://aka.ms/tellpress

We know you're busy, so we've kept it short with just a few questions. Your answers go directly to the editors at Microsoft Press. (No personal information will be requested.) Thanks in advance for your input!

Stay in touch

Let's keep the conversation going! We're on Twitter: *http://twitter.com/MicrosoftPress*

CHAPTER 1

Getting started with Microsoft Azure SQL Database

—Leonard Lobel

In this chapter, you will create your first database on the Microsoft Azure SQL Database platform—completely from scratch. *From scratch* means that all you need to follow along is a web browser (the chapter uses Internet Explorer) and Internet access. You will sign up for a Microsoft account (if you don't already have one), and use your Microsoft account to create and access a free trial subscription to Microsoft Azure. Then we'll introduce you to the Microsoft Azure management portal, and you'll quickly get a server and database up and running in the cloud. Finally, you'll use the SQL Database management portal to design, populate, and query the database.

Note We'll often refer to Microsoft Azure SQL Database simply as *SQL Database*. The term *SQL Server* refers exclusively to *on-premises* database instances, while the term *SQL Database* always means the cloud-based Microsoft Azure SQL Database.

Although this book is focused on Microsoft Azure SQL Database, you'll find it helpful to understand SQL Database in the broader context of the Microsoft Azure platform, and cloud computing in general. This understanding will greatly enhance your appreciation of SQL Database. So, before signing up for a Microsoft account, here's a brief high-level discussion of cloud computing with Microsoft Azure.

Cloud computing: The concept

Microsoft Azure is Microsoft's cloud-computing platform. But what exactly is cloud computing? The fact is, there really is no precise definition; indeed, *cloud computing* is an ambiguous term. Many different types of services exist today that run "in the cloud." Fundamentally, then, *cloud computing* refers to the evolution of Internet hosting in which providers (such as Microsoft, Google, Amazon, and others) offer services to consumers and businesses that run on redundant hardware, with system maintenance that's either partially or fully automated. This is a level of service beyond traditional Internet hosting that emerged with the dot-com bubble in the 1990s. With cloud computing, the Internet is not merely used as a medium for sharing information. Indeed, the cloud leverages the

Internet as a way of connecting clients to various infrastructure, platform, and application services with a far greater degree of flexibility and abstraction than previous hosting schemes could possibly offer.

One of the earliest cloud-computing platforms was Amazon Web Services (AWS), introduced back in 2002 by Amazon.com. Still today, AWS is prominently positioned as a serious contender in the cloud service industry. Since the mid-2000s, cloud computing has been rapidly gaining popularity, and in 2009, Microsoft unveiled Microsoft Azure (which was called Windows Azure until the name was changed in April 2014). Even as Azure launched, and steadfastly ever since, Microsoft has been expanding its cloud platform with newer and more robust capabilities.

Instant dynamic provisioning

To start with, provisioning on-premises servers on your own is difficult. First you need to purchase and physically install the hardware. Then you need to get the necessary software license or licenses, install the OS, and deploy and configure your application. You'll also need to ensure acceptable performance levels and continuous uptime in the event of unexpected hardware, software, or network failures. That means configuring load balancing and redundancy using mirroring and clustering technologies. You'll have to devise a backup strategy and attend to it religiously as part of an overall disaster-recovery plan, which you'll also need to establish. And once all that is set up, you'll still need to maintain everything to keep a healthy system running for the lifetime of your application.

Without exaggeration, *moving to the cloud eliminates all these burdens.*

In short, the idea of applications and services running in "the cloud" means that you're dealing with intangible hardware resources, which in turn, translates to a maintenance-free runtime environment. You sign up with a cloud-hosting company (Microsoft, in the case of Azure) for access, pay them for how much power (in terms of resources) your applications require (RAM, CPU, storage, bandwidth, scale-out load balancing, and so on), and let them worry about all the rest. Compared to the manual labor and potential for error involved in doing things yourself, it's both hassle free and risk free.

The Microsoft Azure cloud

With Azure, your applications, services, and data reside in the cloud. The Azure cloud is backed by large, geographically dispersed Microsoft data centers equipped with powerful servers, massive storage capacities, and very high redundancy to ensure continuous uptime.

But the Microsoft Azure environment is much more than a set of conventional web-hosting facilities on steroids. In fact, your cloud-based applications and services don't actually run directly on these server machines. Instead, sophisticated *hypervisor* virtualization technology runs on top of all this physical hardware. Your "code in the cloud," in turn, runs on that virtualization layer. So scaling out during peak season becomes a simple matter of changing a configuration setting that increases the number of running instances to accommodate the increase in demand. When the busy season is over, it's the same simple change to reduce the instance count and scale back down. Microsoft Azure manages the scaling by dynamically granting more or less hardware processing power to the virtualized runtime environment. The process, often referred to as *elastic scaling*, is practically instantaneous.

Now consider the same scenario with conventional infrastructure. You'd need to purchase and install servers, bring them online, and add them as members to a load-balanced farm. And then you'd need to take them offline to be decommissioned later when the extra capacity is no longer required. That requires a great deal of work and time—either for you directly or for your hosting company—compared to tweaking some configuration with only a few mouse clicks.

Because cloud solutions can be delivered in lots of different ways, many new terms and buzzwords have infiltrated our vocabulary in recent years. Among them are the various "as-a-service" acronyms, including Infrastructure as a Service (IaaS), Platform as a Service (PaaS), and Software as a Service (SaaS). All these terms obviously refer to *services*; their differences lie in the *level* of service. It's often helpful to think of these terms as gradations of abstraction, starting with the lowest level of the underlying hardware infrastructure. When you're on-premises, you have no abstraction at all, and you are intimately involved with and responsible for everything from the hardware on up. When you move to the cloud, you can go IaaS, Paas, or SaaS as your needs dictate, where each of those approaches provide increasingly greater abstractions.

Infrastructure as a Service

With IaaS, Microsoft Azure effectively gives you virtual machines (VMs) that are entirely under your control. Just as in an on-premises environment, you'll be responsible for installing the OS and configuring the machine. It's easy to build virtual machine images from scratch—or to customize existing virtual machines from a library of preconfigured VMs—and then deploy them to run in the cloud with full network connectivity (even Virtual Private Network [VPN] connections) and configurability. But unlike working on-premises, you'll never need to handle screwdrivers, hard drives, cables, racks, power supplies, motherboards, RAM, or anything like that ever again. This is true IaaS—abstraction of hardware (networking, storage, severs, virtualization), and nothing else.

With this capability, you could certainly create a VM on Microsoft Azure that runs Microsoft SQL Server; that is, a virtual machine in the cloud that itself is running the full *on-premises* version of SQL Server. There might be situations where that is entirely justified and valid—for example, if you require full compatibility with on-premises SQL Server, which SQL Database does not provide. (We discuss the differences between these two platforms in Chapter 3, "Differences between SQL Server and Microsoft Azure SQL Database.") A prime example of this scenario is to deliver cloud reporting with SQL Server Reporting Services (SSRS) running in a Microsoft Azure VM (which you learn how to do in Chapter 6, "Cloud reporting"). But understand that running SQL Server in an Azure VM is completely different than using Microsoft Azure SQL Database. Going with IaaS and SQL Server means that you are still responsible for maintaining your virtual machine or machines in the cloud. This includes installing the operating system from scratch (unless you choose to upload a preconfigured VM from the gallery), installing SQL Server, configuring instances, keeping the software up to date, protecting VMs from faulty software, and backing up data. If your VM crashes, then it's *your* crisis. SQL Database is entirely different, which is what makes it a PaaS solution.

Platform as a Service

With PaaS, the abstraction level gets raised above IaaS so that you are also shielded from the operating system, middleware, and runtime layers. This means that Microsoft Azure also provides a *platform* for your applications and services to run on. You have no control over the platform; you get to manage only applications and data, while the cloud provider manages the rest of the infrastructure. You still get to create and test your applications locally and then upload them to run on Microsoft Azure. (We cover this in Chapter 10, "Building cloud solutions."). This gives your application incredible scalability without requiring the investment in expensive hardware that such scalability would normally require in any on-premises scenario.

SQL Database, too, is a PaaS solution. It's still SQL Server, but to deliver a relational database *platform* (as opposed to infrastructure), certain features that are available on-premises are not supported. With SQL Database, you can provision servers and databases on the fly, without ever interacting with the OS or other underlying infrastructure. You will never need to know or care if your data and log files are stored on a C drive or a D drive, because SQL Database handles all details of physical storage for you. As you'll learn about in Chapter 3, enjoying the benefits of virtually instantaneous provisioning and risk-free, care-free maintenance also means incurring some loss of control that you normally get to exercise when working with SQL Server on-premises.

Software as a Service

SaaS is at the high end of the abstraction spectrum, where everything from the hardware up to and including the end-user application is handled by the service. There are many cloud SaaS offerings available today, including Office 365, CRM, and Salesforce.com.

You can create your own SaaS solutions with SQL Database by layering a service or website—also hosted on Azure—over the database. (You'll do this in Chapter 10.) You could then offer this as a complete solution to your customers, who interact only with the application through their browser or mobile device. Your customers are not concerned with any aspects of infrastructure or platform. They just connect to your application. So, from their perspective, you have delivered true SaaS.

Getting signed up for SQL Database

To start using SQL Database, you need two things: a Microsoft account and a Microsoft Azure subscription. It's quite possible that you already have a Microsoft account, which was formerly known as a Windows Live ID. This is the same account you might be using today for logging in to various Microsoft websites and services, such as Outlook.com, Hotmail, Xbox LIVE, Windows Phone, OneDrive (formerly SkyDrive), and other Microsoft offerings.

Creating a Microsoft account

The very first step before you can use any Microsoft Azure service is to acquire a Microsoft account if you don't already have one. This is essentially an email address and password combination you will use to create and access your Microsoft Azure subscription. If you already have a Microsoft account, you can use it now to create a new Azure subscription. There's no need to create another account, so you can just skip ahead to the next section, "Creating a Microsoft Azure subscription." Otherwise, you'll need to create one now.

Tip If you already have a Microsoft account but you want to use a different email address for any reason, you still don't need to create a new account. You can either rename the existing account or create an alias. See *http://windows.microsoft.com/en-US/hotmail/get-new-outlook-address* for more information.

If you do create a new Microsoft account, the user name can be an email address you already own. Alternatively, you can create a new email address for the account that ends either with *@outlook.com* or *@hotmail.com*. It really makes no difference which you choose, as long as the name you provide has not already been taken by someone else at either @outlook.com or @hotmail.com. If you do choose to create a new email address, you will also get a new mailbox account at that address, and Microsoft will communicate with you via that mailbox any time it needs to notify you about important information regarding your account.

Whether you use an existing email address or create a new one, you'll also need to assign a strong password to protect the Microsoft account. Some additional personal information is also required, such as your name, gender, one of two forms of identity confirmation, your country, and your postal/Zip code.

Follow these steps to create your new Microsoft account:

1. Using Internet Explorer, browse to **http://signup.live.com**. This displays the Create An Account page, as shown in Figure 1-1.

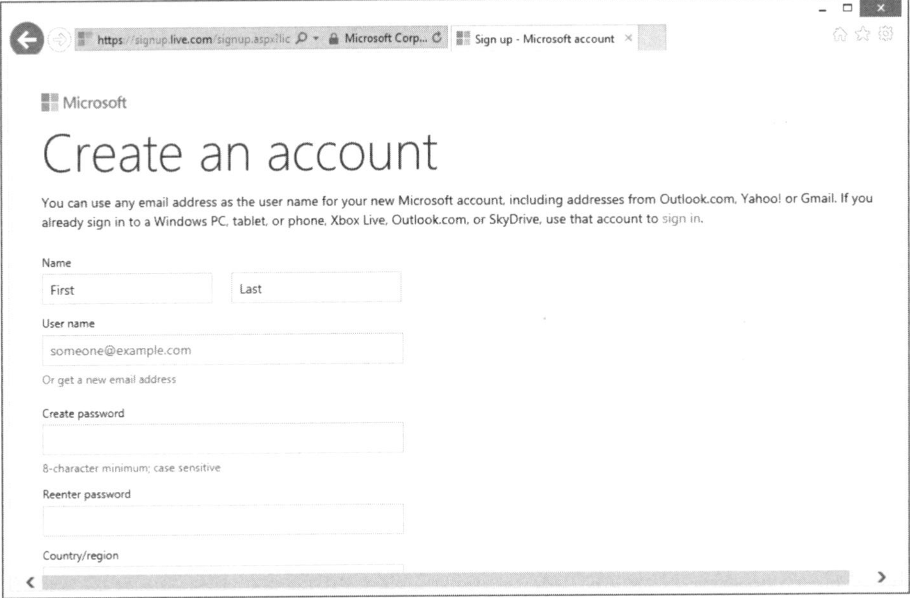

FIGURE 1-1 Signing up for a new Microsoft account

2. Provide your first name and last name.
3. For the Microsoft account user name (which is what you will be logging on to the Microsoft Azure portal with), provide an existing email address. Or click the Or Get A New Email Address link to create a new one available on either @outlook.com or @hotmail.com.
4. Supply a password, and then reenter it to confirm. The account requires a strong password of at least eight characters that must contain a combination of mixed case, numbers, and symbols.
5. Provide your country and postal/Zip code, birthdate, and gender.
6. Provide a phone number or alternate email address. You must provide at least one of these identity-confirmation methods.
7. Type the random characters generated to prove that you're a real person.
8. Click the Create Account button.

If you created a new email address in step 3, a mailbox is created for it and you are directed immediately to the Account Summary page. If you provided an existing email address, you will receive an email at that address from the Microsoft account team shortly after clicking Create Account. This email is sent to verify that you do, in fact, own the email address you provided. Your new Microsoft account will not become activated until you click on the verification link provided in the email.

Creating a Microsoft Azure subscription

Now that you have your Microsoft account, it's time to create an Azure subscription. The subscription is essentially your Microsoft Azure billing account, and that opens the gateway to the full range of services available on Microsoft Azure—including, of course, SQL Database.

In the procedure that follows, you will create a free trial subscription to Microsoft Azure. At the time of this writing, the free trial gives you $200 of credit for 30 days with access to all services. This requires providing credit card information that will be used to bill your subscription after your trial expires.

Important Microsoft Azure pricing and special offers are subject to ongoing change. We strongly recommend that you visit *http://www.windowsazure.com/en-us/pricing/purchase-options/* to review the latest pricing structures available. Furthermore, special pricing is available for MSDN subscribers. See *http://www.windowsazure.com/en-us/pricing/member-offers/msdn-benefits/* for more information.

Follow these steps to create your new Microsoft Azure subscription:

1. Using Internet Explorer, browse to **http://www.windowsazure.com**.
2. Click the green Try For Free button.
3. On the next page, click the green Try It Now button.
4. If you are not already logged in to your Microsoft account, log in now.
5. You will be taken to the Free Trial Signup page, as shown in Figure 1-2.

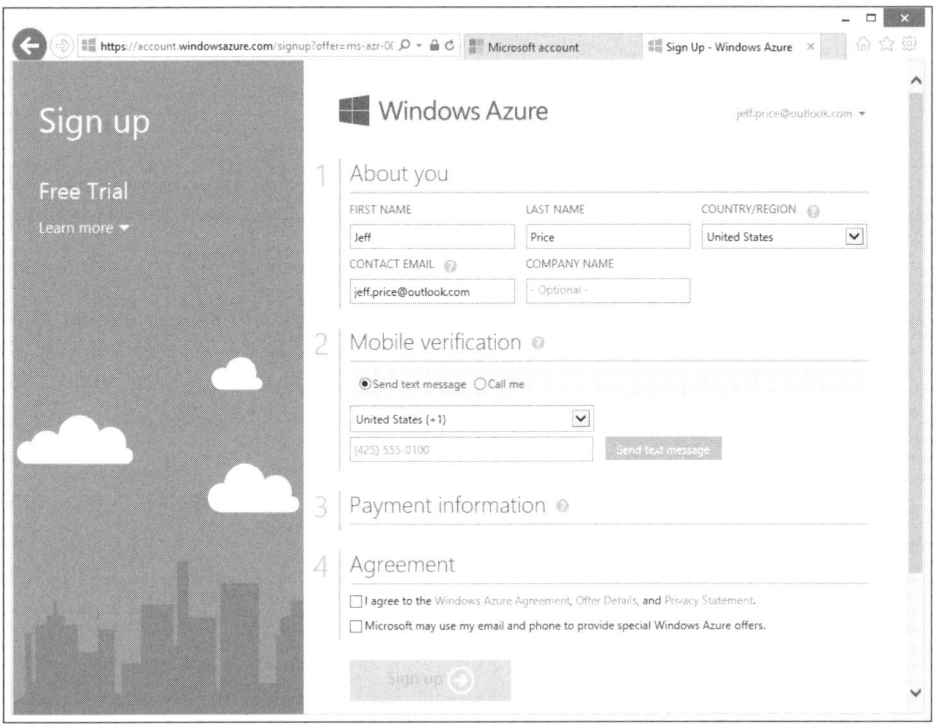

FIGURE 1-2 Signing up for a new free trial Microsoft Azure subscription

6. Choose to either receive a text message or phone call as the method to receive a verification code.
7. Enter the code received via the text message or phone call, and click Verify Code.
8. Provide the credit card payment details for billing after the free trial expires.
9. Select the box to indicate that you agree to all the terms.
10. Click the green Sign Up button.

It takes just a few moments to complete setting up your new Azure subscription, and then you're ready to get started working with SQL Database and all the other Microsoft Azure services.

Creating a server

It's easy to create a server, which is akin to an instance of SQL Server in the sense that it can host multiple databases. All you need to do is create an administrator account user name with a strong password, and specify the geographical region where the server should be located physically. To achieve the best performance, you should choose the region closest to your consumers. As we discuss in Chapter 2, "Configuration and pricing," you will also want to be sure that any Microsoft Azure cloud

Web sites and services (such as the ones you'll create in Chapter 10) are hosted in the same region as the SQL Database servers they communicate with. By locating both in the same region, you will avoid the bandwidth-based fee that gets incurred when your cloud sites, services, and databases communicate across different Azure regions. You will also reduce latency, which results in significantly better performance.

SQL Database also has special *firewall rules* you can set to control exactly which computer or computers can access your database server in the cloud. Minimally, you'll need to add a rule granting access to the IP address of your computer so that you can access the server from your local machine. For production, you might need to add rules granting access to blocks of IP addresses. You will learn more about firewall rules in Chapters 2 and 5.

Follow these steps to create a new server:

1. Log in to the Microsoft Azure portal at **https://manage.windowsazure.com**. This brings you to the main portal page showing ALL ITEMS, as shown in Figure 1-3.

> **Note** The first time you log into the portal, you are welcomed with a message that offers to give you a brief tour. You can take the tour if you wish, or close the message to proceed to the main portal page.

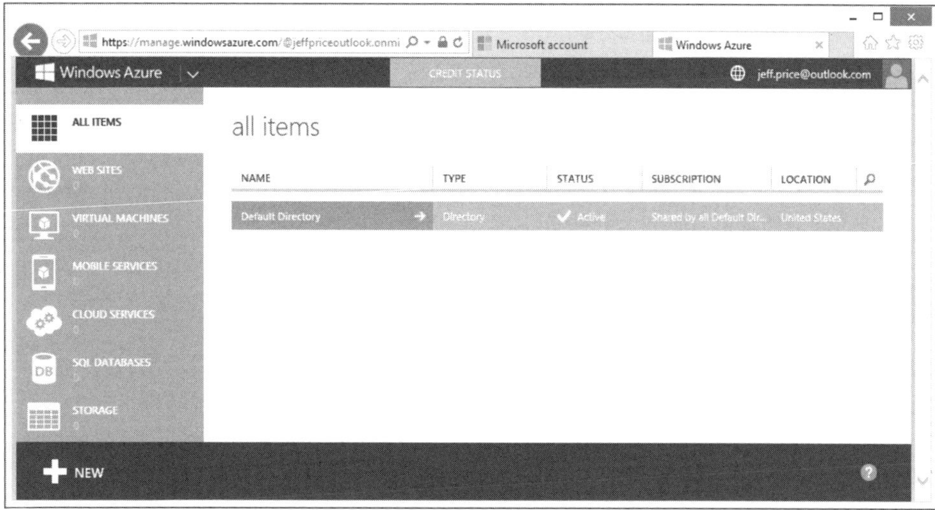

FIGURE 1-3 The Microsoft Azure Management Portal with no services yet configured

2. As illustrated in Figure 1-4, first click SQL DATABASES in the vertical navigation pane on the left, then click SERVERS at the top of the page, and then click CREATE A SQL DATABASE SERVER.

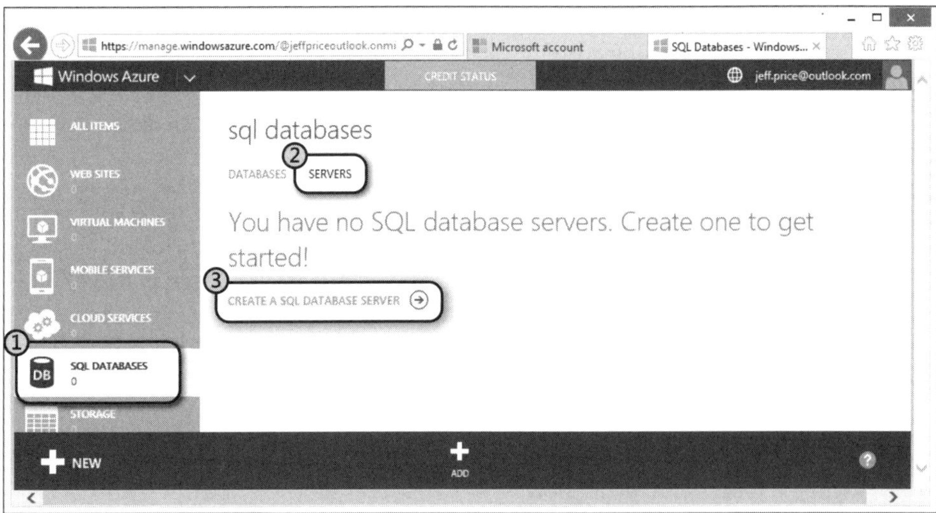

FIGURE 1-4 The CREATE A SQL DATABASE SERVER link on the SQL DATABASES page

3. Provide a new server login name—for example, **saz**.
4. Supply a password for the new server, and then reenter it to confirm. Typical strong password rules apply, which require you to use a combination of mixed case, numbers, and symbols.
5. Choose a region from the drop-down list—for example, East US. For best performance, pick the region you are located in or nearest to.
6. Be sure to leave the ALLOW WINDOWS AZURE SERVICES TO ACCESS THE SERVER check box selected. This makes the server accessible to the Microsoft Azure cloud services that you'll create or use in other chapters (Microsoft Azure was formerly called Windows Azure). The page should appear similar to Figure 1-5.

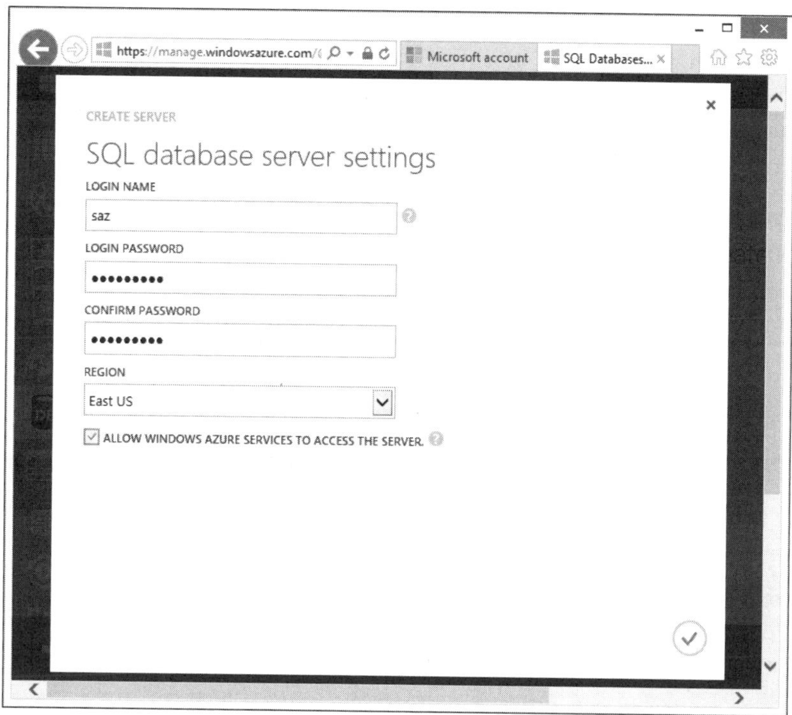

FIGURE 1-5 The CREATE SERVER dialog

7. Click the checkmark icon on the lower-right side of the dialog to complete the settings. After just a few moments, the new server is provisioned and ready to use, as shown in Figure 1-6.

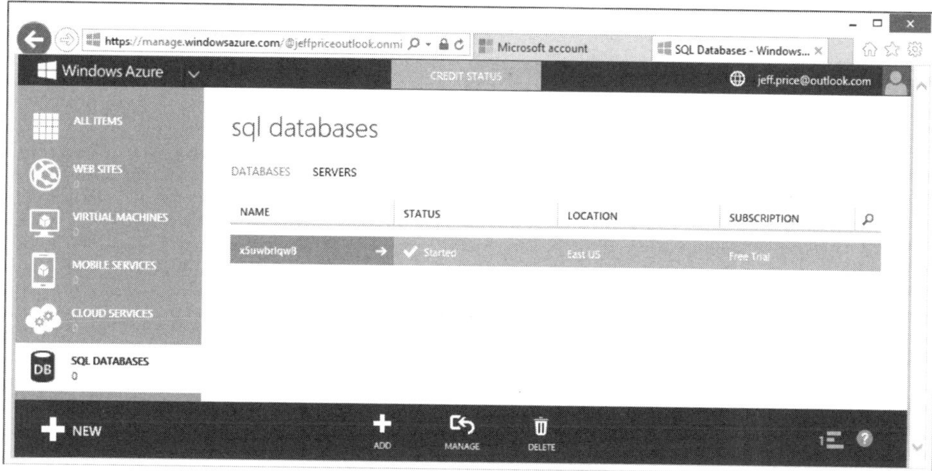

FIGURE 1-6 The new SQL Database server

If you've ever prepared a new on-premises server from scratch yourself, you can really appreciate the time and effort you just saved. This server is now available and ready to host databases in the cloud, and SQL Database has automatically assigned a randomly unique (but relatively short) name by which it can be accessed. But before access is granted, the server firewall must be configured. So the next step is to add a firewall rule so that you can connect to the server from your local machine.

The check box mentioned in step 6 added the special IP address 0.0.0.0, which allows cloud services running on Microsoft Azure to access the SQL Database server. However, you still need to add the IP address of your local machine to access the server from the SQL Database management portal and other tools (such as SQL Server Management Studio and SQL Server Data Tools in Microsoft Visual Studio, which you learn more about in later chapters).

To add a firewall rule for the IP address of your local machine, follow these steps:

1. Click the server name, and then click the CONFIGURE link at the top of the page.
2. To the right of your current detected IP address, click ADD TO THE ALLOWED IP ADDRESSES, as shown in Figure 1-7. A new firewall rule for your IP address is added.

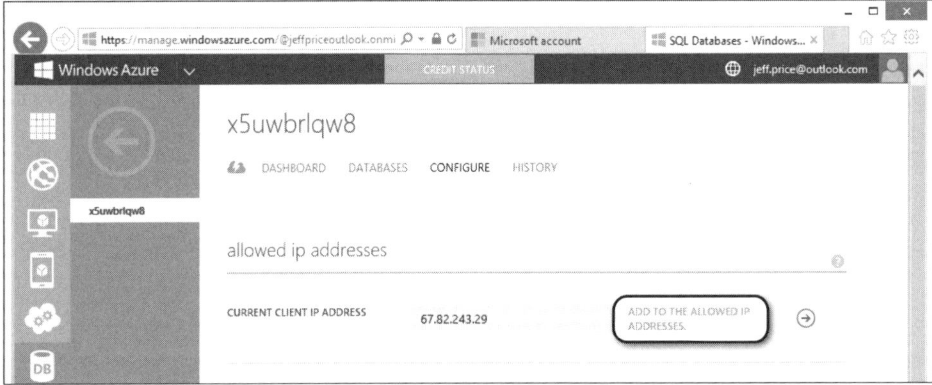

FIGURE 1-7 Adding your local IP address to the list of IP addresses allowed though the firewall

3. Click SAVE at the bottom of the page.
4. Click the back icon (the large back-pointing arrow) to return to the SQL DATABASES page for the new server.

You might need to wait a few moments for the new firewall rule to take effect, although typically it happens very quickly (often within five to ten seconds). If you don't wait long enough, however, and the rule has not yet taken effect, you can be quite certain that you will not be able to connect to the server from your local machine until it does.

Creating a SQL Database instance

It will be just about as easy to create a database as it was to create the server. You simply need to choose a name for the new database, an edition, a maximum size, a default collation, and of course, the server to host the database on.

In Chapter 2, you'll learn more about the different options for database edition and maximum size. For right now, the important thing to know is that all these settings (except for the default collation) can be easily changed later on. As part of the elastic scaling provided by SQL Database, you can freely switch back and forth between the Web and Business editions. You can also switch up and down between the sizes (1 GB or 5 GB for the Web edition, or 10 GB through 150 GB for the Business edition) as your changing needs dictate. And if 150 GB is still too small for you, you can partition your database using special *sharding* techniques, as we explain in Chapter 8, "Designing and tuning for scalability and high performance."

Follow these steps to create a new SQL Database:

1. If you are continuing from the previous procedure, click the DATABASES link at the top of the page and then skip to step 4. Otherwise, if you have logged out since then and are starting fresh, continue with step 2.
2. Log in to the Microsoft Azure portal at **https://manage.windowsazure.com**. This brings you to the main portal page showing ALL ITEMS, as shown in Figure 1-3 earlier.
3. Click SQL DATABASES in the vertical navigation pane on the left.
4. Click CREATE A SQL DATABASE, as shown in Figure 1-8. This opens the NEW SQL DATABASE dialog.

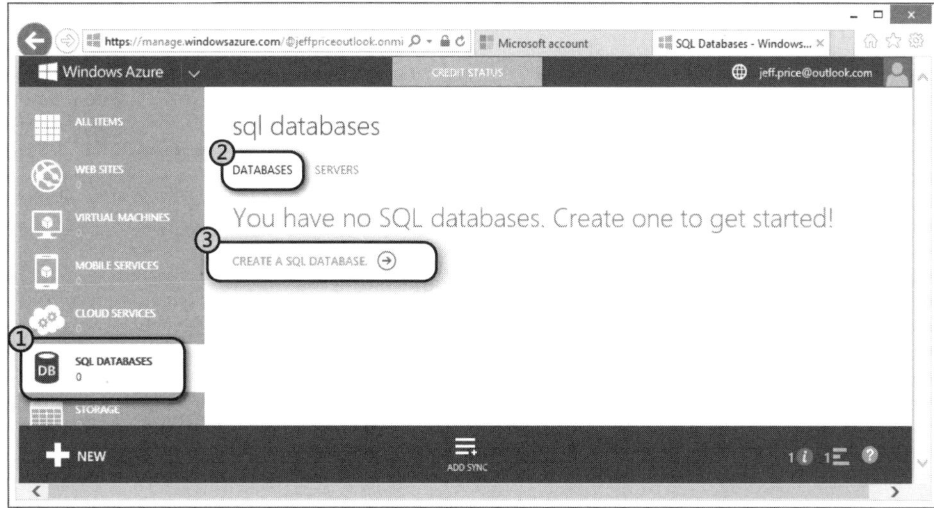

FIGURE 1-8 The CREATE A SQL DATABASE link on the portal's SQL DATABASES page

5. Type the name for the new database, **WineCloudDb** (yes, you'll be in the wine business).

6. Leave the default settings to create a Web edition database up to 1 GB in size using the *SQL_Lating1_GeneralCP1_CI_AS* collation.

> **Note** Chapter 2 discusses the Web and Business editions, the maximum database sizes, and the significance of SQL Database collations.

7. Choose the server you created in the previous procedure from the drop-down list. The page should appear similar to Figure 1-9.

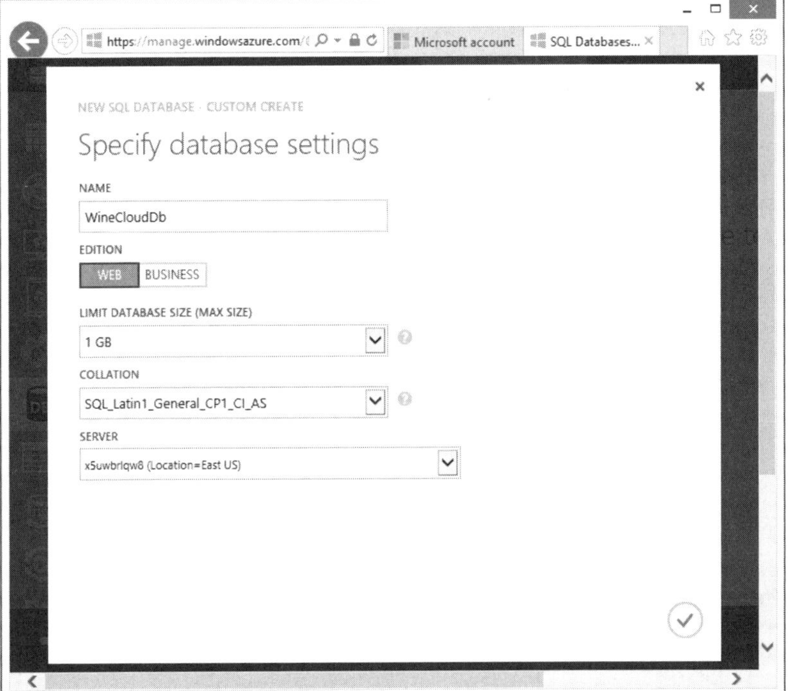

FIGURE 1-9 The NEW SQL DATABASE dialog

8. Click the checkmark icon in the lower right of the dialog to complete the settings.

After a few more moments, the new *WineCloudDb* database is created and ready to use, as shown in Figure 1-10.

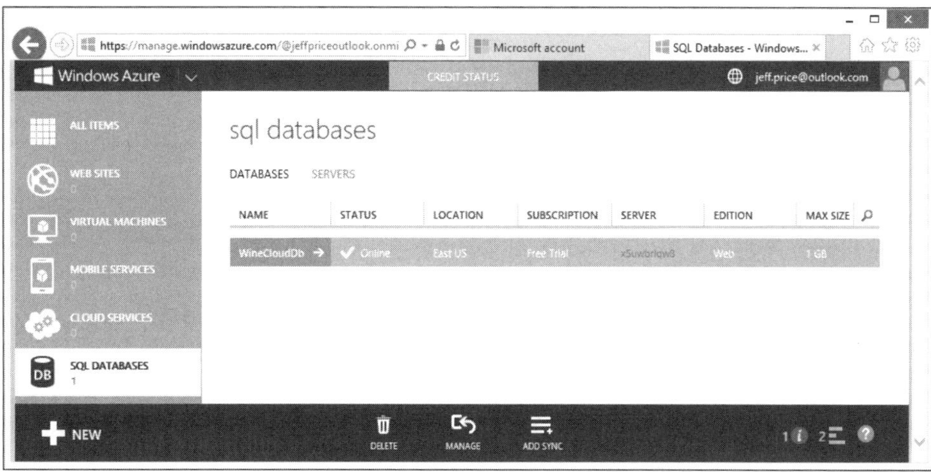

FIGURE 1-10 The new *WineCloudDb* SQL Database

Using the SQL Database management portal

Up to this point, you've used the Microsoft Azure management portal to create a SQL Database server and database. The Azure management portal is an HTML-based interface, which—parenthetically—replaced the earlier Silverlight-based interface back in mid-2012. Actually *designing* a database, however, is performed using a different portal, the SQL Database management portal, which is still Silverlight-based at the time of this writing. In this section, you'll learn how to access the SQL Database management portal from the Microsoft Azure management portal.

Follow these steps to access the SQL Database management portal:

1. If you are continuing from the previous procedure, skip to step 4. Otherwise, if you have logged out, continue with step 2.
2. Log in to the Microsoft Azure portal at **https://manage.windowsazure.com**. This brings you to the main portal page showing ALL ITEMS, as shown in Figure 1-3 earlier.
3. Click SQL DATABASES in the vertical navigation pane on the left.
4. Click the *WineCloudDb* database.
5. Click the DASHBOARD link at the top of the page.
6. Scroll the page down a bit, and find the MANAGE URL link in the quick glance section at the right of the page, as shown in Figure 1-11.

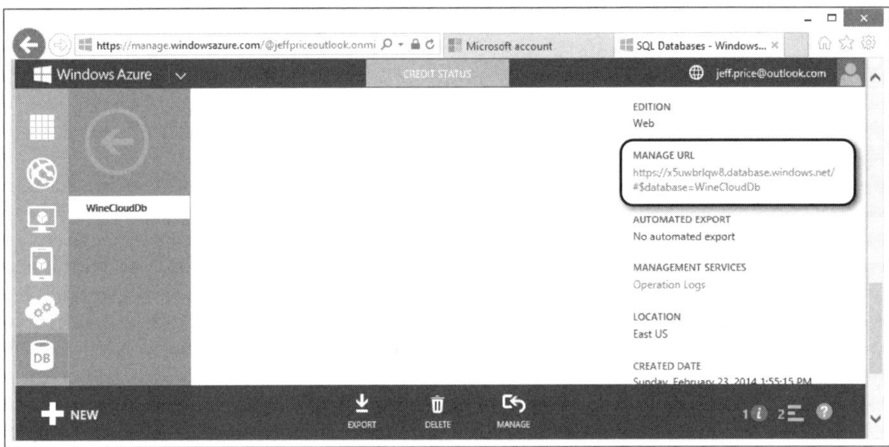

FIGURE 1-11 Finding the link to the SQL Database management portal for database *WineCloudDb*

7. Click the MANAGE URL link. This opens a new browser tab to the SQL Database portal's login page.

Note The SQL Database portal is Silverlight-based. If you don't have Silverlight installed, you will first be prompted to download it before you can use the portal.

8. Type the user name (for example, **saz**) and password you specified when you created the server, as shown in Figure 1-12.

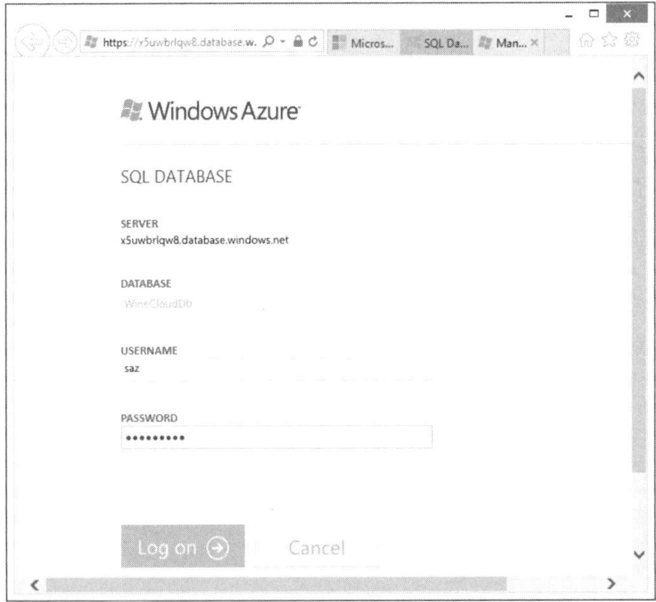

FIGURE 1-12 The SQL Database management portal login page

9. Click Log On. Once you have authenticated, you are taken to the Summary view of the Administration tab for the database, as shown in Figure 1-13.

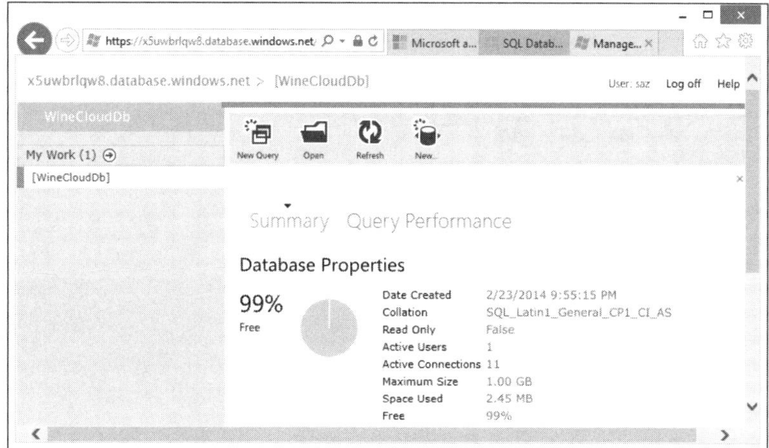

FIGURE 1-13 The Summary view shows properties for the *WineCloudDb* database

Designing tables and relationships

Now you're ready to create some tables. You'll create two tables now, though you will extend this design a bit more in other chapters. It's easy to create a new table, as you'll see in the next procedure. Just click the Design tab on the left side of the page and then click New Table, as shown in Figure 1-14.

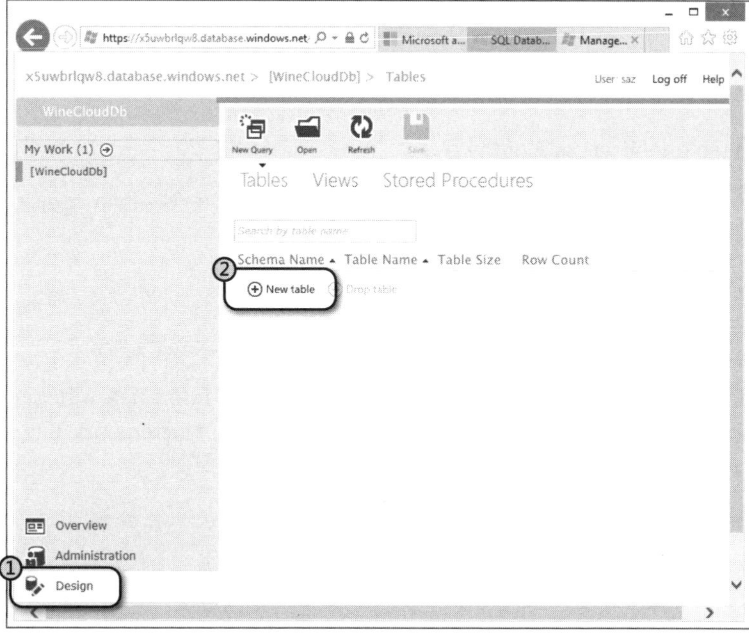

FIGURE 1-14 Creating a new table

This opens the table designer, which you'll use now to create a table for storing wine products, as shown in Figure 1-15.

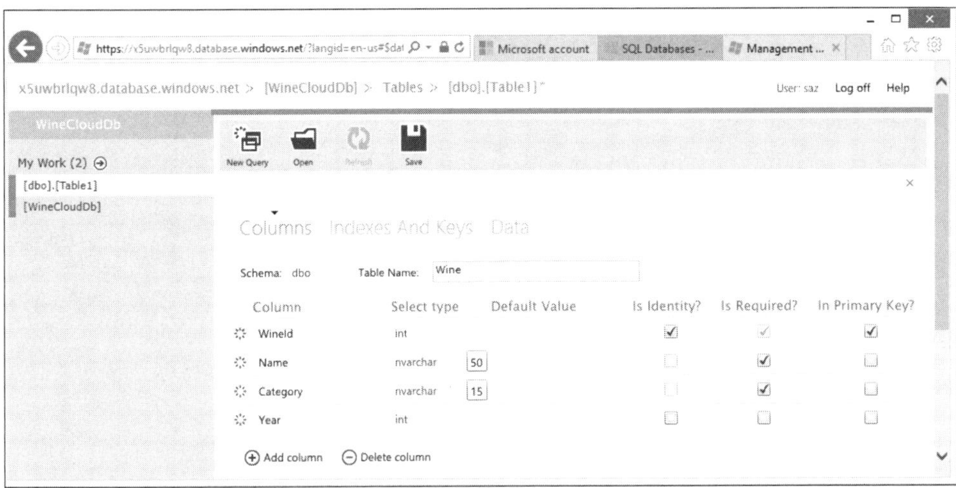

FIGURE 1-15 Defining the *Wine* table using the portal's table designer

Creating the Wine table

First create the *Wine* table. Every row in this table is another wine product that your company sells to customers, so you'll design the *Wine* table to include the columns *WineId* (the primary key that uniquely identifies each individual wine product), *Name*, *Category*, and *Year*.

To create the *Wine* table, follow these steps:

1. Log in to the SQL Database management portal for the *WineCloudDb* database, as described in the previous procedure.
2. Click the Design tab on the left side of the page.
3. Click New Table. The table designer opens with a default name of *Table1*, an integer *ID* column, and two string columns named *Column1* and *Column2*.
4. Change the Table Name to **Wine**.
5. Change the *ID* column name to **WineId**, leaving it as the required primary key.
6. Select the Is Identity? check box for the *WineId* column. When you insert new wine products into the table, this setting tells SQL Database to automatically assign incremental integer values for this column in each new row.
7. Change the *Column1* column name to **Name**, leaving it as a required *nvarchar(50)* string.
8. Change the *Column2* column name to **Category**, leaving it as a required *nvarchar(15)* string.
9. Click Add Column. This adds another integer column named *Column1* to the table design.

10. Change the new column name to **Year**, and leave it as an optional integer (meaning you do not select the Is Required? check box).
11. Click Save in the toolbar at the top of the designer.

You have now created the *Wine* table, which should appear similar to the image shown in Figure 1-15 earlier.

Creating the Customer table

Now follow a similar procedure to create the *Customer* table, with the columns *CustomerId* (the primary key), *FirstName*, *LastName*, and *FavoriteWineId*. The *FavoriteWineId* column relates to the *WineId* primary key column in the *Wine* table, so *FavoriteWineId* in the *Customer* table is a *foreign key*. After creating the *Customer* table, you will establish a relationship between its *FavoriteWineId* foreign key column and the primary key column *WineId* in the *Wine* table.

To create the *Customer* table, follow these steps:

1. Click the [WineCloudDb] tab on the top left side of the page.
2. Click the Design tab on the bottom left. This takes you to the same page you used before when you created the *Wine* table. (See Figure 1-14.)
3. Click New Table.
4. Change the Table Name to **Customer**.
5. Change the *ID* column name to **CustomerId**, leaving it as the required primary key.
6. Select the Is Identity? check box for the *CustomerId* column.
7. Change the *Column1* column name to **FirstName**, leaving it as a required *nvarchar(50)* string.
8. Change the *Column2* column name to **LastName**, leaving it as a required *nvarchar(15)* string.
9. Click Add Column.
10. Change the new column name to **FavoriteWineId**, leaving it as an optional integer (meaning you do not select the Is Required? check box).
11. Click Save.

Now the database has *Wine* and *Customer* tables. These tables store (obviously) your wine products and your customers, though (equally obviously) they are both empty at this point.

Defining the table relationship

Before populating the tables with data, you will establish the foreign-key relationship between *FavoriteWineId* in the *Customer* table and *WineId* in the *Wine* table. Note that it isn't strictly necessary to do this. However, it's best practice to let SQL Database know about the relationships between tables so that it can enforce referential integrity in your data. (For example, SQL Database will ensure that the integer value in each customer's *FavoriteWineId* column refers to an existing row in the *Wine* table that can be located by *WineId*.) It also helps SQL Database devise more efficient query plans internally when you join on table relationship in your queries.

The SQL Database management portal offers a foreign-key management experience that makes defining the relationship easy, as shown in Figure 1-16.

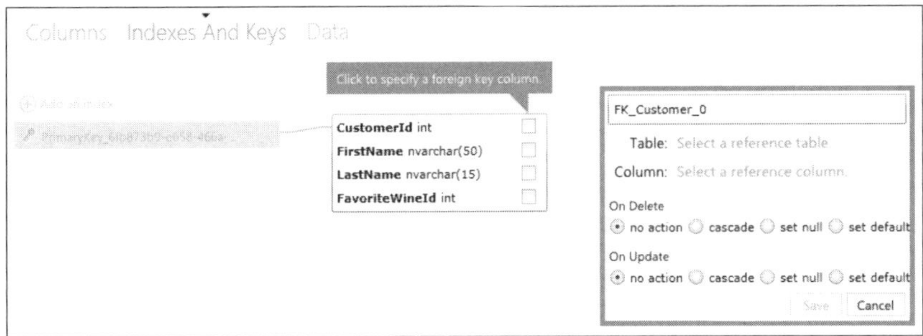

FIGURE 1-16 Defining table relationships using the foreign-key designer

To define the relationship between the two tables, follow these steps:

1. While still in the *Customer* table design page, click Indexes And Keys at the top of the page.
2. On the right side of the page, click Add A Foreign Key Relationship. The foreign-key designer appears as shown in Figure 1-16.
3. Select the *FavoriteWineId* column in the *Customer* table. This specifies the foreign-key column.
4. Change the foreign-key name (assigned as *FK_Customer_0* by default) to **FK_Customer_Wine**.
5. Click Select A Reference Table, and choose *Wine*.
6. Click Select A Reference Column, and choose *WineId*.
7. Click Save.

The relationship is created, and the designer should now appear similar to Figure 1-17.

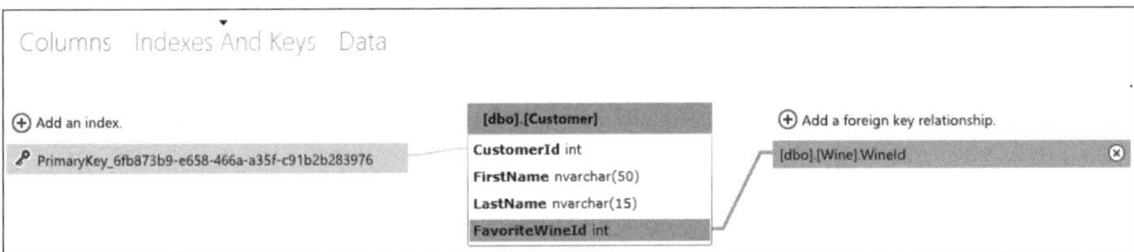

FIGURE 1-17 A completed table relationship in the foreign-key designer

Inserting data

Most likely, you'll be migrating from existing on-premises SQL Server databases (as we cover in Chapter 4, "Migrating databases"), or perhaps you'll be building applications that load data into the database (covered in Chapter 10). But for quick and raw data entry, the SQL Database management portal offers a convenient way to interactively insert rows of data into tables (as you can see in Figure 1-18), without coding Transact-SQL (T-SQL) *INSERT* statements.

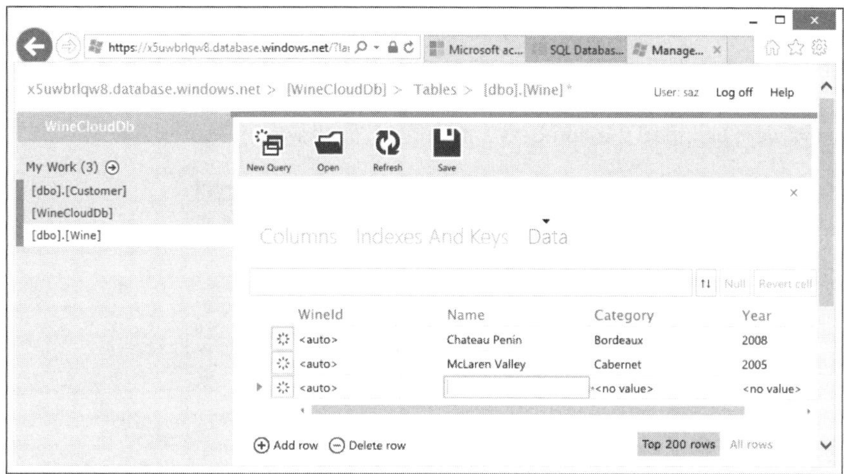

FIGURE 1-18 Populating a table with data

To populate the *Wine* table with sample products, follow these steps:

1. Log in to the SQL Database management portal for the *WineCloudDb* database, and navigate to the *Wine* table design page, as you did in previous procedures.
2. Click Data at the top of the page.
3. Click Add Row.
4. Enter a row with *Name*, *Category*, and *Year* values of **Chateau Penin**, **Bordeaux**, and **2008**, respectively.

> **Note** Because you selected the Is Identity? check box for the *WineId* column when you designed the table, the designer displays *<auto>* to indicate that SQL Database will automatically assign a value for *WineId* when you save these rows to the database.

5. Repeat steps 3 and 4 to enter three more wines to add to the table as follows:

    a. Enter a row for **McLaren Valley**, **Cabernet**, **2005**.

    b. Enter a row for **Mendoza**, **Merlot**, **2010**.

    c. Enter a row for **Valle Central**, **Merlot**, **2009**.

6. Click Save in the toolbar at the top of the page.

None of the data you entered is actually saved to the database until you click Save in step 6. At that point, the rows are inserted and the display is refreshed to show the *WineId* primary-key values that were automatically assigned by SQL Database. Being the very first four rows added to the table, those primary keys were assigned the numbers 1 through 4, as shown in Figure 1-19.

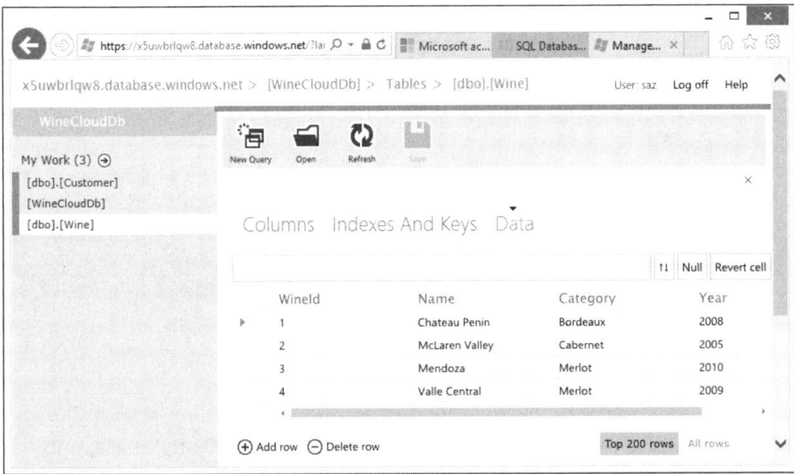

FIGURE 1-19 The *Wine* table populated with rows of data with automatically assigned primary-key identity values

Now add some data to the *Customer* table. You'll use the same procedure you just followed for the *Wine* table. The only additional consideration to keep in mind is that each customer has a foreign-key value that identifies that customer's favorite wine. Because you informed SQL Database about this foreign-key relationship in a previous procedure, you can only supply a value of 1 through 4 for each customer's *FavoriteWineId* column (or other integers for rows that are added to the *Wine* table in the future). Your only other option is to supply *NULL*, because *FavoriteWineId* is optional (meaning that it's OK if the customer's favorite wine is unknown). Otherwise, as we'll demonstrate, SQL Database will not permit you to add a customer row with a non-*NULL* value for *FavoriteWineId* that does not have a related row in the *Wine* table.

To populate the *Customer* table, follow these steps:

1. Navigate to the *Customer* table design page.

2. Click Data at the top of the page.

3. Click Add Row

4. Enter a row with *FirstName*, *LastName*, and *FavoriteWineId* values of **Jeff**, **Hay**, and **4**, respectively.

5. Click Add Row again to enter another row for **Mark**, **Hanson**, **3**.

6. Click Save to save the rows to the database. The two rows are automatically assigned primary key values of 1 and 2 for the *CustomerId* column.

7. Click Add Row again to enter a third row for **Jeff**, **Phillips**, but this time type a **6** for the *FavoriteWineId*.

8. Click Save. Now SQL Database complains of an error.

9. Expand the Error Details as shown in Figure 1-20. This displays the error message describing the foreign-key conflict that occurred because there is no row in the *Wine* table with a *WineId* of 6.

FIGURE 1-20 Error message displayed when attempting to violate a defined foreign-key relationship

10. Correct the problem by changing the 6 to a **2**.

11. Click Save. Now Jeff Phillips gets saved to the *Customer* table. (See Figure 1-21.)

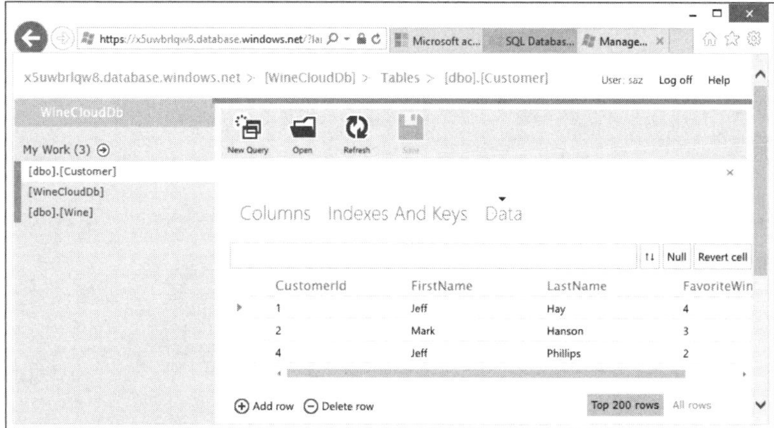

FIGURE 1-21 The *Customer* table populated with several rows of data

Interestingly, the Jeff Phillips row was assigned a primary key value of 4, skipping over the next available value (which, after Mark Hanson, would have been 3). This is because the number 3 got "used up" during the failed insert attempt that occurred with the foreign-key conflict,

Querying the database

Now you have a database with two related, populated tables. The next logical step is to query this data. Because SQL Database is essentially an adapted version of on-premises SQL Server tailored for running on Microsoft Azure, most typical queries can be expressed using the same T-SQL syntax that works with on-premises SQL Server. So the *Customer* and *Wine* tables can be easily joined together to display the names of each customer's favorite wine. Furthermore, they can be filtered to limit the results by some specific criteria.

The SQL Database management portal has an ad-hoc query window that lets you run T-SQL queries and view their results. To query for customers and their favorite wines, follow these steps:

1. Log in to the SQL Database management portal for the *WineCloudDb* database.
2. Click New Query at the top of the page to open a new query window.
3. Type the following T-SQL code into the query window:

```
SELECT
  c.FirstName,
  c.LastName,
  w.Category,
  w.Name
 FROM
  Customer AS c
  LEFT OUTER JOIN Wine AS w ON c.FavoriteWineId = w.WineId
 ORDER BY
  c.LastName, c.FirstName;
```

4. Click Run at the top of the page. SQL Database executes the query and displays the results in the bottom portion of the query window, as shown in Figure 1-22.

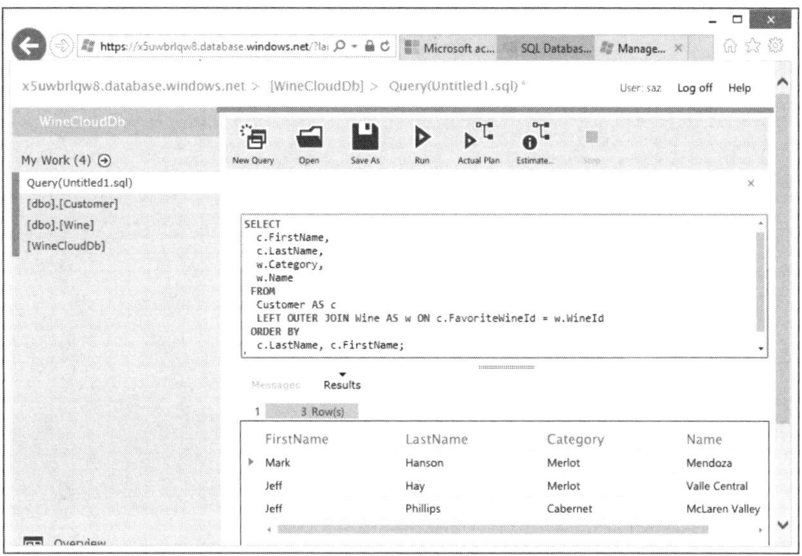

FIGURE 1-22 Creating and running a query that joins customers with their favorite wine

5. Modify the query by adding a *WHERE* clause. Just before the *ORDER BY* clause, type **WHERE w.Category = 'Merlot'**

6. Click Run again. The query executes once more, this time returning only customers whose favorite wine is a Merlot, as shown in Figure 1-23.

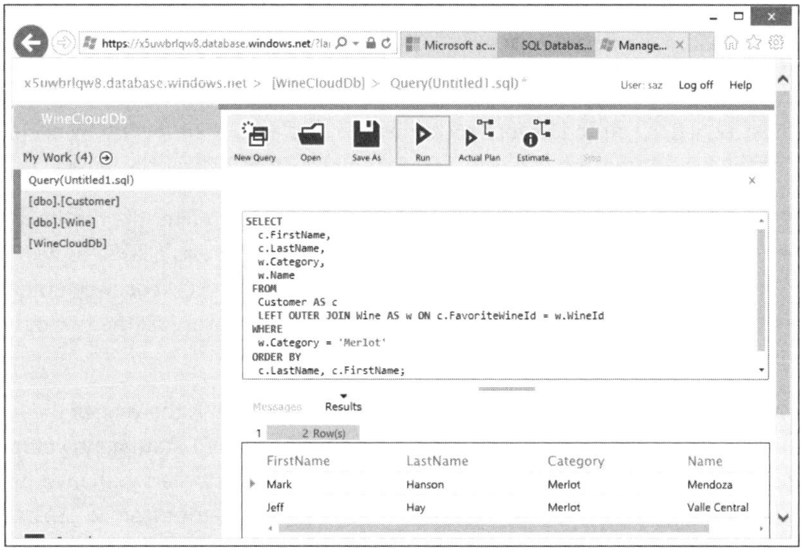

FIGURE 1-23 Applying a query filter using the *WHERE* clause

7. Change the *WHERE* clause of the query from *w.Category = 'Merlot'* to **w.Year < 2010**.

8. Click Run once more. This time, the query filters on the wine year, as shown in Figure 1-24.

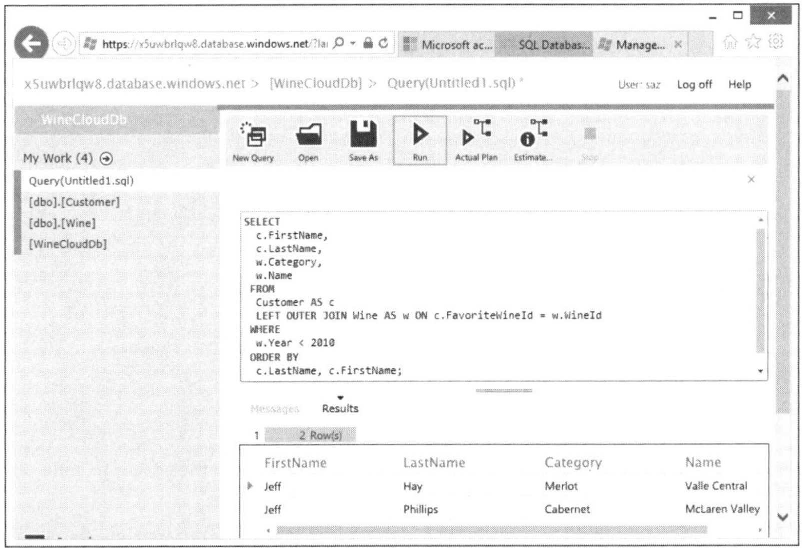

FIGURE 1-24 Filtering on the customer's favorite wine year

In step 3, notice how you joined the *Customer* and *Wine* tables in the query's *FROM* clause. The *LEFT OUTER JOIN* ensures that customer rows are returned even if they contain a *NULL* in *FavoriteWineId*—that is, even if they have no favorite wine. Using an *INNER JOIN* instead would automatically exclude customers without a favorite wine.

The initial version of this query had no *WHERE* clause, and with a *LEFT OUTER JOIN*, there was no filtering at all. So, at first, it returned every customer and displayed their favorite wine. (*NULL* would be returned for the wine name and category for customers without a favorite wine.)

By adding the *WHERE* clause in step 5, you asked SQL Database to filter the results to include only customers whose favorite wine is any kind of Merlot. The *Wine* table was aliased as *w* in the *FROM* clause, so *w.Category* in the *WHERE* clause refers to, and filters by, the *Category* column in the row joined in from the *Wine* table. Running this version of the query returns just the two customers with Merlot as their favorite wine category.

In step 7, you changed the *WHERE* clause to filter by *w.Year*, which is the year of the wine. Notice how this column is not actually in the result set returned by the *SELECT* statement, yet it is perfectly valid to filter on it. This version of the query now returns the two customers with favorite wines (in any category) older than 2010. These are Jeff Hay (with a Velle Central Merlot from 2009) and Jeff Phillips (with a McLaren Valley Cabernet from 2005). Mark Hanson's favorite wine is the Mendoza Merlot, but he is filtered out from these results because that wine is from 2010, and the query is returning only customer rows with favorite wines that are older than 2010.

Exploring additional portal capabilities

In just this first chapter alone, you've already accomplished quite a lot with SQL Database. You've created a server and a database, defined tables with relationships, populated data, and executed queries. And you've done all those things with nothing more than a browser, using the Microsoft Azure management portal and the Microsoft Azure SQL Database management portal. But all that is still just scratching the surface of what's possible.

The SQL Database management portal has matured greatly since the early days of Microsoft Azure (when it was called the *SQL Azure management portal*). And you can expect it to continue evolving—quite possibly even by the time this book goes to press. Before concluding the chapter, we recommend you take the time to examine some of these additional capabilities available in the current SQL Database management portal at the time of this writing.

Creating views

Views are essentially encapsulated queries that are stored in the database. In most respects, your queries can treat views just as ordinary tables.

For example, you could create three views that encapsulate the three versions of the query from the previous section "Querying the database." You might name those three views as follows:

- *CustomersWithFavoriteView*
- *CustomersWIthFavoriteMerlotView*
- *CustomersWithFavoritePre2010View*

With those views in place, it becomes much easier to query the database. For example, you can just select from the *CustomersWithFavoriteMerlotView*, instead of writing the lengthier version of the query that joins the *Customer* and *Wine* tables.

Creating stored procedures

Like views, stored procedures can also encapsulate queries, but they can also do much more than that. In addition to returning data from queries, stored procedures can contain any T-SQL logic. They can also accept parameters, update data, and call other stored procedures.

Stored procedures are commonplace in professional relational databases. They are often used to protect underlying tables from inappropriate usage. They can also build on views, implement business logic, or further abstract details of the underlying database structure—hiding the way that tables, views, and columns are named; how the table relationships are defined; and so on. Essentially, and particularly from the perspective of designing multitiered layered architectures, stored procedures can be effectively leveraged to implement a service layer over your data, at the database level.

Here's a stored procedure you can create that joins the *Customer* and *Wine* tables to return customers with their favorite wine, just as you did in the previous query. But this stored procedure will have some added flexibility; it will accept a *@FavoriteWineId* parameter so that the results can be limited to returning just those customers whose favorite wine matches the value passed in through this parameter. If *NULL* is specified for *@FavoriteWineId*, the stored procedure will return all customers. As before, you will use an *OUTER JOIN*, so if no parameter value is passed, even customers with no favorite wines will be returned (and *NULL* will be returned for the name of their favorite wine). You will aptly name this stored procedure *GetCustomers*.

To create the *GetCustomers* stored procedure, follow these steps:

1. Log in to the Microsoft Azure SQL Database portal.
2. Click the Design tab on the left side of the page.
3. Click Stored Procedures at the top of the page.
4. Click New Stored Procedure. The stored procedure designer opens with a default name of *Stored Procedure1*.
5. Change the Stored Procedure name to **GetCustomers**.
6. Click Add Parameter to create a new parameter named *@Parameter1* with a data type of *nvarchar(50)*.
7. Change the parameter name to **@FavoriteWineId**.
8. Click the drop-down list beneath Select Type to change the parameter data type to *int*.
9. Type the following code into the code window:

```
SELECT
  c.FirstName, c.LastName, w.Category, w.Name
 FROM
  Customer AS c
  LEFT OUTER JOIN Wine AS w ON c.FavoriteWineId = w.WineId
 WHERE
  (@FavoriteWineId IS NULL) OR (c.FavoriteWineId = @FavoriteWineId)
 ORDER BY
  c.LastName, c.FirstName;
```

10. Click Save at the top of the page.

Your screen show appear similar to Figure 1-25.

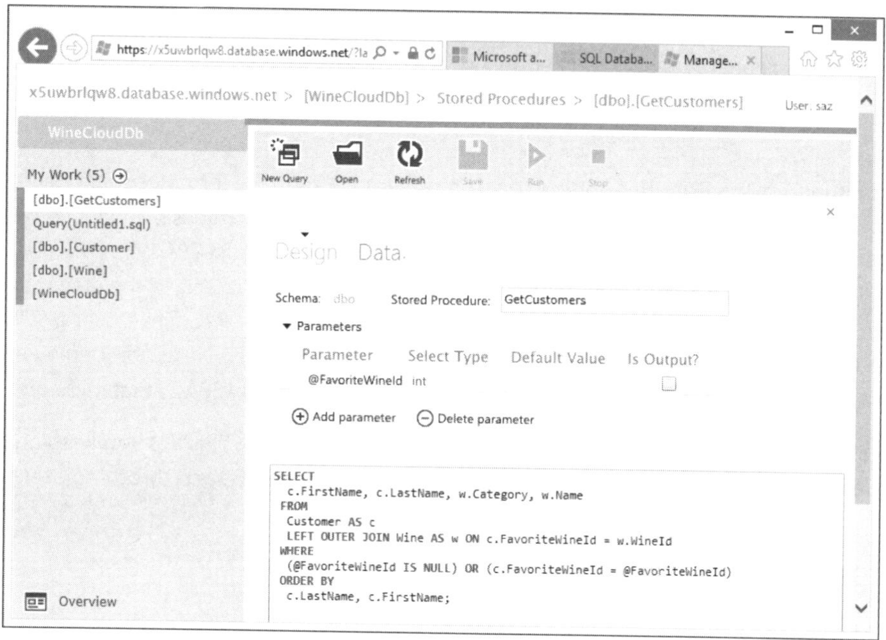

FIGURE 1-25 Designing the *GetCustomers* stored procedure

As we explained, this stored procedure accepts an integer parameter named *@FavoriteWineId*. The stored procedure encapsulates the same join logic between *Customer* and *Wine* in the *FROM* clause you've already seen, but it also adds logic in the *WHERE* clause to determine if a favorite wine was requested (that is, if the value for the *@FavoriteWineId* parameter was not passed in as *NULL*). It therefore returns either all customers (if *NULL* was passed in for *@FavoriteWineId*) or only those customers with favorite wines that match the value in *@FavoriteWineId*.

To test the stored procedure, follow these steps:

1. Click New Query at the top of the page to open a new query window.
2. In the new query window, type **EXEC GetCustomers @FavoriteWineId = NULL**.
3. Click Run at the top of the page to execute the stored procedure, passing in *NULL* for the *@FavoriteWineId* parameter. SQL Database returns all three customers and the names of their favorite wine.
4. Modify the *EXEC* statement from step 2 by changing *NULL* to **3**, which is the *WineId* for the 2010 Mendoza Merlot.
5. Click Run again. This time, only Mark Hanson is returned, because (currently) he's the only customer that has selected 2010 Mendoza Merlot as his favorite wine.

Database administration features

The SQL Database management portal also offers several database administration features you should be aware of, such as DACPAC and BACPAC support (for migration and backup) and event tracking.

The portal supports the Data-tier Application Component Package file format, commonly referred to as *DACPAC files*. A DACPAC file contains the complete definition of a database, and it can be leveraged for streamlined incremental deployments of the database design. A BACPAC file is similar, except that in addition to the definition of the database, it includes actual data as well. In the management portal, there is full support for importing and exporting DACPAC and BACPAC files. Locally, SQL Server Data Tools (SSDT) in Visual Studio can also be used to define DACPAC files and deploy them to Microsoft Azure SQL Database. You will learn more about DACPAC and BACPAC in later chapters.

You can also track events from the SQL Database management portal. This lets you keep an eye on things like database connections (whether they succeed or fail), deadlocks, and throttling events.

Summary

This chapter got you acquainted with Microsoft Azure SQL Database. We began with an overview of Azure and cloud computing, and then demonstrated how easy it is to get signed up for a Microsoft account and an Azure subscription. You then used the Microsoft Azure management portal to quickly create a new server, and then create a new database on that server.

You also learned how to use the SQL Database portal (which you launched from the Microsoft Azure portal using a special management URL) to design the database. You created and populated two related tables, and then you opened a query window to run a few *SELECT* queries that joined the tables. You also learned about creating views, creating stored procedures, and the availability of other database administration features in the SQL Database management portal.

Now that we've introduced you to the SQL Database platform, you're ready to move on to Chapter 2, where we will delve more deeply into the details of setup and configuration.

CHAPTER 2

Configuration and pricing

—Leonard Lobel

Now that you have your first database up and running, you're ready to explore additional options for managing the setup and configuration of SQL Database. You'll learn more capabilities of the Microsoft Azure management portal you started working with in Chapter 1, "Getting started with Microsoft Azure SQL Database" as well as Microsoft SQL Server Management Studio (SSMS) and Windows PowerShell, all of which can be used to administer SQL Database.

In this chapter, we show you how to use the aforementioned tools to create and drop (delete) databases. Many other chapters in this book also use SSMS to perform more detailed actions and specific tasks. After acquainting you with these tools, the chapter concludes with a discussion of pricing and provides helpful tips for reducing the cost of using SQL Database.

Using the Microsoft Azure platform management portal

As you saw in Chapter 1, the Microsoft Azure management portal provides a good basic interface for creating and provisioning new SQL Database servers and databases. In this section, you'll learn more about how the portal can be used to create databases with the Quick Create and Custom Create options, allow client access with firewall rules, obtain connection strings, and delete databases.

Creating a new database

The management portal offers three options for creating a new database: Quick Create, Custom Create, and Import.

Quick Create is the fastest and easiest way to create a database. If you are fine with a 1-gigabyte (GB) Web edition database and the default collation for North American and Western European languages, use the Quick Create option. (The different editions are explained later in this chapter in the section "Configuring the database edition and size.") If you need to customize the language settings to support other language types stored in the database, or if you want to preset the database for a larger size than 1 GB, use the Custom Create option. Finally, if you already have an existing database (either a Microsoft Azure SQL Database on another server or an on-premises SQL Server database) that you want to bring into a particular Microsoft Azure SQL Database server, use the Import option.

Warning You can change the database edition and size at a later time, but *not* the collation. So if most users of this database are outside of the U.S. and western Europe, make sure to set the appropriate collation to support the required languages when you create the database.

Quick Create

With Quick Create, you need to supply only two pieces of information to create a database: The name of the new database, and the name of the existing server that the new database should be hosted on (although, indeed, Quick Create will allow you to create a new server for the database on the fly, at the same time the database is created.

To create a new SQL Database using Quick Create, follow these steps:

1. Log in to the Microsoft Azure portal at **https://manage.windowsazure.com**. This brings you to the main portal page showing ALL ITEMS.
2. Click SQL DATABASES in the vertical navigation pane on the left.
3. Click the NEW button at the bottom of the page.
4. Click QUICK CREATE, as shown in Figure 2-1.

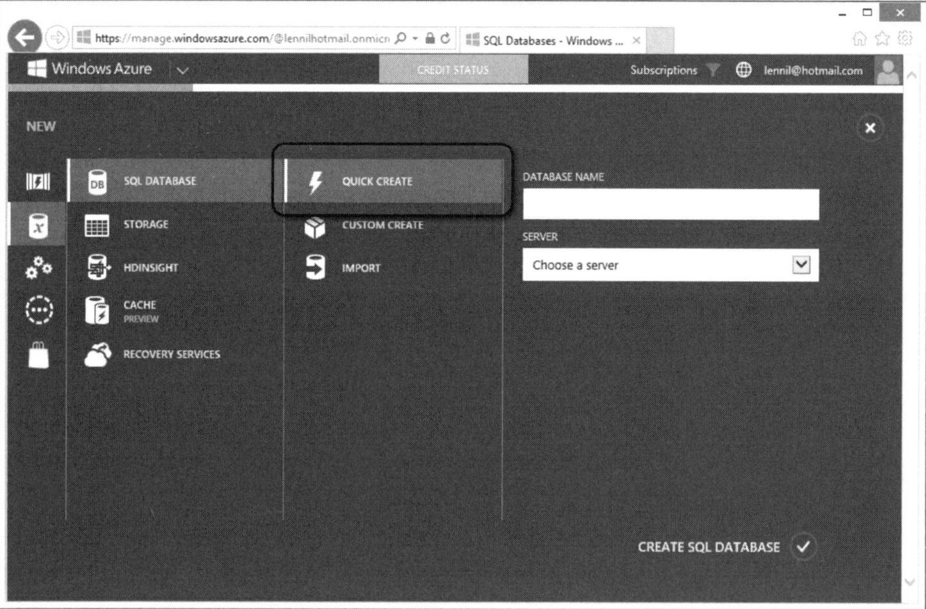

FIGURE 2-1 Using Quick Create to create a new database.

5. For DATABASE NAME, type **MyQuickCreateDb**.

6. For SERVER, choose any available server from the drop-down list to host the database (or choose New SQL Database Server from the drop-down list to create a new server on the fly).

7. Click CREATE SQL DATABASE.

After a brief moment, the *MyQuickCreateDb* database is created and ready for use. This is a 1-GB Web Edition SQL Database with the default collation.

Custom Create

With Custom Create, you have control over the options for the new database that you don't get with Quick Create. These options include the database edition, size, and collation. Indeed, you used Custom Create in Chapter 1 to create the *WineCloudDb* database, you just invoked it differently, by clicking the CREATE A SQL DATABASE link. (Refer back to Figure 1-9.)

Database editions and size are discussed later in this chapter in the section "Configuring the database edition and size," but the important thing to know up front is that you can always change these settings later on, after the database is created. The collation, however, cannot be changed once the database is created. Collation is important when you need to use languages other than western European languages. For example, if your main audience needs its data stored in Mandarin, Cyrillic, or Arabic, you should set the collation appropriately.

Follow these steps to create a new SQL Database using Custom Create:

1. Log in to the Microsoft Azure portal at **https://manage.windowsazure.com**. This brings you to the main portal page showing ALL ITEMS.

2. Click SQL DATABASES in the vertical navigation pane on the left.

3. Click the NEW button at the bottom of the page.

4. Click CUSTOM CREATE. This opens the NEW SQL DATABASE dialog, as shown in Figure 2-2.

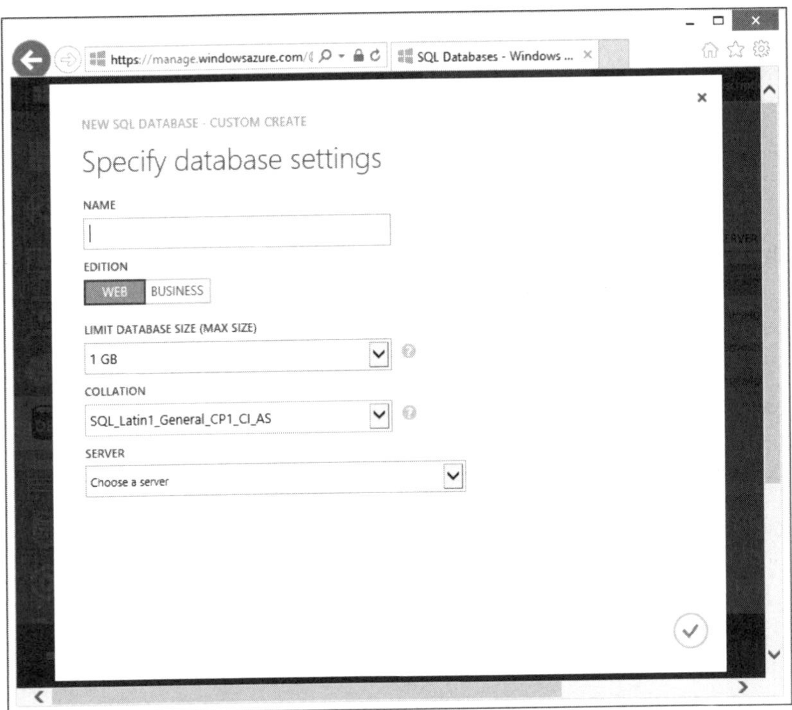

FIGURE 2-2 Using the NEW SQL DATABASE dialog with Custom Create.

5. For DATABASE NAME, type **MyCustomCreateDb**.
6. Choose the edition (Web for 1 to 5 GB, or Business for 10 to 150 GB).
7. Select the collation appropriate for your data.
8. For SERVER, choose any available server from the drop-down list to host the database (or choose New SQL Database Server from the drop-down list to create a new server on the fly).
9. Click the checkmark "finish" button to complete the settings.

After a brief moment, the *MyCustomCreateDb* database is created and configured with the edition, size, and collation you specified.

Importing a database

A third way of creating a database in the portal is to import an existing database from a BACPAC file. A BACPAC file is, essentially, a backup of an entire database (schema and data), stored as a binary large object (BLOB).

You can create a BACPAC file from a local SQL Server (on-premises) database or from a SQL Database on Azure. Once you have a BACPAC file, you can import it to SQL Database. This makes it easy to back up or migrate databases across multiple SQL Server instances and Microsoft Azure SQL Database servers, datacenters, and subscriptions.

Importing (and exporting) databases on Azure is facilitated by storing BACPAC files in Azure Blob Storage. This, in turn, requires the creation of a Microsoft Azure Storage Account, which is simply an account that provides access to cloud storage for your BACPAC files. The entire process is explained in Chapter 4, in the section "SQL data-tier applications."

Setting firewall rules

Most of the time, you want your production SQL Databases to be accessed by only your production cloud services. Thus, the firewall settings for the server are set up by default to limit access only within the Microsoft Azure datacenters. However, you (and others) will sometimes need to access the databases directly from tools (such as SSMS and Microsoft Visual Studio) running on your own local machines. To do so, you need to create an allow list of the IP address of users attempting to access the database over the Internet.

It is important to understand that the IP address that needs to be specified is not your IP address on your local network, but the IP address that the Microsoft Azure datacenter sees when you attempt to access something. So if you are accessing the database from your office, it is the public static IP address of the office router that needs to be specified. For example, if you have IP addresses as shown in Figure 2-3, the address you need for the firewall configuration is the public static IP address 123.456.789.012.

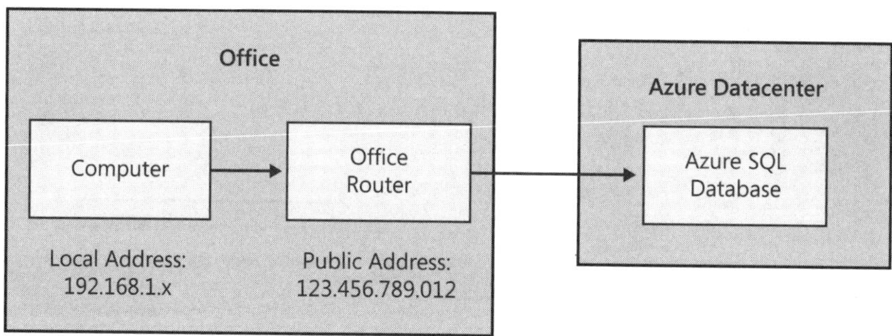

FIGURE 2-3 Public IP address of Internet Gateway Router requires access to SQL Database in the Microsoft Azure datacenter.

The method by which you find the appropriate IP address differs depending on whether you are behind that same public router or not. The next two sections describe how to enable the firewall rules in these two scenarios.

Enabling access to the local network

In Chapter 1, you already added the public IP address for your local machine. (Refer back to Figure 1-7.) This section shows you how to add additional IP addresses; for example, if you were at home when you worked on Chapter 1, and now you're working on Chapter 2 from work.

To update the firewall rules with another IP address, follow these steps:

1. Log in to the Microsoft Azure portal at **https://manage.windowsazure.com**. This brings you to the main portal page showing ALL ITEMS.
2. Click SQL DATABASES in the vertical navigation pane on the left. This shows a list of available databases, which should include the *WineCloudDb* database you created in Chapter 1.
3. Click on the database name *WineCloudDb*. This displays a page of quick-start links for the database.
4. Click the Set Up Windows Azure Firewall Rules For This IP Address link, as shown in Figure 2-4 (Microsoft Azure was formerly called Windows Azure). Again, if you already added the same IP address as in Chapter 1, you will receive an error message stating that the IP address has already been added to the firewall rules (which is expected, of course).

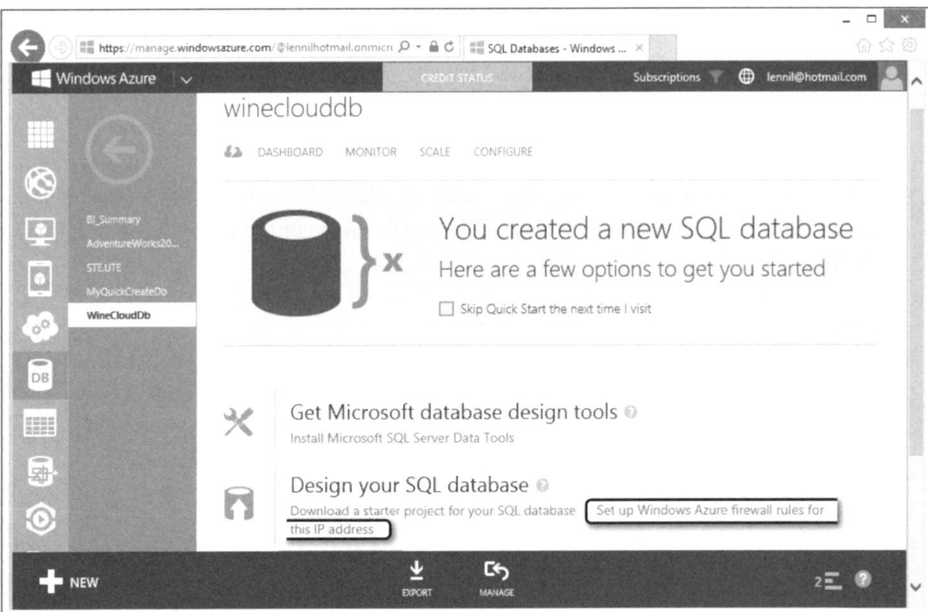

FIGURE 2-4 The quick-start link to create a firewall rule for the local network.

5. When prompted to update the firewall rules, as shown in Figure 2-5, click YES.

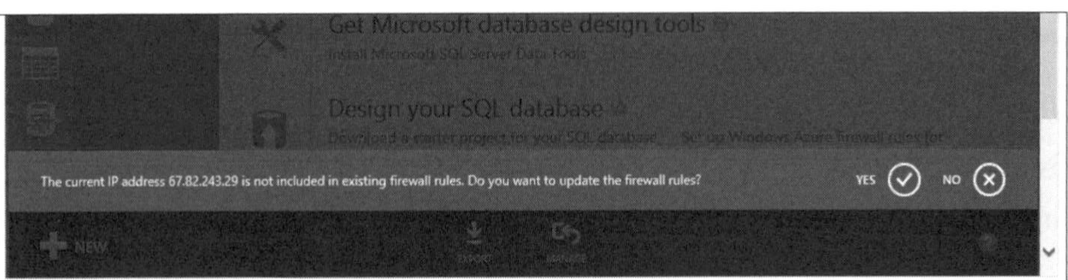

FIGURE 2-5 Automatically set up a firewall for this address.

Enabling access to a remote IP address

The previous scenario works if your computer is on the same network with the same public IP address as your computer or other computers that should be authorized to log in to the database. But what if you need to authorize some other computer at a different location on the Internet to be able to access the database? You need to find the public IP address of those other computers and add those IP addresses to the firewall rules as well.

To open the firewall for a remote user who needs access to the database, you normally need to contact a network administrator to learn the IP address or addresses. If you can't or don't want to reach out to the administrator, you can open the firewall for the remote user by working cooperatively, with the help of *whatismyipaddress.com*.

To do so, follow these steps:

1. Ask the remote user to log on to a computer on her network.
2. Have the user open a browser and navigate to the website **http://whatismyipaddress.com**.
3. Have the user read the IP address that the website reports to them and write it down.
4. Log in to the Microsoft Azure portal at **https://manage.windowsazure.com**. This brings you to the main portal page showing ALL ITEMS.
5. Click SQL DATABASES in the vertical navigation pane on the left.
6. Click the server name of the database to which the remote user needs access.
7. Click the CONFIGURE link at the top of the page. You will see a page that shows all the allowed IP addresses (the allow list), which should already include the one for your local machine that was previously added automatically.
8. In the RULE NAME text box, enter a descriptive name (no spaces allowed) for the remote user or group to which you are granting access to the database—for example, **RemoteDevOffice**.
9. Enter the IP address you wrote down in step 3 (the one the remote user reported from *whatismyipaddress.com*) into both the START IP ADDRESS and END IP ADDRESS text boxes. (In this scenario, you are creating a rule for a single address, but these text boxes can also be used to specify a range of IP addresses as desired.) The page should appear similar to Figure 2-6.

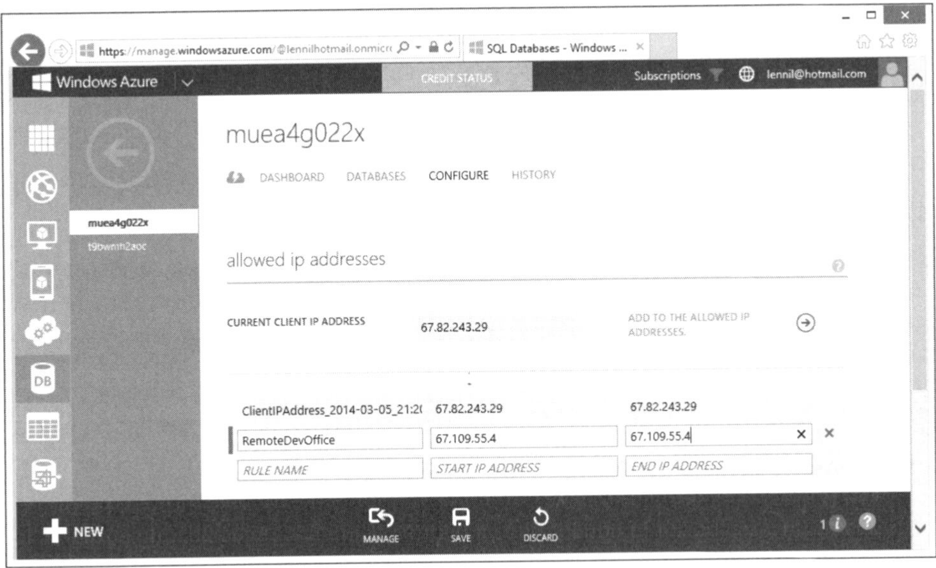

FIGURE 2-6 Adding a new IP address to the firewall rules for a server.

10. Click the SAVE button at the bottom of the page.

The specified IP address can now reach the database.

Obtaining connection strings

If you are building a client application that connects to this SQL Database, you'll need the connection string for the database. You can obtain connection strings in a number of different formats that are suitable for the most common database clients, including ADO.NET, ODBC, PHP, and JDBC.

To obtain the connection string of the *WineCloudDb* database for various database clients, follow these steps:

1. Log in to the Microsoft Azure portal at **https://manage.windowsazure.com**. This brings you to the main portal page showing ALL ITEMS.
2. Click SQL DATABASES in the vertical navigation pane on the left. This shows a list of available databases, which should include the *WineCloudDb* database you created in Chapter 1.
3. Click on the database name *WineCloudDb*. This displays a page of quick-start links for the database.
4. Click the View SQL Database Connection Strings For ADO.Net, ODBC, HPP, And JDBC link, as shown in Figure 2-7. Also, take note of the server name beneath the link, which is always suffixed with *.database.windows.net*. You will need this server name to connect to SQL Database using SSMS a bit further on in the chapter.

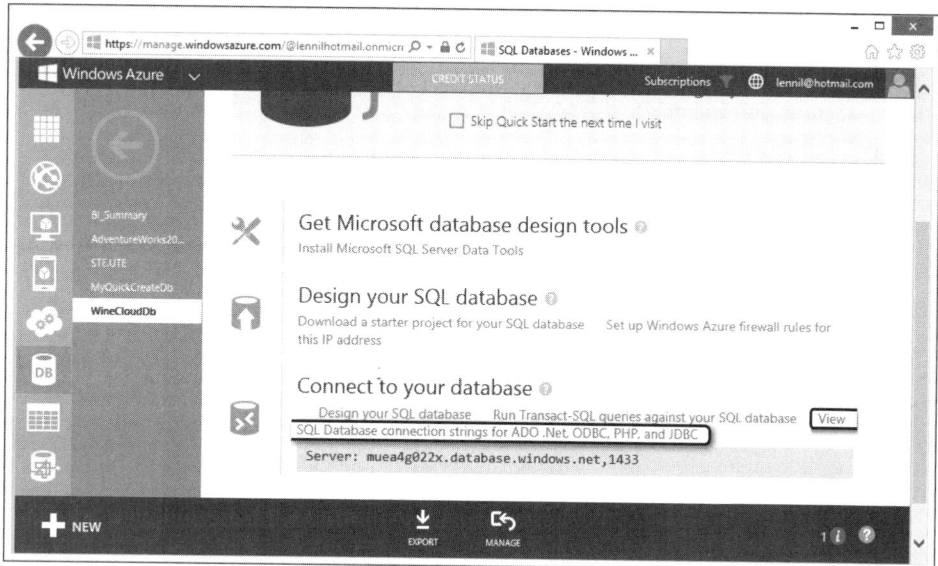

FIGURE 2-7 The quick-start link to display database connection strings.

5. The page displays the connections strings, as shown in Figure 2-8. Each connection string appears in a text box (that scrolls, if necessary), from which you can easily copy and paste into your client application.

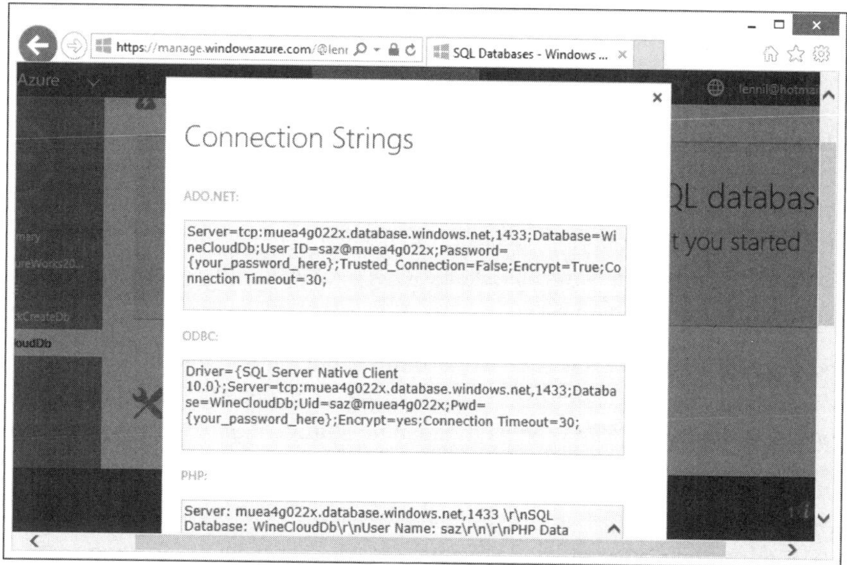

FIGURE 2-8 Viewing the database connection strings for ADO.NET, ODBC, PHP, and JDBC.

Deleting a database

When you no longer need a database (or server), you can use the management portal to delete it. In this section, you will delete the *MyQuickCreateDb* and *MyCustomCreateDb* databases you created earlier in this chapter.

To delete the unwanted databases, follow these steps:

1. Log in to the Microsoft Azure portal at **https://manage.windowsazure.com**. This brings you to the main portal page showing ALL ITEMS.
2. Click SQL DATABASES in the vertical navigation pane on the left. This shows a list of available databases, which should include the *MyQuickCreateDb* and *MyCustomCreateDb* databases you created earlier in this chapter.
3. Click to select the row for *MyQuickCreateDb*. (Don't click in the NAME or SERVER columns.)
4. Click the DELETE button at the bottom of the page.
5. Click YES, DELETE when prompted that the database will be permanently deleted.
6. Repeat steps 3, 4, and 5 to delete the *MyCustomCreateDb* database.

The management portal is great for working with SQL Database from any computer with a web browser, without requiring any other special software or tools. Alternatively, there are a number of local tools available that can also connect to and work with SQL Database. This includes SSMS and PowerShell, which are covered next in this chapter, as well as SQL Server Data Tools (SSDT), which is covered in Chapter 10.

Using SQL Server Management Studio

You can also administer SQL Database using SQL Server Management Studio (SSMS), which (as of SSMS 2008 R2) has partial support for Microsoft Azure SQL Database built in. This section explains how to use SSMS to connect to your SQL Database server. You will then learn how to create, alter, and drop SQL Databases from within SSMS.

You must already have SSMS installed to follow the procedures in this section. If you don't already have SSMS, you can download it for free (either by itself, or along with SQL Server Express edition). Instructions for downloading SSMS can be found in the Introduction.

Once you connect with SSMS, you can use Object Explorer to navigate between objects in SQL Database just as you can with an on-premises SQL Server database. However, most of the other graphical designers and dialogs are not available. For example, if you try to design a table or create a new database, SSMS will open a new query window with template Transact-SQL (T-SQL) script for you to edit, rather than opening the table designer or the New Database dialog, as you might expect. This is because these features rely on SQL Server Management Objects (SMO), which SQL Database has only limited support for. Therefore, almost everything needs to be done via T-SQL script when using SSMS to configure SQL Database.

Note SQL Server Data Tools (SSDT), which runs inside Visual Studio, can also connect to SQL Database, and it works very similar to SSMS. Unlike SSMS, however, SSDT does not rely on SMO, so the SSDT table designer and other SSDT graphical dialogs *are* supported for SQL Database just the same as they are for on-premises SQL Server. You will learn much more about SSDT in Chapter 10.

Connecting to SQL Database

To connect to SQL Database from SSMS, follow these steps:

1. From the Windows Start screen, launch SSMS. You can either scroll through the app tiles to find it (in the Microsoft SQL Server 2012 category) or just type **sql server management studio** to run a search, and then click on the tile, as shown in Figure 2-9. After a brief moment, the Connect To Server dialog appears.

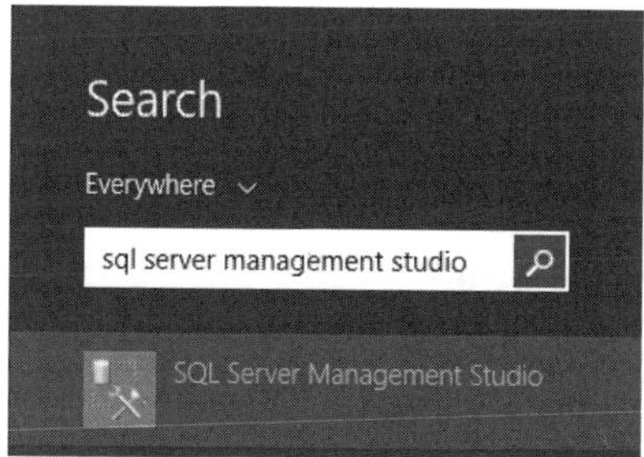

FIGURE 2-9 Launching SQL Server Management Studio from the Windows Start screen.

2. For Server Name, type ***<servername>*.database.windows.net**. This is the fully qualified name to the SQL Database server, where *<servername>* should be replaced by the name assigned to your server.

Tip If you have trouble figuring out the server name, you can easily find it at the bottom of the quick-start links page, as shown in Figure 2-7. You can also discover the server name by viewing the Connection Strings dialog, as shown in Figure 2-8.

3. For Authentication, select SQL Server Authentication from the drop-down list. (SQL Database does not support Windows Authentication.)

4. For Login and Password, type the user name and password you assigned the server when you created it in Chapter 1. The dialog should appear similar to Figure 2-10.

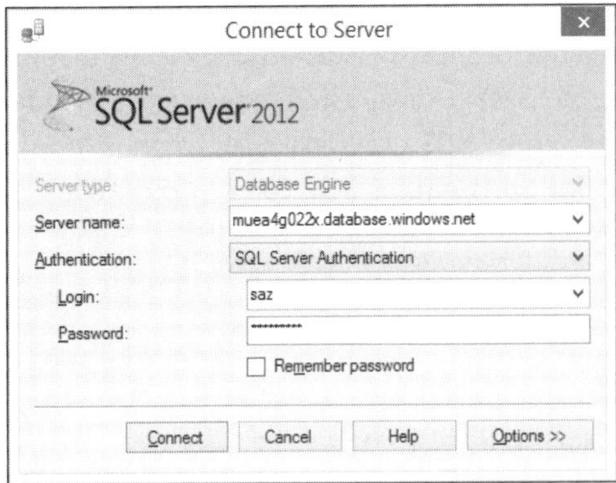

FIGURE 2-10 Connecting to SQL Database from the Connect To Server dialog in SSMS.

5. Click the Connect button.

After a brief moment, the connection is made, and you can then use SSMS to manage SQL Database. If SSMS fails to connect, the most likely cause is that your public IP address has not been added to the firewall rules, as described earlier in this chapter. The error message will make it clear if this is the problem. If the connection fails with a more generic error message, ensure that port 1433 is open on your local firewall. (SQL Database, like SQL Server, uses port 1433 to communicate.)

Once connected, you can drill through Object Explorer to the *WineCloudDb* database, as shown in Figure 2-11.

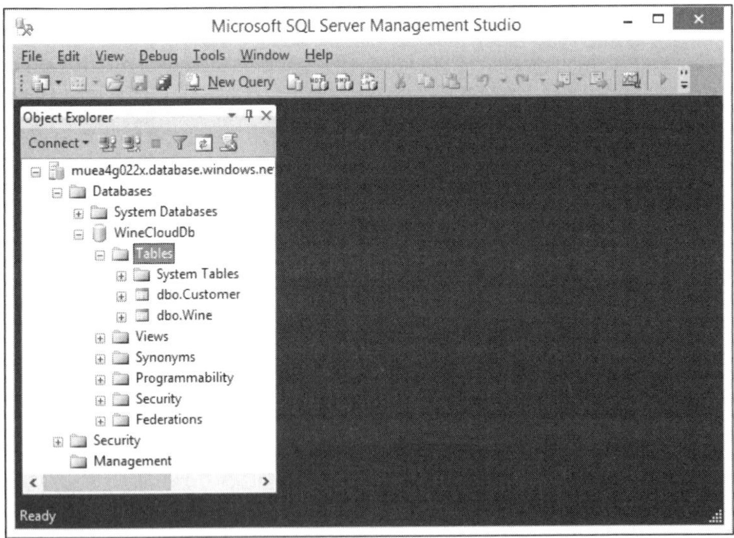

FIGURE 2-11 Drilling down to the tables in a database using Object Explorer in SSMS.

Creating a new database

As we mentioned, the usual New Database dialog in SSMS is not available when you are connected to SQL Database. Instead, SSMS will simply open a query window with the T-SQL script for the *CREATE DATABASE* statement templated in, which is a bit confusing. So the simpler way to create a SQL Database using SSMS is to just go straight to a blank query window and issue a basic *CREATE DATABASE* statement.

To create a new database using an SSMS query window, follow these steps:

1. Connect to a SQL Database server, as described in the previous procedure.
2. In Object Explorer, right-click the server and choose New Query.
3. In the new query window, type **CREATE DATABASE MyDb**. The SSMS window should appear similar to Figure 2-12.

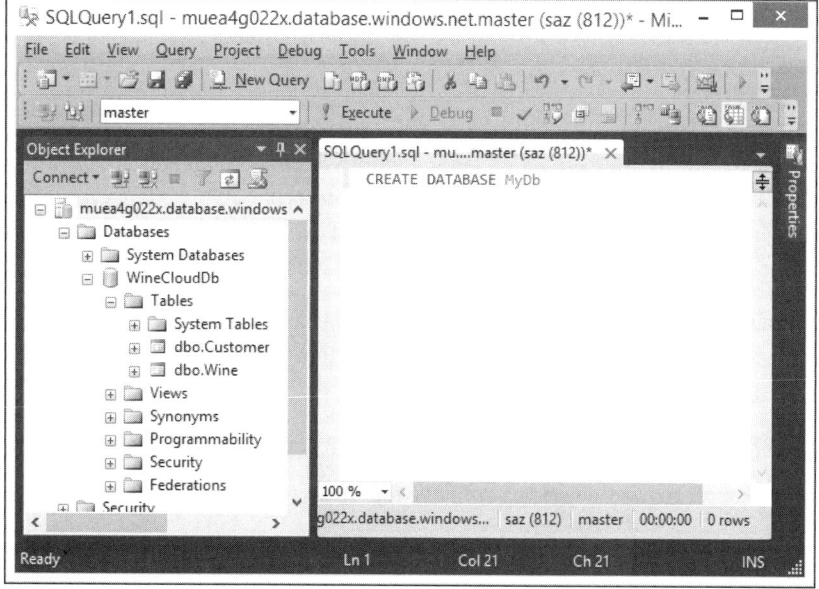

FIGURE 2-12 Creating a new database by executing T-SQL script in an SSMS query window.

4. Press F5 (or click Execute on the toolbar) to execute the statement. It should take only a few moments for execution to complete.

Changing the database edition and maximum size

The *MyDb* database created by the previous procedure has the default configuration, which is Web edition and a size of 1 GB, just like a database created using Quick Create. If you want to change the edition and size, you can do so by issuing an *ALTER DATABASE* statement. For example, to change from Web edition to Business edition with a maximum database size of 10 GB, execute the following T-SQL command in the query window:

```
ALTER DATABASE MyDb MODIFY (EDITION='business', MAXSIZE=10GB)
```

Deleting a database

Dropping a SQL Database is like dropping any SQL Server database. Either right-click on the database in Object Explorer and choose Delete, or execute the following T-SQL command in the query window:

```
DROP DATABASE MyDb
```

Using PowerShell

PowerShell is Microsoft's modern scripting language for system administration that supports a wide variety of tasks by executing commands (known as *cmdlets*, pronounced *command-lets*) from the PowerShell command line. Microsoft has also developed PowerShell cmdlets for managing Microsoft Azure, including a number of useful SQL Database commands.

Even if you already have PowerShell installed, these special cmdlets for Microsoft Azure need to be installed separately. The following section describes how to download and install the cmdlets.

Installing the Microsoft Azure PowerShell cmdlets

To install the Microsoft Azure PowerShell cmdlets, follow these steps:

1. Navigate your web browser to **https://www.windowsazure.com/en-us/downloads**.
2. Scroll down to Command-Line Tools, and click the Install link beneath Windows PowerShell, as shown in Figure 2-13.

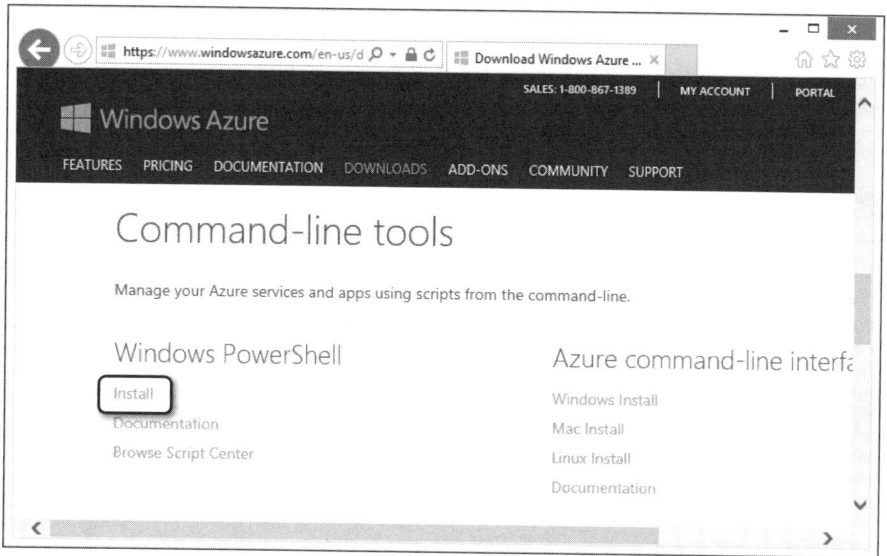

FIGURE 2-13 Downloading the Microsoft Azure cmdlets for PowerShell.

3. When prompted to run or save, click Run.
4. If the User Account Control dialog appears, click Yes.
5. In the Web Platform Installer dialog (shown in Figure 2-14), click Install.

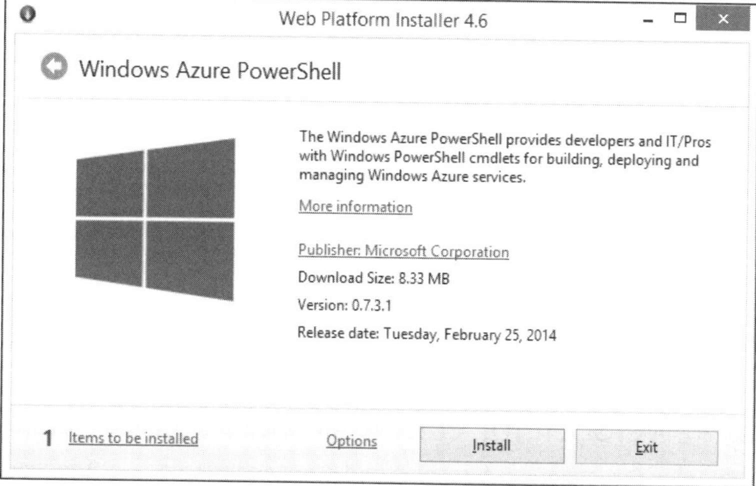

FIGURE 2-14 Installing the Azure cmdlets for PowerShell.

6. Click I Accept to start the installation.
7. When installation completes, click Finish.
8. Click Exit to close the Web Platform Installer dialog.

Using the PowerShell Integrated Scripting Environment

Although you can use a simple text editor (even Notepad) to write PowerShell scripts, the PowerShell Integrated Scripting Environment (ISE) is a much more productive environment. As you'll see, it offers some nice features, such as syntax highlighting and IntelliSense-style auto-completion.

There is no app tile for the PowerShell ISE on the Windows Start screen, so it needs to be launched from the command line. To start the PowerShell ISE and view help information for the Azure SQL Database cmdlets, follow these steps:

1. Open a command prompt. (An app tile for it can be found on the Start screen in the Windows System category, or you can just type **command prompt** to search for it.)
2. At the command prompt, type **powershell_ise**.
3. At the PowerShell ISE prompt, type **get-help get-azuresql**, and then pause. In a moment, a popup window appears showing all the cmdlets that start with *get-azuresql*, as shown in Figure 2-15.

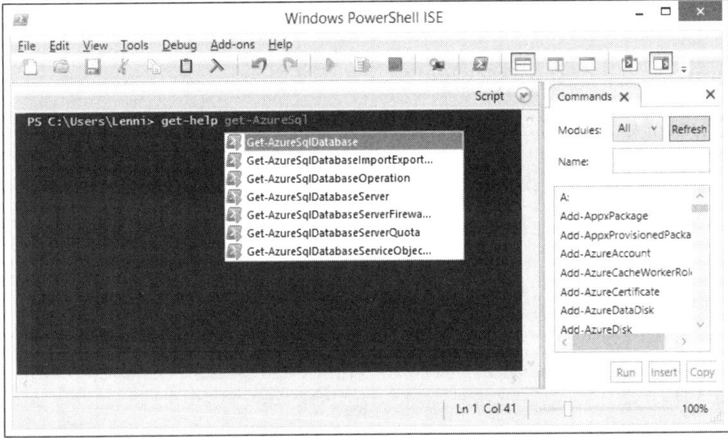

FIGURE 2-15 Obtaining help on the Microsoft Azure SQL Database PowerShell cmdlets.

4. Double-click on any of the cmdlets to complete the command, and then press Enter to view help for the selected cmdlet.

Configuring PowerShell for your Microsoft account

Before you can start using PowerShell to manage Azure, you need to configure it for your account. This is simply a matter of logging in to the portal, and then running a few PowerShell commands to retrieve your account information from Azure and import it into PowerShell. This section walks you through the process.

To configure PowerShell for your Microsoft account, follow these steps:

1. Log in to the Microsoft Azure portal at **https://manage.windowsazure.com**. This step is necessary for PowerShell to identify your account. If you don't log in first, you will be prompted to log in when you try to retrieve your account settings in PowerShell.
2. Start the PowerShell ISE, as explained in the previous procedure.
3. Type **Get-AzurePublishSettingsFile** to retrieve your account settings. Internet Explorer will open up automatically and download a *.publishsettings* file with your account information.
4. Click Save to save the *.publishsettings* file to your default Downloads folder.

Important The *.publishsettings* file should be kept safe and private, because it effectively provides access to the Azure subscriptions on your Microsoft account.

5. Back in the PowerShell ISE, type **Import-AzurePublishSettingsFile *<.publishsettings file>***, where *<.publishsettings file>* is the complete file name (with path) of the account settings file you just saved to your default Downloads folder. (This is typically *C:\Users\<username>\Downloads\<subscription-name>.publishsettings*.)

Note The file name might be long, but the PowerShell ISE auto-complete feature helps with an IntelliSense-style drop-down list as you type. Just press the Tab key to auto-complete your way through the command, and through the folder names and file name of the *.publishsettings* file.

The PowerShell ISE doesn't boast with a message when the settings are imported successfully. You'll only get an error message if it fails. Otherwise, you'll know that all went well if you are silently returned back to the PowerShell command-line prompt.

As you learned in Chapter 1, every SQL Database is hosted on a server. Recall how you used the Microsoft Azure management portal to first create a server, and then to create a database on that server. You also used the portal to set firewall rules to allow access to your SQL Database from designated IP addresses. You will now perform those very same tasks using just a few simple PowerShell commands.

Creating a new server

First, create a new server and add a firewall rule for your IP address so that the server will allow you to connect to it using PowerShell. To do this, follow these steps in the PowerShell ISE:

1. Type **New-AzureSqlDatabaseServer –Location "East US" –AdministratorLogin "*<new-login>*" –AdministratorLoginPassword "*<new-password>*"**, where *<new-login>* and *<new-password>* are the credentials you want to assign for the new server. The server is created, and PowerShell responds by displaying the new server name, as shown in Figure 2-16.

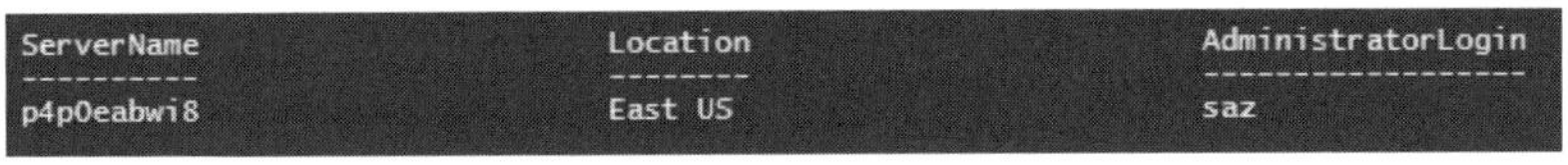

```
ServerName          Location          AdministratorLogin
----------          --------          ------------------
p4p0eabwi8          East US           saz
```

FIGURE 2-16 Creating a new server with PowerShell.

2. Type **New-AzureSqlDatabaseServerFirewallRule –ServerName *<server-name>* –RuleName *<any-name>* –StartIpAddress *<your-ip-address>* –EndIpAddress *<your-ip-address>***, where *<server-name>* is the name of the new server created in step 1, *<any-name>* is an arbitrary name for the new rule (no spaces permitted), and *<your-ip-address>* is the IP address of your machine. This command creates a new firewall rule to allow PowerShell access to the server from your IP address, as shown in Figure 2-17.

Note If you don't know your IP address, you can find out what it is by using *whatismyipaddress.com*, as explained in the section "Enabling access to a remote IP address" earlier in the chapter.

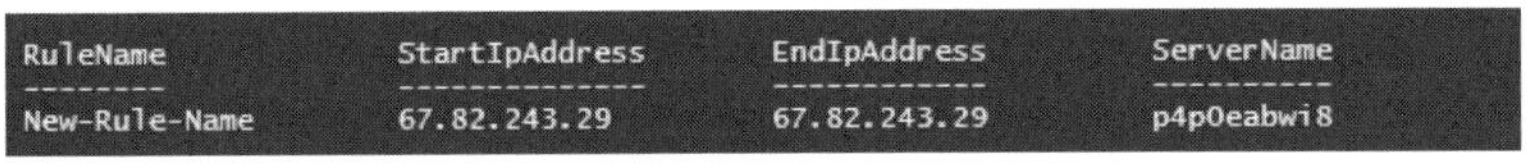

```
RuleName          StartIpAddress     EndIpAddress      ServerName
--------          --------------     ------------      ----------
New-Rule-Name     67.82.243.29       67.82.243.29      p4p0eabwi8
```

FIGURE 2-17 Creating a new server firewall rule with PowerShell.

Creating a new database

The *New-AzureSqlDatabase* cmdlet creates a new database. Before you can use this cmdlet, you must first create an object with your credentials, and then you use those credentials to create a context associated with the server that you want to create the new database on. You store the server context in a variable, and then you specify the server context variable with the *New-AzureSqlDatabase* cmdlet to create the database (as well as all other cmdlets you might run for that particular server).

To create a new database now, follow these steps in the PowerShell ISE:

1. Type **$creds = new-object System.Management.Automation.PSCredential ("*<login-name>*", ("*<login-password>*" | ConvertTo-SecureString –asPlainText –Force))**, where *<login-name>* and *<login-password>* are the administrator login and password you assigned when you created the server in the previous procedure. This stores those administrator credentials in a secure string named *$creds*.

2. Type **$context = New-AzureSqlDatabaseServerContext –ServerName *<server-name>* –Credential $creds**, where *<server-name>* is the name of the server you created in the previous procedure. (The server name is displayed when you create the server, as shown in Figure 2-16.) This creates a context associated with the credentials you created in step 1 and the server you created in the previous procedure, and it stores that context in an object named *$context*.

3. Type **New-AzureSqlDatabase –Context $context –DatabaseName MyNewDb**. This creates a new database named *MyNewDb*. The database is created on the server associated with *$context*, using the credentials associated with *$creds*. When the database is created, PowerShell displays information about the new database, as shown in Figure 2-18.

```
Name                                       : MyNewDb
CollationName                              : SQL_Latin1_General_CP1_CI_AS
Edition                                    : Web
MaxSizeGB                                  : 1
ServiceObjectiveName                       : Shared
ServiceObjectiveAssignmentStateDescription : Complete
CreationDate                               : 12/14/2013 3:22:40 PM
```

FIGURE 2-18 Creating a new database with PowerShell.

4. It's often useful to view all the databases that exist on the server. To do so, type **Get-AzureSqlDatabase –Context $context**. As shown by this cmdlet's output in Figure 2-19, the server includes a *master* database, just as an on-premises SQL Server does.

```
Name                                       : master
CollationName                              : SQL_Latin1_General_CP1_CI_AS
Edition                                    : Web
MaxSizeGB                                  : 5
ServiceObjectiveName                       : System Standard
ServiceObjectiveAssignmentStateDescription : Complete
CreationDate                               : 12/12/2013 2:18:08 AM

Name                                       : MyNewDb
CollationName                              : SQL_Latin1_General_CP1_CI_AS
Edition                                    : Web
MaxSizeGB                                  : 1
ServiceObjectiveName                       : Shared
ServiceObjectiveAssignmentStateDescription : Complete
CreationDate                               : 12/14/2013 3:22:40 PM
```

FIGURE 2-19 Listing all the databases that exist on the server.

The database you just created with *New-AzureSqlDatabase* is, by default, a Web edition database with a maximum size of 1 GB and the default collation. This is the same type of database that gets created when you use Quick Create in the Microsoft Azure management portal. To override these defaults, specify the *–Edition*, *–MaxSizeGb*, and *–Collation* switches with an edition, maximum size, and collation of your own choosing. For example, the following statement creates a Business edition database with a maximum size of 150 GB (the largest possible):

```
New-AzureSqlDatabase -Context $context -DatabaseName MyBigDb -Edition Business -MaxSizeGB 150
```

You can also change the edition and maximum size (but not the collation) of an existing database by using the *Set-AzureSqlDatabase* cmdlet with the *–Edition* and *–MaxSizeGb* switches. For example, you can use the following command to reconfigure the *MyNewDb* database you just created as a Business edition database with a maximum size of 20 GB:

```
Set-AzureSqlDatabase -Context $context -DatabaseName MyNewDb -Edition Business -MaxSizeGB 20
```

Deleting a database

The *Remove-AzureSqlDatabase* cmdlet deletes a SQL Database. To delete the *MyNewDb* database you just created in the previous section, follow these steps:

1. Type **Remove-AzureSqlDatabase –Context $context –DatabaseName MyNewDb**.
2. When prompted to confirm, click Yes.

If you are using *Remove-AzureSqlDatabase* to write scripts you intend to run with no user intervention, you can include the *–Force* switch. This switch causes the database to be deleted immediately, without being prompted to confirm.

Budgeting for SQL Database

The final section of this chapter covers various cost-related items you need to consider when using SQL Database. Specifically, we discuss pricing for the SQL Database storage and bandwidth that you consume. There are no procedures to follow in this section.

Warning As mentioned in the Introduction, Microsoft Azure pricing is subject to change. The following information is based on current pricing at the time this book was written. We strongly recommend that you visit the Microsoft website for the latest figures. Pricing for SQL Database can be found at *http://www.windowsazure.com/en-us/pricing/details/sql-database*.

The information in this section will help you figure out the right configuration and give you tips as to how to save money on your SQL Database deployments. You should also take a look at the online pricing calculator, which quickly calculates pricing based on your input. The online pricing calculator is available at *http://www.windowsazure.com/en-us/pricing/calculator*.

SQL storage

The biggest cost of using SQL Database is for the actual disk space required for storage in Microsoft Azure. Table 2-1 shows current pricing for SQL Database storage.

TABLE 2-1 SQL Database storage pricing

Database Size	Price per Database per Month
Under 100 MB	Flat $4.995
100 MB to 1 GB	Flat $9.99
1 GB to 10 GB	$9.99 for first GB + $3.996 for each additional GB
10 GB to 50 GB	$45.954 for first 10 GB + $1.996 for each additional GB
50 GB to 150 GB	See *http://www.windowsazure.com/en-us/pricing/details/sql-database/*

If you already have an on-premises SQL Server database and would like to calculate the size of the database for estimating the migration cost to SQL Database, you can query the *reserved_page_count* column in the *sys.dm_db_partition_stats* dynamic management view. That column value is expressed in pages, so you can use the following query to sum the total page count: multiply by 8192 (the number of bytes per page), and then divide by 1024 twice to convert the result into megabytes (the first division converts from bytes to kilobytes, the second from kilobytes to megabytes):

```
SELECT (SUM(reserved_page_count) * 8192) / 1024 / 1024 AS DbSizeInMB
 FROM sys.dm_db_partition_stats
```

Client bandwidth

If you connect to your SQL database from within the same datacenter, you do not incur any bandwidth charges for the data flowing either in to or out of the database. If you connect to the database from outside the datacenter, your database incurs only "egress" charges for bandwidth usage, which means that data flowing out of the database to clients is charged, while "ingress" flows (data coming into the database) are free.

The charges are also different in different areas of the world. Client bandwidth pricing is based on the location of the Microsoft Azure datacenter, regardless of where the client accessing the database is located. Again, noting that pricing details are subject to change, the data-transfer pricing details at the time of this writing are shown in Table 2-2.

TABLE 2-2 SQL Database client bandwidth pricing

Data Transfer (Outbound Only)	United States and Europe (per month)	Asia (per month)
Under 5 GB	Free	Free
5 GB to 10 TB	$0.12 per GB	$0.19 per GB
10 TB to 50 TB	$0.09 per GB	$0.15 per GB
50 TB to 150 TB	$0.07 per GB	$0.13 per GB
150 TB to 500 TB	$0.05 per GB	$0.12 per GB
Over 500 TB	Contact Microsoft at wapteams@ microsoft.com	Contact Microsoft at wapteams@ microsoft.com

Backup storage space

When you use Azure Storage to manage your BACPAC files for backups, the storage space for the BACPAC files incurs usage costs. The prices vary with sizes, but using Azure Storage to hold your backups is generally much cheaper than using SQL Database storage. (See Table 2-3.)

For a very small (100-MB) database, the cost of the database is $4.95 per month, while the price for backup storage is only $0.035 (less than 1/100th the cost). As you go up in size, backup storage prices get relatively more expensive, but they are still cheaper than database storage. At 100 GB, the SQL Database cost is $175 per month, while the Azure Storage cost is only $7 per month for a single backup (1/20th the cost). Be careful though, because charges can accrue quickly if you have a backup strategy that requires storing a large number of backups. However, if you maintain a simple incremental backup strategy, in which you keep one backup for the latest hour, day, week, month, and year, then for a 100-MB database you are paying only $0.175 per month for backup, and for a 100-GB database you're paying only $35—a relatively small price to pay to ensure the security of your data.

Alternatively, you can enable geo-replication on your storage account. This is an attractive option for backups because it builds in geographic distribution for disaster recovery, and it does so more cheaply than paying for storage in a separate datacenter as well as paying bandwidth costs to get to that datacenter.

TABLE 2-3 Backup storage space pricing

Storage	Geographically Redundant	Locally Redundant
Under 1 TB	$0.095 per GB	$0.07 per GB
1 TB to 50 TB	$0.09 per GB	$0.065 per GB
50 TB to 500 TB	$0.07 per GB	$0.06 per GB
500 TB to 100 TB	$0.065 per GB	$0.055 per GB
1000 TB to 5000 TB	$0.06 per GB	$0.045 per GB
5000 TB to 9000 TB	$0.055 per GB	$0.037 per GB
Over 9000 TB	Contact Microsoft at wapteams@ microsoft.com	Contact Microsoft at wapteams@ microsoft.com

Backup storage bandwidth

The main difference between offsite and onsite backup costs is bandwidth usage for sending your backups to a different datacenter. The bandwidth usage charges are the same as for the database itself, so you can look at Table 2-2 to understand the charges. Like database access, bandwidth charges are incurred only one way; you won't get double-charged for bandwidth out of one datacenter and into the other. So if you have a 100-MB database and you have backups taken every day, your bandwidth charges are as follows:

0.1 GB X $0.12/GB X 30 days = $0.36/month

If you choose to take backups each hour, your bandwidth charges would be as follows:

0.1 GB X $0.12/GB X 24 hours/day X 30 days = $8.64/month

If you choose to run those backups within the same datacenter, the bandwidth is free.

Another option to consider is to use geo-replicated storage, as mentioned in the previous section, which also provides the protection of storing backups in different datacenters. In this scenario, the storage account you set up for your database backups has geo-replication turned on, and the data is automatically replicated out to another datacenter *within the same region*. For example, if your storage account is in the North Central datacenter, the replica of the data might be in the South Central datacenter, where both datacenters are in the U.S.; it would not be in some datacenter in Europe or Asia.

The main reason why geo-replicated storage is attractive is cost. Imagine you have a 100-MB database and take backups every hour to a remote storage account. If you have hourly, daily, weekly, monthly, and yearly backups, you pay the following:

0.1 GB X $0.070/GB/month X 5 backup files = $0.035/month for the storage plus another $8.64 per month in bandwidth charges, for a total of about $8.69 for backups

If you pay the higher amount for geo-replicated storage, it actually saves you money. The cost for the geo-replicated storage for the same database would be as follows:

0.1 GB X $0.095/GB/month X 5 backup files = $0.0475/month for the storage

However, because it is already geo-replicated, you do not have to pay for the bandwidth to do the replication. Your total amount for backup storage in that case is only $0.0475, instead of $8.69 in the manually replicated scenario.

Support

When discussing costs, one thing that is frequently overlooked is the cost of a support package. Microsoft offers several support tiers, which can be viewed at *http://www.windowsazure.com/en-us/support/plans*, as shown in Figure 2-20.

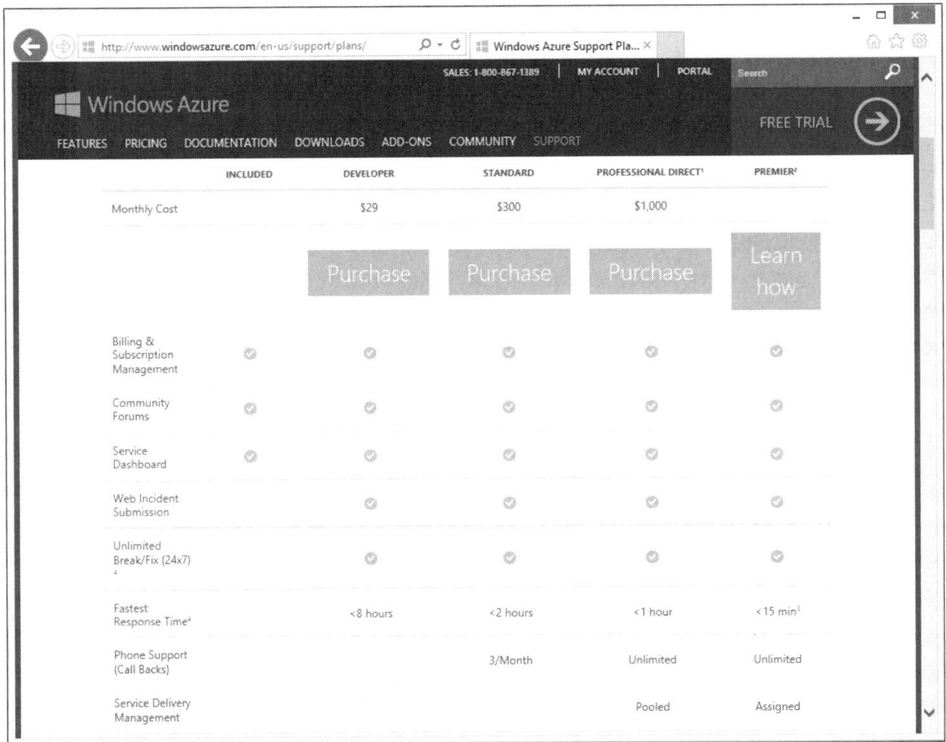

FIGURE 2-20 Browsing the available Azure support plans.

When you're just getting started and need some help, it's easy to get by on just the forums and other online resources. But once your applications start becoming more complex and you start supporting lots of users, it is a good idea to have a support plan in place. We have found that in the early stages of trying to diagnose issues with deployments, it is useful to have Microsoft personnel help with troubleshooting. We recommend that, after your trial period ends, you start off with at least the Developer support plan.

Optimizing your costs

To optimize your costs on SQL Database, here are the things you should think about:

- Don't store BLOBs in the database. Use Azure Blob Storage for image, video, and text files that you might otherwise store as *varbinary(max)* or *image* column in the database. The cost of Blob Storage is much less than SQL Database. A 100-GB SQL Database costs $175 per month, but Blob Storage costs only $7 per month. To reduce costs and improve performance, put these large items in your Blob Storage, and just store the Blob Storage record key in your database to reference it. This strategy will have a huge effect on price if you store files in your database.

- Cycle out old records and tables in your database. This saves money, and knowing what you can or cannot delete is important if you hit your database Max Size and you need to quickly delete records to make space for new data.
- Place your SQL Database in the same datacenter as your websites, mobile services, and other Azure components that will be clients of the database. Co-locating the applications with the database not only prevents you from incurring data bandwidth charges for data going between two datacenters, but also makes your application run faster.
- Use a strategy for removing old backups such that you maintain history but reduce storage needs. If you maintain backups for the last hour, day, week, month, and year, you have good backup coverage while not incurring more than 25 percent of your database costs for backup. If you have a 1-GB database, your costs would be $9.99 per month for the database and only $0.10 per month for the backup space.
- Instead of using a remote storage account for your backups, use geo-replicated storage to keep from incurring bandwidth charges.
- If you intend to use a substantial amount of Azure resources for your application, you can choose to use a volume purchase plan. These plans allow you to save 20 to 30 percent of your datacenter costs for larger applications.

Configuring the database edition and size

You've seen that when you create a SQL Database, you also specify the database edition and size (or at least, you allow it to default to a 1-GB Web edition database). This section explains the meaning of the database edition and size settings.

In the past, Microsoft has talked about the possibility of including more features in the Business edition than the Web edition. However, at this time, the features are the same for both editions. So then, what (if any) is the purpose of the edition and size settings? It essentially comes down to controlling cost. The database edition dictates your maximum size, and your maximum size is there for cost containment, as shown in Table 2-4.

TABLE 2-4 SQL Database editions and sizes

Edition	Maximum Size Options
Web	1 GB, 5 GB
Business	10 GB, 20 GB, 30 GB, 40 GB, 50 GB, 100 GB, 150 GB

Note At the time this book went to press, Microsoft announced the Preview availability of SQL Database Premium. This is a more costly option than the standard Web and Business editions of SQL Database, and it supports a maximum database size of 500 GB. As we explain in Chapter 8, SQL Database Premium also lets you scale up for performance using dedicated CPU and memory.

Monthly charges for SQL Database are based on the data that is actually stored in the database, not the maximum size. So if you are using 2 GB of space in a database with a maximum size of 150 GB, you are charged only for that 2 GB of space. You should therefore set the maximum size to an amount that will comfortably contain the data for your application and still give you some room to grow. The ceiling on the data size prevents some inadvertent programming error from adding too many records and running up your bills.

When your database reaches the maximum size, it will no longer allow you to insert data, although you may still update and delete data. You should plan ahead for this scenario. One option is to create space by deleting unnecessary records. Note that it can take a bit of time after you delete records for the space to free up, so don't expect to be able to recover instantaneously after the cleanup. Your other option is to increase the limit on your database, whether permanently (for example, to accommodate expected business growth) or temporarily (for example, to accept new records while you sort out your longer term strategy for reducing the database size).

As a preventative measure, you should talk to your users about aging policies for certain types of records so that you can cycle old unused records out of the system. That is a good conversation to have before you hit your database size limit. Also, watch the size of your database as it grows over time so that you can anticipate when you'll hit the limit of your database. Chapter 9 has more information about how to monitor your system.

As you saw earlier in this chapter, it's easy to change the edition and size of a SQL Database at any time using both T-SQL and PowerShell. If you prefer a user interface, you can also use the Microsoft Azure management portal to configure the edition and size through the browser.

Summary

In this chapter, you learned how to use the Microsoft Azure management portal, SQL Server Management Studio, and PowerShell to create and configure a Microsoft Azure SQL Database. You saw how to connect each of these tools to Azure, and use them to create and manage servers, firewall rules, and databases.

The chapter then proceeded to discuss cost, pricing, and budget. We detailed the estimation and optimization of costs, and we explained all the cost-related elements you need to consider, including storage and bandwidth, as well as the database edition and maximum size settings.

CHAPTER 3

Differences between SQL Server and Microsoft Azure SQL Database

—Leonard Lobel

One of the most attractive aspects of Microsoft Azure SQL Database is that it shares virtually the same codebase and exposes the same tabular data stream (TDS) as on-premises Microsoft SQL Server. Thus, to a great extent, the same tools and applications that work with SQL Server work just the same and just as well with SQL Database. Notice that we said *to a great extent*, because despite their commonality, there are quite a few SQL Server features that SQL Database does not support. In this brief chapter, we discuss how and why these two platforms differ from one another, and we explain the SQL Database constraints you need to be aware of if you have previous experience with SQL Server.

SQL Server and SQL Database differ in several ways—most notably, in terms of size limitations, feature support, and T-SQL compatibility. In many cases, these constraints are simply the price you pay for enjoying a hassle-free, self-managing, self-healing, always-available database in the cloud. That is, Microsoft cannot responsibly support features that impair its ability to quickly replicate, relocate, and scale a SQL Database instance. This is why SQL Database places limits on database size and doesn't support certain specialized features, such as FILESTREAM.

Another common reason why a particular feature or T-SQL syntax might not be supported in SQL Database is that it's simply not applicable. With SQL Database, administrative responsibilities are split between Microsoft and you. Microsoft handles all the physical administration (such as disk drives and servers), while you manage only the logical administration (such as database design and security). This is why any and all T-SQL syntax that relates to physical resources (such as path names) are not supported in SQL Database. For example, you don't control the location for primary and log file groups. This is why you can't include an *ON PRIMARY* clause with a *CREATE DATABASE* statement, and indeed, why SQL Database does not permit a file group reference in *any* T-SQL statement. Plainly stated, everything pertaining to physical resources (that is, infrastructure) is abstracted away from you with SQL Database

Yet still, in some cases, a certain SQL Server feature or behavior might be unsupported merely because Microsoft has just not gotten around to properly testing and porting it to SQL Database. Azure is constantly evolving, so you need to keep watch for updates and announcements. This small chapter is a great starting point, but the best way to stay current is by reviewing the "Guidelines and Limitations" section of the SQL Database documentation on the MSDN website. (See *http://msdn.microsoft.com/en-us/library/ff394102.aspx*.)

Size limitations

With the exception of the free, lightweight Express edition of SQL Server, there is no practical upper limit on database size in any edition of SQL Server. A SQL Server database can grow as large as 524,272 terabytes. (For SQL Server Express edition, the limit is 10 gigabytes.)

In contrast, SQL Database has very particular size limitations. As explained in Chapter 2, "Configuration and pricing," you can set the maximum size by choosing between the Web and Business editions. With a Web edition database, you can set the maximum database size to either 1 or 5 gigabytes (GB). With a Business edition database, the maximum database size can range from 10 to 150 GB. The absolute largest supported database size is 150 GB, although partitioning strategies can be leveraged for scenarios that require databases larger than 150 GB (as explained in Chapter 8, "Designing and tuning for scalability and high performance").

Note At the time this book went to press, Microsoft announced the Preview availability of SQL Database Premium. This is a more costly option than the standard Web and Business editions of SQL Database (which have been rebranded as Basic and Standard), and it supports a maximum database size of 500 GB. As we explain in Chapter 8, SQL Database Premium also lets you scale up for performance using dedicated CPU and memory.

Connection limitations

SQL Database is far less flexible than SQL Server when it comes to establishing and maintaining connections. Keep the following in mind when you connect to SQL Database:

- SQL Server supports a variety of client protocols, such as TCP/IP, Shared Memory, and Named Pipes. Conversely, SQL Database allows connections only over TCP/IP.
- SQL Database does not support Windows authentication. Every connection string sent to SQL Database must always include a login user name and password.
- SQL Database often requires that @<*server*> is appended to the login user name in connection strings. SQL Server has no such requirement.
- SQL Database communicates only through port 1433, and it does not support static or dynamic port allocation like SQL Server does.
- SQL Database *does* fully support Multiple Active Result Sets (MARS), which allows multiple pending requests on a single connection.

- Because of the unpredictable nature of the Internet, SQL Database connections can drop unexpectedly, and you need to account for this condition in your applications. Fortunately, several options are available to cope with this:
  - The latest version of the Entity Framework (EF6, Microsoft's recommended data access API for .NET) has a new Connection Resiliency feature, which automatically handles the retry logic for dropped connections.
  - The Microsoft Enterprise Library Transient Fault Handling Application Block, covered in Chapter 4, lets you define and implement retry strategies to deal with dropped connections.
  - The ADO.NET *SqlConnection* class has an *OpenWithRetry* extension method that handles the retry logic based on the default retry policy (which must be defined using the Microsoft Enterprise Library Transient Fault Handling Application Block).

Unsupported features

This section lists many SQL Server capabilities that are not supported in SQL Database, and here we suggest workarounds where possible. Again, because this content is subject to change, we recommend you check the MSDN website for the latest information. (See *http://msdn.microsoft.com/en-us/library/ff394102.aspx*.)

- **Agent Service** You cannot use the SQL Server Agent service to schedule and run jobs on SQL Database.
- **Audit** The SQL Server auditing feature records server and database events to either the Windows event log or the file system, and it is not supported in SQL Database.
- **Backup/Restore** Conventional backups with the *BACKUP* and *RESTORE* commands are not supported with SQL Database. However, SQL Database supports an automated backup schedule that creates transactionally consistent backups in the form of BACPAC files created in Azure storage. You can also create BACPAC files manually; however, this does not provide transactional consistency for changes made during the export operation. To ensure transactional consistency for a manual backup, you can either set the database as read-only before exporting it to a BACPAC, use the Database Copy feature to create a copy of the database with transactional consistency and then export that copy to a BACPAC file. See Chapter 5, "Security and backup," for more information.
- **Browser Service** SQL Database listens only on port 1433. Therefore, the SQL Server Browser Service, which listens on various other ports, is unsupported.
- **Change Data Capture (CDC)** This SQL Server feature monitors changes to a database, and it captures all activity related to change tables. CDC relies on a SQL Server Agent job to function and is unsupported in SQL Database.

- **Common Language Runtime (CLR)** The SQL Server CLR features (often referred to simply as *SQL CLR*) allow you to write stored procedures, triggers, functions, and user-defined types in any .NET language (such as Microsoft C# or Visual Basic) as an alternative to using traditional T-SQL. In SQL Database, only T-SQL can be used; SQL CLR is not supported. Note, however, that this limitation does not apply to SQL Server data types implemented internally using the CLR (such as *xml*, *geography*, and *geometry*, all of which are supported in SQL Database).
- **Compression** SQL Database does not support the data-compression features found in SQL Server, which you use to compress tables and indexes.
- **Database object naming convention** In SQL Server, multipart names can be used to reference a database object in another schema (with the two-part name syntax *schema.object*), in another database (with the three-part name syntax *database.schema.object*), and (if you configure a linked server) on another server (with the four-part name syntax *server.database.schema.object*). In SQL Database, two-part names can also be used to reference objects in different schemas. However, three-part names are limited to reference only temporary objects in *tempdb* (that is, where the database name is *tempdb* and the object name starts with a # symbol); you cannot access other databases on the server. And you cannot reference other servers at all, so four-part names can never be used.
- **Extended events** In SQL Server, you can create extended event sessions that help to troubleshoot a variety of problems, such as excessive CPU usage, memory pressure, and deadlocks. This feature is not supported in SQL Database.
- **Extended stored procedures** You cannot execute your own extended stored procedures (which are typically custom-coded procedures written in C or C++) with SQL Database. Only conventional T-SQL stored procedures are supported.
- **File streaming** SQL Server native file-streaming features, including FILESTREAM and FileTable, are not supported in SQL Database. Instead, you can consider using Azure Blob Storage containers for unstructured data files, but it will be your job at the application level to establish and maintain references between SQL Database and the files in blob storage, though note that there will be no transactional integrity between them using this approach.
- **Full-Text Searching (FTS)** The FTS service in SQL Server that enables proximity searching and querying of unstructured documents is not supported in SQL Database. However, there is a third-party text search engine library available from Lucene that does work with SQL Database. For more information, visit *http://www.lucene.net*.
- **Mirroring** SQL Database does not support database mirroring, which is generally a non-issue because Microsoft is ensuring data redundancy with SQL Database, so you don't need to worry about disaster recovery. This does also mean that you cannot use SQL Database as a location for mirroring a principal SQL Server database running on-premises. However, if you want to consider the cloud for this purpose, you can host SQL Server inside an Azure virtual machine (VM) against which you can mirror an on-premises principal database. This solution requires that you also implement a virtual private network (VPN) connection between

your local network and the Azure VM, although it will work even without the VPN if you use server certificates.

- **Partitioning** With SQL Server, you can partition tables and indexes horizontally (by groups of rows) across multiple file groups within a database, which greatly improves the performance of very large databases. SQL Database has a maximum database size of 150 GB (or 500 GB, for the newly announced Premium edition) and gives you no control over file groups, thus it does not support table and index partitioning.
- **Replication** SQL Server offers robust replication features for distributing and synchronizing data, including merge replication, snapshot replication, and transactional replication. None of these features are supported by SQL Database; however, SQL Data Sync can be used to effectively implement merge replication between a SQL Database and any number of other SQL Databases on Microsoft Azure and on-premises SQL Server databases. See Chapter 7, "Microsoft Azure SQL Data Sync," for more information.
- **Resource Governor** The Resource Governor feature in SQL Server lets you manage workloads and resources by specifying limits on the amount of CPU and memory that can be used to satisfy client requests. These are hardware concepts that do not apply to SQL Database, so the Resource Governor is unsupported.
- **Service Broker** SQL Server Service Broker provides messaging and queuing features, and it is not supported in SQL Database.
- **System stored procedures** SQL Database supports only a few of the system stored procedures provided by SQL Server. The unsupported ones are typically related to SQL Server features and behaviors not supported by SQL Database. At the same time, SQL Database provides a few new system stored procedures not found in SQL Server that are specific to SQL Database (for example, *sp_set_firewall_rule*).
- **Tables without a clustered index** Every table in a SQL Database must define a clustered index. By default, SQL Database will create a clustered index over the table's primary key column, but it won't do so if you don't define a primary key. Interestingly enough, SQL Database will actually let you create a table with no clustered index, but it will not allow any rows to be inserted until and unless a clustered index is defined for the table. This limitation does not exist in SQL Server.
- **Transparent Data Encryption (TDE)** You cannot use TDE to encrypt a SQL Database like you can with SQL Server.
- **USE** In SQL Database, the *USE* statement can refer only to the current database; it cannot be used to switch between databases as it can with SQL Server. Each SQL Database connection is tied to a single database, so to change databases, you must connect directly to the database.
- **XSD and XML indexing** SQL Database fully supports the *xml* data type, as well as most of the rich XML support that SQL Server provides, including XML Query (XQuery), XML Path (XPath), and the *FOR XML* clause. However, XML schema definitions (XSD) and XML indexes are not supported in SQL Database.

Summary

In this brief chapter, you learned about the important differences between on-premises SQL Server and SQL Database on Microsoft Azure. We explained the SQL Database limitations on size, as compared to a virtually unlimited database size supported by SQL Server. We also discussed connection limitations, and important considerations to keep in mind with respect to dropped connections, which occur with relative frequency in SQL Database. The chapter concluded by enumerating the many SQL Server features that are either unsupported or have limited support in SQL Database, and offered workarounds where possible.

The information in this chapter will help you decide whether or not SQL Database is suitable for your particular scenario. Of course, if you determine that it is not, always remember that you can run on-premises SQL Server in an Azure VM (we show you how in Chapter 6). This IaaS approach provides you with full SQL Server functionality in the cloud, compared to the PaaS approach of going with SQL Database.

CHAPTER 4

Migrating databases

—Eric Boyd

In our experience helping customers develop and migrate applications to Microsoft Azure, there has always been a need to migrate data along with those applications, even for "all new development" projects. So you really need to know about the solutions that are available for migrating your data to SQL Database and to understand their strengths and weaknesses. In this chapter, you will work with multiple tools and techniques for migrating data to SQL Database, including Transact-SQL (T-SQL) scripts, SQL Data-Tier Applications (BACPAC), bulk copy (bcp), and the SQL Database Migration Wizard.

Note As mentioned in Chapter 1, "Getting started with Microsoft Azure SQL Database," and practiced throughout this book, the term *SQL Database* refers specifically to *Microsoft Azure SQL Database* in the cloud, whereas the term *SQL Server* refers specifically to local (on-premises) SQL Server.

In addition to the tools and techniques discussed in this chapter, there are many other solutions available from both Microsoft and third-party vendors that might also fit your scenario and requirements. For example, SQL Server Integration Services (SSIS) is a great solution if you need to import data from data sources beyond SQL Server, like Excel spreadsheets, or other database platforms like Oracle. If you are starting with an existing database in SQL Database and you want to apply incremental changes and updates to your database, third-party tools like Red-Gate SQL Compare and Data Compare are also good solutions. You should explore these and all other available solutions to help you migrate data from your on-premises data stores and database servers to SQL Database. You need to understand the capabilities and limitations of each option so that you can effectively choose a solution that best fits your scenario.

Making the case for data migration

The percentage of an IT budget that gets spent on maintenance versus new software projects is a popular metric that technology and business executives like to monitor and measure. It is always the goal to minimize maintenance and be able to invest more in innovation and new projects. Software development and technical teams typically prefer to work on new projects (often referred to as *greenfield* projects) rather than maintaining and extending existing codebases (*brownfield* projects).

However, if you've been in the IT industry for any length of time, you know how much time is invested in maintaining and managing existing codebases and data stores.

The existing code and data we manage (often referred to as *legacy*, even if it was born in the last year) drives us to consider migration strategies when evaluating the public cloud and Microsoft Azure. In this chapter, we demonstrate various ways to move data into SQL Database from existing legacy systems and on-premises SQL Server servers, and we discuss other things to consider when migrating data to SQL Database.

Migrating data using Transact-SQL scripts

SQL Database uses virtually the same Transact-SQL (T-SQL) syntax as "regular" SQL Server, which is a significant advantage if you are already familiar with SQL Server. Thus, one simple option for populating data in SQL Database is to run T-SQL scripts.

In the next section, you will use SQL Server Management Studio (SSMS) to write T-SQL scripts that create and populate a local SQL Server database. Note that you can also use SQL Server Data Tools (SSDT) inside Microsoft Visual Studio to build and run T-SQL scripts. (You will learn much more about SSDT in Chapter 10, "Building cloud solutions.") Also, note that all the scripts in this chapter can be downloaded from the book's companion website. (See the Introduction for details.)

Setting up a local SQL Server database

To get started, you will set up the Wine database from previous chapters in your local environment. Doing this requires a local SQL Server database.

If you have access to a SQL Server instance that you can create a local database on, you can use that SQL Server instance. Otherwise, you will need to install the SQL Server Express edition to host the database on your local machine. A step-by-step procedure for doing so can be found in the Introduction, in the section "Installing the SQL Server Express edition."

Note This chapter assumes you are using the SQL Server Express edition for your local SQL Server database, which has a server instance name of *.\sqlexpress*. If you are using another edition, you must replace the instance name *.\sqlexpress* specified in the instructions with the name of server instance you are using. For example, if you are running a primary instance of the SQL Server Developer edition on your local machine, you can simply specify the dot (.) symbol, or *localhost*. If you are running a named instance on your local machine, append a backslash followed by the name of the instance (for example, *.\myinstance* or *localhost\myinstance*).

The T-SQL code to create the local *WineDb* database is shown in Listing 4-1. This script creates the *WineDb* database, and then creates the *Customer*, *Order*, and *Wine* tables. It also establishes all the foreign-key relationships between the tables. This is a similar design as the *WineCloudDb* database found in other chapters throughout this book.

LISTING 4-1 Creating the local *WineDb* database

```
CREATE DATABASE WineDb
GO

USE WineDb
GO

CREATE TABLE Wine(
  WineId int IDENTITY PRIMARY KEY,
  Name nvarchar(50) NOT NULL,
  Category nvarchar(15) NOT NULL,
  Year int,
  Price MONEY DEFAULT 0 NOT NULL,
  AddedOn datetime2 DEFAULT SYSDATETIME() NOT NULL,
  UpdatedOn datetime2)

CREATE TABLE Customer(
  CustomerId int IDENTITY PRIMARY KEY,
  FirstName nvarchar(50) NOT NULL,
  LastName nvarchar(50) NOT NULL,
  FavoriteWineId int,
  CONSTRAINT FK_Customer_Wine FOREIGN KEY (FavoriteWineId) REFERENCES Wine(WineId))

CREATE TABLE [Order](
  OrderId int IDENTITY PRIMARY KEY,
  OrderedOn datetime2 DEFAULT SYSDATETIME() NOT NULL,
  CustomerId int NOT NULL,
  WineId int NOT NULL,
  Quantity int NOT NULL,
  Price MONEY NOT NULL,
  CONSTRAINT FK_Order_Customer FOREIGN KEY (CustomerId) REFERENCES Customer(CustomerId),
  CONSTRAINT FK_Order_Wine FOREIGN KEY (WineId) REFERENCES Wine(WineId))
```

To create the *WineDb* database using this T-SQL, follow these steps:

1. Launch SSMS. An easy way to do this is to press the Windows key, type **sql server management studio** on the Start screen, and press Enter.
2. In the Connect To Server dialog, connect to your local SQL Server instance using the appropriate credentials, as shown in Figure 4-1.

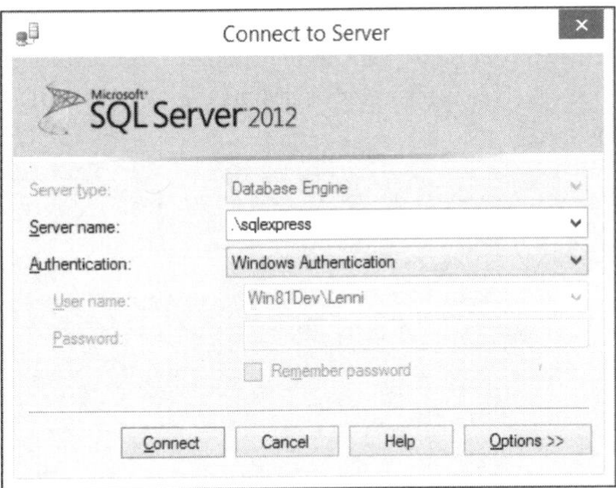

FIGURE 4-1 Connecting to SQL Server from the Connect To Server dialog in SSMS

3. Once you are connected, your SQL Server instance will be listed in the Object Explorer pane. Right-click on your SQL Server instance, and choose New Query as shown in Figure 4-2. This opens a new query window.

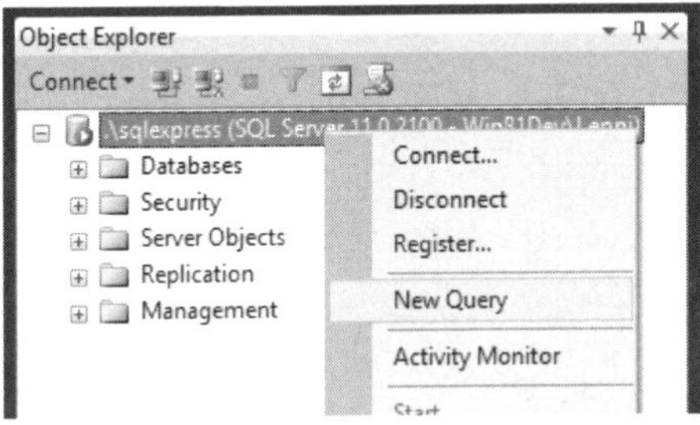

FIGURE 4-2 The New Query context menu option in SSMS Object Explorer

4. Type the code shown in Listing 4-1 into the query window (or paste it in from the listing file downloaded from the book's companion website).
5. Press F5 (or click the Execute button in the toolbar) to run the script.
6. Expand the Databases node beneath your SQL Server instance in Object Explorer (or, if it's already expanded, right-click it and choose Refresh). The *WineDb* database now appears.
7. Expand the *WineDb* database node, and then expand the Tables node beneath it to view the *Customer*, *Order*, and *Wine* tables.

There is now a *WineDb* database running on your local SQL Server instance. This is the source database you will migrate to Microsoft Azure using various tools and techniques throughout the rest of this chapter.

Creating the T-SQL scripts

You are now ready to populate the local *WineDb* database tables with data. In this section, you will create simple T-SQL scripts to populate the *Customer* and *Wine* tables with records. One of the great benefits of SQL Database is that you can use the same T-SQL syntax you use when working with SQL Server. So the same scripts can be used to insert data into either SQL Server or SQL Database.

Listing 4-2 shows the T-SQL script you will run in the next procedure. This script populates the *Wine* table with 15 rows of data and the *Customer* table with 3 rows of data. Notice how the *IDENTITY_INSERT* setting is turned on before inserting rows into a table, and then turned off again after. Turning this setting on allows the script to provide explicit values for each new record's primary key, which would normally be assigned automatically by SQL Server because the primary keys were designated with *IDENTITY*. (Refer to Listing 4-1 earlier.)

LISTING 4-2 Populating the local *WineDb* database

```
SET IDENTITY_INSERT Wine ON
INSERT Wine (WineId, Name, Category, Year) VALUES (1, 'Chateau Penin', 'Bordeaux', 2008)
INSERT Wine (WineId, Name, Category, Year) VALUES (2, 'McLaren Valley', 'Cabernet', 2005)
INSERT Wine (WineId, Name, Category, Year) VALUES (3, 'Mendoza', 'Merlot', 2010)
INSERT Wine (WineId, Name, Category, Year) VALUES (4, 'Valle Central', 'Merlot', 2009)
INSERT Wine (WineId, Name, Category, Year) VALUES (5, 'Mendoza', 'Malbec', 2010)
INSERT Wine (WineId, Name, Category, Year) VALUES (6, 'Tuscany', 'Brunello', 2007)
INSERT Wine (WineId, Name, Category, Year) VALUES (7, 'Willamette Valley', 'Pinot Noir',
2009)
INSERT Wine (WineId, Name, Category, Year) VALUES (8, 'Bordeaux', 'Cabernet', 2009)
INSERT Wine (WineId, Name, Category, Year) VALUES (9, 'Barossa Valley', 'Shiraz', 2010)
INSERT Wine (WineId, Name, Category, Year) VALUES (10, 'Napa Valley', 'Syrah', 2010)
INSERT Wine (WineId, Name, Category, Year) VALUES (11, 'Barossa Valley', 'Grenache', 2006)
INSERT Wine (WineId, Name, Category, Year) VALUES (12, 'La Mancha', 'Mourvedre', 2009)
INSERT Wine (WineId, Name, Category, Year) VALUES (13, 'Beaujolais', 'Gamay', 2011)
INSERT Wine (WineId, Name, Category, Year) VALUES (14, 'Sonoma', 'Zinfandel', 2011)
INSERT Wine (WineId, Name, Category, Year) VALUES (15, 'Tuscany', 'Sangiovese', 2010)
SET IDENTITY_INSERT Wine OFF

SET IDENTITY_INSERT Customer ON
INSERT Customer (CustomerId, FirstName, LastName, FavoriteWineId) VALUES
 (1, 'Jeff', 'Hay', 4)
INSERT Customer (CustomerId, FirstName, LastName, FavoriteWineId) VALUES
 (2, 'Mark', 'Hanson', 3)
INSERT Customer (CustomerId, FirstName, LastName, FavoriteWineId) VALUES
 (3, 'Jeff', 'Phillips', 2)
SET IDENTITY_INSERT Customer OFF
```

To populate the database with this T-SQL script, follow these steps:

1. Open a new query window in SSMS (or delete all the code in the same query window you used in the previous procedure).
2. Type the code shown in Listing 4-2 into the query window (or paste it in from the listing file downloaded from the book's companion website).
3. Press F5 (or click the Execute button in the toolbar) to run the script.

Generating T-SQL scripts

At this point, you have set up the *WineDb* database on your local SQL Server instance and populated it with some data. Of course, you could now execute the same T-SQL script to create the schema for a SQL Database instance, and execute the T-SQL script to add rows and populate data in that SQL Database. But creating T-SQL scripts like this for large amounts of data is tedious and time consuming.

You might be thinking there must be a better way, and of course, there is. SSMS can examine the database and generate a T-SQL script with *INSERT* statements for all the data in the tables. In this next procedure, you will use SSMS to automatically generate a T-SQL script from your local *WineDb* SQL Server database that you can then use to populate your *WineCloudDb* SQL Database, effectively migrating the data from SQL Server to SQL Database.

1. If you've closed SSMS since the previous procedure, start it up again and connect to your local SQL Server instance that contains the *WineDb* database.
2. In Object Explorer, expand the node for your SQL Server instance name.
3. Beneath your SQL Server instance name, expand the Databases node to display the list of databases.
4. If the *WineDb* database does not appear, right-click the Databases node and choose Refresh.
5. Right-click on the *WineDb* database, and choose Tasks | Generate Scripts. This launches the Generate And Publish Scripts wizard.
6. On the Introduction page, click Next to display the Choose Objects page.
7. On the Choose Objects page, you have the option of scripting the entire database or selecting specific objects you want to script. This is not limited to tables; it can also include other database objects, such as views, stored procedures, triggers, and so on. Leave the default option selected to script the entire database, and click Next to display the Set Scripting Options page.
8. On the Set Scripting Options page, click the Advanced button to display the Advanced Scripting Options dialog.

9. Scroll down to the Script For The Database Engine Type property. (It's towards the bottom of the General category.) By default, this option is set to Stand-alone instance. You can also choose SQL Azure Database to generate scripts compatible with SQL Database. In our current scenario, we want to use SQL Database, so choose SQL Azure Database.

10. Scroll down to the Types Of Data To Script property. (It's the last property in the General category.) By default, this option is set to script only the database schema. You can also choose to script only data or both schema and data. In our current scenario, we only want to script the data, so choose Data Only, as shown in Figure 4-3.

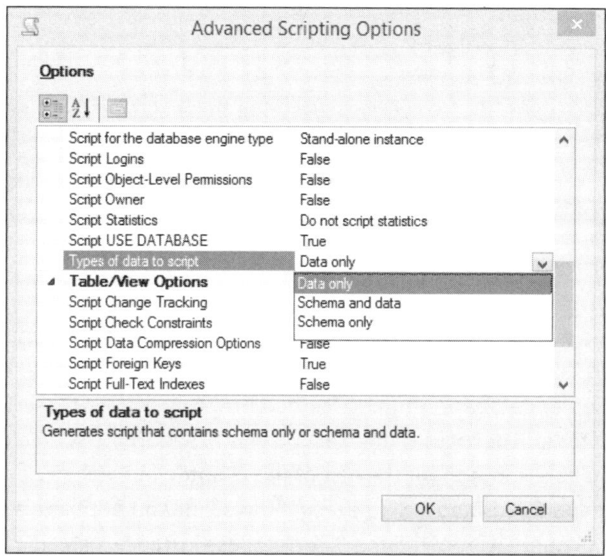

FIGURE 4-3 Advanced Scripting Options in the Generate Scripts wizard

11. Click OK to return to the Set Scripting Options page.

12. Choose the Save To New Query Window radio button.

13. Click Next to advance to the Summary page.

14. Click Next to advance to the Save Or Publish Scripts page.

15. Click Finish to generate the script, which is then displayed in a new query window, as shown in Figure 4-4.

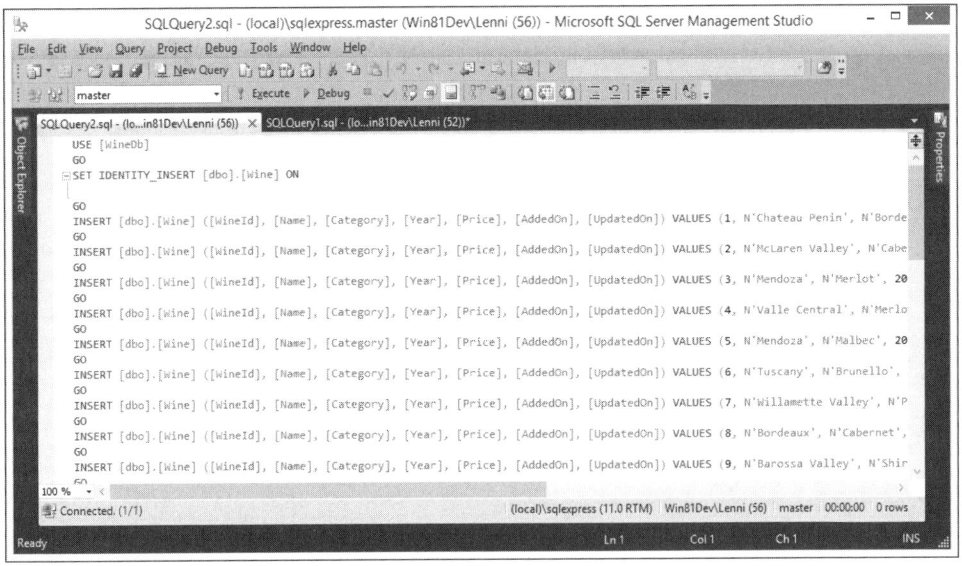

FIGURE 4-4 Viewing the generated T-SQL in SSMS

At this point, you have created a *WineDb* database, with both schema and data, in your local SQL Server instance. You created T-SQL scripts by hand that you executed to create the schema and insert data into your local SQL Server database. You also learned how to generate these T-SQL scripts using SQL Server Management Studio. The focus of this section was to set up the source database that will be migrated to SQL Database throughout the rest of this chapter, but you can execute this same T-SQL script in SQL Server and SQL Database. To execute this script and populate a SQL Database instance, connect your SSMS query window to the SQL Database instance instead of the local SQL Server database, and execute the T-SQL script in that window. You can also execute these T-SQL scripts using the SQL Database management portal as mentioned in the "Creating a SQL Database instance" section found in Chapter 1.

SQL Data-Tier Applications

Data-Tier Applications (DACs) provide a simple but powerful way to develop, deploy, and manage database and instance objects. DAC enables developers to package SQL Server and SQL Database objects into a single DAC package (a .dacpac file) for convenient deployment across development, test, and production environments.

When migrating a database from on-premises SQL Server to SQL Database, you often want to migrate your data along with your database and instance objects, and that is when BACPAC (.bacpac files) becomes useful. BACPAC is similar to DACPAC, but in addition to the database objects (schema), it also includes the actual data from the database in the package.

To migrate data to SQL Database using BACPAC, you first need to create a .bacpac file from your on-premises SQL Server database and upload it to a *blob container* in Microsoft Azure Storage. Then you can import the uploaded .bacpac file into SQL Database. This section walks you through these steps.

Creating a Microsoft Azure Storage account

First, you need a place to store your .bacpac in Microsoft Azure, and that place is in a Microsoft Azure Storage blob container. In this section, you will create a blob container using the Storage service, which first requires you to create a Storage account.

Microsoft Azure Storage accounts authenticate access using one of two 512-bit storage access keys (a primary and a secondary). These keys are automatically generated for you when you create a storage account. You can regenerate these keys at any time in the Microsoft Azure management portal (and via the Microsoft Azure Service Management API). To help keep your storage account secure, it is recommended that you regenerate your access keys periodically. Changing authentication credentials to services that other services and applications depend on without causing downtime can be challenging. Microsoft Azure simplifies this by providing the two access keys, which allows you to rotate access keys without causing downtime.

To create a Microsoft Azure Storage account you can use to upload and store your .bacpac file, follow these steps:

1. Log in to the Microsoft Azure portal at **https://manage.windowsazure.com**. This brings you to the main portal page showing ALL ITEMS.
2. Click STORAGE in the vertical navigation pane on the left.
3. Click the NEW button at the bottom of the page.
4. Click the QUICK CREATE link.
5. In the data entry area to the right of the QUICK CREATE link, do the following:
    a. For URL, type **mywinestorage**. This will be the name of your storage account. (It can be any name from 3 to 24 lowercase letters and numbers.) This must be a globally unique name, so you'll need to choose something other than *mywinestorage* if the portal informs you that the specified storage account name is already in use (which is very probable).
    b. For LOCATION/AFFINITY GROUP, select the Microsoft Azure data center where you want to create your storage account from the drop-down list. This should be the same data center that hosts your SQL Database server. (See Chapter 2, "Configuration and pricing," to understand the pricing implications of choosing a data center location.)
    c. For REPLICATION, leave the default Geo-Redundant setting, which enables geo-replication. This synchronizes a copy of your data with another Microsoft Azure data center, to enable recovery in the event of a data center disaster. (Again, we say more on this in Chapter 2.) The portal should appear similar to Figure 4-5.

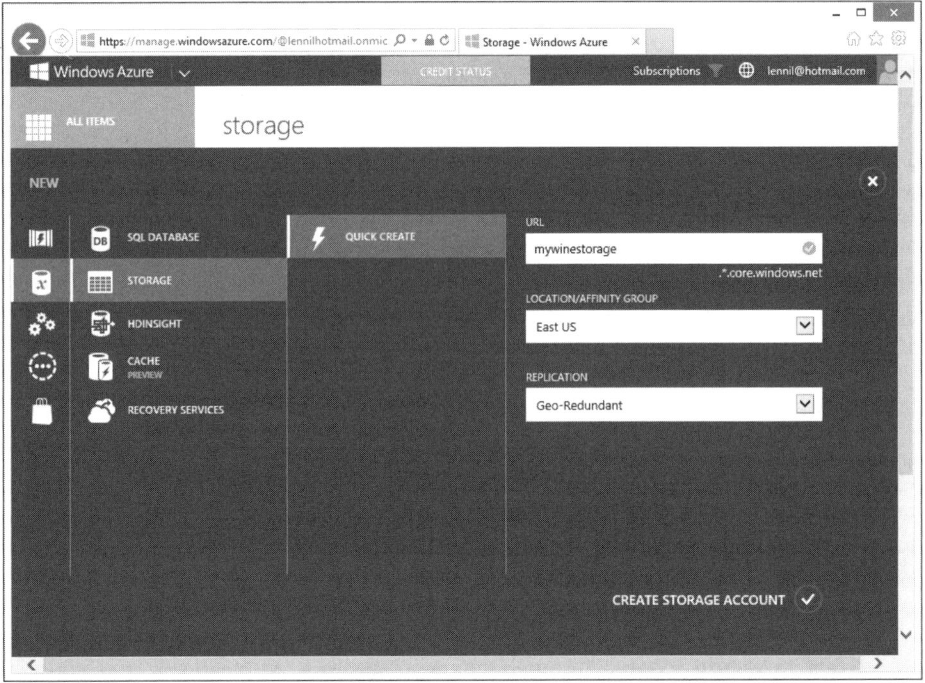

FIGURE 4-5 Creating a new Microsoft Azure Storage account in the management portal

6. Click CREATE STORAGE ACCOUNT to start provisioning the new storage account. In a few moments, you will see it appear in the portal with an Online status, as shown in Figure 4-6.

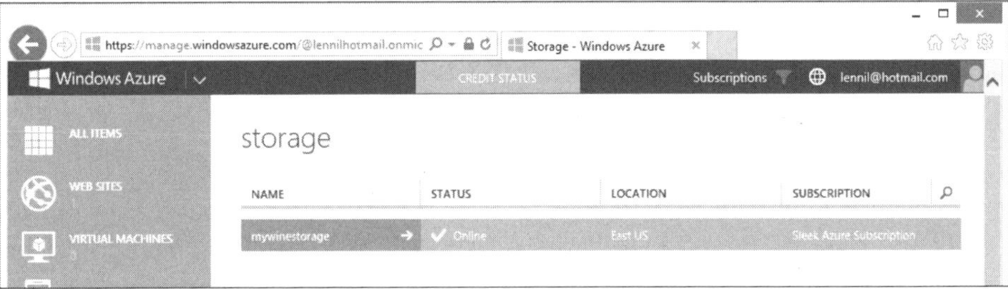

FIGURE 4-6 Viewing the new storage account in the management portal

7. Click on the storage account name (*mywinestorage*, or whatever name you assigned in the previous procedure).

8. Click the MANAGE ACCESS KEYS button at the bottom of the page to display the Manage Access Keys dialog. This displays the Primary Access Key and Secondary Access Key, as shown in Figure 4-7. These keys are used for authentication to your storage account, and you will need the primary access key shortly to upload a .bacpac file.

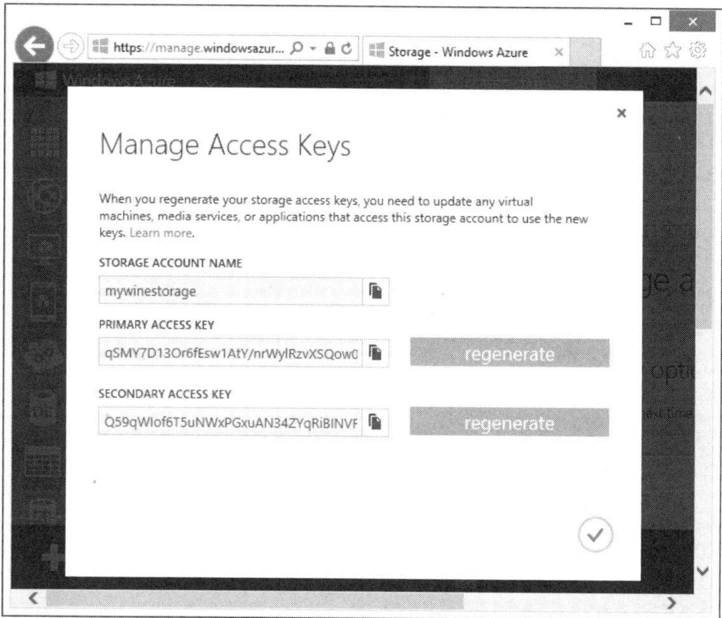

FIGURE 4-7 Viewing the primary and secondary access keys generated for the new storage account

9. Click the copy button to the right of the PRIMARY ACCESS KEY text box (the icon that looks like two documents) to copy the primary access key to the clipboard. You will paste this key in a later step, so be sure not to copy anything else to the clipboard until then.

10. If you are prompted by the browser to permit clipboard access, click Allow Access.

11. Click the checkmark icon in the lower-right side of the dialog to return to the Storage Account home screen.

Now that you have created a storage account, the next step is to create a blob container for it. Then you will be able to upload a .bacpac file to the blob container within the storage account, and finally import the .bacpac file to SQL Database. To create the blob container, follow these steps:

1. Click the CONTAINERS link at the top of the page, as shown in Figure 4-8.

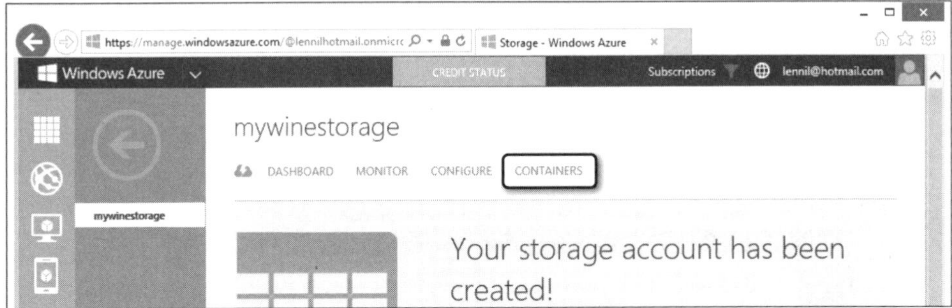

FIGURE 4-8 Creating a new blob container for the storage account

2. Click the ADD button at the bottom of the page to display the New Container dialog.
3. For NAME, type **dbimport**.
4. For ACCESS, leave the default Private setting, which ensures that only the account owner (you) can access the new container.
5. Click the checkmark icon in the lower-right side of the dialog to create the container. When the process is complete, you'll see a notification at the bottom of the portal.
6. Click OK to dismiss the notification that the container was created.

Exporting a BACPAC to Microsoft Azure Storage

You are now ready to create a .bacpac file from the local *WineDb* database. In the following steps, you will export a .bacpac file and upload it to the blob container in the Microsoft Azure Storage account you just created:

1. If it's not still opened from an earlier procedure, launch SSMS and connect to your local SQL Server instance that contains the *WineDb* database.
2. In the Object Explorer, expand the node for your SQL Server instance name.
3. Beneath your SQL Server instance name, expand the Database node to display the list of databases.
4. Right-click on the *WineDb* database, and choose Tasks | Export Data-Tier Application, as shown in Figure 4-9. This launches the Export Data-Tier Application wizard.

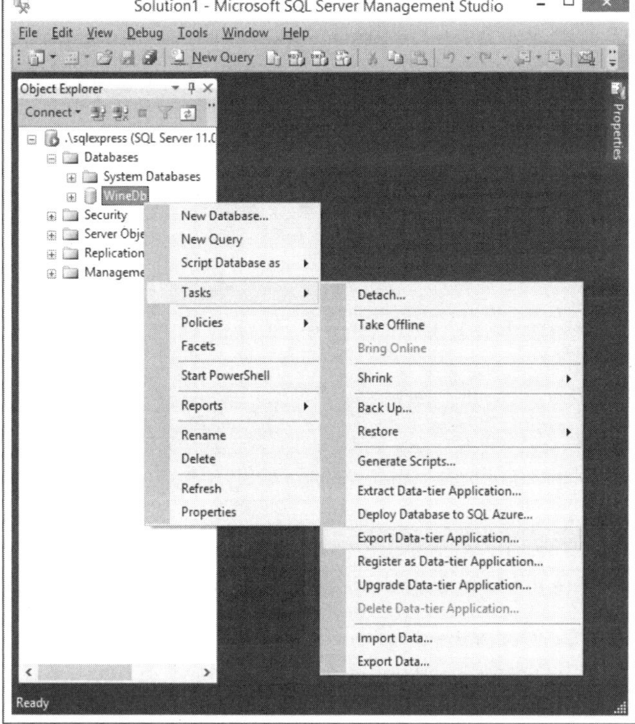

FIGURE 4-9 The Export Data-Tier Application menu item in SSMS

5. On the Introduction page, click Next to advance to the Export Settings page.
6. In the Settings tab on the Export Settings page, click the Save To Microsoft Azure radio button.

> **Tip** If you don't want to include the entire database in the .bacpac file, you can choose just the database objects you want to export in the Advanced tab of the Export Settings page.

7. Click the Connect button to launch the Connect To Microsoft Azure Storage dialog.
8. For Storage Account, type **mywinestorage** (or whatever globally unique name you assigned to the storage account when you created it). Notice that the HTTPS check box at the bottom of the dialog gets selected automatically when you type the account name. This is expected, and you should leave it selected.

9. In the Account Key text box, right-click the mouse and choose Paste (or press CTRL+V) to insert the primary access key you copied to the clipboard when you created the storage account. (If the key is no longer available from the clipboard, return to the Manage Access Keys dialog in the portal to copy it again, as shown in Figure 4-7.) The Connect To Windows Azure Storage dialog should now appear as shown in Figure 4-10.

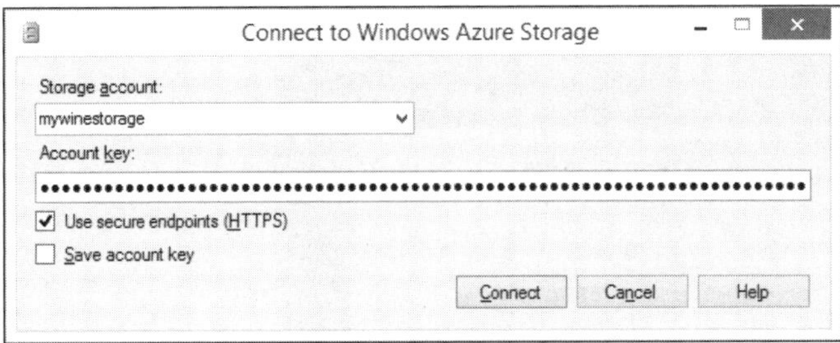

FIGURE 4-10 The Connect To Microsoft Azure Storage dialog

10. Click the Connect button. The wizard connects to the storage account and returns to the Export Settings page, where the Container drop-down list has now become enabled.

11. For Container, select *dbimport* from the drop-down list. (This is the container you created in the previous procedure.) The wizard should now appear as shown in Figure 4-11.

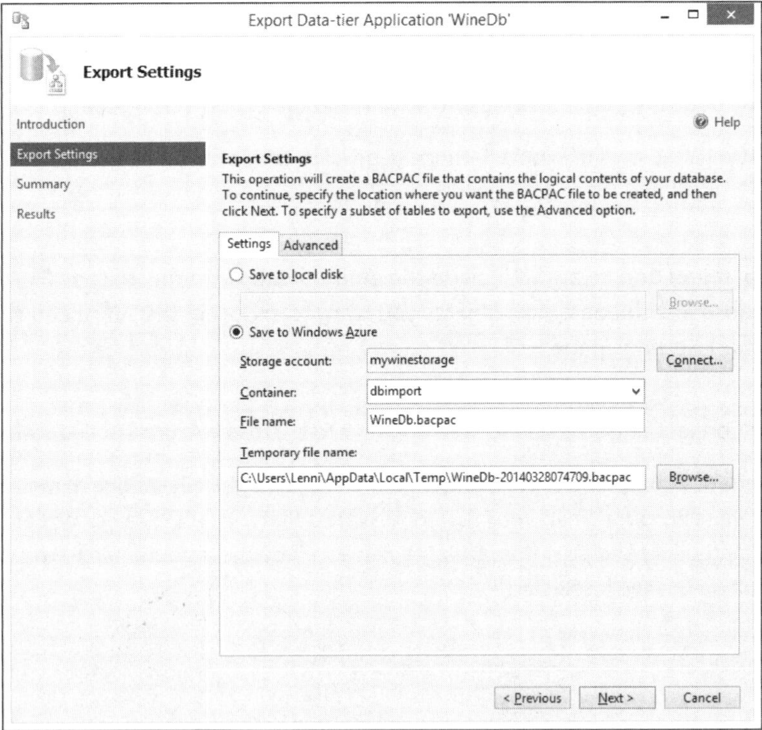

FIGURE 4-11 Exporting a .bacpac file to Microsoft Azure Storage

12. Click Next to advance to the Summary page.
13. Review the Summary page. If everything looks correct, click Finish to begin the export.

Once the export has finished successfully, the wizard displays the Results page with a list of all the tasks it completed. The .bacpac file has now been exported and uploaded to your Microsoft Azure Storage account. You can now click Close to close the Export Data-Tier Application wizard.

Importing a BACPAC to Microsoft Azure SQL Database

At this point, you have created a storage account with a blob container, into which you have uploaded a .bacpac file exported from an existing on-premises SQL Server database. The last thing to do is import this .bacpac file into a new SQL Database instance.

To import the .bacpac file, follow these steps:

1. Log in to the Microsoft Azure portal at **https://manage.windowsazure.com**. This brings you to the main portal page showing ALL ITEMS.
2. Click SQL DATABASES in the vertical navigation pane on the left
3. If you have a *WineCloudDb* database in your list of databases from previous chapters, delete it now:
    a. Click on the any column to the right of the Name column to select the *WineCloudDb* database. (Don't click on the database name itself.)
    b. Click the DELETE button at the bottom of the page.
    c. Click YES, DELETE when prompted to confirm.
    d. If that was the only database on the SQL Database server, you will also be asked if you also want to delete the server. Because you are going to import your .bacpac file into a new database on this server, click NO.
    e. Click OK to dismiss the notification message that the database was deleted.
4. Click the NEW button at the bottom of the page.
5. Click IMPORT, as shown in Figure 4-12. This displays the IMPORT DATABASE dialog box.

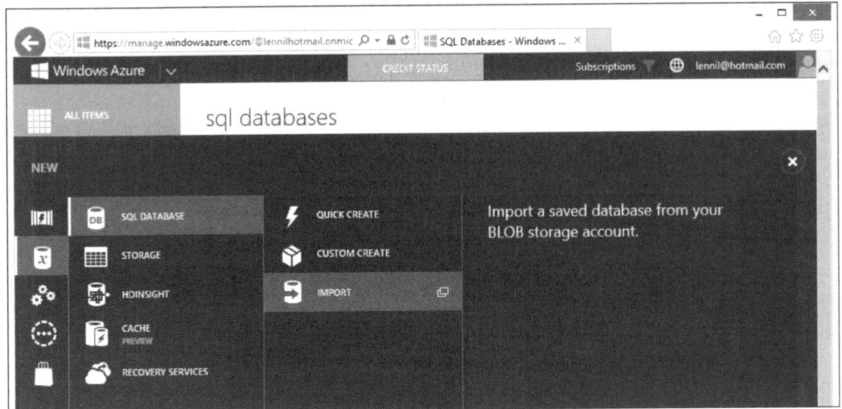

FIGURE 4-12 Creating a new database by using the Import option in the management portal

6. Click the folder icon to the left of the BACPAC URL text box. This opens the BROWSE CLOUD STORAGE dialog box.
7. An explorer tree that displays your Microsoft Azure Storage accounts and their containers appears on the left side of the dialog. Expand your storage account to display the *dbimport* container inside of it.
8. Click the *dbimport* container to display its contents on the right. You can see the *WineDb.bacpac* file you recently uploaded to the container, as shown in Figure 4-13.

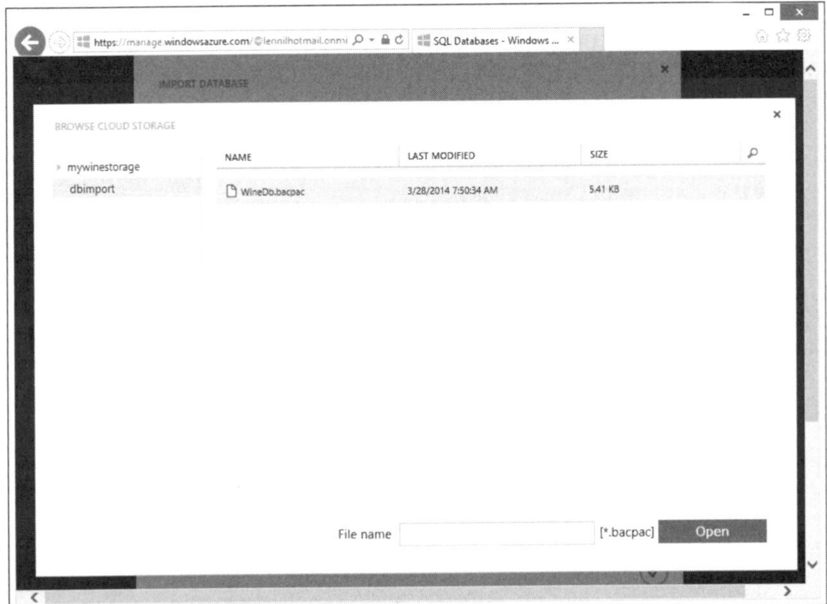

FIGURE 4-13 The contents of the *dbimport* container displayed in the BROWSE CLOUD STORAGE dialog

9. Click the *WineDb.bacpac* file to select it.

10. Click the Open button. This returns you to the IMPORT DATABASE dialog with the URL of the .bacpac file populated in the BACPAC URL text box.
11. For NAME, change the database name from *WineDb* (the name of the local SQL Server database, which was discovered from the .bacpac file that the database was exported to) to **WineCloudDb**, which is the actual name you want to give the new SQL Database instance.
12. For SERVER, choose any available server from the drop-down list to host the database (or choose New SQL Database Server from the drop-down list to create a new server on the fly). Once you choose a server, the SERVER LOGIN NAME and SERVER LOGIN PASSWORD text boxes appear. The SERVER LOGIN NAME text box is automatically populated with your administrator login name.

> **Important** If you create the storage account and the SQL Database server in different regions, you will incur additional Microsoft Azure billing charges for network bandwidth between the two regions. In this event, the Microsoft Azure management portal will alert you with a warning message. See Chapter 2 for more information on pricing for Microsoft Azure.

13. For SERVER LOGIN PASSWORD, type the password for your login. The IMPORT DATABASE dialog should appear similar to Figure 4-14.

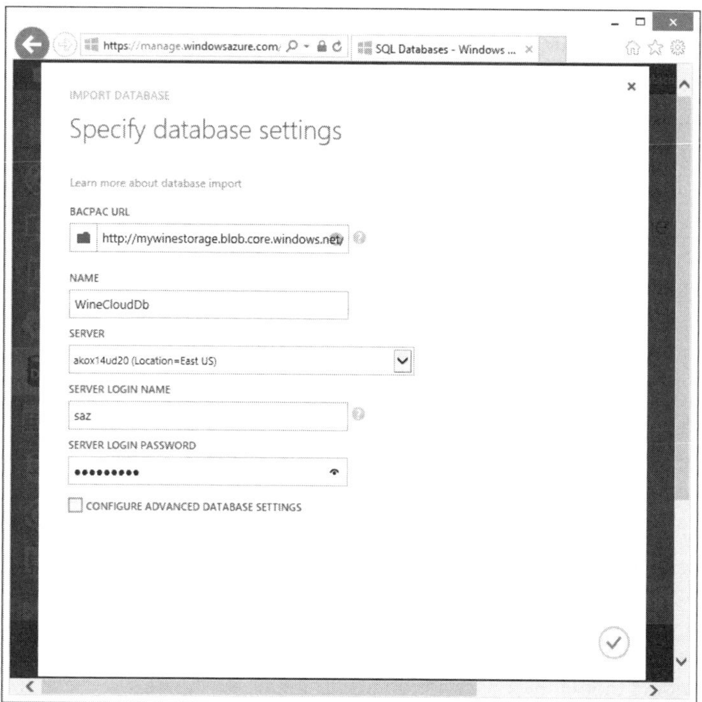

FIGURE 4-14 Importing a .bacpac file from Microsoft Azure Storage into a new SQL Database instance

Note By default, a database imported from a .bacpac file will be a 1-GB, Web edition database. If you need a larger database, select the CONFIGURE ADVANCED DATABASE SETTINGS check box at the bottom of the Import Database dialog. This converts the simple IMPORT DATABASE dialog into a two-page wizard, where the second page provides you with options to set the SQL Database edition and size. For more information, see the section "Configuring the database edition and size" in Chapter 2.

14. Click the checkmark icon in the lower-right side of the dialog to begin the import. Once the import has completed, a notification that the import was successful appears at the bottom of the page, and the new *WineCloudDb* database appears in the list of SQL databases. (Sometime, it is necessary to refresh the page by pressing F5 to get the new database to appear.)

Using BACPAC Data-Tier Applications is one of the simplest ways to migrate both the database schema and data to a SQL Database instance. You can also use DACPAC Data-Tier Applications to migrate only the schema, if that meets your migration requirements. One of the things that makes SQL Data-Tier Applications easy to work with is that you can use familiar tooling, including SQL Server Management Studio (SSMS) and SQL Server Data Tools (SSDT) in Visual Studio. As you just saw, you can perform a database migration entirely using only the familiar SQL Server tools and the Microsoft Azure management portal, which makes this technology accessible for almost all Microsoft developers.

You should be aware of one limitation of using BACPAC: you cannot import a .bacpac file into an SSDT database project. (Chapter 10 covers SSDT database projects.) If you need to make any schema modifications between exporting your database and importing your database into SQL Database, you cannot achieve this with a .bacpac file. Instead, you can import .dacpac files (which contain only schema information) into SSDT database projects, but you would not have the data in your package using a DACPAC. Because of feature limitations and syntax differences between SQL Server and SQL Database, you will often need to make schema changes before deploying your databases to SQL Database. As a result, you will either need to extract .dacpac files without data or make any necessary schema and syntax changes to your local SQL Server database prior to exporting your .bacpac files.

SQL Server Bulk Copy (bcp)

SQL Server Bulk Copy (bcp) is a command-line utility that is intended to be used for high-performance, bulk-data migrations to and from SQL Server and SQL Database. Migrating data using bcp is a two-step process; first, you export data from the source table into a bcp data file, and then you import data into your destination table from the exported data file.

In this section, you will learn how to use the bcp utility to export data files from a source SQL Server database and import them into a destination SQL Database instance.

Migrating Schema

To use SQL Server Bulk Copy (bcp) to migrate your database to Microsoft Azure, you must first have the destination database schema deployed to a SQL Database instance. This is because the bcp utility moves only data—it will not migrate any database objects (such as table definitions or other schema). To create your database objects, you can build and run T-SQL scripts, design and publish a database project using SSDT (as shown in Chapter 10), or you could even manually design your tables using the SQL Database management portal (as shown in Chapter 1).

For the purposes of this exercise, you will drop and re-create the *WineCloudDb* tables populated by the BACPAC migration you performed in the previous section. To do this, you will use the SQL Database management portal to run the T-SQL script shown in Listing 4-3. (Remember, though, you can also run T-SQL scripts against a SQL Database instance using any of the familiar locally installed tools, such as SSMS or SSDT.) You'll notice that this script is almost exactly the same as the one in Listing 4-1 that you used to create a new local SQL Server database at the start of the chapter. The only difference is that this T-SQL script starts with three *DROP TABLE* statements that delete the existing tables (populated by the BACPAC migration you performed in the previous section), which are then re-created as empty. This has the net effect of migrating just the schema of a database without any data.

LISTING 4-3 T-SQL script to drop and re-create the local *WineCloudDb* tables

```
DROP TABLE [Order]
DROP TABLE [Customer]
DROP TABLE [Wine]

CREATE TABLE Wine(
  WineId int IDENTITY PRIMARY KEY,
  Name nvarchar(50) NOT NULL,
  Category nvarchar(15) NOT NULL,
  Year int,
  Price MONEY DEFAULT 0 NOT NULL,
  AddedOn datetime2 DEFAULT SYSDATETIME() NOT NULL,
  UpdatedOn datetime2)

CREATE TABLE Customer(
  CustomerId int IDENTITY PRIMARY KEY,
  FirstName nvarchar(50) NOT NULL,
  LastName nvarchar(50) NOT NULL,
  FavoriteWineId int,
  CONSTRAINT FK_Customer_Wine FOREIGN KEY (FavoriteWineId) REFERENCES Wine(WineId))

CREATE TABLE [Order](
  OrderId int IDENTITY PRIMARY KEY,
  OrderedOn datetime2 DEFAULT SYSDATETIME() NOT NULL,
  CustomerId int NOT NULL,
  WineId int NOT NULL,
  Quantity int NOT NULL,
  Price MONEY NOT NULL,
  CONSTRAINT FK_Order_Customer FOREIGN KEY (CustomerId) REFERENCES Customer(CustomerId),
  CONSTRAINT FK_Order_Wine FOREIGN KEY (WineId) REFERENCES Wine(WineId))
```

To run this T-SQL script, follow these steps:

1. Log in to the Microsoft Azure portal at **https://manage.windowsazure.com**. This brings you to the main portal page showing ALL ITEMS.
2. Click SQL DATABASES in the vertical navigation pane on the left.
3. Click the *WineCloudDb* database. (This is the database you imported from a BACPAC file in the previous section.)
4. Click the DASHBOARD link at the top of the page.
5. Scroll the page down a bit, find the MANAGE URL link in the "Quick Glance" section at the right of the page, and click the link. This opens a new browser tab to the SQL Database portal's login page.

Note The SQL Database portal is Silverlight-based. If you don't have Silverlight installed, you will first be prompted to download it before you can use the portal.

6. For USERNAME and PASSWORD, type the administrator login name and password for the server, respectively, and click Log On.
7. Click the New Query button in the toolbar at the top of the SQL Database management portal to open a blank query window.
8. Type the code shown in Listing 4-3 into the query window (or paste it in from the listing file downloaded from the book's companion website).
9. Click the Run button in the toolbar to execute the script.

The *WineCloudDb* SQL Database instance now has empty *Wine*, *Customer*, and *Order* tables that are ready for migration with bcp. Before running your first bcp command, it's a good idea to become acquainted with bcp syntax. Table 4-1 shows the common bcp parameters that need to be specified for a typical import or export operation.

TABLE 4-1 Common SQL Server Bulk Copy (bcp) parameters

Parameter	Description
source | *target*	**Database Object** For export, it specifies the table, view or T-SQL query to be used as the source for the export operation. For import, it specifies the table to be used as the target for the import operation.
in | *out* | *queryout*	**BCP Operation** To import data into a table or view, specify in. To export data to a data file from a table or view, specify out. To export data to a data file from a query, specify queryout.
data file	**Data File** For export, it specifies the name of the data file to create from the table, view, or T-SQL query. For import, it specifies the name of the data file to retrieve data for the table being imported. This parameter must include the full path to the data file.
–S server	**Server Name** Specifies the server name of the SQL Server or Microsoft Azure SQL Database that bcp should connect to.

Parameter	Description
–T	**Windows Authentication** Use a trusted connection that doesn't require a user name and password. It cannot be combined with –U and –P. Trusted connections are supported only for SQL Server. When connecting to SQL Database, you must use –U and –P for SQL Server authentication instead.
–U login	**SQL Server Authentication Login** Combine with –P to connect using SQL Server authentication with either SQL Server or SQL Database. Cannot combine with –T.
–P password	**SQL Server Authentication Password** Combine with –U to connect using SQL Server authentication with either SQL Server or SQL Database. Cannot combine with –T.
–n	**Use Native Data Types** Recommended when migrating between SQL Server, SQL Database, or both. For non-Microsoft databases, this switch is not supported, and bcp will prompt you for the data type of each column (or you can define the data types in a separate format file).
–q	**Support Quoted Identifiers** Allows you to use a database, owner, table, or view name that contains a space or single quotation mark (executes the SET QUOTED_IDENTIFIERS ON statement).

Note that bcp is very particular about the first three parameters. The database object, operation, and data file parameters must always be specified in that order. The remaining switch parameters can appear in any order on the command line.

Exporting data

As you might have already inferred by its syntax, the bcp utility migrates data into and out of individual tables and not an entire database. The local *WineDb* database contains three tables: *Wine*, *Customer*, and *Order*. The *Wine* and *Customer* tables both have data, and the *Order* table is empty, so you will export data from the database by running the bcp utility twice: once for the *Wine* table and a second time for the *Customer* table.

To export data from your local *WineDb* database into bcp data files, follow these steps:

1. Launch a command-prompt window. An easy way to do this is to press the Windows key, type **cmd** on the Start screen, and press Enter.
2. Type **bcp WineDb.dbo.Wine out Wine.dat –S .\sqlexpress –T –n –q**, and press Enter.
3. Type **bcp WineDb.dbo.Customer out Customer.dat –S .\sqlexpress –T –n –q**, and press Enter.

Note These instructions assume you are using the SQL Server Express edition, which has a server name of *.\sqlexpress*. If you are using another edition, you must replace the server name *.\sqlexpress* specified in the instructions with the name of server you are using. Furthermore, if your server doesn't support Windows authentication, you cannot specify *–T*, and must instead use the *–U* and *–P* switches for SQL Server authentication.

When bcp runs, it displays status information, including the number of rows exported, the packet size, the duration of the export, and the average throughput, as shown in Figure 4-15.

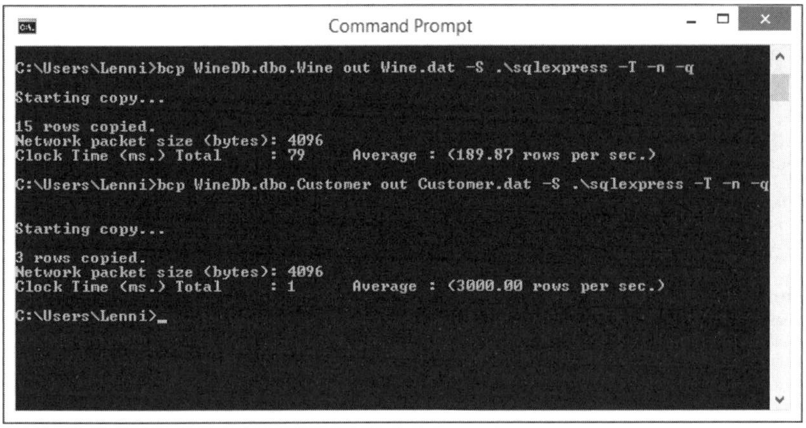

```
Command Prompt
C:\Users\Lenni>bcp WineDb.dbo.Wine out Wine.dat -S .\sqlexpress -T -n -q
Starting copy...
15 rows copied.
Network packet size (bytes): 4096
Clock Time (ms.) Total     : 79      Average : (189.87 rows per sec.)
C:\Users\Lenni>bcp WineDb.dbo.Customer out Customer.dat -S .\sqlexpress -T -n -q

Starting copy...
3 rows copied.
Network packet size (bytes): 4096
Clock Time (ms.) Total     : 1       Average : (3000.00 rows per sec.)
C:\Users\Lenni>_
```

FIGURE 4-15 Exporting SQL Server tables to data files with bcp

Importing data

Now you will use bcp once more to import the data files you just exported into the *WineCloudDb* SQL Database instance, only this time you will specify *in* to perform an import operation.

When importing with bcp, you need to pay attention to the size of the data file being imported. If your data set is large, you will likely need to split it up into multiple chunks. You can easily do this using the *–b* switch parameter to specify the number of rows to import as one batch. Each batch is imported and logged as a separate database transaction so that if an error occurs, only inserts from the current batch are rolled back. By default, bcp imports all rows in a data file as one batch, but if you are importing large numbers of rows, you will likely experience connection loss and throttling from SQL Database if you don't specify a smaller batch size. You might need to experiment with your data set to determine the right batch size to avoid throttling and connection loss with bcp.

The bcp syntax provides special switches to support batched import operations and to let you specify hints that enable other options. These additional switch parameters are shown in Table 4-2.

TABLE 4-2 SQL Server Bulk Copy (bcp) import parameters

Parameter	Description
–b batch_size	**Batch Size** Specifies the number of rows to process for a batched import operation.
–F first_row	**First Row** When batching with –b, specifies the starting row in the data file to use as the starting point for the import operation.
–L last_row	**Last Row** When batching with –b, specifies the ending row in the data file to use as the stopping point for the import operation.
–h hints	**Hints** Enable other options. For example, you can sort and order the data using the ORDER hint, force constraints to execute during the import operation using the CHECK_CONSTRAINTS hint, and lock the table during the import operation using the TABLOCK hint.

It is also a recommended practice to disable nonclustered indexes, triggers, and constraints on the destination database during the import process and then re-enable them again after. Doing so can significantly improve the performance and speed of the import. Given the simplicity and size of the *WineDb* database, there is nothing to disable, nor is there any need to break up the import operation into batches (although we will still demonstrate batching with the 15-row *Wine* table, just so you can learn how to do it with much larger tables).

To import the data files exported from the local *WineDb* SQL Server database into the *WineCloudDb* SQL Database instance, follow these steps:

1. If it's not still opened already from the previous export operation, launch a new command prompt.
2. Type **bcp WineCloudDb.dbo.Customer in Customer.dat –S tcp:<*server*>.database.windows.net –U <*login-id*>@<*server*> –P <*password*> –n**, and press Enter. This command imports the entire *Customer.dat* data file into the *Customer* table. When the command is completed, bcp displays status information as shown in Figure 4-16.

Note Replace <*server*>, <*login-id*>, and <*password*> with the server name, administrator user name, and administrator password of the SQL Database server hosting your *WineCloudDb* database.

Command Prompt

```
C:\Users\Lenni>bcp WineCloudDb.dbo.Customer in Customer.dat -S tcp:akox14ud20.da
tabase.windows.net -U saz@akox14ud20 -P          -n

Starting copy...

3 rows copied.
Network packet size (bytes): 4096
Clock Time (ms.) Total     : 94      Average : (31.91 rows per sec.)

C:\Users\Lenni>_
```

FIGURE 4-16 Importing a data file to a SQL Database table with bcp

3. Type **bcp WineCloudDb.dbo.Wine in Wine.dat –S tcp:<*server*>.database.windows.net –U <*login-id*>@<*server*> –P <*password*> –n –b 5 –F 1 –L 5 –h "TABLOCK"**, and press Enter. This imports the first batch of rows (rows 1 through 5) from the *Wine.dat* file into the *Wine* table. The *–h* switch specifies the *TABLOCK* hint, which tells bcp to lock the *Wine* table while importing.

4. Type **bcp WineCloudDb.dbo.Wine in Wine.dat –S tcp:<*server*>.database.windows.net –U <*login-id*>@<*server*> –P <*password*> –n –b 5 –F 6 –L 10 –h "TABLOCK"**, and press Enter. This imports the second batch of rows (rows 6 through 10) from the *Wine.dat* file into the *Wine* table, which gets locked during the process.

5. Type **bcp WineCloudDb.dbo.Wine in Wine.dat –S tcp:<*server*>.database.windows.net –U <*login-id*>@<*server*> –P <*password*> –n –b 5 –F 11 –L 15 –h "TABLOCK"**, and press Enter. This imports the third (and last) batch of rows (rows 11 through 15).

You have now imported both the *Wine* and *Customer* tables from the local *WineDb* SQL Server database into the *WineCloudDb* SQL Database instance using the bcp utility. In our example, we migrated a very small data set to SQL Database, so it wasn't really necessary to break the Wine table up into 3 batches of 15 rows each (but now you've learned how). In fact, bcp was designed to efficiently migrate large amounts of data into and out of SQL Server. So if you have large tables of data to migrate into and out of SQL Database (and/or SQL Server), this exercise has shown you how to batch the overall import operation with bcp.

SQL Database Migration Wizard

SQL Database has a number of noteworthy differences and limitations when compared to SQL Server. (These are detailed in Chapter 3, "Differences between SQL Server and Microsoft Azure SQL Database.") These differences need to be factored into your database migration projects. Your database schemas and T-SQL scripts must conform to the supported features and syntax of SQL Database, but inspecting your SQL Server schemas and scripts for unsupported features and syntax can be a lengthy, painful, and error-prone process. The great news is that the Microsoft Azure SQL Database Migration Wizard greatly simplifies and reduces the pain of this otherwise tedious process.

All the database migration tools and solutions we've explored to this point are built into the Microsoft SQL Server tools or Visual Studio. However, there are other nice and useful tools outside of the commercial Microsoft toolset, and the Microsoft Azure SQL Database Migration Wizard is one of them. This is a free, open source tool that interactively walks you through the process of migrating a database to SQL Database. The migration wizard was created by George Huey, a Principal Architect at Microsoft, back in the early days of Microsoft Azure SQL Database when it was still called *SQL Azure*. It has been battle-tested by thousands of users and is often updated with bug fixes and feature enhancements, often as a result of great community feedback.

Note Even though this tool was created by a Microsoft employee, it is not an official Microsoft product and is not supported by Microsoft.

If you have an existing SQL Server database, and you're not sure it satisfies the requirements and limitations of SQL Database, the Microsoft Azure SQL Database Migration Wizard is a great place to start. It will not only deploy schema and data from SQL Server to SQL Database, but it will also identify compatibility issues, and it can even resolve certain compatibility issues automatically.

The Microsoft Azure SQL Database Migration Wizard greatly simplifies migrating databases to SQL Database by doing these three things very well:

- Analyzes a SQL Server database, SQL Profiler trace, or T-SQL script for SQL Database compatibility issues
- Generates T-SQL scripts for creating database schema in SQL Database
- Migrates data to SQL Database using the bcp utility

You already worked with T-SQL scripts and migrated data to SQL Database using BACPAC and bcp. But one thing you haven't done to this point is analyze the database for incompatibilities, and that's one of the major benefits of the Microsoft Azure SQL Database Migration Wizard.

Downloading the tool

To get started with the SQL Database Migration Wizard, you need to download it from Codeplex and install it. The SQL Database Migration Wizard has dependencies on SQL Server assemblies, which requires that SQL Server already be installed.

At the time of this writing, there are two different versions of the SQL Database Migration Wizard. Version 3.X supports SQL Server 2008 R2, and version 4.X supports SQL Server 2012. We assume you are running SQL Server 2012, so you should install version 4.X. It's reasonable to expect that future versions of the tool will be released to work with future versions of SQL Server, so you just need to pay attention to which version of the tool you are downloading.

To download and install the SQL Database Migration Wizard, follow these steps:

1. Navigate your web browser to **http://sqlazuremw.codeplex.com**. This takes you to the tool's dedicated Codeplex page. (Note that the URL has a reference to "SQL Azure" in it, because the tool was created back when SQL Database was named *SQL Azure*.)
2. Click the DOWNLOADS button at the top of the page. This takes you to a page that lists all the available SQL Database Migration Wizard downloads.
3. Scroll down to find and click the download link for SQLAzureMW v4.0.18 Release Binary for SQL Server 2012 (or, as mentioned, find and click the Release Binary link with the version number that corresponds with the version of SQL Server you are running).
4. When prompted to Open or Save, click Save to begin the download.
5. When prompted, click Open Folder to launch an Explorer window to the location on your computer where you saved the downloaded *.zip* file.

6. Right-click the *.zip* file, and choose Properties.

7. In the Properties dialog, click the Unblock button, as shown in Figure 4-17. If you don't unblock the *.zip* file, you will still be able to extract it, but you won't then be able to run the tool from the extracted location.

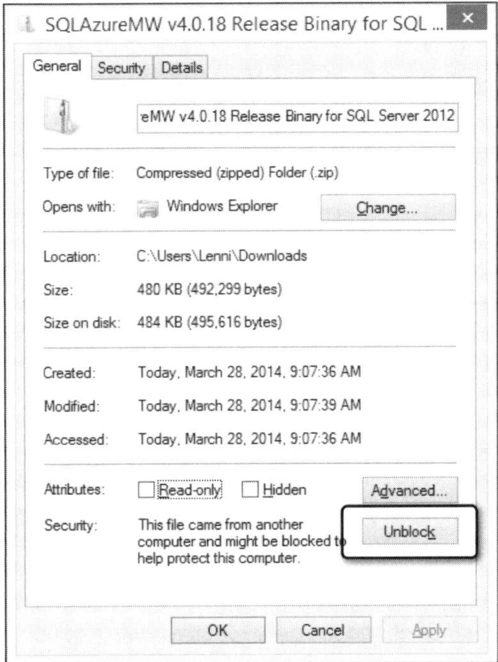

FIGURE 4-17 Unblocking the downloaded *.zip* file using the Properties dialog

8. Click OK to close the Properties dialog.

9. Right-click the *.zip* file, and choose Extract All.

10. Click Extract to extract the contents of the *.zip* file to a new folder in the same location and with the same name as the *.zip* file.

After the *.zip* file is extracted, the folder with the extracted files opens up automatically in a new Explorer window, and you are ready to begin using the tool.

Migrating a database

To use the SQL Database Migration Wizard to migrate the *WineDb* database, follow these steps:

1. In the Explorer window opened to the extracted files, double-click the file *SQLAzureMW.exe* to launch the tool. This displays the wizard's Select Process page, as shown in Figure 4-18.

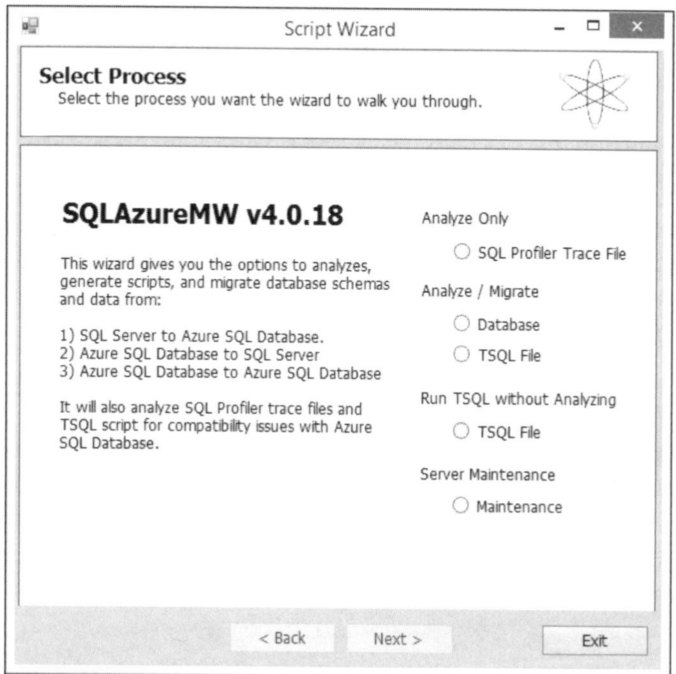

FIGURE 4-18 The Select Process page of the SQL Database Migration Wizard

2. In the options on the right, choose the Database radio button beneath Analyze / Migrate, and click Next. This displays the Connect To Server dialog.

Note The TSQL File radio button is useful if you already previously scripted your database objects to a T-SQL file, in which case the tool can also analyze and migrate using that T-SQL file.

3. For Server Name, type **.\sqlexpress** (or the name of your local SQL Server instance that contains the *WineDb* database).
4. If your local server requires SQL Server authentication, choose the Use A Specific User ID And Password radio button and supply your login name and password.
5. Leave the other options set to their defaults, and click the Connect button at the bottom of the dialog.
6. The Select Source page now displays a list of the databases installed on the local SQL Server instance you just connected to. Select the *WineDb* database, and click Next.
7. The Choose Objects page appears. By default, this page is set to script all the database objects, but you can select specific database objects if you want. Leave the default option selected to script the entire database, and click Next.

8. The Script Wizard Summary page now appears. Take a moment to expand the information and review it for correctness, and then click Next.

9. When prompted to generate the SQL script, Click Yes. This creates a script to generate the database schema and runs bcp to export the individual tables from the local *WineDb* database.

10. When processing completes, the wizard displays the Results Summary page, as shown in Figure 4-19. You should encounter no errors with the *WineDb* database. However, if there are errors, this is where you will discover them, because the wizard will refuse to migrate the database until you resolve the errors.

Note The Results Summary page uses color coding to make it easy for you to spot problems. Green and blue indicate success, but if there are compatibility issues, they will show up in either red or dark red. Red indicates an error that prevents migration, which you need to resolve, while dark red text indicates that an incompatibility was found, but the SQL Database Migration Wizard knows that it can resolve the issue automatically.

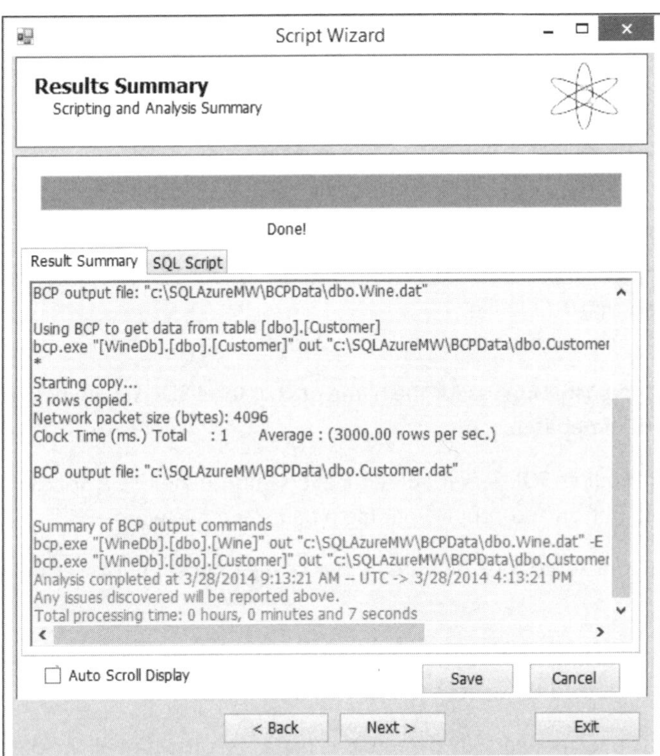

FIGURE 4-19 The Results Summary page after successfully generating and running a script

11. Click the SQL Script tab to view the T-SQL schema creation script that the SQL Database Migration Wizard has generated, as shown in Figure 4-20.

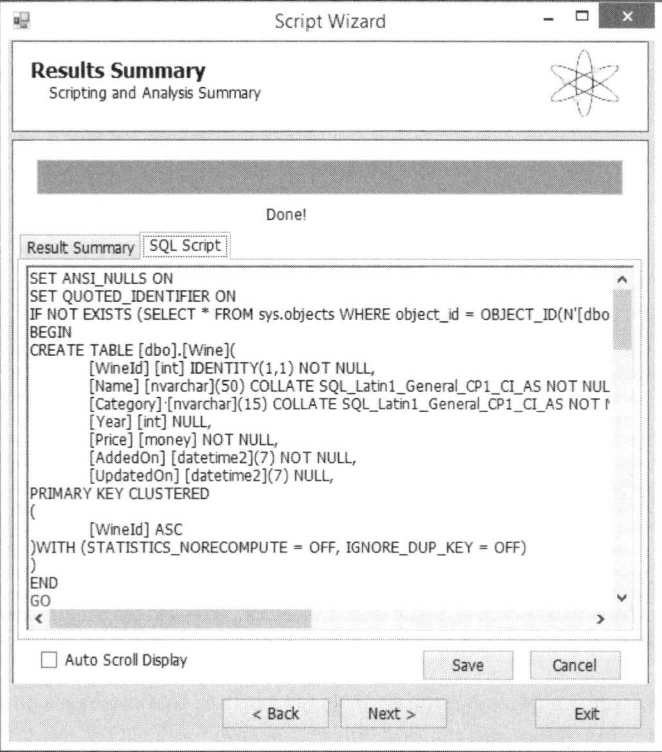

FIGURE 4-20 The SQL Script tab displays the generated schema creation script

12. If you would like to save the script to a file for later use or review, click Save and select a location to save the file.

13. Click Next to begin configuring the deployment to SQL Database. This launches the Connect To Server dialog.

14. In the Connect To Server dialog, do the following:

    a. For Server Name, type **<*server*>.database.windows.net** (replace <*server*> with the name of your SQL Database server).

    b. For User Name, type **<*login-id*>@<*server*>** (replace <*login-id*> with the server's administrator user name, and replace <*server*> with the name of your SQL Database server).

    c. For Password, type the type server's administrator password. The Connect To Server dialog should appear similar to Figure 4-21.

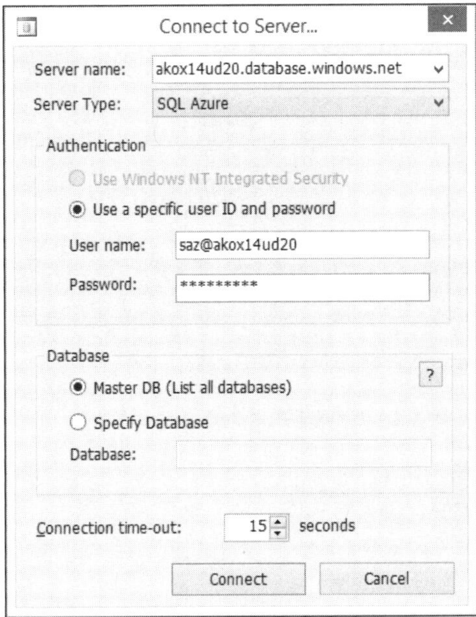

FIGURE 4-21 Connecting to SQL Database to deploy using the SQL Database Migration Wizard

   d. Click Connect to connect to your SQL Database server. This closes the Connect To Server dialog and returns to the wizard.

15. The Setup Target Server Connection page appears, and lists all the databases on the server. If you have been following along with the previous procedures, you will see the *WineCloudDb* database appear in the list. You want to begin with an empty database, so delete the current one as follows:

   a. Click the *WineCloudDb* database.

   b. Click the Delete Database button at the bottom of the dialog.

   c. When prompted to confirm, click Yes to return to the wizard.

16. Click the Create Database button at the bottom of the dialog. This launches the Create Database dialog.

17. For Enter Database Name, type **WineCloudDb**. The Create Database dialog should appear similar to Figure 4-22.

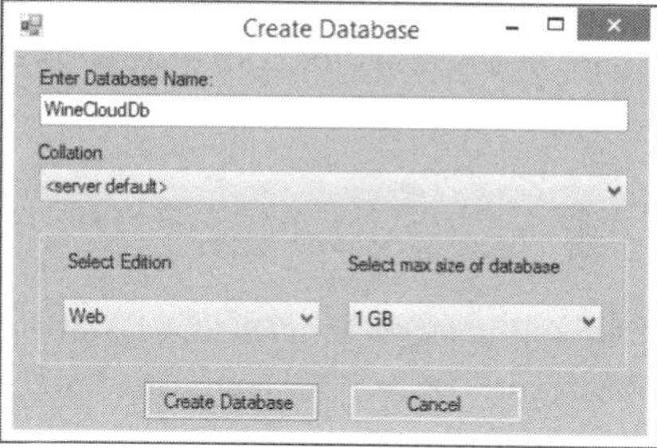

FIGURE 4-22 Creating the target database for deployment with the SQL Database Migration Wizard

18. Click the Create Database button. This creates an empty SQL Database named *WineCloudDb*, closes the Create Database dialog, and returns to the wizard.
19. Select the newly created *WineCloudDb* database in the list, and click Next.
20. When prompted to execute the script, click Yes.
21. As the deployment progresses, you will see status updates written to the Target Server Response page. When the deployment completes successfully, the Target Server Response page should appear similar to Figure 4-23.

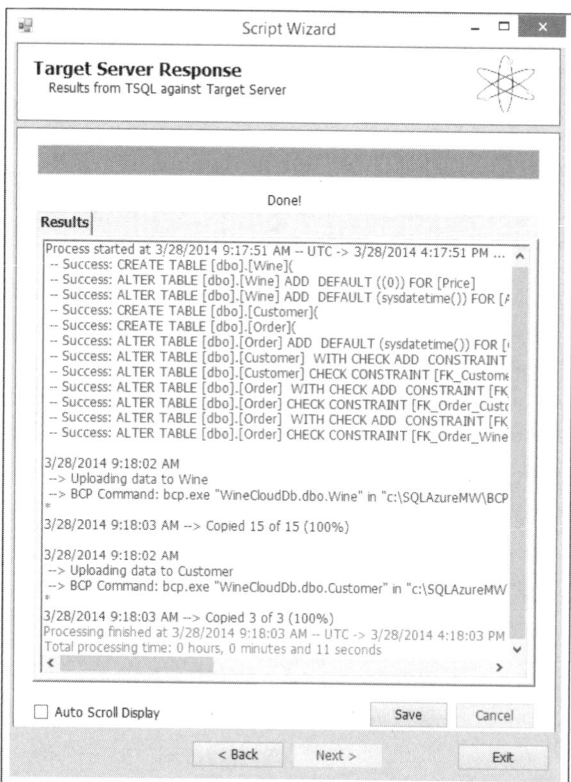

FIGURE 4-23 The Target Server Response page after a successful deployment

Note The Target Server Response page also uses color coding to indicate success (green and blue) and failure (red).

22. Click Exit to close the wizard.

You have now deployed both the schema and data to the *WineCloudDb* SQL Database instance using an intuitive step-by-step tool, thanks to the Microsoft Azure SQL Database Migration Wizard. Beyond deploying both your database schema and data, it also analyzed your schema for compatibility issues when migrating from SQL Server to SQL Database.

To summarize, the tool performed the following actions:

1. Generated T-SQL scripts for all the database objects (schema) in the local SQL Server database
2. Exported data into data files using bcp
3. Analyzed the generated T-SQL script with a pattern matching rules engine that uncovers known incompatibilities and limitations
4. Deployed the database schema to SQL Database by executing the generated (and potentially autocorrected) T-SQL scripts
5. Imported data into SQL Database from the exported data files using bcp

All these steps (with the exception of the analysis step) could have been performed independently, as you did in the previous sections of this chapter. The SQL Database Migration Wizard just packages everything up in an easy-to-use tool that visually and interactively walks through the process, without you needing to use multiple tools and command prompts. But the rules engine analysis that the SQL Database Migration Wizard conducts on your local database schema is not something you can do with the other tools. This analysis is a unique and extremely compelling capability of the wizard.

The Microsoft Azure SQL Database Migration Wizard is open source, and you can look at the internals of this tool if you want. If you discover an incompatibility between SQL Server and SQL Database that the tool doesn't catch, or you're just curious about the predefined syntax rules, you can easily view the rules. They are defined in an XML file named *NotSupportedByAzureFile.Config*, which can be found in the same directory as the *SQLAzureMW.exe*. If you are comfortable with regular expressions, you can even add your own rules to the SQL Server Migration Wizard by modifying this XML file with a text editor.

Summary

It is rare to work on a project that is entirely greenfield and all new development. You're much more likely to work on a project involving Microsoft Azure SQL Database that will require the migration of existing databases. There are many ways to migrate your SQL Server databases to SQL Database, and they each have their own pros and cons to fit different scenarios. In this chapter, we walked through a number of tools and techniques for migrating existing SQL Server databases to SQL Database, including T-SQL scripts, .bacpac files, bcp, and the SQL Database Migration Wizard.

For lightweight scenarios, you saw how T-SQL scripts can be generated from a SQL Server database and executed against a SQL Database instance. SQL Data-Tier Application .bacpac files make it easy to package an entire database, including both schema and data, and import that into a SQL Database instance, but it operates at the database level and doesn't allow you to migrate individual database objects. Furthermore, for larger databases, the size of the .bacpac file can make it difficult to migrate to SQL Database. Bulk Copy with bcp is an efficient and high-performance way to migrate large amounts of data to SQL Database, but it doesn't do anything to migrate your database objects (schema). Finally, the Microsoft Azure SQL Database Migration Wizard is a free, open source project on Codeplex that is not commercially supported by a software vendor that brings together the process of migrating the schema and data to SQL Database while generating T-SQL scripts and automating bcp.

CHAPTER 5

Security and backup

—*Eric Boyd*

The topics of security, availability, and disaster recovery top the list of concerns that customers raise when considering the public cloud. These are certainly not new concerns introduced with the cloud; customers have been architecting solutions to deal with these same concerns since long before the cloud. The cloud is simply unfamiliar territory that causes these foundational concerns to be revisited. Thus, customers need these top concerns addressed with reasonable solutions before the public cloud is a viable option. Microsoft does a great job of putting customers' concerns at ease on these topics with the security processes and certifications that are in place in Microsoft Azure, along with the features of the platform that provide customers with the control and visibility they need.

In this chapter, we discuss security and backup concerns in the cloud. We start by explaining the general security responsibilities of any public cloud vendor, and then talk more specifically about security in Microsoft Azure and Microsoft Azure SQL Database. You will learn how to secure SQL Database by configuring the firewall as you create custom firewall rules and define users and permissions.

Security and backup often go hand in hand. Notwithstanding all other security-related concerns, how "secure" is your business if you have no backup in the event of an unforeseen disaster? So toward the end of this chapter, you will also learn how to copy and back up SQL Database, and how to schedule automated backups.

Addressing major cloud concerns

Two of the most common concerns users raise when considering public cloud platforms are security and business continuity, sometimes referred to as *disaster recovery*. Security is an overloaded term, and it can mean a lot of different things depending on the individual and context. So it is easier to think about security concerns by dividing them into two major categories: security concerns that are the sole responsibility of the public cloud vendor (Microsoft, in the case of Azure), and security concerns that are either the customer's responsibility or the combined responsibility of the customer and public cloud vendor.

Security responsibilities of the public cloud vendor

Some security concerns can be managed and addressed only by public cloud vendors, because customer access is limited to higher-level abstractions over the raw computing infrastructure, resources, and services. The customer typically cannot gain direct access to things like network routers, switches, and firewalls, as well as physical servers and the hypervisor, which is the software layer that virtualizes the hardware for multiple operating systems to run on a single physical server. As a result, it is very important to have a reputable cloud vendor with a successful history that you can count on and trust. But you cannot rely only on faith in a vendor, you also need transparency and insight into the resources and practices of your cloud vendor, and this includes their security practices and procedures, as described in the following sections.

Physical data center

Access to the physical data center—including entry inside the outermost security fence, entry into the building, and access to the physical infrastructure and hardware—must be managed with secure policies that are consistently enforced. You want it to be extremely difficult, and ideally impossible, for an unauthorized person to gain physical access to your servers.

Privacy from vendor personnel

The personnel who are authorized to gain access to the computing infrastructure and resources should still not be able to access your data, unless you explicitly grant them permission to do so. Because you don't manage the foundational infrastructure, the vendor must ensure that it's secure with the appropriate safeguards to prevent their personnel from accessing your data without your permission.

Isolating tenants

As is the case with vendor personnel, you don't want other tenants of the cloud vendor to be able to gain access to your data and applications. (*Multitenancy* is an architecture in which a single infrastructure component serves multiple customers, where each customer is called a *tenant*.) When you are using multitenant services, this is a concern that must be managed by the vendor.

Preventing cyber attacks

A malicious attack, such as a denial-of-service attack, could occur against your applications and services, or at a broader level against the cloud vendor's services. When these kinds of attacks occur, you want the cloud vendor to detect them and prevent them from causing a service outage.

Shared security responsibilities

Other security concerns are either the customer's responsibility or are shared between the customer and the cloud vendor. Whenever a security concern can be affected by the customer's configuration, implementation, or software, it cannot be the responsibility of the cloud vendor alone. The customer must secure aspects of their application to resolve these security concerns.

Meeting compliance requirements

A number of industries and organizations must meet regulatory requirements because of the nature of their businesses and the data they handle. These requirements often span the physical data center, applications running in the data center, and management processes across both of these areas. As a result, you need to understand what compliance certifications your cloud vendor has achieved. But you also need to understand that you also have a responsibility to meet the requirements that are outside of the cloud vendor's control that are application-centric and specific to your implementation.

Auditing activities

Much like compliance, knowing who did what and when they did it is a responsibility that is shared between the cloud vendor and the customer. Only the cloud vendor can track and provide an audit log of the activities that occur in the platform services. But it's the customer's responsibility to track the application-level activities. Because accurate and detailed auditing is a common requirement for most compliance certifications, it's an important capability both for your cloud vendor and your applications to provide. A core requirement for effective auditing requires you to provide unique credentials for every user and ensure that users do not share their credentials. If multiple users share a single account, you cannot possibly know exactly who performed an activity logged for that account.

Keeping electronic intruders out

Let's not forget the hackers who try to profit from stealing data and other hackers who just want to be malicious and aim to create chaos. You need to keep both of those types of hackers out. The cloud vendor must protect the infrastructure and core services and keep the electronic intruders out at that level. It's your responsibility to protect your applications from exploitations, and if you manage the virtual machines (VMs) in an Infrastructure-as-a-Service (IaaS) model, you must patch and secure your operating system whenever it is exploited.

Security in Microsoft Azure

Microsoft invests a lot of effort and talent into making sure Azure is a secure and reliable public cloud. Microsoft also does a great job being transparent and providing insight into the security and privacy practices of Microsoft Azure. One of the ways they do this is via a website called the Microsoft Azure Trust Center, which can be found at *http://azure.microsoft.com/en-us/support/trust-center/*. The Microsoft Azure Trust Center provides detailed information on Microsoft's practices that enable security, privacy, and compliance in Microsoft Azure. It is a great resource to gain a deeper understanding of security in Microsoft Azure and to find answers to your Microsoft Azure security questions.

Although Microsoft invests a lot of effort into ensuring SQL Database is a secure and reliable service, you still need to do a number of things to create a secure experience when using it. In the following sections, you will walk through step-by-step procedures that help to secure SQL Database. You will begin by securing access to and communication with SQL Database. Then you will walk through application-level security concerns such as SQL injection attacks and data encryption.

Securing SQL Database

SQL Database provides security features for authentication and authorization that are similar to those found in SQL Server. In addition to those features, SQL Database provides capabilities to secure access based on the client's IP address and ensures that the communication channels are encrypted and secure. In the following step-by-step procedures, you will walk through securing your SQL Database service.

Creating a SQL Database

To demonstrate various security and backup practices, the procedures in this chapter work a *WineCloudDb* SQL Database similar to the one you've created in other chapters. If you don't already have this database (or if you deleted it), you can create it now to follow along with this chapter. Otherwise, if you have a *WineCloudDb* database already on a SQL Database server from any other chapter in this book, you can skip ahead to the next procedure, "Configuring SQL Database Firewall."

You will use SSMS to create the database. Then you will execute the script in Listing 5-1 to create some tables and populate them with some data.

LISTING 5-1 Script to create the *WineCloudDb* database

```
CREATE TABLE Wine(
  WineId int IDENTITY PRIMARY KEY,
  Name nvarchar(50) NOT NULL,
  Category nvarchar(15) NOT NULL,
  Year int);

CREATE TABLE Customer(
  CustomerId int IDENTITY PRIMARY KEY,
  FirstName nvarchar(50) NOT NULL,
  LastName nvarchar(50) NOT NULL,
  FavoriteWineId int,
  CONSTRAINT FK_Customer_Wine FOREIGN KEY (FavoriteWineId) REFERENCES Wine(WineId));

SET IDENTITY_INSERT Wine ON;
INSERT Wine (WineId, Name, Category, Year) VALUES
 (1, 'Chateau Penin', 'Bordeaux', 2008),
 (2, 'McLaren Valley', 'Cabernet', 2005),
 (3, 'Mendoza', 'Merlot', 2010),
 (4, 'Valle Central', 'Merlot', 2009);
SET IDENTITY_INSERT Wine OFF;

SET IDENTITY_INSERT Customer ON;
INSERT Customer (CustomerId, FirstName, LastName, FavoriteWineId) VALUES
 (1, 'Jeff', 'Hay', 4),
 (2, 'Mark', 'Hanson', 3),
 (3, 'Jeff', 'Phillips', 2);
SET IDENTITY_INSERT Customer OFF;
```

To create the *WineCloudDb* database, follow these steps:

1. Launch SSMS. An easy way to do this is to press the Windows key, type **sql server management studio** on the Start screen, and press Enter.
2. In the Connect To Server dialog, do the following:
    a. For Server Name, type **<*servername*>.database.windows.net**. This is the fully qualified name to the SQL Database server, where <*servername*> should be replaced by the name assigned to your server.
    b. For Authentication, select SQL Server Authentication from the drop-down list. (SQL Database does not support Windows Authentication.)
    c. For Login and Password, type the user name (we've been using *saz*) and password you assigned the server when you created it.
    d. Click the Connect button. The server now appears as a node in the Object Explorer.
3. Right-click the server node in the Object Explorer, and choose New Query to open a new query window connected to the *master* database.
4. In the new query window, type **CREATE DATABASE WineCloudDb** and press F5 to execute the script. This creates a new *WineCloudDb* database on the server.
5. Expand the Databases node in the Object Explorer. If the new *WineCloudDb* database is not visible, right-click the Databases node and choose Refresh.
6. Right-click the *WineCloudDb* database in the Object Explorer, and choose New Query to open a new query window connected to the *WineCloudDb* database.
7. Type the code shown in Listing 5-1 into the query window (or paste it in from the listing file downloaded from the book's companion website).
8. Press F5 to execute the script.
9. Close the query window. (You don't need to save the changes unless you want to.)

Configuring SQL Database Firewall

In a typical SQL Server deployment, SQL Server is set up inside the firewall, not in a perimeter network, which is a subnetwork that exposes externally-facing services to a larger and untrusted network. In this manner, an on-premises SQL Server database is not accessible outside of the internal network. In the cloud, however, services are intended to be accessible and thus they cannot be limited to the internal network. These networking requirements make it more difficult to reduce the surface area for attack in the cloud than it is to do the same with SQL Server in your data center. Microsoft Azure closes this gap with a feature that is unique to SQL Database called SQL Database Firewall.

SQL Database Firewall restricts access to SQL Database based on the origin IP address of the connection. It is an opt-in model, which means that by default all connections to SQL Database are blocked unless a rule has been added that explicitly allows an IP address to connect. Rules can be defined for individual IP addresses as well as IP address ranges. SQL Database Firewall rules allow connections to be made to a SQL Database server, they do not authorize access to objects within the SQL Database instance. Once a connection has been permitted and established, SQL Database will authenticate the user and then authorize access to the requested database objects.

Tip In addition to server-level firewall rules created using the Microsoft Azure management portal, you can configure database-level firewall rules using the *sp_set_database_firewall_rule* stored procedure found in each database. For more information on configuring database-level firewall rules, visit *http://msdn.microsoft.com/en-us/library/jj553530.aspx*.

SQL Database server-based firewall rules are defined for an entire SQL Database server, they are stored in the *master* database, and they allow clients to connect to any database within that server. These rules can be edited directly in the *master* database, and they can also be managed using the Microsoft Azure management portal. SQL Database firewall rules have a name, a starting IP address, and an ending IP address. This arrangement allows you to create a single rule for multiple consecutive IP addresses, for example, and an entire IP subnet. You can also create a rule for a single IP address by making the starting IP address and ending IP address the same.

Creating custom firewall rules

SQL Database Firewall will prevent all connections to SQL Database unless explicitly allowed via a firewall rule. This includes your attempts to connect to SQL Database even using the SQL Database management portal. As a result, the IP address you are trying to connect from needs to be included in the firewall rules.

Follow these steps to add your IP address to the server-based firewall rules:

1. Log in to the Microsoft Azure management portal at **https://manage.windowsazure.com**. This brings you to the main portal page showing ALL ITEMS.
2. Click SQL DATABASES in the vertical navigation pane on the left.
3. Click the SERVERS link at the top of the page. This displays a list of your Microsoft Azure SQL Database servers, as shown in Figure 5-1.

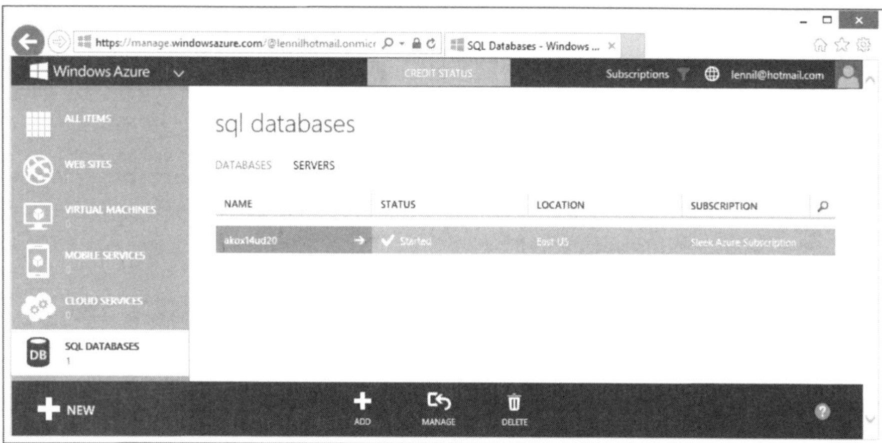

FIGURE 5-1 List of SQL Database servers in the Microsoft Azure management portal

4. In the NAME column, click the server that contains the *WineCloudDb* database. This opens a page with links for the selected server.

5. Click the CONFIGURE link at the top of the page. This displays the SQL Database server firewall configuration, as shown in Figure 5-2.

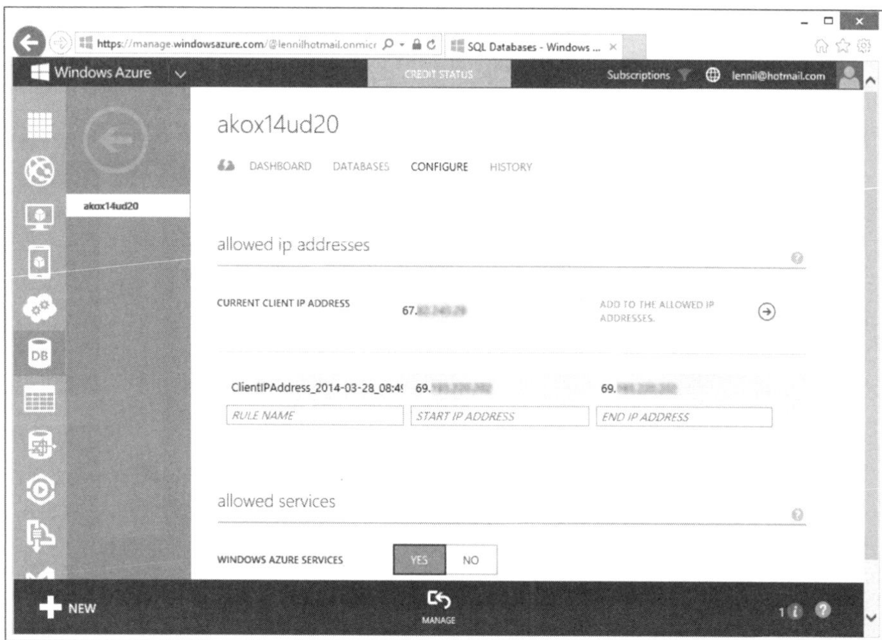

FIGURE 5-2 SQL Database server firewall configuration

6. If you followed similar procedures in Chapter 1, "Getting started with Microsoft Azure SQL Database," and Chapter 2, "Configuration and pricing," you should already see one rule named

ClientIPAddress_yyyy-mm-dd_hh:mm:ss in place for your current IP address, or at least, for the IP address you were using at the time if you are now in a different location. In this case, click the X to the right of the rule (the X appears only when you hover the mouse over the rule) to remove it now.

7. In the Allowed IP Addresses section, your current IP address should appear to the right of CURRENT CLIENT IP ADDRESS. Click the ADD TO THE ALLOWED IP ADDRESSES link to the right of your IP address to add it now.

With this change, you will be able to connect to the SQL Database server from your current IP address, wherever you happen to be. Of course, if you are connecting from the same IP address you used in Chapters 1 and 2, the new rule you just added is the same rule as the one you just removed in the previous step. In this case, the purpose of this exercise was solely to demonstrate how to delete a rule.

New firewall rules don't take effect until you click the SAVE button at the bottom of the page. Before you do that, add another rule so that you can also connect from your home office. To create the home office rule, follow these steps:

1. In the RULE NAME text box beneath the list of existing rules, type **Home Office**. Note that the rule name cannot contain either forward slash (/) or backslash (\) characters, nor can it end with a period (.) character.
2. In the START IP ADDRESS and END IP ADDRESS boxes, type the IP address range of your home office. (Type the same IP address in both text boxes to specify a single IP address rather than a range.) The page should appear similar to Figure 5-3.

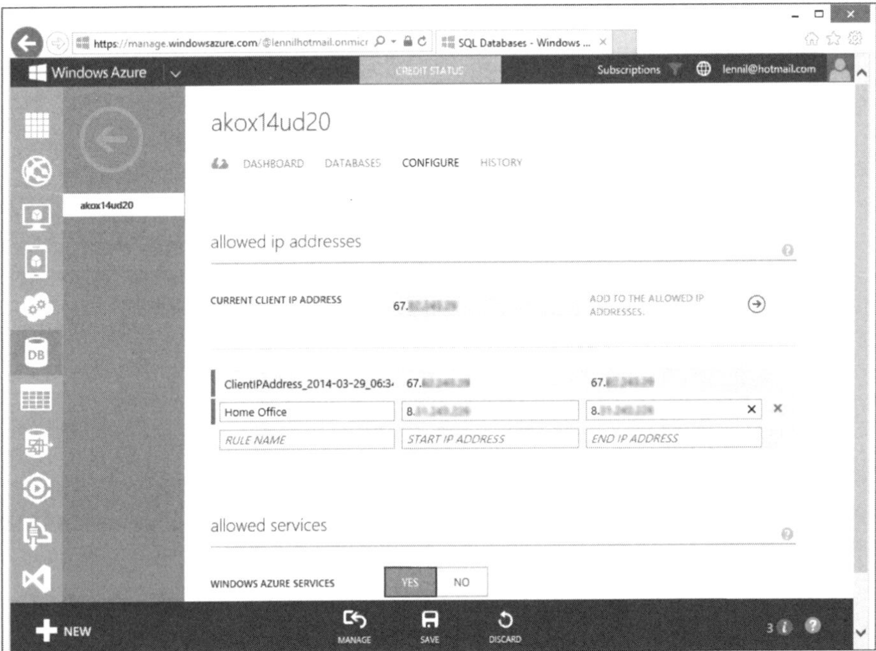

FIGURE 5-3 New firewall rules for the current location and the Home Office

3. Click the SAVE button at the bottom of the page.

You have now updated the firewall rules. Prior to doing so, the home office IP address or addresses you specified would be blocked from connecting to your SQL Database server using any mechanism, including SQL Server Management Studio (SSMS), SQL Server Data Tools (SSDT), your own custom applications using ADO.NET or Entity Framework, and even the SQL Database management portal itself.

Allowing Microsoft Azure services to connect

If you want, Microsoft Azure services can also be blocked from connecting to your SQL Database server. Finding out the IP addresses of the Microsoft Azure originating requests can be difficult and complex to manage, so SQL Database provides a feature that enables you to allow or block requests from other Azure services without having to know the specific IP addresses for the request. If you allow Azure services to connect to your SQL Database server using this feature, all Azure services are allowed to connect through the SQL Database server firewall. They will still need to authenticate and be authorized in your SQL Database server to do anything with your databases, but they won't be blocked from connecting by the firewall.

When you create a server, you'll see a check box you can select to enable Microsoft Azure services to access your SQL Database server. (You used this check box in Chapter 1; see Figure 1-5.) This check box is selected by default, and if you left it selected when you created your SQL Database server (and as we instructed in Chapter 1), Azure services are allowed to connect to your SQL Database server. Once the server has been created, you can easily toggle the setting to allow or block Azure services through the firewall by clicking the YES and NO options for WINDOWS AZURE SERVICES beneath Allowed Services at the bottom of the firewall rules page. (See the bottom of Figure 5-3.)

When you choose to allow Microsoft Azure services, a firewall rule is added to your SQL Database server with an IP range of 0.0.0.0 to 0.0.0.0. This is a special range that allows all Microsoft Azure services to connect to your SQL Database server, and it does not appear with your other rules on the firewall rules page. (You can determine whether or not the 0.0.0.0 rule is in place based on whether YES or NO is selected for WINDOWS AZURE SERVICES at the bottom of the page.)

In addition to managing server-based firewall rules in the Microsoft Azure management portal as you've just done, the SQL Database Management REST API can also be used in scenarios where you want to manage the SQL Database firewall from an application or script. (The REST API is explained in Chapter 8, "Designing and tuning for scalability and high performance.")

Authenticating and authorizing users

Once a client connection is permitted through the SQL Database Firewall, SQL Database then needs to authenticate credentials and log in users. SQL Database manages and authenticates users using SQL Server Authentication, just like on-premises SQL Server. Unlike SQL Server, however, Windows Authentication is not supported. (More information about differences between Microsoft Azure SQL Database and SQL Server can be found in Chapter 3, "Configuration and pricing.")

When Microsoft Azure creates a SQL Database server, it also creates a *master* database on the server. One of the responsibilities of the *master* database is managing SQL Database server logins. The initial login is created from the user name and password you provide when creating a SQL Database server. (We've been using *saz* in our examples.) That user name and password gets used as the server-level principal for your SQL Database server, similar to the *sa* user in SQL Server. You can use that login to connect to your SQL Database server from your applications, but doing so is not a good practice because this login has full permissions in the database and does not allow you to provide fine-grained access. To restrict access and achieve more fine-grained access control, you need to create new SQL Database logins and users.

Creating SQL Database logins

To create a new login and user in SQL Server, you could use the graphical interface in SQL Server Management Studio. Unfortunately, those dialogs and forms are not available in SSMS when you are connected to a SQL Database server. As a result, you will need to execute direct T-SQL commands inside a query window instead.

Follow these steps to create a new SQL Database server login:

1. Launch SSMS. An easy way to do this is to press the Windows key, type **sql server management studio** on the Start screen, and press Enter.
2. In the Connect To Server dialog, enter the appropriate credentials, as shown in Figure 5-4. Be sure to choose the server that has the *WineCloudDb* database on it. Also, remember that the server name must be suffixed with *.database.windows.net* and you must provide the login you specified when you created the server. (We've been using *saz* in our examples.)

FIGURE 5-4 The Connect To Server dialog in SQL Server Management Studio

3. Click the Connect button.
4. Once connected, your SQL Database server will be listed in the Object Explorer pane. Right-click on the server name, and choose New Query as shown in Figure 5-5. This opens a new query window connected to the *master* database.

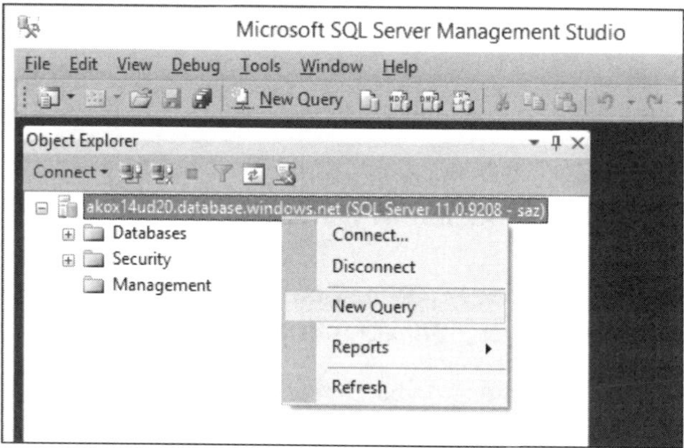

FIGURE 5-5 Opening a new query window for the *master* database in SQL Server Management Studio

5. Type the following T-SQL statement:
   CREATE LOGIN WineCloudDbLogin WITH PASSWORD='<Password>'

> **Note** Replace *<Password>* with a strong password that you select for your new login. The password must satisfy the requirements of the password policy. For more information about the strong password policy, see *http://msdn.microsoft.com/en-us/library/ms161962.aspx*.

6. Press F5 (or click the Execute button in the toolbar) to run the script.

You have now created a new SQL Database server login; however, this login isn't authorized to do anything with the SQL Database server. You now need to create a user for this login and then either grant the user server-level or database-level permissions.

Granting server-level permissions

SQL Database has two server-level security roles, *loginmanager* and *dbmanager*, as shown in Table 5-1. These roles make it possible for users other than the server-level principal to manage security and databases. A user must be created for a login in the *master* database to assign server-level roles.

TABLE 5-1 SQL Database server-level roles

Role	Description
loginmanager	This role has permissions to create logins in the SQL Database server, similar to the securityadmin role in SQL Server.
dbmanager	This role has permissions to create databases in a SQL Database server, similar to the dbcreator role in SQL Server.

As when creating and managing logins, you will need to manage users and role assignments using T-SQL scripts, because the SQL Server Management Studio user interfaces are not available when you are connected to a SQL Database server. Working in the same query window that's connected to your SQL Database server from the previous procedure, follow these steps to create a new user with server-level permissions:

1. Delete the T-SQL code in the query window left over from the previous procedure.
2. Type the following T-SQL statements into the code window:
   CREATE USER WineCloudDbUser FROM LOGIN WineCloudDbLogin
   GO
   EXEC sp_addrolemember 'loginmanager', 'WineCloudDbUser'
   EXEC sp_addrolemember 'dbmanager', 'WineCloudDbUser'
3. Press F5 (or click the Execute button in the toolbar) to run the script. This code creates a new user named *WineCloudDbUser* that is associated with the existing login named *WineCloudDbLogin* that you created in the previous procedure, and then adds the new user to the *loginmanager* and *dbmanager* roles.

You have now created a new user in the *master* database named *WineCloudDbUser* and granted this user permissions to manage logins and databases within the scope of the SQL Database server. This will allow you to delegate permissions to others to manage the SQL Database server without needing to distribute the server-level principal credentials.

Granting database-level permissions

One of the goals when working on security is to minimize the surface area and reduce exposure to attack. One of the principles that gets applied to this problem is the principle of *least privilege*, which basically means, give users just enough access to perform their required job functions, and not any more or less. This minimizes users' access, which in turn minimizes the overall surface area for attack.

When using SQL Database, you don't want to grant all users server-level permissions; instead, you want to give users just enough permissions to do what they need. For example, if you have an application that only needs to read data from a database, you don't want to give the user the application is connecting as permissions to write data. In this case, you can create a new user who has read-only database permissions. This involves creating a new login in the *master* database and then creating a new user associated with that login in the *WineCloudDb* database. Create the new read-only user now by following these steps:

1. Delete the T-SQL code in the query window left over from the previous procedure. (Remember that this query window is still connected to the *master* database.)
2. Type the following T-SQL statement into the code window:
   CREATE LOGIN WineCloudDbReadonlyLogin WITH PASSWORD='<Password>'

Note Once again, replace *<Password>* with a strong password for the new login.

3. Press F5 (or click the Execute button in the toolbar) to run the script. This code creates a new login named *WineCloudDbReadonlyLogin* in the *master* database.
4. In Object Explorer, expand the Databases node to reveal the list of databases on the server (which should include the *WineCloudDb* database).
5. Right-click the *WineCloudDb* database, and choose New Query, as shown in Figure 5-6. This opens a new query window connected to the *WineCloudDb* database.

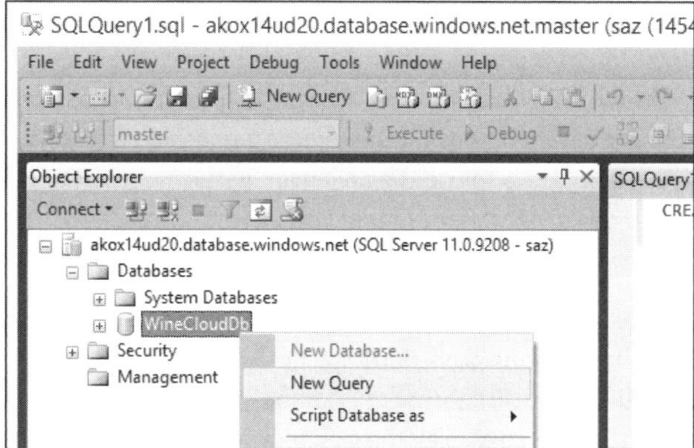

FIGURE 5-6 Opening a new query window for the *WineCloudDb* database

6. Type the following T-SQL statements into the code window connected to *WineCloudDb*:
CREATE USER WineCloudDbReadonlyUser FROM LOGIN WineCloudDbReadonlyLogin
GO
EXEC sp_addrolemember 'db_datareader', 'WineCloudDbReadonlyUser'

You have now created a new login in the *master* database of your SQL Database server. You created a user for that login in the *WineCloudDb* database and granted that user permissions to read data. Granting database-level permissions enables you to grant least-privilege permissions to users and minimize the attack surface of your SQL Database server.

Connecting to a SQL Database server with database-level permissions

The previous procedure walked through creating a SQL Database login named *WineCloudDbReadonlyLogin* and an associated user named *WineCloudDbReadonlyUser* that is granted read-only permission for the *WineCloudDb* database. This login could be used by a custom application connecting to the database, or you might want to grant a developer read-only access to a database in order to diagnose a production issue. In the latter scenario, it is likely that the developer would want to use SSMS. However, when that developer attempts to connect with SSMS using the *WineCloudDbReadonlyLogin* credentials, SSMS will display an error message as shown in Figure 5-7.

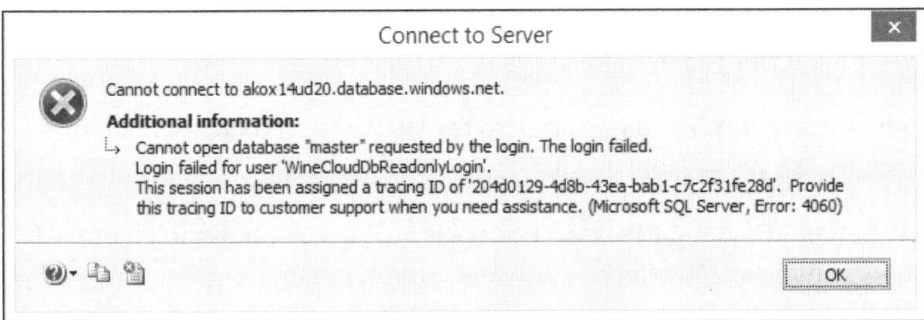

FIGURE 5-7 The SSMS Connect To Server error message when the login doesn't have access to *master*

This error occurs because, by default, SSMS attempts to access the *master* database when it connects, but the login provided has no permissions on the *master* database—it just has read-only permissions on *WineCloudDb*. The resolution is to use the advanced version of the Connect To Server dialog, which allows you to specify a particular database that you want to access other than *master*, which in our case, is *WineCloudDb*. To use the advanced Connect To Server dialog in SSMS, follow these steps:

1. If you've closed SSMS since the previous procedure, start it up again to display the Connect To Server dialog. If SSMS is still open, click Connect | Database Engine in the Object Explorer toolbar menu as shown in Figure 5-8 to display the Connect To Server dialog.

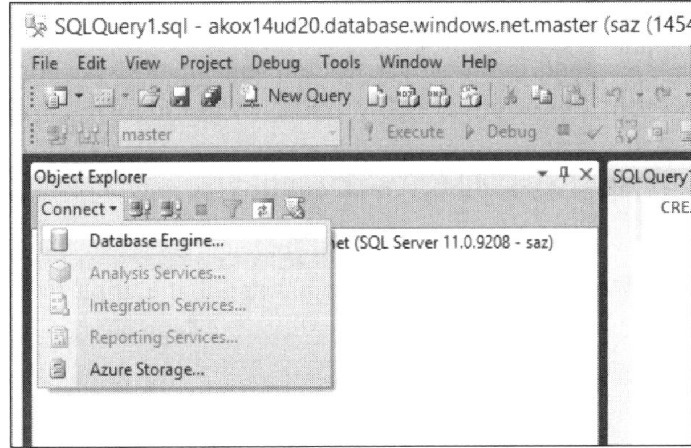

FIGURE 5-8 Connecting to Database Engine in the SSMS Object Explorer

2. For Server name, type the name of your SQL Database server that contains the *WineCloudDb* database. (Remember to add the suffix *.database.windows.net*.)

3. For Authentication, choose SQL Server Authentication.

4. For Login, type **WineCloudDbReadonlyLogin**.

5. For Password, type the password you assigned to *WineCloudDbReadonlyLogin* in the previous procedure.

6. Click the Options button at the bottom right of the dialog. This changes the Connect To Server dialog to its advanced version, which includes a Connect To Database text box with which you can specify a database for the connection other than *master*.

7. In the Connect To Database text box, type **WineCloudDb** as shown in Figure 5-9.

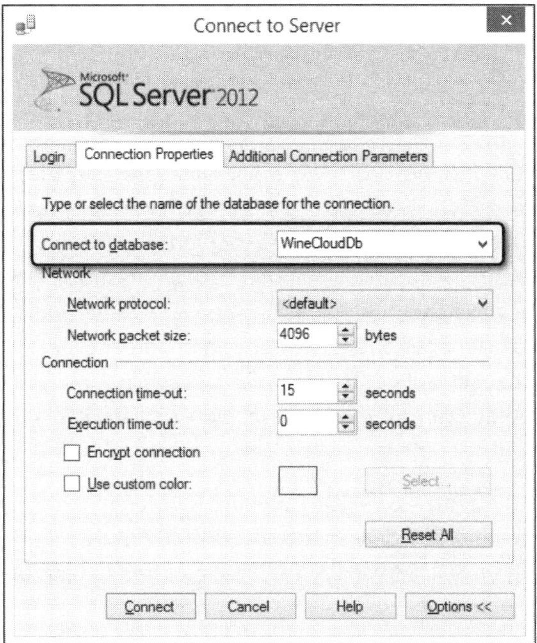

FIGURE 5-9 The advanced Connect To Server dialog lets you specify a particular database for the connection

8. Click the Connect button. Now, instead of displaying the error message shown in Figure 5-8, SSMS connects successfully.

You have now connected to the *WineCloudDb* SQL Database using SSMS with a limited access account that has only *db_datareader* permissions. As explained, this is useful when you need to give a team member read-only access to a production database to diagnose issues or conduct some analysis on the data.

Microsoft Azure SQL Database provides security capabilities that include firewall and server-level roles. You can also secure SQL objects with database-level roles and permissions in just the same way as you can with SQL Server. This enables you to follow the principle of least privilege and grant users only the permissions they need, no more and no less. Doing so reduces the attack surface and helps maintain security. It is a good practice to follow this principle when developing applications that connect to your SQL Database, and when providing other team members credentials for SQL Database to use for development, troubleshooting, and analysis.

Backing up SQL Database

The inconvenient truth is that disasters do occur, and they come in various shapes and sizes. A disaster could result from a malicious attack, a service outage, or something as simple as bad code that deleted or corrupted data. When disaster strikes, you need to be able to recover from it and continue on with your business. Having a good business continuity and disaster recovery plan is the key to successfully working through a catastrophe. One essential component of your disaster recovery plan is backups. Beyond recovering from disasters, backups are commonly used to set up new environments and to troubleshoot issues that might be occurring only in a specific environment.

When developers are initially introduced to Microsoft Azure SQL Database, they often mistakenly think that backups are not needed because SQL Database provides high-availability features by default. The need for backups is similar but different than the need for high availability. High-availability capabilities help ensure that your database is accessible when small-scale infrastructure downtime occurs—for example, when there is excessive load on a server or when a server needs to be rebooted during routine maintenance. High availability does not help when something unexpected deletes or corrupts the database, because those changes will get replicated across all high-availability nodes. So you need a backup-and-restore strategy even with the built-in, high-availability features of SQL Database.

The backup-and-restore process in Microsoft Azure SQL Database is different than what you might be used to in SQL Server, because the traditional T-SQL statements *BACKUP* and *RESTORE* are not supported. Instead of traditional backups in SQL Server, BACPAC files are used to back up and restore with SQL Database.

Copying a database

Transactional consistency is important to maintain when backing up a transactional system like SQL Database or SQL Server. BACPAC files do not provide transactional consistency, because a BACPAC is by copying tables individually, and modifications could occur between the time that the first table and last table are copied. So the first thing you need to do when backing up a SQL Database server is create a copy of the database that isn't being modified using the Database Copy feature.

The Database Copy feature creates a new database from an existing SQL Database that is transactionally consistent when the copy finishes. It does this by replicating any changes that are made to the source database while the database is copying at the end of the process. Database copies can be created either on the same SQL Database server or on a different server within the same region.

Follow these steps to create a copy of the *WineCloudDb* database:

1. In SSMS, connect to your SQL Database server that contains the *WineCloudDb* database using the login you used to create the server. (We've been using *saz* in our examples.) Once connected, the SQL Database server will be listed in the Object Explorer pane on the left.

2. Right-click on the server name, and choose New Query as shown in Figure 5-5. This opens a new query window connected to the *master* database.

3. Type the following T-SQL statement into the code window:
   CREATE DATABASE WineCloudDbCopy AS COPY OF WineCloudDb

4. Press F5 (or click the Execute button in the toolbar) to run the script. This starts the process of copying the *WineCloudDb* database to a new database named *WineCloudDbCopy*.

You have now started copying your *WineCloudDb* database to a new database named *WineCloudDbCopy*. In this procedure, you copied a source database to a destination database on the same SQL Database server, but you could also copy your database to another SQL Database server, as long as the destination database server is within the same Microsoft Azure region as the source database server. You can do this by executing the *CREATE DATABASE* statement in a query window connected to the *master* database on the destination server. Then just prefix the source database name in the *CREATE DATABASE...AS COPY OF* statement with the name of the source server—like so, for example:

```
CREATE DATABASE WineCloudDbCopy AS COPY OF muea4g022x.WineCloudDb
```

Monitoring the progress of a database copy operation

When you execute the *CREATE DATABASE...AS COPY OF* statement to copy a database, it returns with success or failure quickly. However, copying a database is an asynchronous process and the result of the *CREATE DATABASE...AS COPY OF* statement is not actually the result of copying the database—it is just the result of beginning the asynchronous copy operation. You can determine the status of the database copy operation running in the background by querying the *sys.databases* and *sys.dm_database_copies* views.

While the database is copying, the *state_desc* column of the *sys.databases* view will return COPYING. If the copy process fails, the *state_desc* column returns SUSPECT. And if the copy completes successfully, the *state_desc* column returns ONLINE.

The new destination database gets created early in the database copy process. If a failure occurs at any time during the database copy, the database will be left in an incomplete state and you will need to delete the new database using the *DROP DATABASE* statement. You can also cancel the database copy operation while it is running by executing the *DROP DATABASE* statement on the new destination database.

Follow these steps to monitor the copy database progress:

1. In SSMS, connect to your SQL Database server that contains the *WineCloudDbCopy* database you created in the previous procedure, using the login you used to create the server. (We've been using *saz* in our examples.) Once connected, the SQL Database server will be listed in the Object Explorer pane on the left.

2. Right-click on the server name, and choose New Query as shown earlier in Figure 5-5. This opens a new query window connected to the *master* database.

3. Type the following T-SQL statement into the code window:
SELECT name, state_desc
 FROM sys.databases
 WHERE name = 'WineCloudDbCopy'

4. Press F5 (or click the Execute button in the toolbar) to run the script. This returns the state of the new destination database from the *sys.databases* view, as shown in Figure 5-10. Of course, if you allowed enough time for the copy operation to complete since starting it in the previous procedure, the *state_desc* column will report ONLINE, not COPYING.

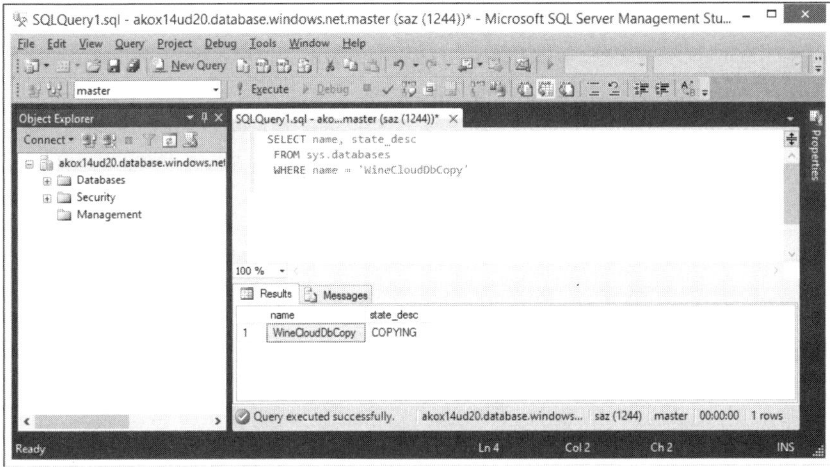

FIGURE 5-10 The results from the *sys.databases* query during a database copy operation

You can obtain additional details about the copy operation (start date, completion percentage, error details, and more) by joining the *sys.databases* view with the *sys.dm_database_copies* view on the *database_id* column as follows:

```
SELECT *
 FROM sys.dm_database_copies AS c INNER JOIN sys.databases AS d ON c.database_id = d.database_id
 WHERE d.name = 'WineCloudDbCopy'
```

Note The *sys.dm_database_copies* view will return a result only while the copy is in progress. Once the copy has completed, this view returns no results.

The database copy operation can also be monitored in the Microsoft Azure management portal, as shown in Figure 5-11.

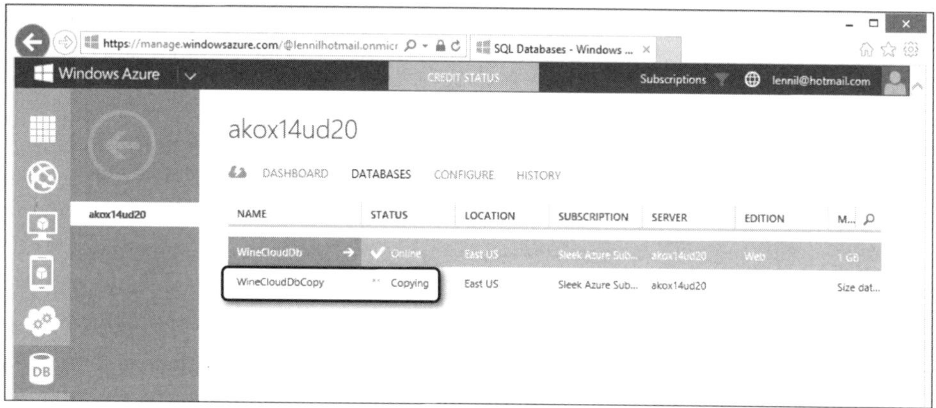

FIGURE 5-11 The Microsoft Azure management portal database list during a database copy operation

Once the operation completes, you have created a transactionally consistent copy of your database, and you are now ready to export it as a BACPAC.

Exporting a BACPAC

As you learned in Chapter 4, "Creating a Microsoft Azure Storage account," SQL Database provides BACPAC import and export capabilities that enable you to easily migrate databases between SQL Database and SQL Server. These import and export capabilities also provide a simple and reliable way to back up and restore databases in SQL Database (provided that you first create a transactionally consistent copy).

The storage service you use in Microsoft Azure to store BACPAC files is Microsoft Azure Blob Storage. Blob Storage is a service designed for storing binary files that are very large in size. The service supports two types of blobs: *block blobs* and *page blobs*, either of which can be used for storing BACPAC files. At the time of this writing, the maximum size of a block blob is 200 gigabytes (GB) and the maximum size of a page blob is one terabyte (TB).

Blob Storage is an ideal service for storing BACPAC files. To use the SQL Database export feature, you need a Microsoft Azure Storage account. If you haven't already set up a Microsoft Azure Storage Account named *mywinestorage*, follow the steps found in Chapter 4 in the section "Creating a Microsoft Azure Storage account."

Follow these steps to export a BACPAC to the *mywinestorage* storage account:

1. Log in to the Microsoft Azure portal at **https://manage.windowsazure.com**. This brings you to the main portal page showing ALL ITEMS.
2. Click SQL DATABASES in the vertical navigation pane on the left.
3. Click on the *WineCloudDbCopy* database (the transactionally consistent copy of the *WineCloudDb* database you just created).
4. Click the EXPORT button at the bottom of the page to display the Export Database.

5. For FILENAME, you can leave the default name assigned by the portal (*WineCloudDbCopy* suffixed with the current date and time), or enter a name of your own choosing for the BACPAC file.

6. For BLOB STORAGE ACCOUNT, choose your blob storage account from the drop-down list (or choose Create A New Storage Account from the drop-down list to create a new storage account on the fly). Once you choose a storage account, the CONTAINER drop-down list appears.

Tip Best practice is to create the storage account in the same Microsoft Azure region as the SQL Database to avoid data-transfer costs between regions. See Chapter 2 for more information on SQL Database pricing and recommendations.

7. For CONTAINER, you can choose an existing container from the drop-down list (such as the dbimport container you created in Chapter 4), or you can create a new one. For this exercise, choose Create A New Container from the drop-down list.

8. For NEW CONTAINER NAME, type **dbbackups**.

9. For SERVER LOGIN NAME, the text box is automatically populated with your server-principal user. (We've been using *saz* in our examples.)

10. For SERVER LOGIN PASSWORD, enter the password for your login. The EXPORT DATABASE dialog should appear similar to Figure 5-12.

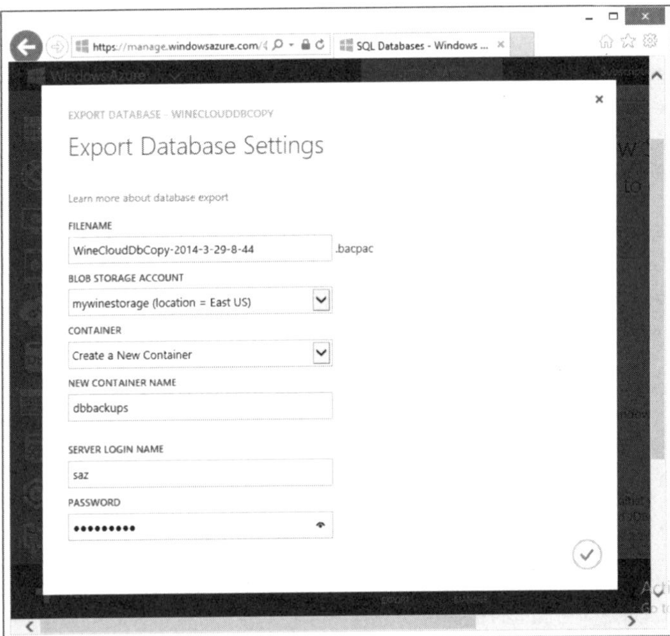

FIGURE 5-12 The Export Database Settings dialog in the Microsoft Azure management portal

11. Click the checkmark icon in the lower-right side of the dialog to begin the export. Once the export has completed, a notification that the export was successful appears at the bottom of the page.

You have now exported your *WineCloudDbCopy* database to a BACPAC file in Blob Storage. The BACPAC file provides a portable backup of your SQL Database that you can archive or restore to another SQL Database on Microsoft Azure, or to a local SQL Server database in your own data center. You can download your exported BACPAC file from the Microsoft Azure management portal or a third-party storage client by browsing to the file in your storage account and container.

Importing a BACPAC

Creating a backup is not very valuable unless you can also restore from it. SQL Database makes restoring a BACPAC file simple using the Import Database feature.

Follow these steps to import your BACPAC:

1. If you've closed the Microsoft Azure Management Portal since the last procedure, log in to the Microsoft Azure management portal at **https://manage.windowsazure.com**. This brings you to the main portal page showing ALL ITEMS.

2. Click SQL DATABASES in the vertical navigation pane on the left.

3. Click the NEW button at the bottom of the page.

4. Click IMPORT, as shown in Figure 5-13. This displays the IMPORT DATABASE dialog.

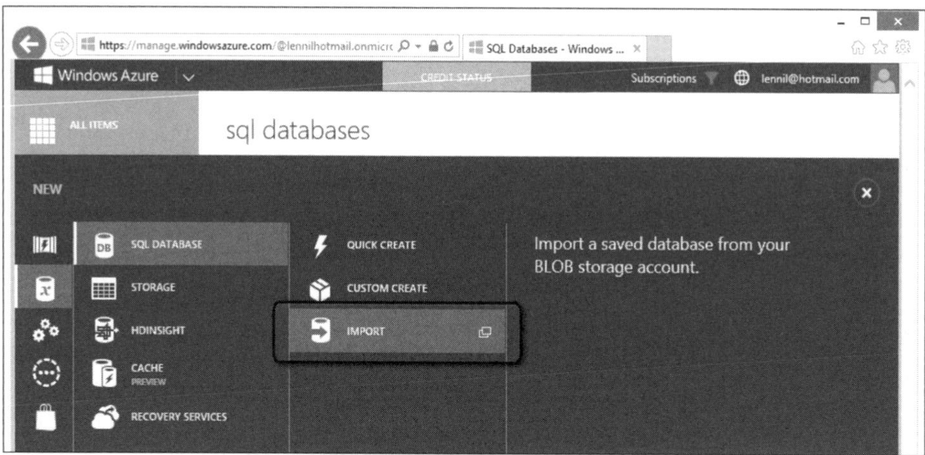

FIGURE 5-13 Restoring a database by using the Import option in the management portal

5. Click the folder icon to the left of the BACPAC URL text box. This opens the BROWSE CLOUD STORAGE dialog.

6. An explorer tree that displays your Microsoft Azure Storage accounts and their containers appears on the left side of the dialog. Expand the *mywinestorage* account you used in the previous Export procedure to display the containers inside of it.

7. Click the *dbbackups* container you used in the previous Export procedure to display its contents on the right. You can see the BACPAC file that got created by the Export operation, as shown in Figure 5-14.

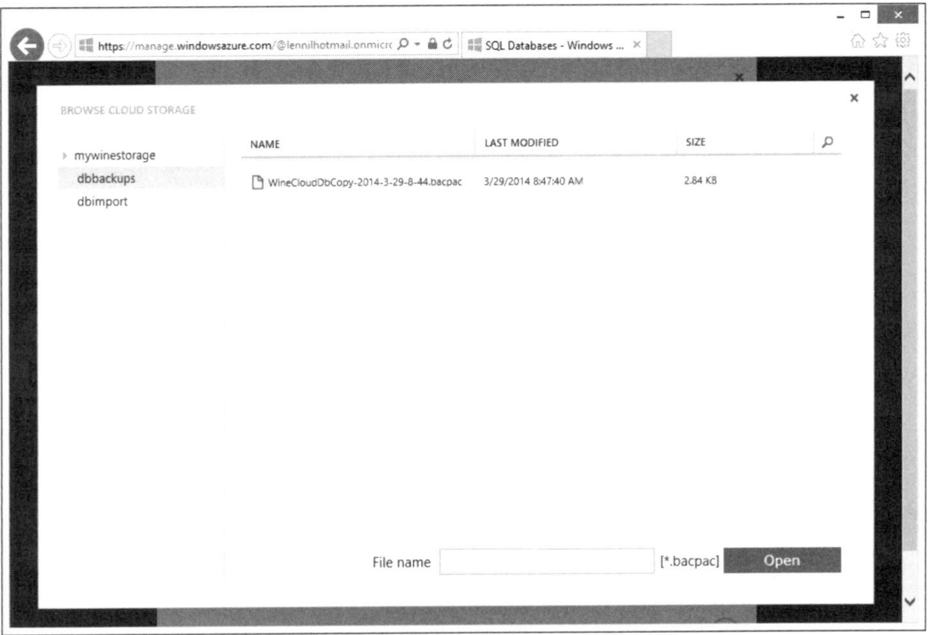

FIGURE 5-14 The contents of the *dbbackups* container displayed in the BROWSE CLOUD STORAGE dialog

8. Click the exported BACPAC file to select it.

9. Click the Open button. This returns you to the IMPORT DATABASE dialog with the URL of the .bacpac file populated in the BACPAC URL text box.

10. For NAME, change the database name to **WineCloudDbRestored**.

11. For SERVER, choose any available server from the drop-down list to host the database. (Always keeping in mind that this should be a server in the same region as the storage account to avoid bandwidth costs.) For this exercise, you can just restore the BACPAC file to the same server you exported the *WineCloudDbCopy* database from, but you can also choose another existing server from the drop-down list. (You can also choose New SQL Database Server from the drop-down list to create a new server on the fly.) Once you choose a server, the SERVER LOGIN NAME and SERVER LOGIN PASSWORD text boxes appear, and the SERVER LOGIN NAME text box is automatically populated with your administrator login name.

12. For SERVER LOGIN PASSWORD, type the password for your login. The IMPORT DATABASE dialog should appear similar to Figure 5-15.

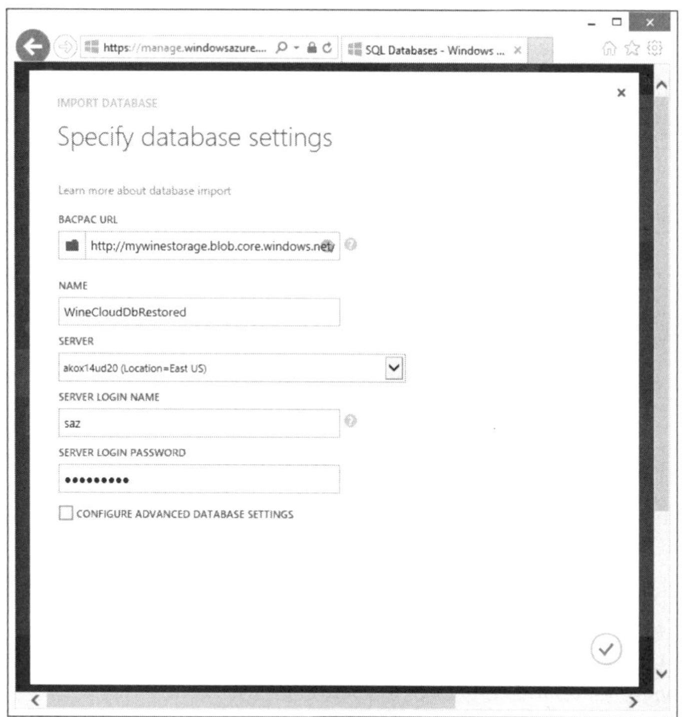

FIGURE 5-15 Importing a BACPAC file from Microsoft Azure Storage into a new SQL Database server.

Note By default, a database imported from a .bacpac file will be a 1-GB, Web edition database. If you need a larger database, select the CONFIGURE ADVANCED DATABASE SETTINGS check box at the bottom of the IMPORT DATABASE dialog. This converts the simple IMPORT DATABASE dialog into a two-page wizard, where the second page provides you with options to set the SQL Database edition and size. For more information, see the section "Configuring database edition and size" in Chapter 2.

13. Click the checkmark icon in the lower-right side of the dialog to begin the import. Once the import has completed, a notification that the import was successful appears at the bottom of the page, and the new *WineCloudDbRestored* database appears in the list of SQL Database instances.

You have now created a database by importing a previously exported BACPAC file. Note that you can also restore your BACPAC to any SQL Database server, including SQL Database servers in other subscriptions, by uploading it to a storage account in the target subscription.

Scheduling BACPAC exports

It is nice to be able to manually export and import BACPAC files. This allows you to easily take a snapshot of a database before making major modifications or capture a database at a point in time to restore into another environment. Manually executing exports is a very efficient and reliable backup strategy. But you will also typically need backups to occur on a regular and consistent schedule. You can do this effectively by scheduling automated backups using the SQL Database Automated Export feature. Automated Export is currently in Preview and is not considered Generally Available (GA), which means it doesn't get the same guarantees and support as features that are GA. It is also free, and that could also change as it leaves Preview and becomes GA.

As we explained, BACPAC files that you create manually do not provide transactional consistency unless you first use the database copy feature to create a transactionally consistent database copy, and then create the BACPAC from the copy. Fortunately, when you schedule a BACPAC export schedule to back up a database automatically, the generated BACPAC *is* transactionally consistent. Thus, automated BACPAC exports provide an effective and reliable backup strategy for SQL Database.

To set up an automated BACPAC export schedule, follow these steps:

1. If you've closed the Microsoft Azure Management Portal since the last procedure, log in to the Microsoft Azure management portal at **https://manage.windowsazure.com**. This brings you to the main portal page showing ALL ITEMS.
2. Click SQL DATABASES in the vertical navigation pane on the left.
3. Click *WineCloudDb* in the NAME column of the database list.
4. Click the CONFIGURE link at the top of the page.
5. For EXPORT STATUS under Automated Export, click the AUTOMATIC button to display the automated export configuration.
6. For STORAGE ACCOUNT, choose *mywinestorage*.
7. For FREQUENCY, configure how often you want the database exported by the entering the export interval in days (with the default being every 7 days) and the start date of the export in UTC time (with the default being today at midnight).
8. For RETENTION, enter the number of days to keep the exports. (The default is 30 days.) Leave the Always Keep At Least One Export File check box selected to guarantee that at least one export will always be retained ever after the retention period expires for all exports.
9. For SERVER LOGIN NAME, type the login you used to create the server. (We've been using *saz* in our examples.)

10. For SERVER LOGIN PASSWORD, type the password for your login, and then wait a brief moment while the password is verified. The CONFIGURE database screen should appear similar to Figure 5-16.

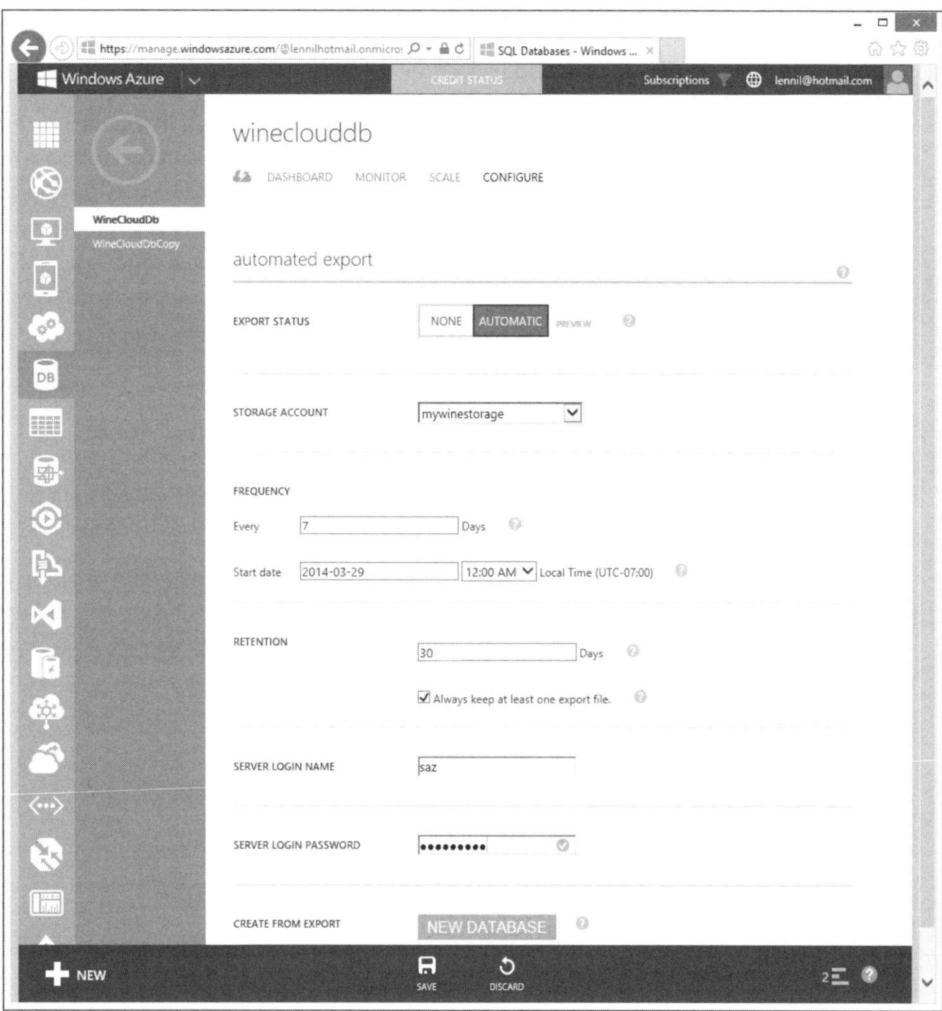

FIGURE 5-16 The automated export configuration of a SQL Database

11. Click the SAVE button at the bottom of the page.

You have now successfully configured an automated backup schedule for the *WineCloudDbCopy* database.

Summary

Security, availability, and disaster recovery are top concerns when you are considering using a public cloud. Microsoft addressed concerns about these issues by providing a secure, reliable, and highly available public cloud platform with Microsoft Azure. It is very important for data services in the public cloud to be secure and have good solutions for disaster recovery.

SQL Database provides good security and disaster-recovery features. In this chapter, you learned how to add security at multiple levels, including IP security policies using SQL Database Firewall and authentication and authorization using SQL Database logins, user, and roles. You also learned about the backup and restore capabilities provided by SQL Database, which helps you simplify disaster-recovery planning by creating transactionally consistent database copies, exporting and importing BACPAC files, and automating transactionally consistent BACPAC export schedules. Using these capabilities of SQL Database, you can create a secure, reliable, and highly available solution using Microsoft Azure and SQL Database.

CHAPTER 6

Cloud reporting

—*Leonard Lobel*

In the database world, getting information into a database is only part of the job. Another major part is extracting meaningful information, strategically analyzing the data you collected, and making valuable sense of it. To that end, an exhaustive suite of Business Intelligence (BI) services and components have evolved and integrated themselves as part of the on-premises Microsoft SQL Server product. Of these, SQL Server Reporting Services (SSRS) is the primary reporting tool. This component of the SQL Server stack provides a rich reporting dialect known as *Report Definition Language (RDL)*, a service to render RDL-based reports, as well as client tools and designers for authoring and deploying RDL files.

In this chapter, you will set up a Microsoft Azure virtual machine (VM) with SSRS and build some simple RDL reports. You will do this using two front-end tools: Report Builder and Microsoft Visual Studio (specifically, the SSDT Business Intelligence add-in for Visual Studio) to author the reports locally, and then deploy them to SSRS on the VM in Microsoft Azure.

What about Microsoft Azure SQL Reporting?

Microsoft formerly offered SQL Reporting as a cloud-based version of SSRS on Azure, but it has recently discontinued the service. At the time of this writing, you cannot create a new Microsoft Azure SQL Reporting server, and existing servers that are still running will be shut down on October 31, 2014.

SQL Reporting was, essentially, a Platform-as-a-Service (PaaS) version of SSRS that ran on Microsoft Azure. It can help to compare Microsoft Azure SQL Reporting with on-premises SSRS in the same way you can compare Microsoft Azure SQL Database with on-premises SQL Server; the former is a PaaS implementation of the latter that is tailored to run on Microsoft Azure and does not support every feature available with the on-premises product.

Unfortunately, there were several problems with SQL Reporting that prompted Microsoft to discontinue the service and to recommend SSRS on a Microsoft Azure VM instead. Arguably, the most significant issue was that SQL Reporting supported only SQL Database as a data source. In contrast, SSRS supports numerous data sources, including multidimensional data stored in a Microsoft SQL Server Analysis Services cube, as well as non-Microsoft data platforms, including Oracle and DB/2. This meant that the only source of the data you can render in reports with SQL Reporting is a relational database hosted on SQL Database. Also, SSRS allows you to embed custom code in your reports and schedule automated report execution and delivery, whereas SQL Reporting did not support either of those features. Finally, there were performance and pricing issues with the SQL Reporting service itself. It ran slower than SSRS, and it could not be shut down when not needed, so charges would accrue steadily even when no reports were being requested and served.

In the end, Microsoft deemed it best to discontinue SQL Reporting and recommend instead the *SSRS-in-a-VM* solution that we cover in this chapter. This means that all on-premises capabilities are available in the cloud as well; for example, you can build reports that run in the cloud that are based on a variety of data sources, not just SQL Database. You can also embed custom code (even code that calls into your own .NET assemblies) into your reports, schedule the execution and delivery of reports, and do everything else that SSRS allows. Because the report server catalog resides on the VM's local disk, performance is similar to the performance you might expect from an on-premises SSRS instance. And when you don't need to serve reports, you can simply shut down the VM to stop compute charges from accruing on your Microsoft Azure subscription.

There are quite a number of procedures in this chapter, and together, they guide you through the process of setting up a VM with SSRS on Microsoft Azure, designing reports locally using authoring tools, and then deploying those reports to the VM.

You will first create a simple report with Report Builder using the *WineCloudDb* database, and deploy the report to the VM. Then you'll move on to creating a report with the SSDT BI tools in Visual Studio. The simple *WineCloudDb* database doesn't have enough schema (tables and columns) and data (rows) to effectively demonstrate more advanced reports, so you'll also download and install *AdventureWorks2012* on SQL Database for the Visual Studio report. The AdventureWorks database (available on Codeplex) has been serving as the standard sample database for SQL Server for many years, and there is a special version of the database designed specifically for Microsoft Azure SQL Database.

Note Many of these procedures are one-time-only installations. Once the VM, tools, and databases are in place, it is actually remarkably fast to put together a report and deploy it. But because the one-time installations can be quite lengthy, you should be prepared to take a lot of coffee breaks while you wait (or perhaps, some wine?).

RDL lies at the heart of SSRS. The RDL format completely describes a report, which essentially consists of three things: how the report *connects* to the database (the data source), how it *queries* for its data (the dataset), and how it actually *looks* (the layout). All that information is contained inside a single RDL file, which is really just a plain XML text file you can view easily in Notepad. While doing so can be very educational and enlightening, Notepad is far from the ideal tool for you to compose RDL. To be productive, there are two primary RDL authoring tools available for both designing and deploying reports:

- Report Builder
- Visual Studio Report Server projects, with the SSDT Business Intelligence add-in

As you progress through this chapter, you will learn how to use both of these tools for creating and deploying simple reports. Of course, there are numerous features and far more complex scenarios that are possible with RDL that fall outside the scope of this chapter. However, you will complete the chapter with a good foundation from which to grow your reporting skills.

Creating a SQL Server Reporting services virtual machine

You will start by creating a VM to host SSRS, although you technically don't actually need an SSRS instance to start building reports. This is because Report Builder and Report Server projects in Visual Studio both provide a preview feature that lets you run and view reports locally as you design them. Once you are satisfied with a report design, you can then deploy it to SSRS in the VM and make the report available to users in the cloud.

In this procedure, you will get a VM up and running quickly by selecting a predefined image from the Microsoft Azure VM gallery. This image already has SQL Server with SSRS installed, which gets you almost all the way there. However, SSRS is not configured in the VM, nor does the VM have the necessary firewall rule to allow access to the SSRS over TCP port 80. Furthermore, a VM endpoint must be configured to match the firewall rule. So in the next few procedures, you will do the following:

1. Create the VM.
2. Configure SSRS in the VM.
3. Create a firewall rule in the VM that allows access to the reporting service.
4. Create a corresponding endpoint for the VM in the Microsoft Azure management portal that allows access to the reporting service.

Note Depending on which SQL Server features you require, you might find it more cost effective to run a licensed copy of SQL Server that you purchase and install separately on the VM. If all you need on the VM is SSRS, you can also consider the free version of Reporting Services that is available with the SQL Server Express With Advanced Services download. The Introduction provides instructions for downloading the SQL Server Express database edition, and you can follow a slightly modified version of those instructions inside a bare-bones Microsoft Azure VM to get SSRS. Just choose the *ENU\x64\SQLEXPRADV_x64_ENU.exe* file (the Express With Advanced Services download that includes SSRS) instead of *ENU\x64\SQLEXPR_x64_ENU.exe* (which includes only the relational database engine) to install a free version of SSRS on the VM.

Creating the virtual machine from the image gallery

To create the VM, follow these steps:

1. Log in to the Microsoft Azure portal. This takes you to the ALL ITEMS page.
2. Click VIRTUAL MACHINES on the left side of the page.
3. Click the NEW button at the bottom of the page.
4. Click QUICK CREATE.
5. In the data entry area on the right, do the following:
    a. For DNS NAME, type a short but meaningful globally unique name to give the VM, We'll use **WineCloudVM** (but you'll need to choose another name if this one is still unavailable).
    b. For IMAGE, choose the latest version of the SQL Server Standard edition running on the latest version of Windows Server from the drop-down list. (At the time of this writing, this is SQL Server 2012 SP1 Standard on Windows Server 2012.)
    c. For USER NAME, type a name for the VM administrator account. We'll use **WineAdmin**.
    d. For NEW PASSWORD and CONFIRM, type and retype a strong password for the VM's administrator account. The password must contain at least eight characters and include a combination of uppercase and lowercase letters, digits, and symbol characters.
    e. For REGION/AFFINITY GROUP, choose the region to host the VM from the drop-down list. To avoid bandwidth charges (as discussed in Chapter 2, "Configuration and pricing"), select the same region in which the SQL Database server with the database you're reporting on is hosted. Your screen should appear similar to Figure 6-1.

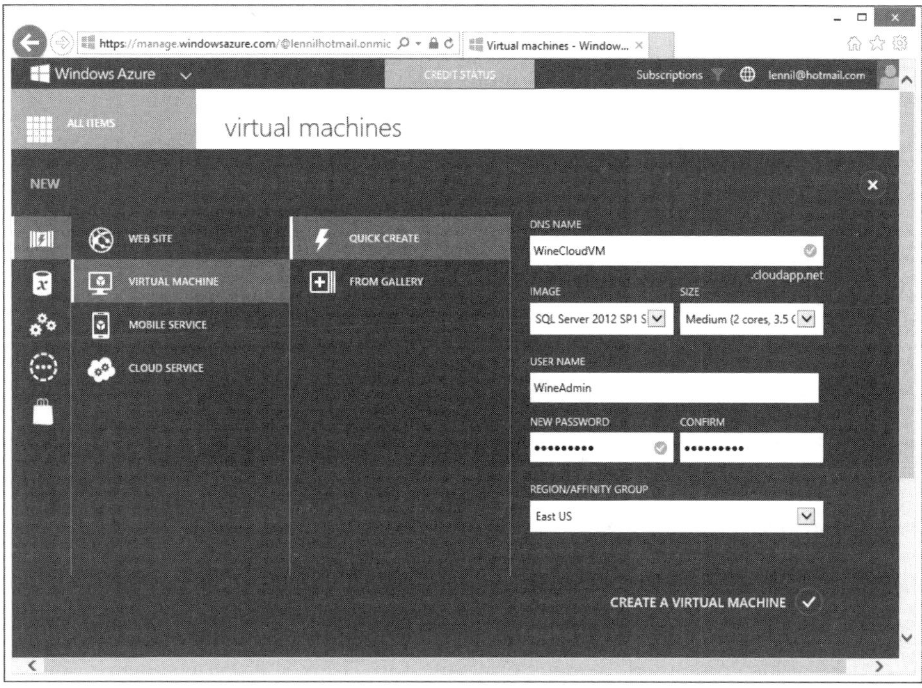

FIGURE 6-1 Creating a new Microsoft Azure VM with SQL Server 2012 SP1 from a predefined gallery image

f. Click CREATE A VIRTUAL MACHINE. It can take a few minutes to create the VM before the portal indicates that it has been started, as shown in Figure 6-2.

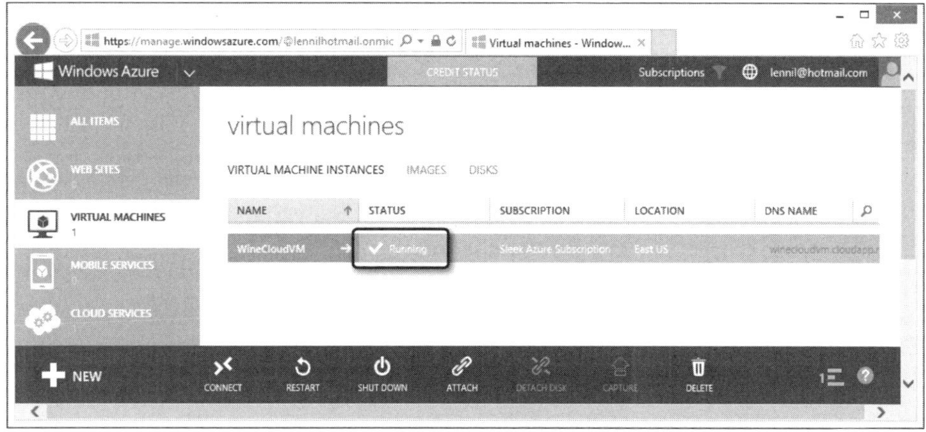

FIGURE 6-2 The Microsoft Azure portal showing that the VM has been started

Important Once the VM starts running, it begins accruing compute charges on your Microsoft Azure subscription. Therefore, you should shut down the VM when you are not working with the procedures in this chapter by clicking the SHUT DOWN button at the bottom of the page.

Configuring SSRS in the virtual machine

The VM you just created from the gallery has SSRS already installed but not yet configured. It's pretty quick and easy to configure SSRS. You just connect to the VM using Remote Desktop and run the SQL Server Reporting Services Configuration Manager to set up the SSRS database and services URL.

Continuing from the previous procedure in the Microsoft Azure management portal, the row for the VM you just created should still be selected. To configure SSRS in the VM, follow these steps:

1. Log in to the VM:

   a. Click the CONNECT button at the bottom of the page. This generates an .rdp file for the remote desktop session and sends it to the browser.

   b. When prompted to open or save the .rdp file, click Open, as shown in Figure 6-3.

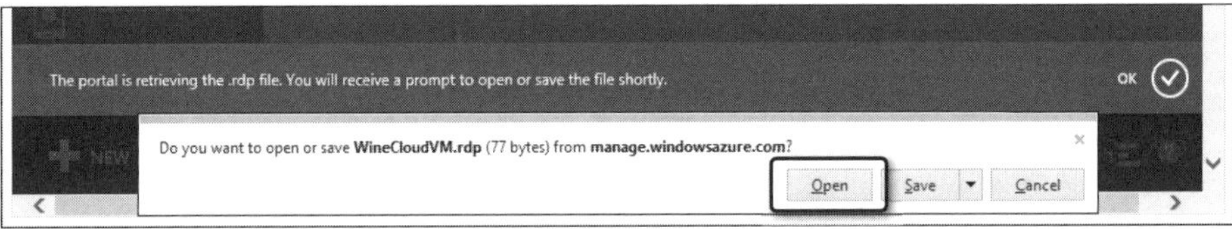

FIGURE 6-3 Downloading the .rdp file to start a Remote Desktop session with the VM

   c. When prompted that the publisher of the remote connection can't be verified, click Connect.

   d. When prompted by the Windows Security dialog, type the user name (**WineAdmin**, for example) and password you assigned to the VM administrator account in the previous procedure. Note that the user name might already be set, and you might only be prompted to supply the password.

   e. Click OK.

   f. When prompted that the identity of the remote computer can't be verified, click Yes. This will start a Remote Desktop session and log you in to the VM.

2. Launch the SQL Server Reporting Services Configuration Manager in the VM.

   a. From the VM's Start screen, you can either scroll through the tiles to find it or just type **reporting services** to run an app search, and then click on the Report Services Configuration Manager tile.

   b. In the Reporting Services Configuration Connection dialog, click Connect. This displays the configuration window for SSRS running in the VM, as shown in Figure 6-4.

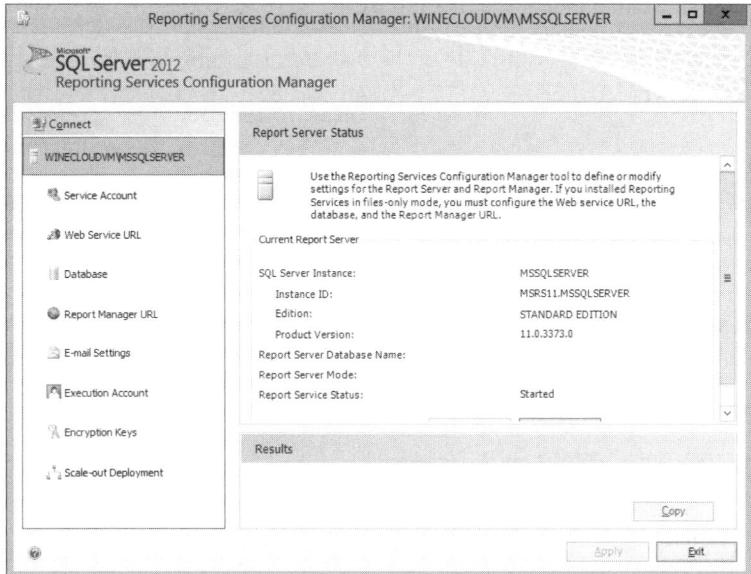

FIGURE 6-4 Running the Reporting Services Configuration Manager inside the VM

3. Create the virtual directory for the reporting service. This will be the web service URL that clients use to deploy and retrieve reports, and perform other SSRS operations. It typically ends with */reportserver*.

   a. Click on Web Service URL in the left panel.

   b. Click Apply in the lower-right side of the dialog. This creates the virtual directory that exposes the reporting service over HTTP through port 80.

4. Create the Reporting Services database. This database will be stored on the local SQL Server instance running on the VM (unlike the SQL Databases that you will be building reports for). This database is used internally by Reporting Services to store metadata about the reports it is hosting.

   a. Click on Database in the left panel.

   b. Click Change Database to open the Report Server Database Configuration Wizard.

c. Click Next all the way through the wizard without changing any default settings, and then wait for the wizard to create the database.

d. Click Finish.

5. Create the virtual directory for Report Manager. This is a friendly front-end website that lets you navigate the report folder hierarchy, render reports, and manage the folder structure, user roles, and permissions. It typically ends with */reports*.

    a. Click on Report Manager URL in the left panel.

    b. Click Apply on the lower-right side of the dialog. This creates the virtual directory that exposes Report Manager over HTTP through port 80.

6. Click Exit.

You've now configured SSRS in the VM. However, until you open the firewall for port 80, all client requests will be blocked by the VM.

Opening firewall access to the report server

The next thing to do is create a firewall rule that opens port 80 in the VM so that the VM can accept SSRS requests from clients over HTTP (TCP).

To open TCP port 80 in the VM, follow these steps:

1. Launch Windows Firewall With Advanced Security in the VM. From the VM's Start screen, you can either scroll through the tiles to find it or just type **firewall** to run an app search, and then click on the Windows Firewall With Advanced Security tile.

2. Click Inbound Rules in the tree view on the left.

3. Click New Rule in the panel on the right.

4. In the New Inbound Rule Wizard, do the following:

    a. On the Rule Type page, choose Port and click Next.

    b. On the Protocols And Ports page, type **80** for Specified Local Ports and click Next.

    c. On the Action page, accept the Allow The Connection default setting and click Next.

    d. On the Profile page, accept all the default settings and click Next.

    e. On the Name page, type **TCP Port 80** and click Finish. The new rule should appear at the top of the list, as shown in Figure 6-5.

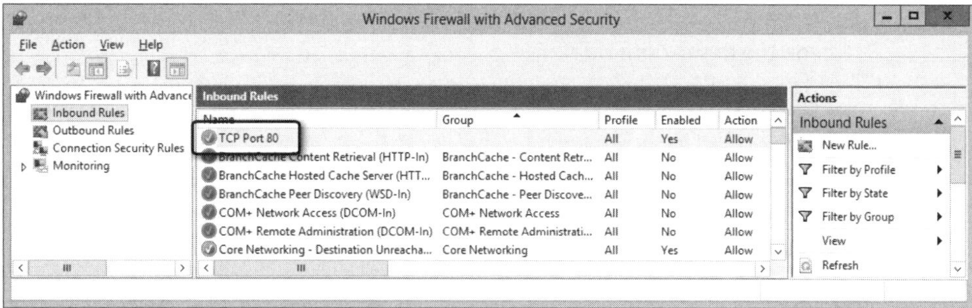

FIGURE 6-5 Creating a firewall rule to open TCP port 80 in the VM and make SSRS accessible to clients

5. Close the Windows Firewall With Advanced Security window.

From this point forward, it is no longer necessary to work with the VM directly over Remote Desktop. SSRS is completely configured in the VM, and it can be accessed by clients directly using the reporting services URL and the Report Manager URL. To log out of the VM now, follow these steps:

1. From the VM's Start screen, click the user account name *WineAdmin* on the upper-right side.
2. Click Sign Out.

This logs you out of the VM, but the VM is still running of course (and it's also billing, as we mentioned previously). There is still one last thing you need to do to make this VM function as an SSRS server in the cloud. You need to create an endpoint for the VM in the Microsoft Azure management portal. Without the endpoint, TCP requests over port 80 will get blocked from ever reaching the VM by Microsoft Azure, and thus the rule you just created in the previous procedure inside the VM would never even have the chance to allow client requests to SSRS.

Back in the Microsoft Azure management portal, the row for the VM should still be selected. To create the endpoint, follow these steps:

1. Click on the name of the VM. This navigates to the Quick Start page for the VM.
2. Click the ENDPOINTS link at the top of the page, as shown in Figure 6-6.

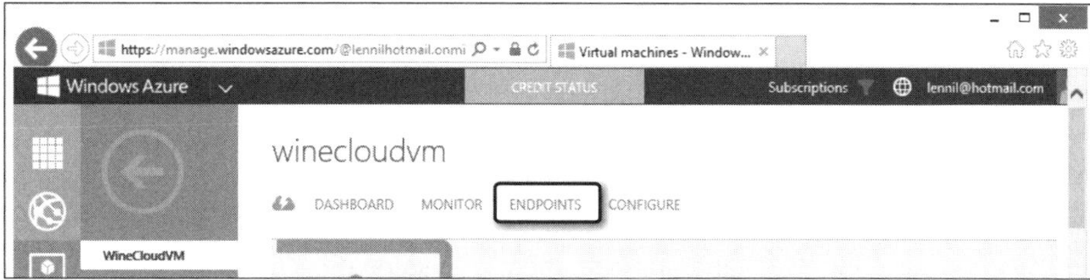

FIGURE 6-6 Clicking the ENDPOINTS link to open TCP port 80 for the VM

3. Click the ADD button at the bottom of the page.

4. Leave the ADD A STAND-ALONE ENDPOINT option selected, and click Next (the right arrow icon on the lower-right side).

5. For NAME, choose HTTP from the drop-down list. This sets the rest of the dialog values for TCP on port 80, as shown in Figure 6-7.

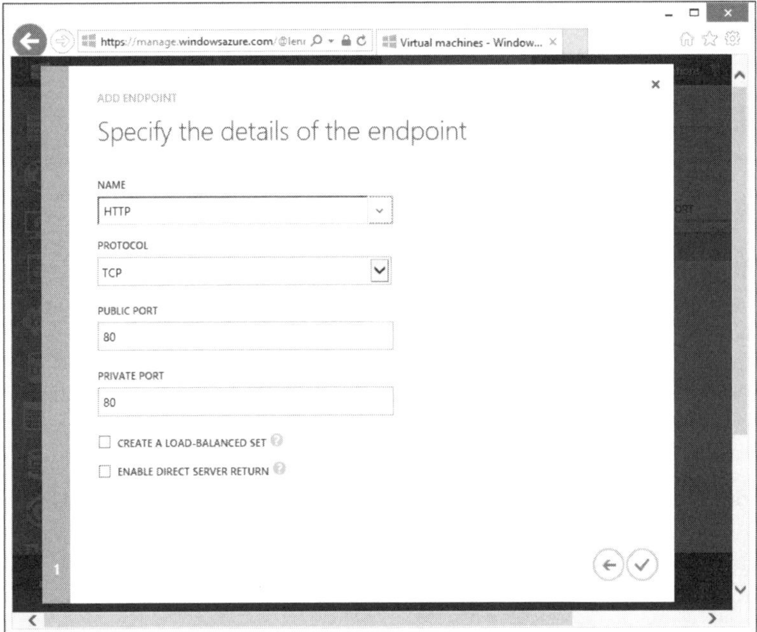

FIGURE 6-7 Creating an HTTP endpoint opens TCP port 80 for the VM

6. Click Finish (the checkmark icon on the lower-right side). It takes a few moments to add the endpoint. Wait until the UPDATE IN PROGRESS message disappears before proceeding.

With SSRS up and running in the VM, you can start thinking about creating your first report. This will be a simple customer list based on a variation of the *WineCloudDb* database you created in Chapter 1, "Getting started with Microsoft Azure SQL Database."

Creating the sample database

For the report in this chapter, you will create a new *WineCloudDb* database very similar to the one used demonstrate in other chapters throughout this book. Listing 6-1 shows the script you will execute to create a few tables and populate them with some data. Once the database is set up, you will create a report that lists each customer's name, that customer's favorite wine, and the total sum of all the customer's orders.

LISTING 6-1 Code to prepare the sample *WineCloudDb* database for reporting

```
CREATE TABLE Wine (
 WineId int PRIMARY KEY,
 Name nvarchar (50),
 Category nvarchar (15),
 Year int,
 Price money)

CREATE TABLE Customer (
 CustomerId int PRIMARY KEY,
 FirstName nvarchar(50),
 LastName nvarchar(15),
 FavoriteWineId int,
 CONSTRAINT FK_Customer_Wine FOREIGN KEY (FavoriteWineId) REFERENCES Wine (WineId))

CREATE TABLE [Order] (
 OrderId int PRIMARY KEY,
 OrderedOn datetime2,
 CustomerId int,
 WineId int,
 Quantity int,
 Price money,
 CONSTRAINT FK_Order_Customer FOREIGN KEY (CustomerId) REFERENCES Customer(CustomerId),
 CONSTRAINT FK_Order_Wine FOREIGN KEY (WineId) REFERENCES Wine(WineId))

INSERT INTO Wine VALUES
 (1, 'Chateau Penin', 'Bordeaux', 2008, 34.90),
 (2, 'McLaren Valley', 'Cabernet', 2005, 48.50),
 (3, 'Mendoza', 'Merlot', 2010, 42.00),
 (4, 'Valle Central', 'Merlot', 2009, 52.00)

INSERT INTO Customer VALUES
 (1, 'Jeff', 'Hay', 4),
 (2, 'Mark', 'Hanson', 3),
 (3, 'Jeff', 'Phillips', 2)

INSERT INTO [Order] VALUES
 (1, '2013-01-01', 1, 1, 5, 34.90),
 (2, '2013-01-03', 2, 3, 1, 42.00),
 (3, '2013-01-05', 1, 2, 3, 48.50),
 (4, '2013-01-06', 2, 4, 2, 52.00),
 (5, '2013-01-06', 3, 3, 2, 42.00),
 (6, '2013-01-08', 1, 1, 1, 34.90)
```

This script creates *Wine*, *Customer*, and *Order* tables and loads some sample data into them. Notice the rows being inserted into the *Order* table at the bottom of the script. The customer ID is the first number after the order date, so you can see that of six orders, three of them were placed by customer 1, two by customer 2, and one by customer 4. The next number is the wine ID, followed by the quantity and price for the order. With this sample data, you will build a report that groups each customer's orders together and calculates the sum of their orders (based on quantity and price).

To create and set up the *WineCloudDb* database, follow these steps:

1. From the Windows Start screen, launch SSMS. You can either scroll through the app tiles to find it (in the Microsoft SQL Server 2012 category) or just type **sql server management studio** to run a search, and then click on the tile. After a brief moment, the Connect To Server dialog appears.
2. In the Connect To Server dialog:
    a. For Server Name, type **<*servername*>.database.windows.net**. This is the fully qualified name to the SQL Database server, where <*servername*> should be replaced by the name assigned to your server.
    b. For Authentication, select SQL Server Authentication from the drop-down list. (SQL Database does not support Windows Authentication.)
    c. For Login and Password, type the user name and password you assigned the server when you created it.
    d. Click the Connect button.
3. In the Object Explorer, expand the Databases node.
4. If the *WineCloudDb* database exists from a previous chapter, delete it now.
    a. Right-click the *WineCloudDb* database, and choose Delete.
    b. In the Delete Object dialog, click OK.
5. Create the database.
    a. In the Object Explorer, right-click the server name and choose New Query to open a new query window connected to the *master* database.
    b. In the query window, type **CREATE DATABASE WineCloudDb**.
    c. Press F5 (or click the Execute button in the toolbar) to create the database.
    d. Close the query window without saving the script.
6. In the Object Explorer, right-click the Databases node and choose Refresh. The *WineCloudDb* database you just created should now appear.
7. Right-click the *WineCloudDb* database, and choose New Query to open a new query window connected to the *WineCloudDb* database.
8. Type the code shown in Listing 6-1 into the query window (or paste it in from the listing file downloaded from the book's companion website).
9. Press F5 (or click the Execute button in the toolbar) to create the database.

You now have a new *WineCloudDb* database that will serve as the data source for your first report.

Note It was necessary to create the database and populate it in two separate query windows because SQL Database does not support the *USE* statement found in SQL Server for switching the connection from the *master* database to the *WineCloudDb* database. See Chapter 3, "Differences between SQL Server and Microsoft Azure SQL Database," for more information.

Now that the VM and database are all set, you're ready to start focusing on the report. You'll use Report Builder to create your first report, and later in the chapter, you'll use Visual Studio to create a more advanced report.

Using Report Builder

Report Builder is a desktop report authoring tool with a Microsoft Office (ribbon) environment. With Report Builder, you can define a report's *data source* (connection information to SQL Database) and *dataset* (data for the report produced by a query). You can then use designers and wizards to lay out the report, customizing fonts and colors, adding tables and matrixes for numeric data, and adding charts and graphs for visual impact.

Once your data source, dataset, and layout are set, Report Builder lets you preview the report so that you can iteratively design and then view your report without deploying it. When you're ready, Report Builder can deploy your report to SSRS, which is essentially just a matter of copying the RDL file from your development environment to the VM where SSRS is running.

Alternatively, you can use Visual Studio to perform the same tasks using similar tools. You will do just that to create another report later in the chapter. Unfortunately, there is (currently) no web-based report designer available on the Microsoft Azure portal to run in the browser, so you need to download either Report Builder or the SSDT BI plug-in for Visual Studio to design reports for SSRS.

Installing Report Builder

To install Report Builder (which is a one-time procedure), follow these steps:

1. Open Internet Explorer, and navigate to **http://www.microsoft.com/en-us/download/details.aspx?id=29072**.
2. Click the large Download button.
3. When prompted to run or save the file, choose Run, as shown in Figure 6-8.

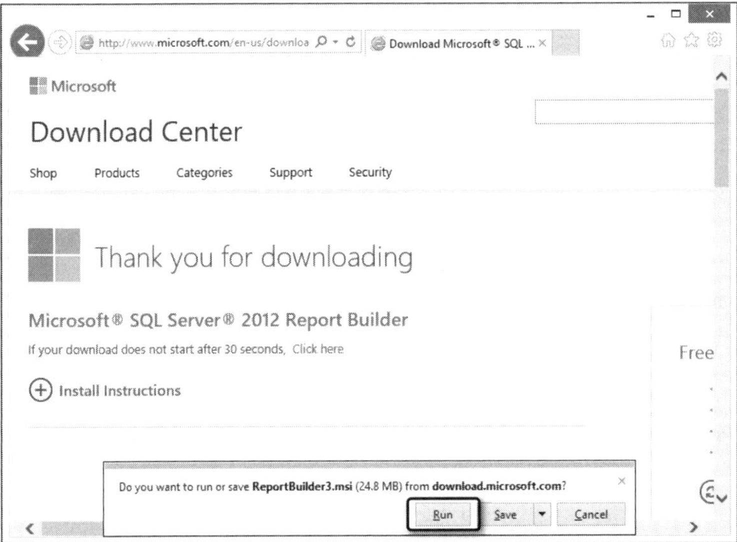

FIGURE 6-8 Downloading Report Builder 3.0

4. When the installation wizard's welcome page appears, click Next, as shown in Figure 6-9.

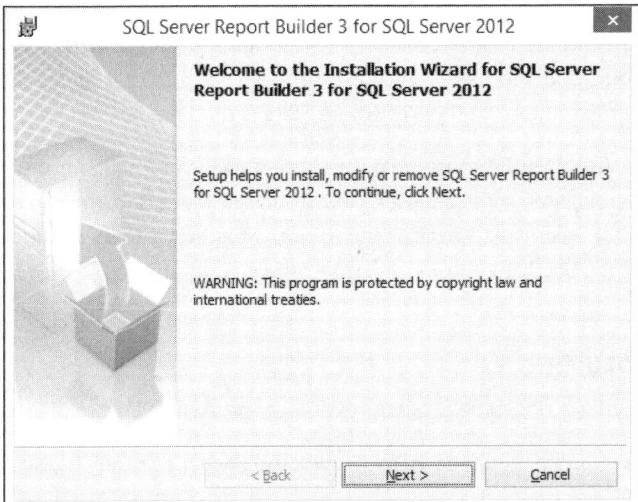

FIGURE 6-9 The Report Builder setup wizard welcome page

5. Choose to accept the license agreement terms, and click Next.
6. On the Feature Selection page, click Next.
7. On the Default Target Server page, leave the default target server URL text box empty and click Next.

8. Click Install.

9. When the User Account Control dialog appears, click Yes to begin the installation.

10. When setup completes, click Finish to close the installation wizard.

Creating a report using Report Builder

When you launch Report Builder, the Getting Started dialog appears. You use this dialog to choose among several wizards, which are designed to help you get started quickly with a variety of report types. For your first report, however, you won't use any of these wizards. Instead, you will start with a clean canvas by choosing to create a blank report.

To launch Report Builder, follow these steps:

1. From the Windows 8 Start screen, launch Report Builder. You can either scroll through the tiles to find it or just type **report builder** to run an app search, and then click on the Report Builder 3.0 tile.

2. On the Getting Started dialog, click Blank Report, as shown in Figure 6-10.

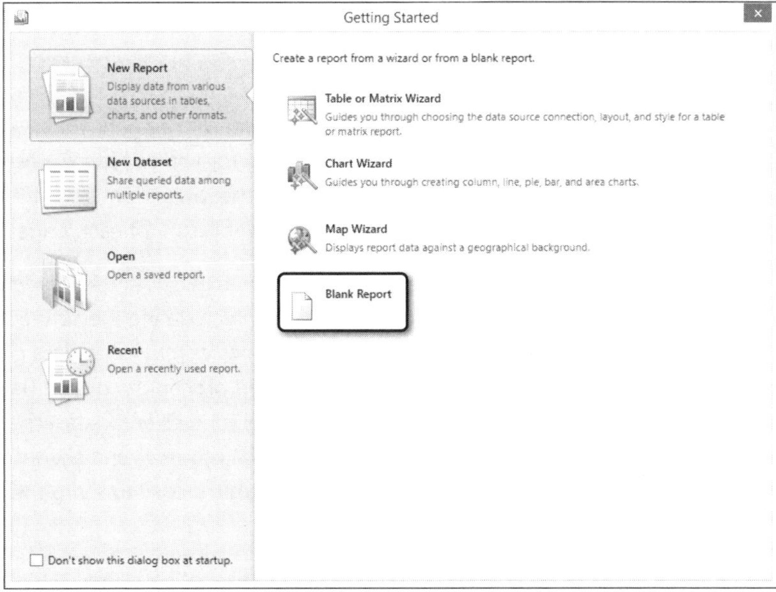

FIGURE 6-10 Choosing to create a blank report from the Getting Started dialog

The Report Builder window should now appear as shown in Figure 6-11.

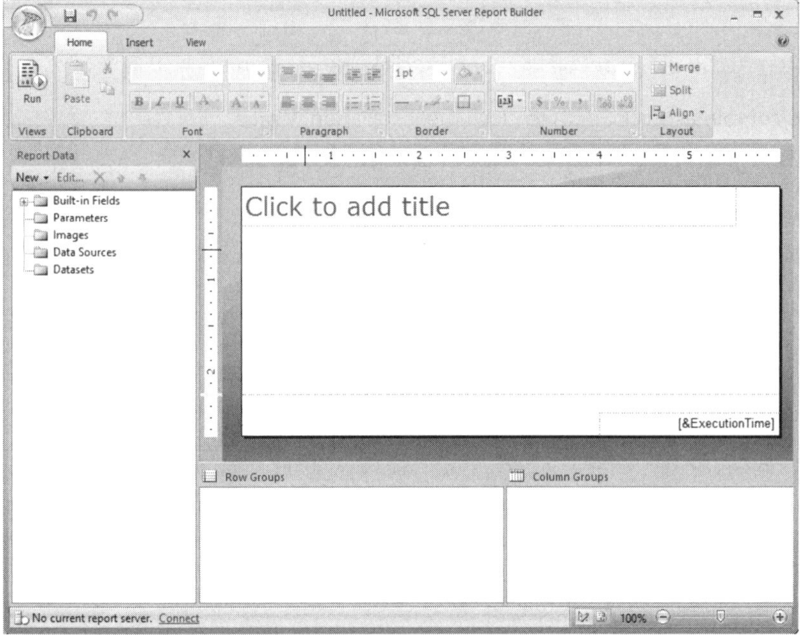

FIGURE 6-11 The Report Builder open and ready to create a new report

Notice the Office-style ribbon user interface—with Home, Insert, and View tabs—and the large round Office button in the upper left corner, which displays a menu with options for saving and deploying reports. The main design surface already has a text box for you to type the report's title, and it also uses the built-in field *&ExecutionTime* in a text box (at the lower right side of the report) to display the date and time at which the report was executed on the bottom of each page.

On the left side of the window, the Report Data pane gives you access to the key elements of your report. The most important of these are your data sources, which define the connection to the SQL Database that the report is querying. Next, your dataset defines exactly what data gets fed to the report. This can be a table or view, the result of calling a stored procedure, or any Transact-SQL (T-SQL) query that gets sent to SQL Database for processing. Data sources and datasets are typically embedded in individual reports, but you can also define *shared* data sources and *shared* datasets and deploy them as reusable objects on the reporting service. This makes it easy to share the same query and provide consistent data across multiple reports.

Once you have at least one data source, and at least one dataset that consumes data from that data source, you are ready to design the layout (and behavior) of the report. To present numerical data, you can use either the table or matrix control. Both of these controls render data in tabular form; the difference lies in the way columns are handled. With both tables and matrixes, there are a variable number of rows in the output. However, tables have fixed columns, while matrixes have variable columns, just like they do on rows.

When you are defining rows and columns, the fields you choose for these axes appear in the Row Groups and Column Groups panes displayed at the bottom of the window. And yes, as implied by those names, both tables and matrixes support grouping both on rows and columns. In fact, the user can even drill down interactively into the levels of the hierarchy defined by your groupings, as you'll see in a report created later in the chapter.

The Report Data pane also lets you define report parameters, which are values that are typically used by the dataset query to filter the report (for example, by date range or by product category). There is also a place to add images to the report, and the pane provides easy access to built-in fields (a set of handy values including things like current date and time, page number, total pages, user ID, and so on) to include in the report.

That's more than enough information for you to get started. So go ahead and create your data source.

Creating a data source for the report

To create the data source for the report, follow these steps:

1. Right-click Data Sources in the Report Data pane on the left side of the Report Builder window, and choose Add Data Source.
2. In the Name text box, replace *DataSource1* with **WineCloudDataSource**.
3. Choose the Use A Connection Embedded In My Report option.
4. Choose Microsoft SQL Azure from the Select Connection Type drop-down list.
5. Click the Build button on the right side of the Connection String text box. This opens the familiar Connection Properties dialog.
6. Supply the connection information to the *WineCloudDb* database you created in the previous section.
    a. For Server Name, type **<*servername*>.database.windows.net** (replacing <*servername*> with the server name that was assigned when you created your server).
    b. Choose the Use SQL Server Authentication option, and type the user name and password you assigned the server when you created it.
    b. Select the Save My Password check box.
    c. In the drop-down list beneath the Select Or Enter A Database Name option, select the *WineCloudDb* database. Or, if the drop-down list appears empty, type **WineCloudDb** directly into it.
    d. Click OK to close the Connection Properties dialog. The Data Source Properties dialog should now appear similar to Figure 6-12.

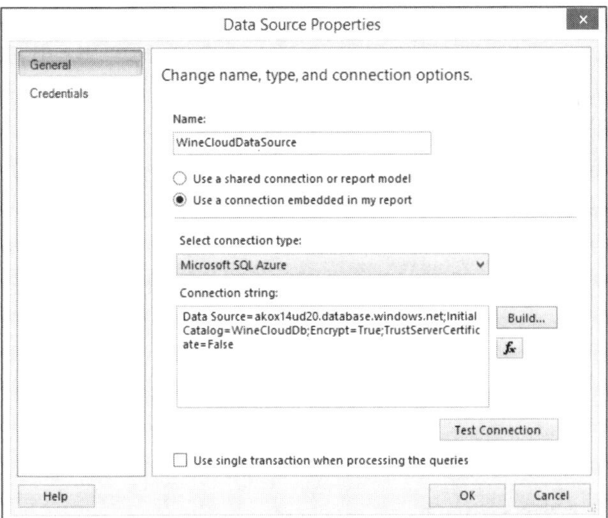

FIGURE 6-12 Creating a data source with the Data Source Properties dialog

7. Click OK to close the Data Source Properties dialog.

In the Report Data pane, *WineCloudDataSource* now appears beneath the Data Sources node. Your next task is to create a dataset.

Creating a dataset for the report

A dataset feeds data to a report. As such, it is generated by some form of database query. This can be as simple as dumping all columns and rows from a single table with *SELECT * FROM Customer*. Or it can be a more complex query that joins on multiple tables, uses expressions to build its output columns, and aggregates data, such as the one shown in Listing 6-2. This query produces a customer list that shows each customer's total order amount. The list also includes each customer's favorite wine, if the customer has one.

LISTING 6-2 Query code for the *CustomerList* report

```
SELECT
  CONCAT(c.LastName, ‘, ‘, c.FirstName) AS [Customer Name],
  CONCAT(w.Name, ‘ (‘, w.Category, ‘)’) AS [Favorite Wine],
  COUNT(*) AS Orders,
  SUM(o.Quantity * o.Price) AS Total
 FROM
  Customer AS c
  LEFT OUTER JOIN Wine AS w ON c.FavoriteWineId = w.WineId
  LEFT OUTER JOIN [Order] AS o ON c.CustomerId = o.CustomerId
 GROUP BY
  c.FirstName, c.LastName, w.Category, w.Name
 ORDER BY
  c.LastName, c.FirstName
```

Notice how the *Customer* and *Wine* tables are joined in the query's *FROM* clause. The *Customer* table is aliased as *c* and the *Wine* table is aliased as *w*, joining on the customer's favorite wine ID. These aliases correspond to the *c* and *w* prefixes used on the names of the first two columns in the *SELECT* list, *[Customer Name]* and *[Favorite Wine]*. The *CONCAT* function combines all the strings passed to it, which formats the customer's name as "last, first" and the customer's favorite wine as "name (category)."

Back in the *FROM* clause, the *Customer* table is also further joined on the *Order* table (aliased as *o*), which returns each customer's orders. This normally results in returning one row per order, which in turn duplicates customer information in each order row belonging to that customer. However, using a *GROUP BY* clause and the *COUNT* and *SUM* functions for the *Total* column, this query *aggregates* (summarizes) the related order rows into a single row with the number of orders and the order total, for each customer. Thus, the query still returns exactly one row per customer. Note that the *SUM* function is dynamically calculating each order's total by multiplying the order quantity and price. This is because our *Order* table doesn't have a total column with this information. (A real database probably would, but our simple *WineCloudDb* database doesn't.) Thus, for each individual order row belonging to a customer, that order's total is calculated as quantity multiplied by price, and then that total is aggregated (summed) across all the order rows for the customer.

In the next procedure, you will create a dataset for the report based on this query. Although you will embed the query from Listing 6-2 directly into the report, you could just as easily create a stored procedure and put the query there. Using a stored procedure offers an alternative to shared datasets for reusing queries across multiple reports, because then even different reports that use their own (nonshared) datasets can still be fed the same data by calling the same stored procedure.

To create the dataset for the report, follow these steps:

1. Right-click Datasets in the Report Data pane on the left side of the Report Builder window, and choose Add Dataset.
2. In the Name text box, replace *DataSet1* with **CustomerListDataset**.
3. Choose the Use A Dataset Embedded In My Report option.
4. Choose WineCloudDataSource from the Data Source drop-down list.
5. Type the code in Listing 6-2 into the Query text box. The Dataset Properties dialog should now appear similar to Figure 6-13.

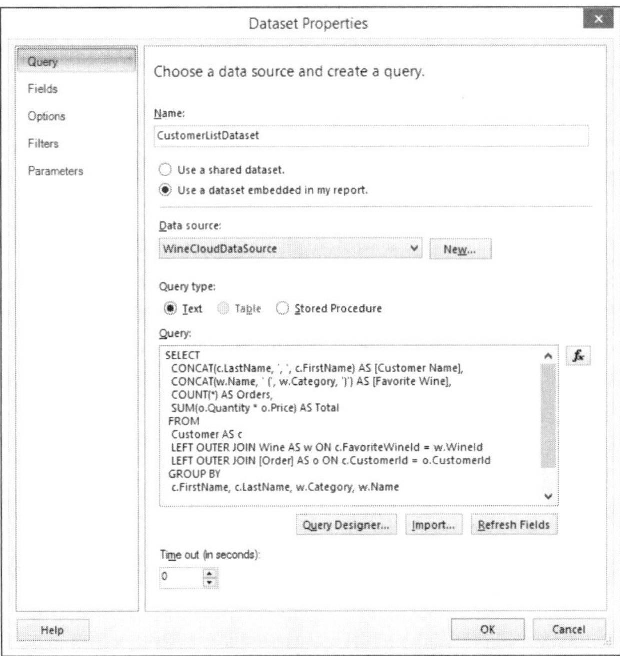

FIGURE 6-13 Creating a dataset with the Data Properties dialog

6. Click OK to close the Dataset Properties dialog.

The Report Builder window should now appear similar to Figure 6-14.

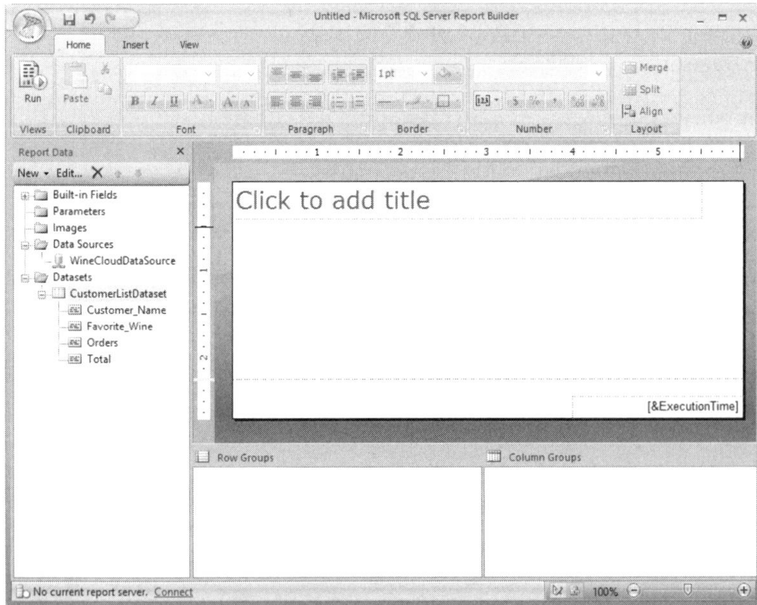

FIGURE 6-14 The Report Builder window with a data source and dataset configured

In the Report Data pane, *CustomerListDataSet* now appears beneath the Datasets node. The fields *Customer_Name*, *Favorite_Wine*, *Orders*, and *Total* also appear nested beneath *CustomerListDataset*. (These fields were created based on Report Builder's discovery of the columns returned by the query.) Now that you have a dataset, you're ready to design the layout of the report.

Designing the report layout

The report designer already has a text box formatted for the report title at the top of the page. In the next procedure, you'll fill in the report title and use the Table Wizard to create a table for the customer list.

To design the layout of the report, follow these steps:

1. Click inside the text box in the upper-left portion of the report's design surface (where it says Click To Add Title), and type **Wine Customers**.
2. Click Insert at the top of the window to display the Insert ribbon.
3. Click Table in the Insert ribbon, and choose Table Wizard, as shown in Figure 6-15. This displays the New Table Or Matrix wizard.

FIGURE 6-15 Invoking the Table Wizard

4. On the Choose A Dataset page, click CustomerListDataset and click Next.
5. In the Available Fields list box, click the first field, Customer_Name.
6. Hold down the SHIFT key and click on the last field, Total. This selects all the available fields.
7. Drag the selected fields from the Available Fields list box, and drop them in the Values list box, as shown in Figure 6-16.

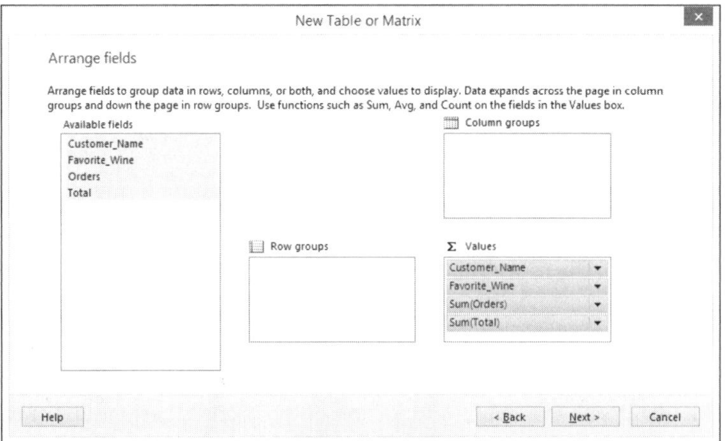

FIGURE 6-16 Selecting all available fields for the report

8. Click Next to advance to the Choose The Layout page.
9. Click Next to advance to the Choose A Style page. The Ocean style is selected by default.
10. Click Finish to complete the wizard, and add the table to the report design surface.
11. Click in any of the table's cells to display the gray selection bars on the left and top sides of the table.
12. Click and drag on the lines between columns in the gray selection bar on the top side of the table to widen the Customer Name column.
13. Repeat the previous step to widen the Favorite Wine column.
14. Click the [Sum(Total)] cell beneath the Total column header.
15. Click the dollar-sign button in the Number panel of the Home ribbon at the top of the window. This will cause the order total value to be formatted as currency in the report (rather than an ordinary decimal number).
16. Click any unused (white) area of the report design surface to hide the gray selection bars from the table. The completed report design should appear as shown in Figure 6-17.

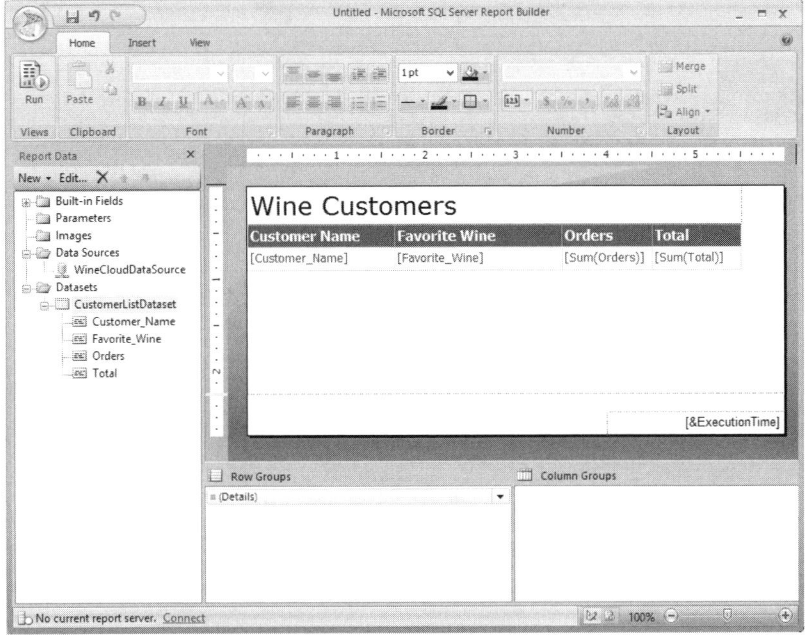

FIGURE 6-17 Viewing the completed report design

Saving and running the report locally

With Report Builder, you can preview the report before deploying it. This speeds report development, because you can iteratively design, save, and preview reports locally, and then deploy them only when desired.

To save and run the report locally, follow these steps:

1. Click the Save icon in the Quick-Access Toolbar at the top of the Report Builder window (above the ribbon), as shown in Figure 6-18. Alternatively, press CTRL+S. This displays the Save As Report dialog which, by default, is set to save the report locally in your Documents folder.

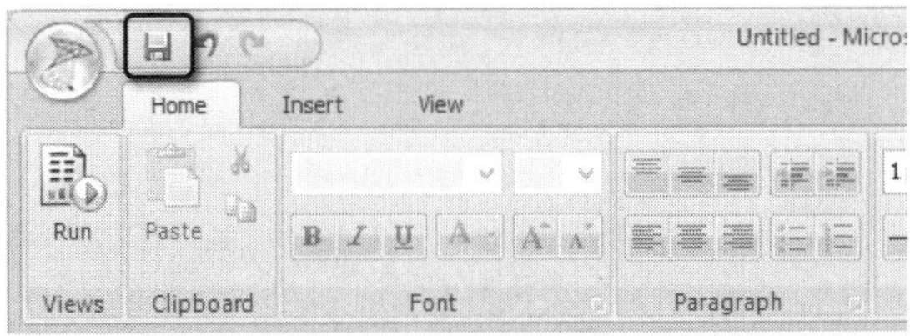

FIGURE 6-18 The Save icon on the Quick-Access Toolbar

2. Type **CustomerListLocal** in the Name text box, as shown in Figure 6-19.

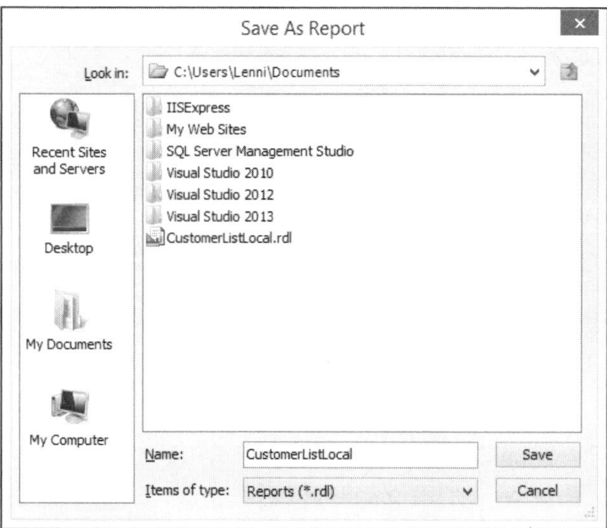

FIGURE 6-19 Saving the report locally

3. Click Save.
4. Click the Run button on the Home ribbon to execute the report, as shown in Figure 6-20.

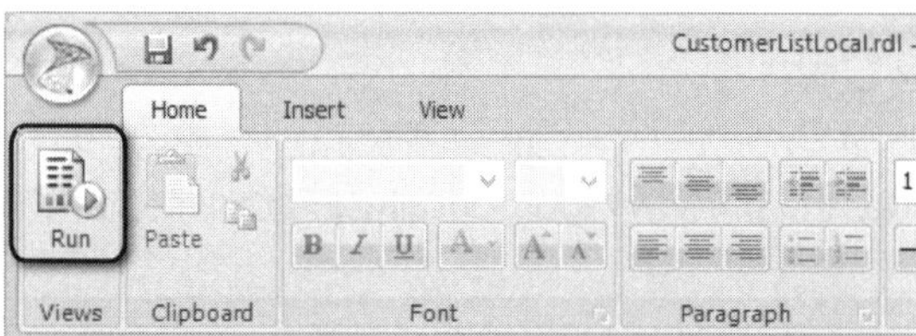

FIGURE 6-20 Clicking the Run button on the Home ribbon

5. The report should appear similar to Figure 6-21. After viewing the report, click the Design button on the Run ribbon to return to the report designer.

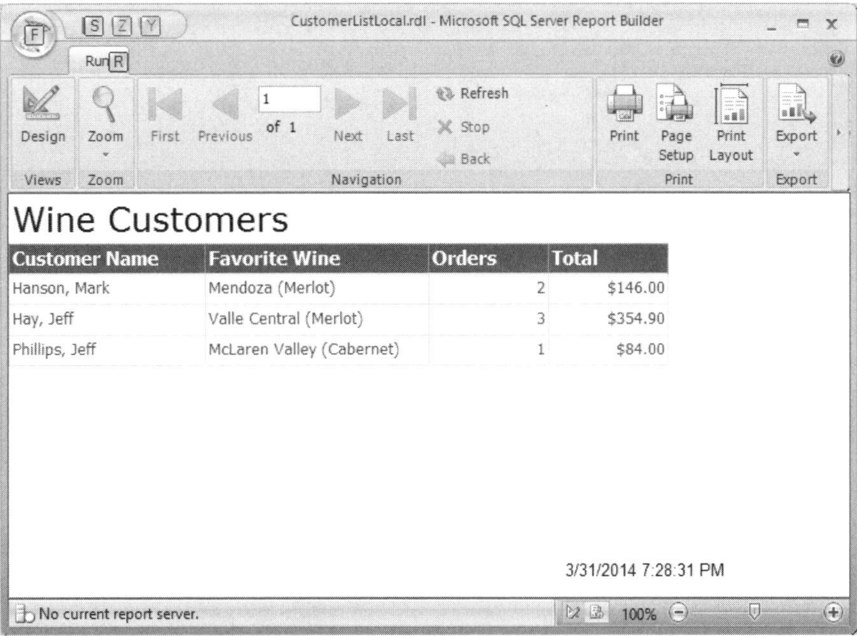

FIGURE 6-21 Running the report locally

The preview shows that the query correctly returned the count and sum of each customer's orders. The query also correctly formatted the customer and wine names. Satisfied with the report, you are now ready to deploy it so that it's available to users in the cloud.

Deploying the report to SSRS on the Microsoft Azure VM

To deploy the report, all you need to know is the URL for SSRS running on the VM. This is always a URL in the form of *http://<vmname>.cloudapp.net/reportserver*, where *<vmname>* is the globally unique name you assigned to the VM when you created it earlier in this chapter. (We've been using *winecloudvm*.)

To deploy the report, follow these steps:

1. In Report Builder, click the round Office button at the top left of the window and click Save As, as shown in Figure 6-22.

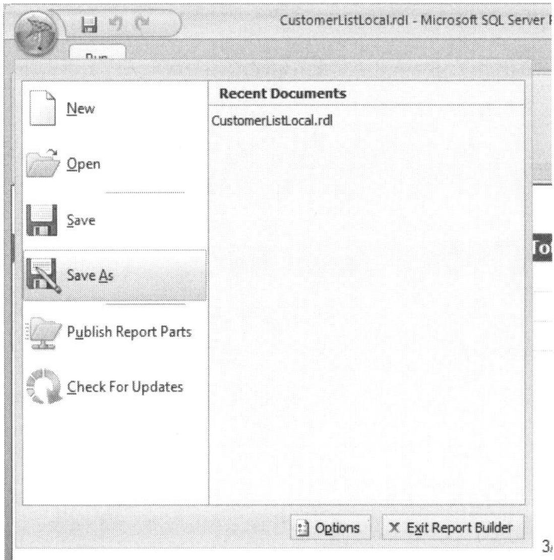

FIGURE 6-22 Clicking the Save As item in the Office menu

2. In the Name text box, type **http://<*vmname*>.cloudapp.net/reportserver** (replacing <*vmname*> with the name you assigned to the VM), and press Enter.
3. In the Connect To Report Server dialog (which can take a few moments to appear), type **WineAdmin** and the password you assigned to the VM's administrator account.
4. Select the Remember My Password check box to prevent Report Builder from prompting you for the credentials when performing future deployments, and then click OK.
5. In the Name text box, type **CustomerList**, as shown in Figure 6-23.

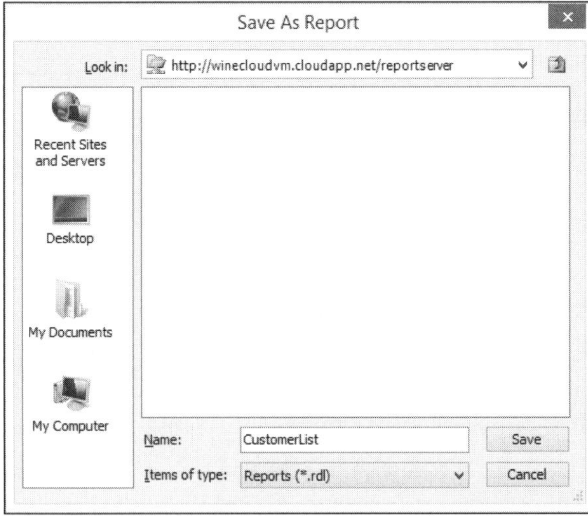

FIGURE 6-23 Saving the report to the Microsoft Azure VM running SSRS

6. Click Save.

The report is now running in the VM on Microsoft Azure, and it can be accessed from any browser. Currently, administrator account *WineAdmin* is the only user, but you can create other users with varying permission levels, as we discuss at the end of the chapter.

Running the report from a browser

There are two ways to run reports from the browser. You can either use the reporting service URL (the one that ends with */reportserver*) or the Report Manager URL (the one that ends with */reports*). Recall that you enabled both of these URLs on the VM when you created it at the beginning of this chapter.

If you navigate your browser to the reporting service URL, you will experience a rather bare-bones interface with simple blue hyperlinks on plain white pages. These hyperlinks let you navigate the folders and subfolders in the hierarchy of reports, and choose any report to render in full fidelity. The Report Manager URL offers a friendlier interface to navigate the report folder hierarchy and render reports. It also provides many other features you can use to manage the hierarchy structure, users, groups, permissions, and roles.

To run the deployed report from your browser using Report Manager, follow these steps:

1. Open a new browser window.
2. Type **http://*<vmname>*.cloudapp.net/reports** (replacing *<vmname>* with the name you assigned to the VM) into the browser's address bar, and press Enter.
3. If prompted for credentials by the Windows Security dialog, type **WineAdmin** and the password you assigned to the VM's administrator account. The Report Manager home page is displayed with links for all the available folders and reports on the server. At this point, there is only one link for the *CustomerList* report in the root folder, as shown in Figure 6-24.

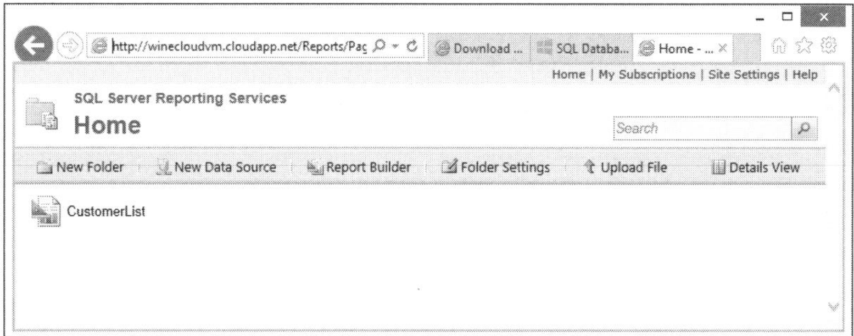

FIGURE 6-24 The Report Manager home page with links to available reports on the VM

4. Click the *CustomerList* report link to run the report, as shown in Figure 6-25.

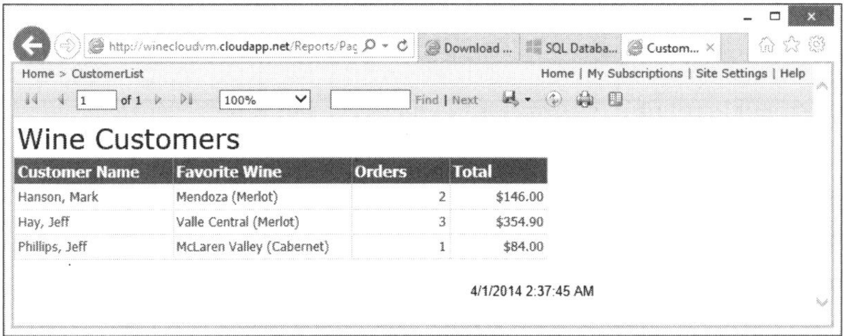

FIGURE 6-25 Running the report in a browser window, served by SSRS in the VM

Before closing the browser, take the time to discover the features exposed by the tool bar at the top of the page. You can page through the report (although this simple report has only one page), increase the magnification, search for text within the report, export the report to various formats, and print the report. These standard capabilities are available for every report rendered by SSRS.

Note Some versions of Internet Explorer require the compatibility view to be set for Microsoft Azure VMs that serve reports using SSRS. Otherwise, the toolbar does not render correctly at the top of the page, and it appears as multiple toolbars with individual items rather than a single toolbar with multiple items, as shown in Figure 6-25. If you experience this behavior, drop down the Tools menu in Internet Explorer and choose Compatibility View Settings. Click Add to set the compatibility view for all *cloudapp.net* websites. Then click Close to close the Compatibility View Settings dialog. Internet Explorer will refresh the page automatically, and the toolbar will render correctly.

Using Visual Studio Report Server projects

While Report Builder is a great standalone tool for ad-hoc reporting, Visual Studio offers a much richer design-time environment with Report Server projects. As with Report Builder, you can use Visual Studio to create Report Server projects with data sources and datasets, leverage wizards and designers for layout, and deploy to SSRS running on a VM. But much more than that, Report Server projects are actual Visual Studio projects, which means that they enjoy many of the same benefits as any Visual Studio project. This includes source control and the ability to participate in a larger multi-project solution alongside other related projects of different types (for example, .NET projects written in Microsoft C# or Visual Basic .NET, or SSDT database projects).

A tool by any other name

For years, Visual Studio has served as the primary authoring tool for SQL Server Reporting Services, although some confusion has arisen by branding changes and release cycles. Until recently, Business Intelligence Developer Studio (BIDS) was the name for this special version of Visual Studio, which also includes similar tooling for Analysis Services and Integration Services. But since 2012, that functionality has been rebranded as SQL Server Data Tools (SSDT).

Unfortunately, the BI project support (whether you call it BIDS or SSDT) has not been very well aligned with the Visual Studio product release cycles. For years after the release of Visual Studio 2010, BIDS ran only under the Visual Studio 2008 shell, requiring developers building .NET applications and reports to toggle between the two Visual Studio versions. Then, in 2012, SSDT replaced BIDS (while introducing new relational database tooling) and finally brought unity to all project types under the single Visual Studio 2010 shell. However, that pleasure was short-lived once Visual Studio 2012 was released, where SSDT lost the BI project support for Reporting Services, Analysis Services, and Integration Services and retained only the new relational database tools and features. And at the time of this writing, Visual Studio 2013 still does not have SSDT BI support. Thus, you need to download and install the SSDT BI support to create Report Server projects in the Visual Studio 2012 shell (a procedure you will see coming up shortly), even if you are running Visual Studio 2013 otherwise.

Essentially, however, it has always been (and continues to be) the Visual Studio shell that provides project templates, designers, and deployment tools for Reporting Services. So despite the sometimes awkward brand names and untimely release cycles, we'll often refer to it simply as *Visual Studio*.

In this section, you will learn how to use Visual Studio to design and deploy Report Server projects to SSRS. But first, you'll do two things in preparation:

- Install the AdventureWorks database for SQL Database.
  - This sample database is much larger than *WineCloudDb*, and it will serve as a better source of reporting data for your next report. Furthermore, it will help you explore many additional reporting capabilities beyond what we cover in this chapter.
- Install the SSDT Business Intelligence project templates for Visual Studio.
  - If you're running Visual Studio 2012, you'll need these project templates to create Report Server projects.
  - If you're running Visual Studio 2013, you'll still need these project templates, which will run in the Visual Studio 2012 shell.
  - If you're running Visual Studio 2010, you already have these project templates.

Installing AdventureWorks2012 for SQL Database

To install AdventureWorks2012 for SQL Database, follow these steps:

1. Open a new browser window.
2. Navigate to **http://msftdbprodsamples.codeplex.com/releases/view/37304**.

Note This URL might have changed by the time this book goes to press. In this case, run an Internet search for "download adventureworks2012 for windows azure sql database" to find the updated link.

3. Beneath RECOMMENDED DOWNLOAD, click the *AdventureWorks2012ForWindowsAzureSQLDatabase* link.
4. When prompted to open or save, click the drop-down portion of the Save button and choose Save As, as shown in Figure 6-26.

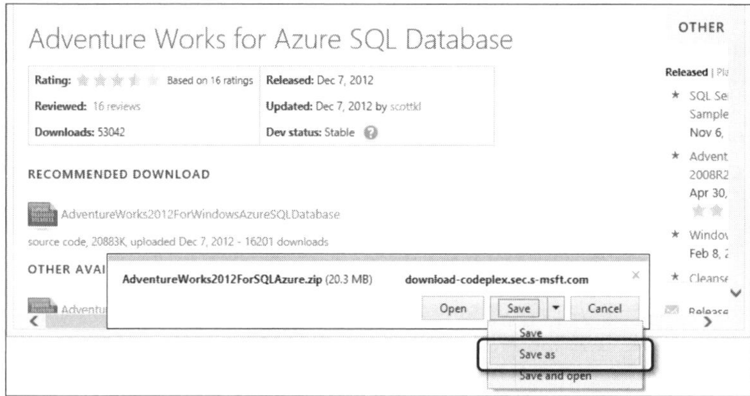

FIGURE 6-26 Saving the *AdventureWorks2012ForSQLAzure.zip* file

5. In the Save As dialog, navigate to any folder of your choice (or accept the default Downloads folder) and click Save.
6. When the download completes, click the Open Folder button. This opens a new Windows Explorer window to the folder where the downloaded *AdventureWorks2012ForSQLAzure.zip* file was saved.
7. Right-click the *AdventureWorks2012ForSQLAzure.zip* file, and choose Extract All.
8. In the Extract Compressed (Zipped) Folders dialog, click Extract to unzip the file and open a new Windows Explorer window to the extracted files.
9. Navigate into the *AdventureWorks* folder by double-clicking on it.

10. Click the File tab on the ribbon, expand the Open Command Prompt item, and then click on Open Command Prompt As Administrator, as shown in Figure 6-27.

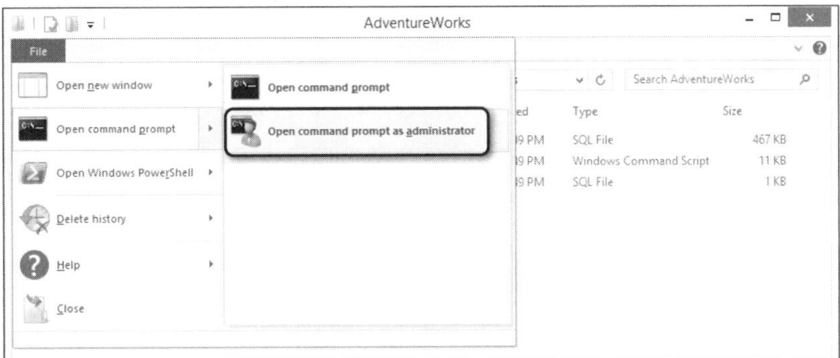

FIGURE 6-27 Opening a command prompt with administrator privileges

11. In the User Account Control dialog, click Yes.

12. In the command-prompt window, type **CreateAdventureWorksForSQLAzure *<servername>*.database.windows.net *<username>*@*<servername>* *<password>***, replacing *<servername>*, *<username>*, and *<password>* with the name of the SQL Database server, administrator account, and administrator password you assigned to the server, as shown in Figure 6-28.

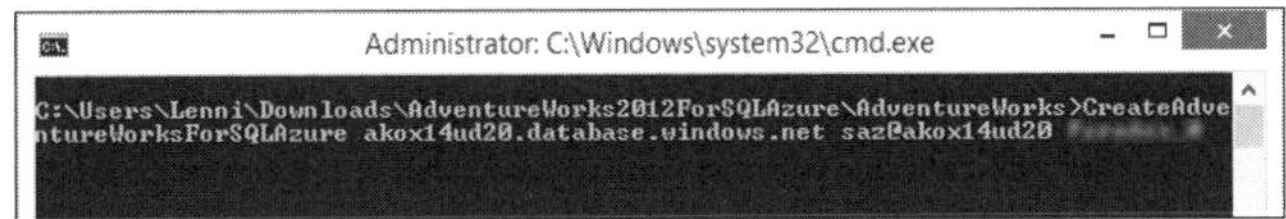

FIGURE 6-28 Deploying the *AdventureWorks2012* database to a Microsoft Azure SQL Database server

Note This step requires the .NET Framework 3.5 (even if .NET Framework 4.5 is installed as part of Visual Studio 2012 or 2013). If it's not already installed, this command will generate errors and a Windows Features dialog will appear prompting you to download .NET Framework 3.5. Click on Download And Install This Feature to install the .NET Framework 3.5. A reboot is required, after which you should open a new Windows Explorer window to the *AdventureWorks* folder and restart this procedure from step 10.

In addition, this step relies on the bcp command-line utility that ships with SQL Server. If you don't have already have SQL Server installed on your local machine, you don't have bcp. However, you don't need to install SQL Server locally just to obtain the bcp utility needed to create the *AdventureWorks2012* SQL Database on Microsoft Azure. The bcp utility can be installed without SQL Server by downloading the Microsoft ODBC Driver 11 for SQL Server from *http://www.microsoft.com/en-us/download/details.aspx?id=36434*, and then downloading the Microsoft Command Line Utilities 11 for SQL Server from *http://www.microsoft.com/en-us/download/details.aspx?id=36433*.

13. After the script completes, log in to the Microsoft Azure portal to verify that the AdventureWorks2012 database is now up and running on your server, as shown in Figure 6-29.

> **Tip** The script creates the database very quickly, but then takes a long time to populate the tables with data. It's not necessary to wait for the script to complete before proceeding to install SSDT Business Intelligence for Visual Studio 2012, which is the next step. Because that installation is also somewhat lengthy, you can save a lot of time by not waiting for the *AdventureWorks2012* database to fully populate before starting the next install, and then waiting for both processes to complete before creating your first Report Server project.

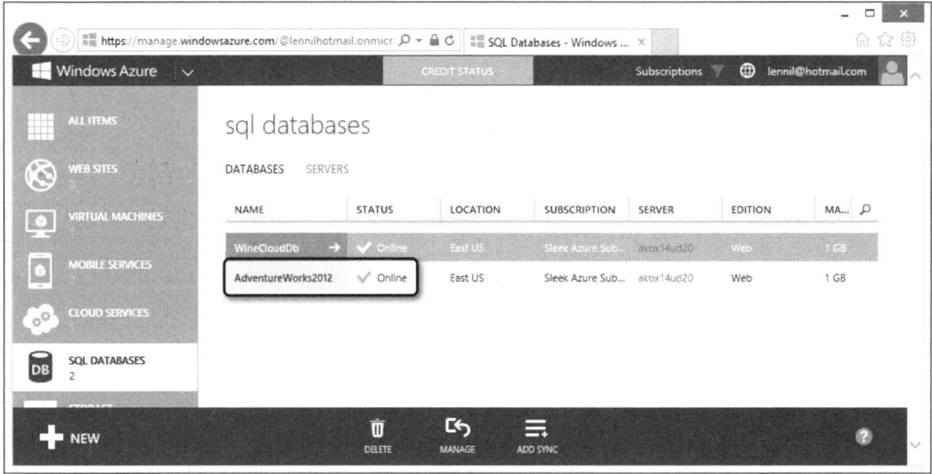

FIGURE 6-29 Viewing the deployed *AdventureWorks2012* database in the Microsoft Azure management portal

Next, you'll install the SSDT BI tools for Visual Studio so that you can start creating Report Server projects.

Installing SSDT Business Intelligence for Visual Studio 2012

Both Visual Studio 2010 and 2012 can be used for building Report Server projects. As we explained, if you are using Visual Studio 2010 and installed SSDT with it, you already have the BI project template support for SSRS available to you, and you can skip the next procedure. Otherwise, whether you are running Visual Studio 2012 or 2013, you need to install the SSDT Business Intelligence tools for Visual Studio 2012 (even if you have "regular" SSDT already installed).

> **Note** During installation, you might be prompted to restart your computer. In this case, click OK, and the installation procedure will resume automatically after your computer restarts.

To install the SSDT Business Intelligence tools for Visual Studio 2012, follow these steps:

1. Open a new browser window.
2. Navigate to **http://www.microsoft.com/en-us/download/details.aspx?id=36843**. This takes you to the Download Center page for Microsoft SQL Server Data Tools - Business Intelligence For Visual Studio 2012, as shown in Figure 6-30.

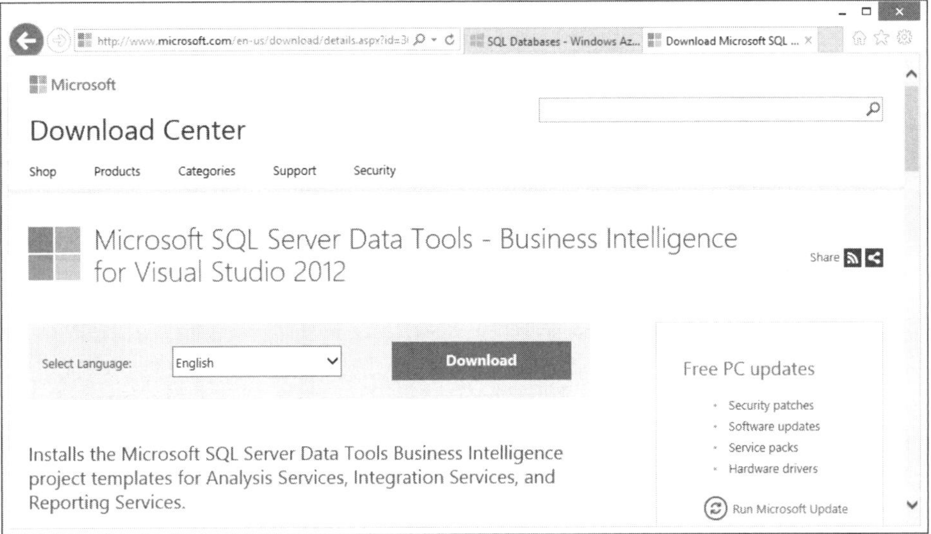

FIGURE 6-30 The Download Center page for Microsoft SQL Server Data Tools - Business Intelligence For Visual Studio 2012

Note This URL might have changed by the time this book goes to press. In this case, run an Internet search for "download business intelligence for visual studio" to find the updated link.

3. Click the Download link. You will be given the choice to Run or Save.
4. Click Run to start the download.
5. When the User Account Control dialog appears, click Yes to start the SQL Server 2012 Setup Wizard.
6. On the License Terms page, select the I Accept The License Terms check box and then click Next.
7. On the Product Updates page, click Next to begin the installation process.

8. If you already have an instance of SQL Server 2012 installed on your machine, the setup wizard will now display an Installation Type page that lets you choose between performing a new installation of SQL Server 2012 and adding features to an existing instance.

    a. Be sure to choose the option for performing a new installation (which is selected by default), *even though SQL Server is already installed*. Otherwise, the setup will fail with an "architecture mismatch" error.

    b. Click Next.

9. On the Feature Selection page, click Select All and then click Next.

10. On the Error Reporting page, click Next. When the installation completes, the Complete page is displayed indicating success, as shown in Figure 6-31. If prompted to restart the computer, click OK.

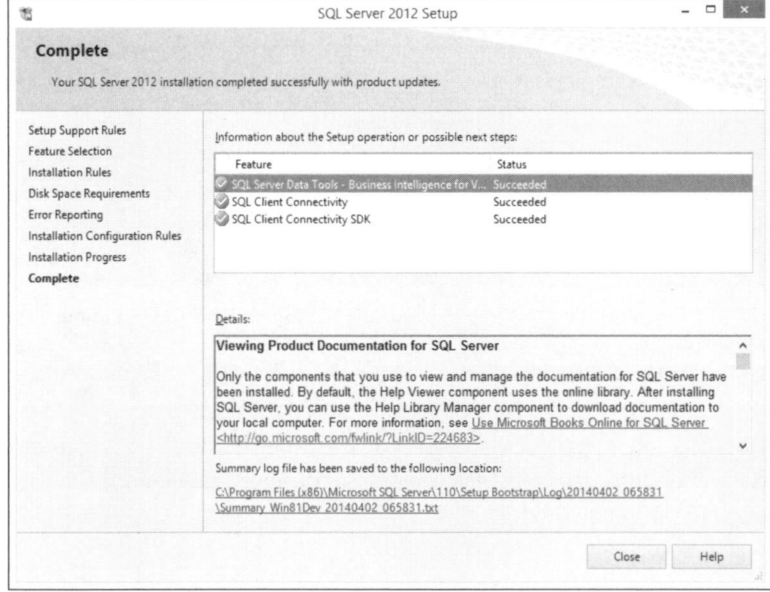

FIGURE 6-31 A successful installation of the Microsoft SQL Server Data Tools - Business Intelligence For Visual Studio 2012

11. Click Close.

Creating a report using Visual Studio

The AdventureWorks database has a lot of data in many tables, and those tables are broken down into schemas, such as *Sales*, *Person*, and *HumanResources*. These schemas are nothing more than logical category groupings—rather than storing all the tables in one flat space (the default *dbo* schema), sales-oriented information is stored in the *Sales* schema, person information in the *Person* schema, and so on.

In this report, you will query the *SalesOrderHeader* and *SalesTerritory* tables in the *Sales* schema. This returns order data, along with related territory information (a hierarchy of country and territory), although our report will summarize the order data to the territory level. (If you can't resist, you can sneak a peek at the final report in Figure 6-46.) The query for the report is shown in Listing 6-3.

LISTING 6-3 The query for this report returns detailed sales information with related territory information

```
SELECT
  soh.SalesOrderID,
  DATEPART(YEAR, soh.OrderDate) AS [Year],
  soh.CustomerID,
  soh.TerritoryID,
  terr.Name as TerritoryName,
  terr.CountryRegionCode as Country,
  soh.TotalDue as TotalSales
 FROM
  Sales.SalesOrderHeader AS soh
  INNER JOIN Sales.SalesTerritory AS terr ON terr.TerritoryID = soh.TerritoryID
 ORDER BY
  [Year]
```

This example differs quite significantly from our previous report of wine customers. Recall from Listing 6-2, that report's query used a *GROUP BY* clause with *COUNT* and *SUM* aggregate functions to summarize order information for each customer, so that the SQL Database query engine performed the aggregation. SSRS merely dumped that information into a table; the number of rows returned by the query is always the same as the number of rows in the report.

In this query, you'll notice that there is no aggregation, meaning that the query engine is returning order-level information that merely *includes* territory information (duplicated across orders in the same territory), and it's the reporting engine that will aggregate those totals to the territory level. That is, the query itself returns 31,465 rows of order data, and the report you will create summarizes that set down to 10 rows, one per territory. This means you can summarize at the database level wherever it makes sense (or is convenient), and then summarize further if needed at the report level. Also, by joining on the territory table and bringing in the country-territory hierarchy, you can deliver automatic drill-down capabilities to your users (in this case, expanding and collapsing the territories within each country). These are some great examples of the flexibility you get with RDL and SSRS.

In another difference from the previous example, this report will use a matrix rather than a table. Notice that the query uses the *DATEPART* function with *YEAR* to extract the year of each order into its own column. You will use this column to create a matrix so that in addition to rendering a variable number of rows (one per territory), the report will render a variable number of columns (one per year) as well.

Using the Report Wizard

The quickest way to create a Report Server project is using the Report Server Project Wizard, and that's what you'll do next. Of course, there's nothing you can do with the wizard that can't also be done as an independent manual step. As you'll see, the wizard walks you through the similar steps of creating a data source, dataset, and defining a report layout, as you did earlier using Report Builder.

To create a Report Server project in Visual Studio, follow these steps.

1. Launch SQL Server Data Tools For Visual Studio 2012. From the VM's Start screen, you can either scroll through the tiles to find it or just type **sql server data tools** to run an app search, and then click on the SQL Server Data Tools For Visual Studio 2012 tile.
2. If this is the first time you have started SQL Server Data Tools for Visual Studio 2012, you will be prompted for default environment settings. In this case, choose Business Intelligence Settings and click the Start Visual Studio button.
3. Click the FILE menu, and then choose New | Project to display the New Project dialog.
4. On the left side of the New Project dialog, expand Templates, Business Intelligence, Reporting Services, and choose Report Server Project Wizard.
5. Name the solution and project **AWReporting**, and choose any desired location, as shown in Figure 6-32.

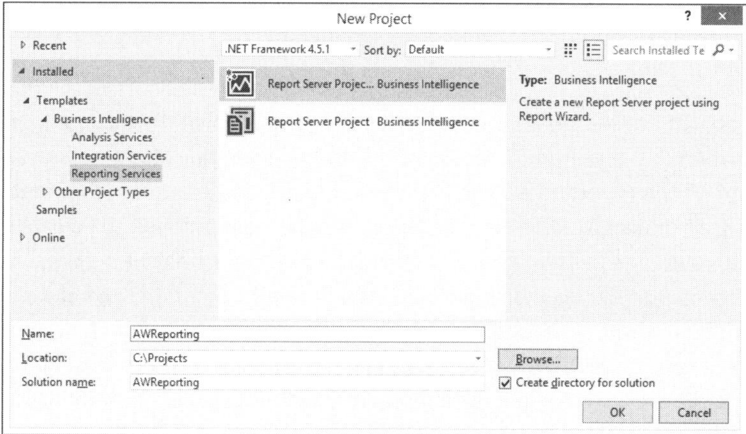

FIGURE 6-32 Creating a new Report Server project using the Report Server Project Wizard

6. Click OK to start the Report Wizard.
7. On the welcome page, click Next.
8. On the Select The Data Source page, do the following:
    a. Name the data source **AWDataSource**.
    b. Choose Microsoft SQL Azure from the Type drop-down list.

c. To the right of the connection string text box, click Edit to open the familiar Connection Properties dialog.

d. For Server Name, type **<*servername*>.database.windows.net** (replacing <*servername*> with the name that was assigned when you created your server).

e. Choose the Use SQL Server Authentication option, and type the user name and password you assigned the server when you created it.

f. Select the Save My Password check box.

g. In the drop-down list beneath the Select Or Enter A Database Name option, select the *AdventureWorks2012* database.

h. Click OK to close the Connection Properties dialog. Your screen should appear similar to Figure 6-33.

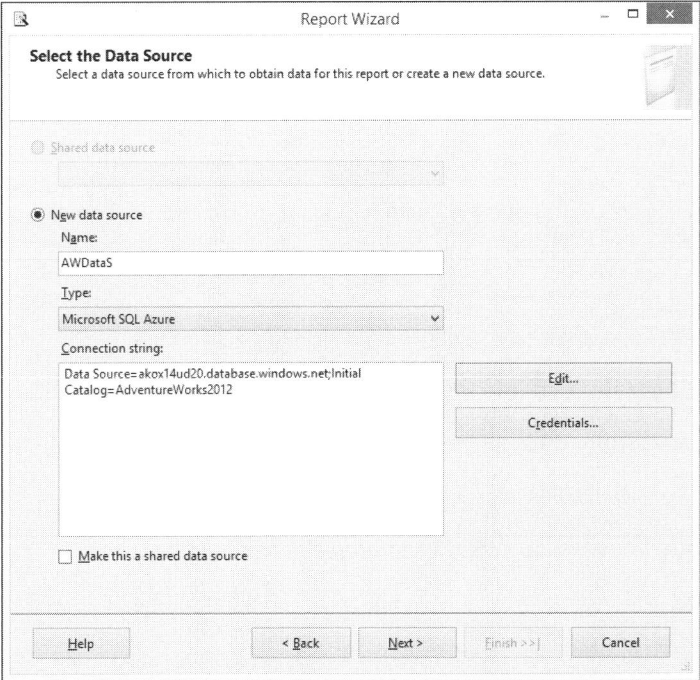

FIGURE 6-33 Defining the report's data source as *AdventureWorks2012* on Microsoft Azure SQL Database

i. Click Next.

9. On the Design The Query page, type the code shown in Listing 6-3 into the Query String text box (or paste it in from the listing file downloaded from the book's companion web site). Your screen should appear similar to Figure 6-34.

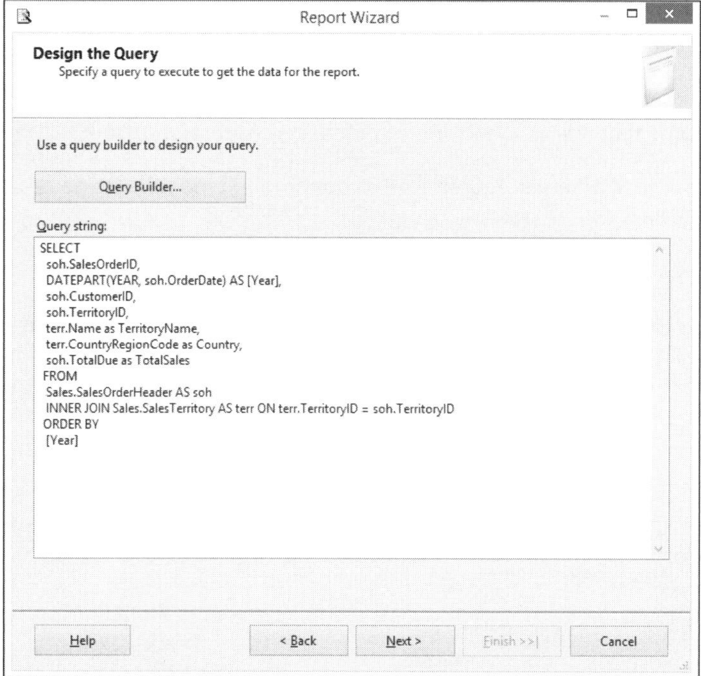

FIGURE 6-34 Defining the report's query to return sales details with territory information

10. Click Next.
11. On the Select The Report Type page, choose Matrix and click Next.
12. On the Design The Matrix page, do the following:
    a. Drag *TotalSales* from Available Fields, and drop it in the Details list.
    b. Drag *Year* from Available Fields, and drop it in the Columns list.
    c. Drag *Country* from Available Fields, and drop it in the Rows list.
    d. Drag *TerritoryName* from Available Fields, and drop it in the Rows list beneath *Country*.
    e. Select the Enable Drilldown check box. The Report Wizard should appear as shown in Figure 6-35.

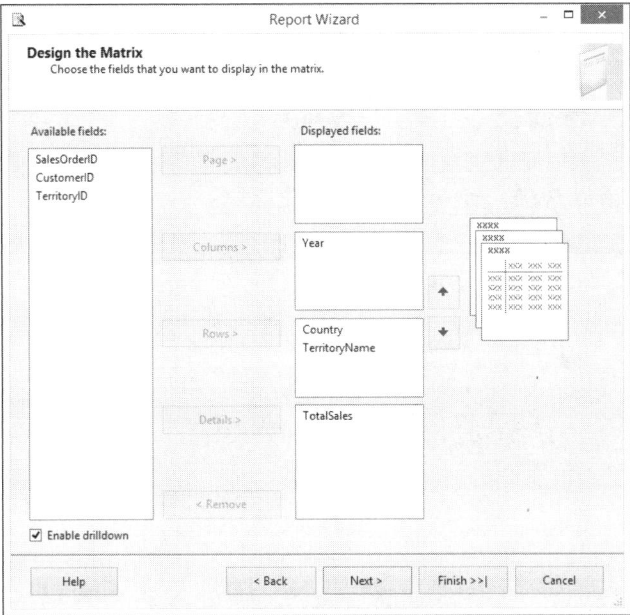

FIGURE 6-35 Designing the report's matrix layout

  f. Click Next.

13. On the Choose The Matrix Style page, click Next.

14. In the Report Server text box on the Choose The Deployment Location page, type **http://<*vmname*>.cloudapp.net/reportserver** (replacing <*vmname*> with the name assigned to your VM), and click Next.

15. In the Report Name text box on the Completing The Wizard page, type **Annual Sales By Territory**.

16. Click Finish to complete the wizard.

The wizard generates the report as shown in Figure 6-36. You can see how Visual Studio provides many of the same features as Report Builder. You get the same report designer surface, flanked on the left by the Report Data pane (expanded in Figure 6-36 to show the data source and dataset) and on the bottom by the row and column groups defined for the matrix. (Notice the country-territory hierarchy in the row groups.) The designer also has a Preview tab to run the report locally, without deploying it.

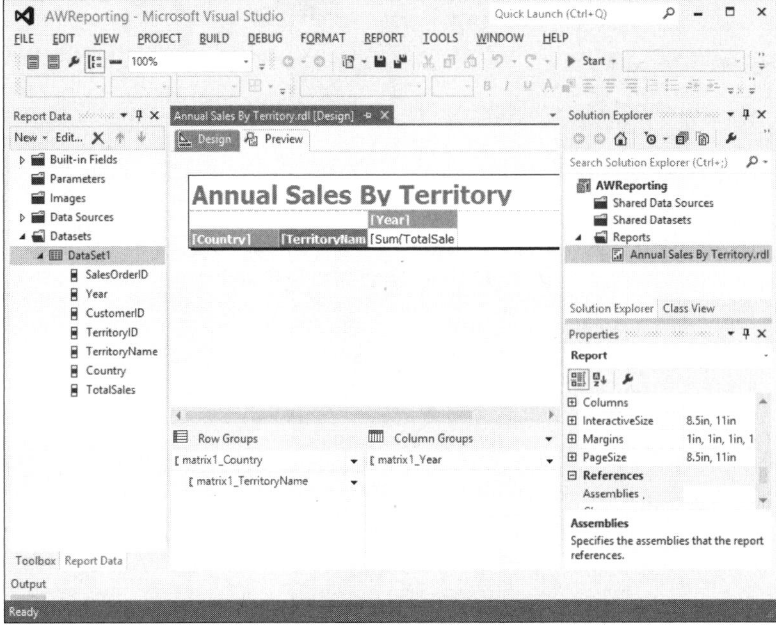

FIGURE 6-36 The project generated by the Report Server Project Wizard, open in design view

The wizard is great for quickly bringing together all the elements of a report, but you'll almost always need to customize or adjust the report that it produces. In our wine customer report, we didn't bother formatting the numbers as currency, but business users usually like to see numbers in the language that counts—money!

Formatting numeric data with the Report Designer

To format the sum of total sales as currency, follow these steps:

1. Right-click the [Sum(TotalSales)] column, and choose Text Box Properties.
2. Click Number in the left navigation pane of the Text Box Properties dialog.
3. Click Currency in the Category list box.
4. Change Decimal Places to **0**. (Pennies are often considered an annoyance.)
5. Select the Use 1000 Separator check box. The Text Box Properties dialog should appear as shown in Figure 6-37.

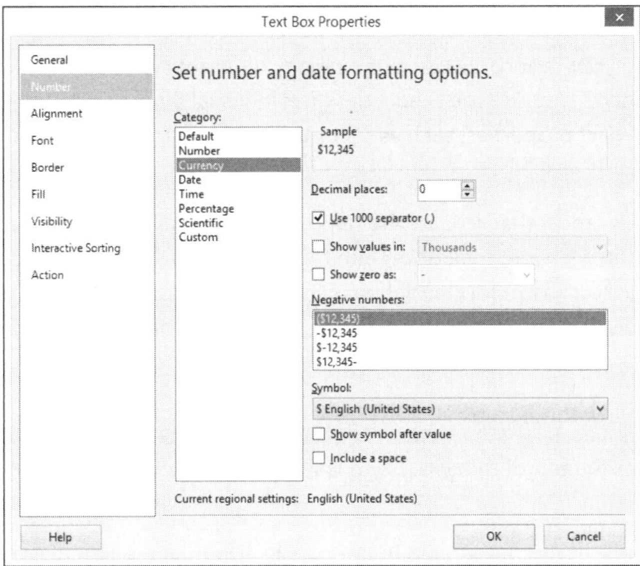

FIGURE 6-37 Formatting the currency text box of the matrix

6. Click OK.

You're all set to preview the report, so click the Preview tab at the top of the window. At first, the report displays only six rows, because the country-territory hierarchy is collapsed, and the report is showing aggregated information at the country level. As it turns out, the AdventureWorks database has only one territory per country except for the U.S., which has territories defined for Central, Northeast, Northwest, Southeast, and Southwest. Click the plus sign next to US to expand those territories and view the total sales for the various regions within the U.S., as shown in Figure 6-38.

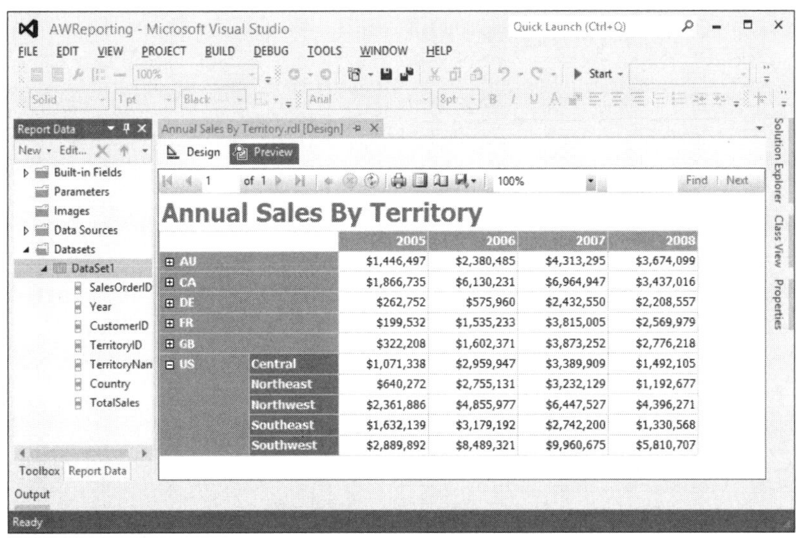

FIGURE 6-38 Previewing the drill-down capabilities of the report

Adding a bar chart to the report

It's very easy to add charts to your reports. RDL supports many different types of charts, including column, line, bar, and area charts. You use the report designer in Visual Studio to define the data for the chart and customize chart properties, such as 3D options, visibility, fill, border, and shadow settings.

Let's add a bar chart to this report that reflects the same information as the table. The chart will show total sales for each country (it won't drill down into the territory level), across all years. You will first enlarge the working space for the report, and then place the chart just beneath the table. To configure the chart data, you will set its values to *TotalSales*, its category groups to *Country*, and its series groups to *Year*.

To create the bar chart, follow these steps:

1. Click the Design tab at the top of the window to leave the report preview and return to design mode.
2. Click the bottom border of the report, and drag down to lengthen the height of the report's design surface. Give it a generous amount of vertical space to accommodate the chart.
3. Click VIEW | Toolbox to display the toolbox (if it's not already currently visible).
4. Click and drag the Chart item from the toolbox, and drop it on the report, just below the table, and all the way to the left.
5. In the Select Chart Type dialog, the Column chart is selected by default, as shown in Figure 6-39. Click OK to choose it.

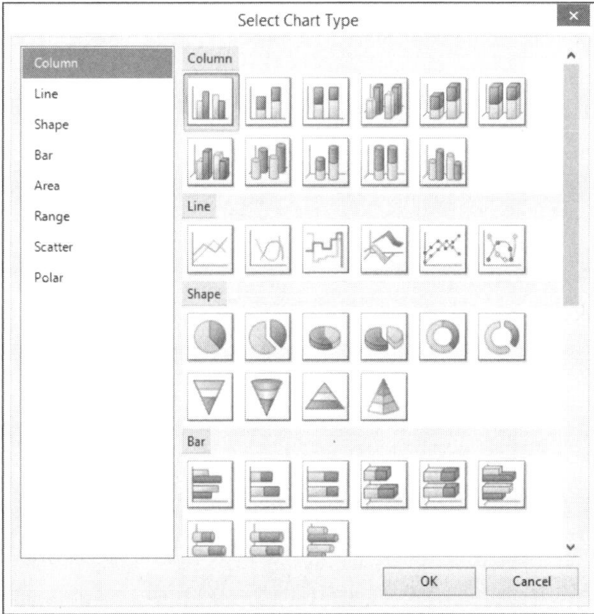

FIGURE 6-39 Viewing the gallery of available chart types

6. Click the sizing handle on the right of the chart, and drag it all the way over to the right to widen the chart across the entire page.
7. Click directly on the chart to open the Chart Data panel.
8. For Values, click the green plus sign and choose *TotalSales*.
9. For Category Groups, click the green plus sign and choose *Country*.
10. For Series Groups, click the green plus sign and choose *Year*. The designer should appear similar to Figure 6-40.

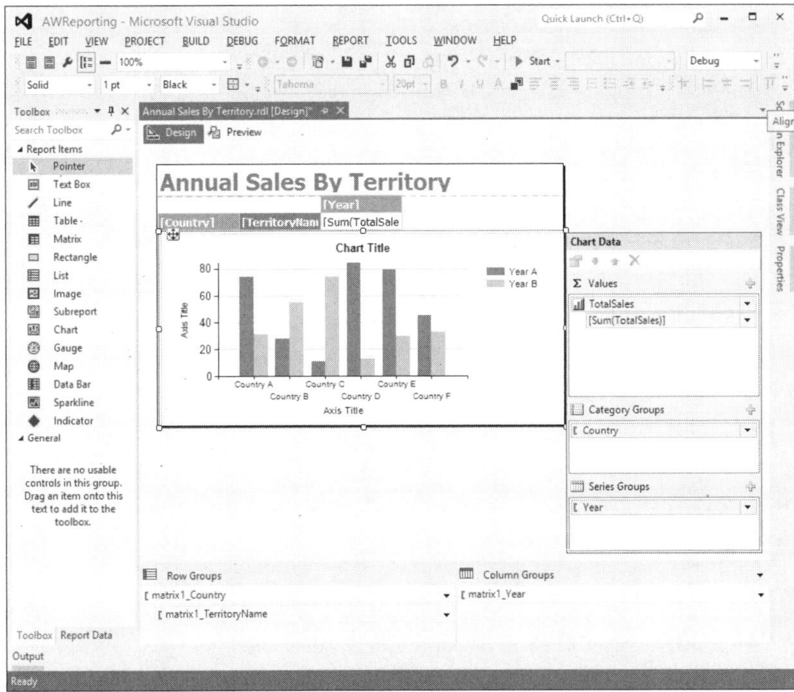

FIGURE 6-40 Setting the values, category groups, and series groups that define the chart's data.

11. Customize the labels:
    a. Click once on the Chart Title to select the text box, and then once again to enter edit mode. Replace Chart Title with **By Country**, and press Enter.
    b. Click once on the vertical Axis Title to select the text box, and then once again to enter edit mode. (The text box will temporarily shift to horizontal display so that you can type.) Replace Axis Title with **Total Sales**, and press Enter.
    c. Click once on the horizontal Axis Title to select the text box, and then once again to enter edit mode. Replace Axis Title with **Country**, and press Enter.
12. Click the Preview tab.

The bar chart now renders beneath the numbers, and it automatically adjusts its location if you drill down on the numbers. For example, if you expand US to drill down on its territories in the preceding table, the chart below moves down to accommodate, as shown in Figure 6-41. Total sales for each country/region are displayed, with bars for the years rendered in a cluster for each country/region.

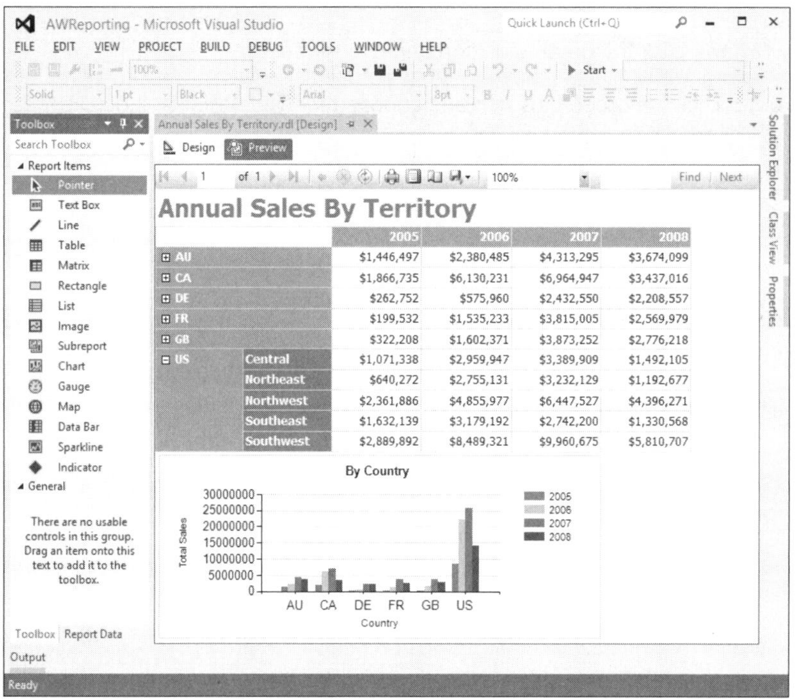

FIGURE 6-41 Previewing the report with a bar chart

Deploying the report to SSRS on the Microsoft Azure VM

Earlier, when you created the report using the wizard, you supplied the VM's SSRS service URL to the report wizard. That URL is stored in the project properties, and it can be changed at any time simply by modifying *TargetServerURL* property. To view the properties now, right-click the *AWReporting* project in Solution Explorer and choose Properties.

As shown in Figure 6-42, the Property Pages dialog shows the *TargetServerURL* set to the URL you supplied to the wizard, along with several other interesting properties. For example, notice the *TargetReportFolder*, which is set to *AWReporting*. This means that, when you deploy, the report itself (which is the file *Annual Sales By Territory.rdl*) will be created beneath a folder called *AWReporting* (named, by default, after the project, but easily changed here if desired). Now click Cancel to close the project Property Pages dialog.

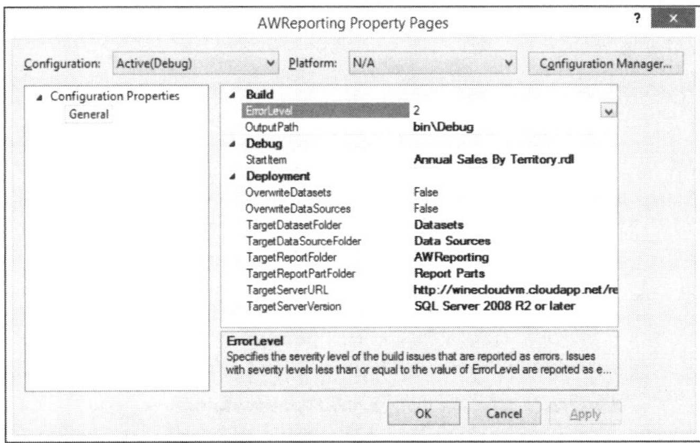

FIGURE 6-42 Viewing the properties of the Report Server project

To deploy the report to SSRS on the VM and then render it, follow these steps:

4. Right-click the *AWReporting* project in Solution Explorer, and choose Deploy.
5. When prompted, enter the administrator user name **WineAdmin** and its password that you assigned when you created the VM, as shown in Figure 6-43.

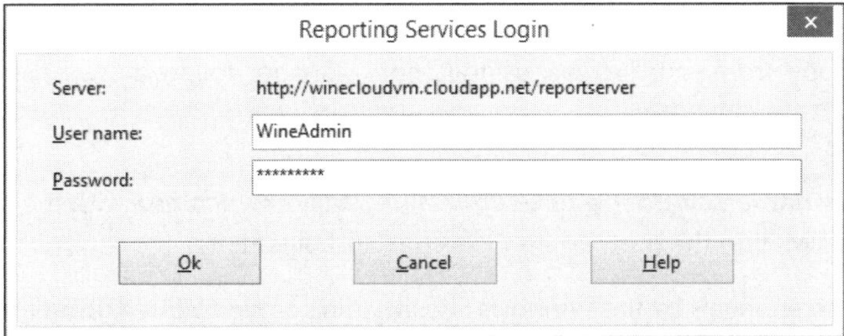

FIGURE 6-43 Entering login information to deploy the report

6. Click OK to deploy. When completed, Visual Studio shows the results in the Output window, as shown in Figure 6-44.

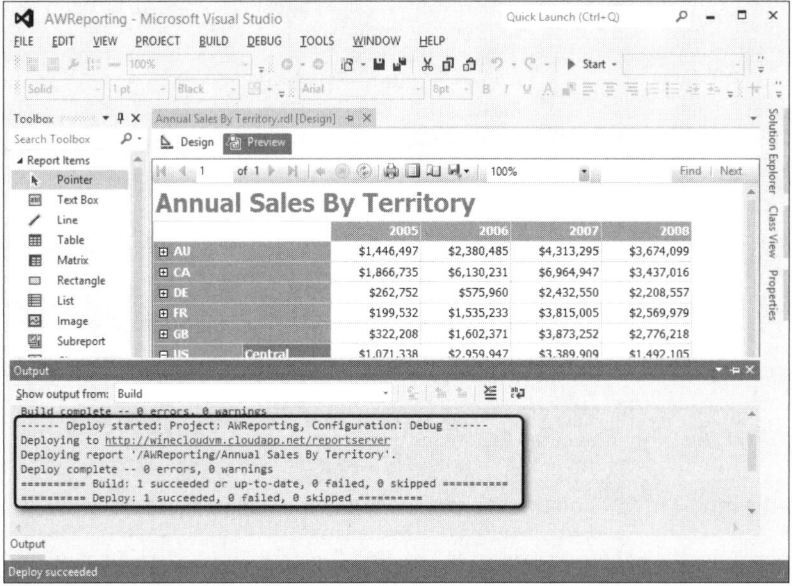

FIGURE 6-44 Viewing the output of a successful deployment

Running the report from a browser

To run the deployed report from your browser using Report Manager, follow these steps:

1. Open a new browser window.
2. Type **http://<*vmname*>.cloudapp.net/reports** (replacing <*vmname*> with the name you assigned to the VM) into the browser's address bar, and press Enter.
3. If prompted for credentials by the Windows Security dialog, type **WineAdmin** and the password you assigned to the VM's administrator account. The Report Manager home page is displayed with links for all the available folders and reports on the server. This includes the *AWReporting* folder that Visual Studio deployed the report to, as shown in Figure 6-45.

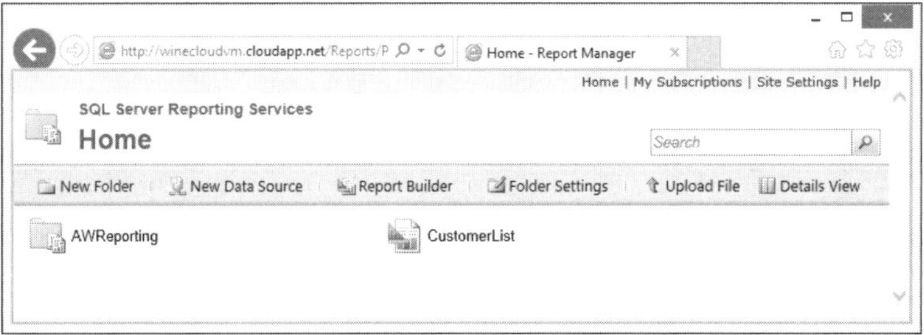

FIGURE 6-45 The Report Manager home page with the *AWReporting* folder link

4. Click the AWReporting link to drill down into the folder.

5. Click the Annual Sales By Territory link to display the report.

As you can see in Figure 6-46, the report looks and works the same in the browser as it did in the designer preview inside Visual Studio.

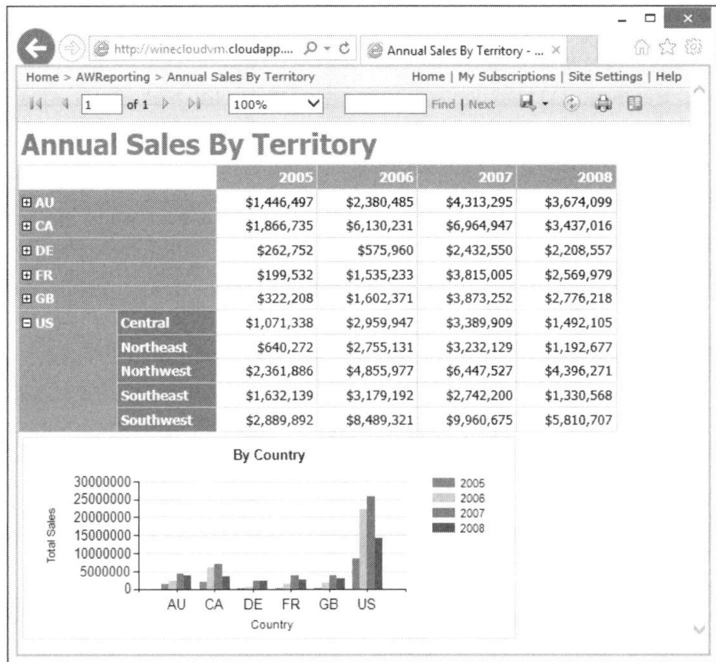

FIGURE 6-46 Viewing the final report in Internet Explorer

By now, you understand the basic steps involved in working with SSRS. Whether you choose to use Report Builder or Visual Studio Report Server projects, you define your data sources or datasets and lay them out in one or more reports (RDL files). You can then preview the report locally and deploy to the cloud whenever desired. After you deploy a report, you need to start thinking about security.

Implementing report security

Anonymous requests are never accepted by SSRS. All users and applications who request access to the report server must be authenticated. By default, SSRS uses Windows Integrated authentication, meaning that standard Windows Active Directory accounts are used to log in to the report server. Throughout this chapter, you used Windows Integrated authentication with the *WineAdmin* account that you created as administrator of the VM. (In this scenario, the Active Directory is stored on the VM, although quite often it is stored on a separate VM designated as a domain controller, and shared by all VMs that are joined in to the domain.) You can create more users on the VM, which adds them to the VM's Active Directory. This enables different individuals to access reports using their own credentials.

Windows authentication is convenient and easy, but it is not the best choice in all situations. SSRS also supports several other types of authentication, including basic authentication, forms-based authentication, and custom authentication. Basic authentication encodes the user name and password in clear text as a base-64 encoded string in the HTTP header, so it is only secure if you also encrypt the channel to make the HTTP header unreadable, typically using Secure Sockets Layer (SSL). Forms-based authentication is a security extension you use to manage your own user store, which can be something like a database table or configuration file. If you have very particular requirements that cannot be met by any of these supported authentication types, you can also implement custom authentication. This is an advanced scenario that requires custom code as well as a good deal of expertise in ASP.NET security.

Authorization is separate and distinct from authentication. Once a user is authenticated, what that user can and cannot do is controlled by role assignments you define using Report Manager. The least privileged role is Browser, which just allows users to view folders and reports. The most privileged role is Content Manager, which allows users to publish reports and gives them total permission (including delete) to folders, reports, and report definitions. You assign users to roles for specific reports or report folders, which determines whether a user can access that particular resource, or if the user can perform a specific operation (for example, delete a report or deploy a report). You can also create groups of users, and then assign groups to a role. This effectively adds every user in the group to the role, which makes it easy to manage multiple users as a single entity.

More Info Security in SSRS is sophisticated and potentially complex. The MSDN online documentation provides a thorough and detailed treatment of SSRS security that you should familiarize yourself with as you contemplate the security model for your particular requirements. The documentation can be found at *http://msdn.microsoft.com/en-us/library/bb522728.aspx.*

Shutting down the SSRS virtual machine

Before concluding the chapter, we strongly recommend shutting down the VM you created to host SSRS, or else your subscription will continue getting charged—even if no users are deploying or viewing reports.

To shut down the VM, follow these steps:

1. Log in to the Microsoft Azure portal. This takes you to the ALL ITEMS page.
2. Click VIRTUAL MACHINES on the left side of the page.
3. Click on the virtual machine to select it. (Click anywhere on the row except in the name column, or the portal will navigate you away to the VM's Quick Start page.)
4. Click the SHUT DOWN button at the bottom of the page.
5. Click YES when prompted to confirm.

The VM uses a virtual hard disk that is stored in Microsoft Azure Blob Storage, so it retains its state while it remains shut down. Whenever you need to start delivering reports again to your users, simply boot the VM from the Microsoft Azure management portal to bring SSRS back online.

Summary

This chapter introduced you to SQL Server Reporting Services (SSRS) and showed you how to create a Microsoft Azure virtual machine (VM) with SSRS to implement cloud reporting. You started by creating the VM and configuring it for SSRS with reporting service and Report Manager URLs. You then used the standalone Report Builder tool to create a simple customer report for the *WineCloudDb* database. In the process, you created a data source and dataset for the report, designed the layout using a table, and deployed the report to SSRS on the Microsoft Azure VM.

You then downloaded the AdventureWorks sample database to use as the data source for an annual sales report built in Visual Studio with a Report Server project. After downloading the SSDT Business Intelligence add-in for Visual Studio 2012, you used the Report Server Project Wizard to create the data source and dataset, and design the table layout. After applying some custom formatting and adding a bar chart to the report, you then deployed the report to SSRS on the Microsoft Azure VM directly from inside Visual Studio. We ended the chapter with a high-level discussion of report security, user authentication, and authorization.

There is certainly much more for you to discover on your own with SSRS and RDL. Now that you understand the most important concepts and features, you have the foundation you need to further explore these technologies and advance your cloud reporting skills.

CHAPTER 7

Microsoft Azure SQL Data Sync

—Leonard Lobel

The Microsoft Azure platform provides a special service called *Microsoft Azure SQL Data Sync*. You can use this service to automatically discover data changes made in one database and replicate those changes to another database (or to any number of other databases). In this chapter, we'll begin with an overview of Microsoft Azure SQL Data Sync, and then dive into a series of procedures for you to follow that put this cloud service to use in a number of common scenarios.

Note In this chapter, we refer to Microsoft Azure SQL Data Sync simply as *SQL Data Sync*. Furthermore, as mentioned in Chapter 1, "Getting started with Microsoft Azure SQL Database," the term *SQL Database* refers specifically to *Microsoft Azure SQL Database* in the cloud, whereas the term *SQL Server* refers specifically to local (on-premises) SQL Server.

Getting to know SQL Data Sync

SQL Data Sync is (at the time of this writing) a free Microsoft Azure service that provides automatic data synchronization across a set of databases. There are many common scenarios in which you can benefit from such a service, including

- Exporting data mastered on-premises to cloud applications
- Importing data in the cloud to on-premises applications
- Sharing data between applications running on premises and in the cloud
- Sharing data between multiple locations
- Scaling out using the cloud

In the sections that follow, we discuss these scenarios and explain how SQL Data Sync can be used to implement a solution for each one of them.

It is incredibly easy to configure and use SQL Data Sync. Everything happens through the Microsoft Azure portal. No local tools are needed. You can use the portal to specify the databases you want synchronized and the datasets within those databases (which tables and columns) to be synchronized. You can also schedule an interval of time that controls how often SQL Data Sync will synchronize the databases automatically, thus controlling how up to date those databases will be. The only time you need to install something locally is when configuring an on-premises SQL Server database for synchronization. This requires the installation of a small *agent* component, a lightweight Windows Service that registers local databases with SQL Data Sync.

The collection of databases to be synchronized (called *reference databases*) are defined within a *sync group*. The reference databases in a sync group can include any number of local (on-premises) SQL Server databases, any number of databases in the cloud (SQL Database), or any combination of on-premises and cloud databases.

Within the sync group, one reference database is designated as the *hub* and all the other reference databases act as *spokes*, in what can be viewed as a *hub-and-spoke* model. In our discussion, we will refer to the spokes as *clients*, because that is the terminology used by the SQL Data Sync service and documentation. In between the hub and each client, you can monitor and apply changes in one direction (from hub to client), the other direction (from client to hub), or bi-directionally (two-way). When two-way synchronization is enabled between a hub and multiple clients, data changes made to the hub are pushed out to all the clients. A data change in any individual client is first pushed to the hub, and then pushed out again to all the other clients. If the same data is changed in two places within a synchronization pass, you can control who "wins" by setting the conflict-resolution behavior for the sync group.

The only requirement in this model is that the hub database absolutely *must* be a SQL Database (that is, it must be a database in the cloud). An on-premises SQL Server database cannot function as the hub of a sync group. All the other reference databases in the sync group (the clients) can be either another SQL Database in the cloud or an on-premises SQL Server database.

Important SQL Data Sync is provided as a "preview" release available to all Microsoft Azure subscribers, so support from Microsoft is not guaranteed. We normally recommend against using preview releases like SQL Data Sync for production applications (as Microsoft does), particularly because it is reasonable to expect that newer and more sophisticated replication services will emerge on Microsoft Azure in the longer term.

However, SQL Data Sync is currently the only synchronization service for SQL Database and SQL Server available from Microsoft on Microsoft Azure. It is also extremely easy to use and reliable, and it has been freely available as a preview release since 2007 (when the service was formerly called *SQL Azure Data Sync*). In fact, there are reports of customers enjoying great success with SQL Data Sync in production environments, and even (under special circumstances) receiving limited Microsoft support. But to reiterate, with preview release software, there are no guarantees. You must carefully consider all these facets before adopting SQL Data Sync and integrating it into your production solution.

Exporting data from SQL Server to SQL Database

SQL Data Sync gives you the ability to synchronize data between SQL Server on-premises and Microsoft Azure SQL Database in the cloud. This capability is ideal when you have existing applications and existing data residing on-premises, and new cloud-based applications are being developed that need to use some of that data—data that is effectively mastered exclusively on-premises.

In this scenario, Data Sync can be used to synchronize one-way, from the SQL Server client up to the SQL Database hub. (See Figure 7-1.) Changes made on-premises in SQL Server will be replicated automatically to SQL Database in the cloud. However, the cloud applications are not able to affect the on-premises SQL Server database in any way, because with one-way synchronization set up in this direction, SQL Data Sync will not monitor the SQL Database hub for changes that might be made in the cloud; thus, it will never modify the SQL Server client database.

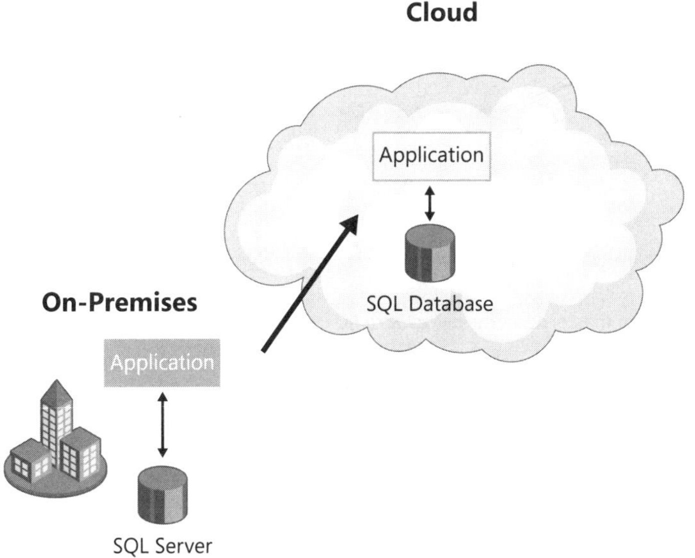

FIGURE 7-1 One-way publishing of data mastered on-premises with SQL Server to SQL Database in the cloud

Importing data from SQL Database to SQL Server

In other cases, you have the exact opposite scenario. You might have cloud-based applications that are inserting, updating, and deleting data in a SQL Database, and those changes are required by applications running on-premises. For example, you can have on-premises Business Intelligence (BI) solutions that analyze data collected in the cloud and pulled down to a local SQL Server database by SQL Data Sync.

In this scenario, a one-way sync in the other direction (from the SQL Database hub down to the SQL Server client) is the requirement. (See Figure 7-2.) By changing the direction of the one-way synchronization, SQL Data Sync will monitor SQL Database only for changes made in the cloud and then push those changes into the on-premises SQL Server database. The on-premises applications are not able to affect the cloud database in any way.

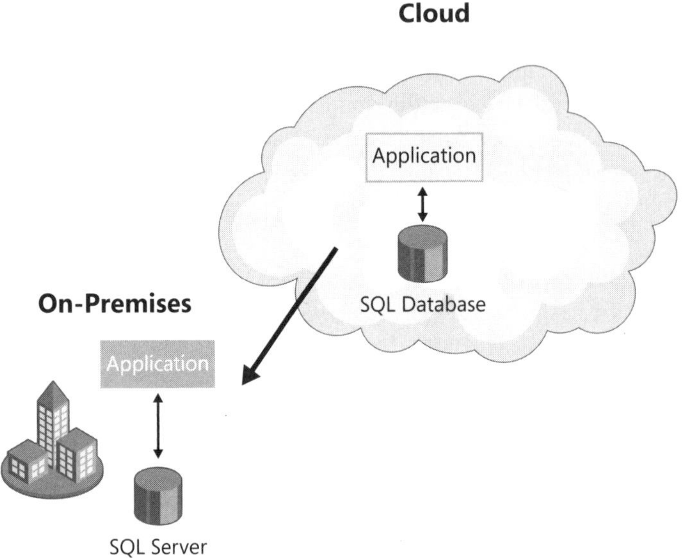

FIGURE 7-2 One-way publishing of data mastered in the cloud with SQL Database to on-premises SQL Server

Sharing data between multiple locations

Yet still, in other scenarios, both on-premises and cloud-based applications operate over a shared database—in which case, full bi-directional (two-way) synchronization is needed. And to extend the scenario a bit further, let's also introduce multiple on-premises locations. These could be restaurants, hotels, retail stores, branch offices, and so on. Figure 7-3 shows only two on-premises locations, although of course, there can be many more.

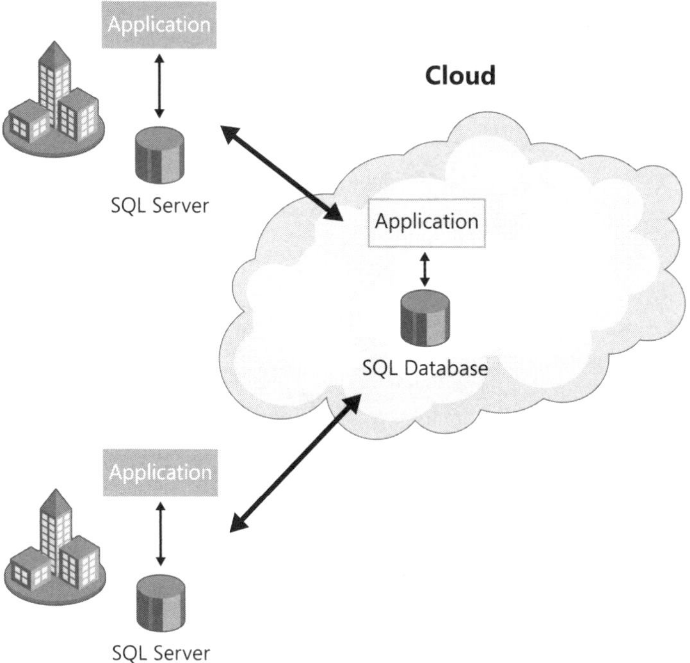

FIGURE 7-3 Two-way publishing of shared data between multiple locations via a centralized hub in the cloud

When you have multiple locations, each location runs its own set of applications and uses data in its own SQL Server database. In some cases, the requirement is to share data between the different SQL Server (on-premises) locations. That is, each location has some data that needs to be kept in sync so that it's available in all the other locations (for example, a product catalog). In this case, SQL Data Sync uses the hub as a conduit through which data is synchronized bi-directionally. Changes are first replicated from the on-premises location to the hub, and then pushed back out to all the other on-premises locations. In this manner, SQL Data Sync can update each location with changes made in any other location, via the SQL Database hub in the cloud.

Another common scenario is to use SQL Database in the cloud as a location to *aggregate* (combine) the data from these multiple locations. Basically, you can use SQL Data Sync to pull the location-specific data from each location and aggregate it into a centralized SQL Database. Then you can create a cloud-based application that consumes the view of that aggregated data across those multiple locations. This is just one example of how SQL Data Sync can provide great insight by pulling distributed data together into a single SQL Database. The cloud-based application can even update data in the SQL Database (either shared data or location-specific data), causing SQL Data Sync to push those changes back down appropriately; the service will send shared data changes to all locations, and location-specific data changes to just the individual corresponding locations.

Scaling out

Finally, you can also synchronize between multiple databases in the cloud, as illustrated in Figure 7-4. This can work in conjunction with the previously described scenarios by including multiple on-premises locations, as depicted on the left side of the diagram. However, this is entirely optional—a local SQL Server database is never required with SQL Data Sync.

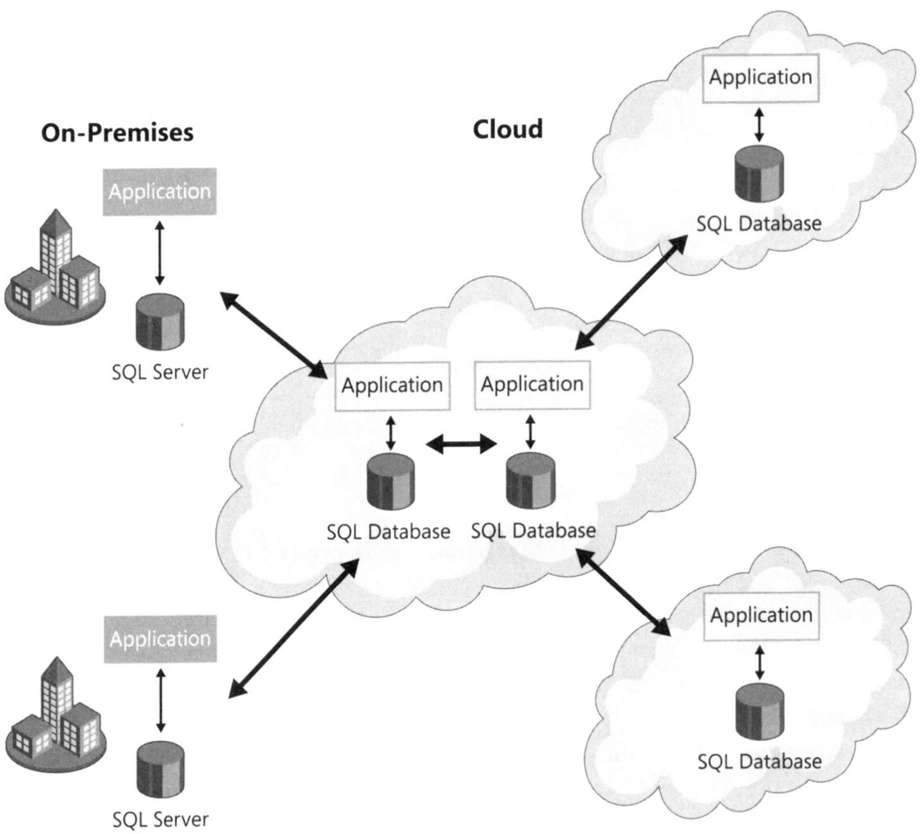

FIGURE 7-4 Synchronizing multiple cloud databases across multiple Microsoft Azure data centers

By maintaining multiple copies of the same data in the cloud (both within a single data center as well as across multiple data centers), you can scale out in significant ways. For example, you can generate one or more replicas of your primary transactional database (often termed the *OLTP* database, for *online transactional processing*), keeping both the OLTP and replica databases hosted within the same data center (as depicted by the two SQL Database instances in the center of the diagram). Then you can run your analysis and reports against a replica, rather than the "live" OLTP database.

Taking this approach greatly reduces the demand on your primary transactional database, which needs to remain responsive to data-entry requests at a fast and furious rate. The OLTP database is primarily focused on (and carefully tuned for) inserting, updating, and deleting small amounts of data within atomic transactions (that is, brief series of operations that succeed or fail as a whole). Although there are also read requests, they are relatively few and typically involve small amounts of data. Because reporting requests tend to involve intensive, potentially long-running read-only queries, they typically have a negative (often severely negative) impact when executed directly on the OLTP database. By comparison, once the OLTP and replica databases are fully synchronized, keeping them in sync has a relatively small impact on the OLTP database as it is queried for fresh changes that have occurred in between each synchronization pass. So this problem is easily remedied by replicating the OLTP database or databases to other databases and then running report and analysis queries against only the replicas.

One of the great things about the Microsoft Azure platform is that Microsoft maintains data centers in multiple regions around the world. This infrastructure makes it easy to geographically locate your own applications around the world as well, if and when the need arises to scale out to that level. Thus, you can keep applications (and their associated data) physically closer to the users consuming those applications. In this case, SQL Data Sync can be used to keep replicated databases (or designated parts of replicated databases) in sync so that the same data (or the same subset of data) is available to all instances of the application worldwide, as depicted on the right side of Figure 7-4.

Important Although the SQL Data Sync service itself is free at the time we are writing this, your Microsoft Azure subscription will most definitely incur normal charges for data transferred between data centers by the service. (See Chapter 2, "Configuration and pricing," for more information.) Furthermore, there will be a performance hit as a result of all the additional network traffic crossing data centers. For these reasons, if possible, you can and should limit synchronization to include only that portion of your database (the minimum number of tables and columns) that absolutely needs to be available globally.

About Microsoft Azure Traffic Manager

SQL Data Sync makes it easy to synchronize the same database for applications hosted in multiple Microsoft Azure data centers, but properly *routing* users to the application running in the data center closest to them is a separate matter. Although routing is a topic that falls beyond the scope of this chapter, you should be aware that Microsoft Azure provides a service called *Traffic Manager* that is specifically designed to handle this concern.

Traffic Manager provides load-balancing capabilities for your applications running on Microsoft Azure in multiple data centers. (Note that this is separate from, and in addition to, the load balancing you can achieve within an individual data center using virtual machines.) It essentially takes the entire collection of Microsoft Azure data centers and places it behind a Domain Name System (DNS) capable of handling the necessary routing. Thus, you can deploy applications to run in multiple data centers, using SQL Data Sync to replicate a copy of the database for each application instance in each data center, and then use Traffic Manager to intelligently direct users to the application instance running in the data center nearest to them, based on their physical location.

Although it's not required to use Traffic Manager in conjunction with SQL Data Sync, it is a highly recommended option. There are solutions available from other companies that similarly use DNS services to route users to the right place based on their location, but such solutions are often quite expensive and can be very complex to implement correctly. Conversely, Traffic Manager is relatively easy to use and accessible as part of the Microsoft Azure platform. And, at the time of this writing, the service is still in preview and available to be used free of charge.

You can learn more about Microsoft Azure Traffic Manager by visiting *http://www.windowsazure.com/en-us/services/traffic-manager.*

Creating the SQL Database

To get started, you will use SQL Server Data Tools (SSDT) inside Visual Studio to quickly create a *WineCloudDb* database similar to the one you've been using throughout this book. The procedure assumes you already created a SQL Database server that you can access through its firewall on which you can create this database, as explained in Chapter 1. If you do not already have a server, it's easy to create one now and open its firewall to your local machine using the Microsoft Azure management portal. (See "Creating a server" in Chapter 1.)

As shown in Listing 7-1, *WineCloudDb* is a simple database that has *Wine* and *Customer* tables and a few rows of data.

Note Because this procedure does nothing more than create a database and execute a script, you can certainly follow similar steps with SQL Server Management Studio (SSMS) instead of Visual Studio and SSDT. Likewise, you can choose instead to use the Microsoft Azure management portal to create the database and the SQL Database management portal to run the script. It's largely a matter of preference, so you should use whichever tool is readily available and most convenient for you.

LISTING 7-1 Script to create the *WineCloudDb* database

```
CREATE TABLE Wine(
  WineId int IDENTITY PRIMARY KEY,
  Name nvarchar(50) NOT NULL,
  Category nvarchar(15) NOT NULL,
  Year int);
```

```
CREATE TABLE Customer(
  CustomerId int IDENTITY PRIMARY KEY,
  FirstName nvarchar(50) NOT NULL,
  LastName nvarchar(50) NOT NULL,
  FavoriteWineId int,
  CONSTRAINT FK_Customer_Wine FOREIGN KEY (FavoriteWineId) REFERENCES Wine(WineId));

SET IDENTITY_INSERT Wine ON;
INSERT Wine (WineId, Name, Category, Year) VALUES
 (1, 'Chateau Penin', 'Bordeaux', 2008),
 (2, 'McLaren Valley', 'Cabernet', 2005),
 (3, 'Mendoza', 'Merlot', 2010),
 (4, 'Valle Central', 'Merlot', 2009);
SET IDENTITY_INSERT Wine OFF;

SET IDENTITY_INSERT Customer ON;
INSERT Customer (CustomerId, FirstName, LastName, FavoriteWineId) VALUES
 (1, 'Jeff', 'Hay', 4),
 (2, 'Mark', 'Hanson', 3),
 (3, 'Jeff', 'Phillips', 2);
SET IDENTITY_INSERT Customer OFF;
```

To create the *WineCloudDb* database using Visual Studio 2013, follow these steps:

1. Start Visual Studio 2013.
2. If the SQL Server Object Explorer is not visible, click the VIEW menu and choose SQL Server Object Explorer.
3. In the SQL Server Object Explorer, right-click SQL Server and choose Add SQL Server to display the familiar Connect To Server dialog.
4. In the Connect To Server dialog, do the following:
   a. For Server Name, type **<*servername*>.database.windows.net**. This is the fully qualified name to the SQL Database server, where <*servername*> should be replaced by the name assigned to your server.
   b. For Authentication, select SQL Server Authentication from the drop-down list. (SQL Database does not support Windows Authentication.)
   c. For Login and Password, type the user name and password you assigned the server when you created it.
   d. Click the Connect button. The server now appears as a collapsed node in the SQL Server Object Explorer.
5. Expand the server node in the SQL Server Object Explorer.
6. Expand the server's Databases node.

7. If a previous version of *WineCloudDb* is present from work you did in an earlier chapter, delete it now:
   a. Right-click the existing *WineCloudDb* database, and choose Delete.
   b. Click OK to confirm.
8. Right-click the Databases node, and choose Add New Database.
9. Type **WineCloudDb**, and press Enter. The new database now appears in the SQL Server Object Explorer.
10. Right-click the *WineCloudDb* database, and choose New Query to open a new query window.
11. Type the code shown in Listing 7-1 into the query window (or paste it in from the listing file downloaded from the book's companion website).
12. Press Ctrl+Shift+E to execute the script (or press the play button icon in the query window's toolbar).
13. Close Visual Studio. (It isn't necessary to save the script.)

Working with SQL Data Sync

The rest of this chapter contains procedures that guide you through the process of setting up a sync group and configuring SQL Data Sync for many of the different scenarios identified in the previous section. You will start by creating a simple sync group to replicate the *WineCloudDb* database to another SQL Database on Microsoft Azure. Then you'll move on to add a local on-premises SQL Server database to the sync group. In other procedures, you will also learn about conflict resolution and how to set an automated synchronization schedule.

Creating a sync group

At a minimum, a sync group requires one SQL Database (the hub) and at least one more SQL Database or on-premises SQL Server database to synchronize with. In the next few procedures, you will create an empty *WineCloudDb* database on a new SQL Database server, and then create a sync group with the populated *WineCloudDb* database (the hub) and the new empty one. You will configure for two-way synchronization, so that SQL Data Sync will first replicate from the hub to the empty database and then subsequently replicate data changes bi-directionally between both databases.

To avoid incurring charges to your Microsoft Azure subscription as you follow along with these procedures, you'll create the new server in the same data center as the one currently hosting *WineCloudDb*. You will create the sync group in the same region as well, for the same reason. This is ideal for scaling out within a data center, but you can just as easily create the server in a different data center (and incur outgoing data-transfer charges between them) if you wanted to geographically disperse the databases and better service global users in closest proximity to their nearest available data center.

Indeed, for this exercise, you don't even really need to create a new server at all; you could use the same server you've been using all along for *WineCloudDb*. SQL Data Sync will happily synchronize two SQL Databases on the same server. Nevertheless, you will still create another server. (Of course, you'd be using separate servers in separate *data centers* if you were actually going to geographically distribute the databases across regions.) If the two databases ran on the same server, you would be forced to name the replica differently (for example, *WineCloudDb2*), whereas you'll be able to name both of them *WineCloudDb* by using separate servers.

Note In Chapter 1, you already created a server, opened the firewall, and created a database. Although the following instructions are very similar to the ones we provided then, you might still want to refer to "Creating a server" in Chapter 1 because the instructions there include screen shots and details that are not repeated here.

To create a new server, follow these steps:

1. Log in to the Microsoft Azure portal at **https://manage.windowsazure.com**. This brings you to the main portal page showing ALL ITEMS.
2. Click SQL DATABASES in the vertical navigation pane on the left.
3. Click the SERVERS link at the top of the page.
4. Click the ADD button at the bottom of the page.
5. Provide a new server administrator login name and password, and then reenter the password to confirm.

Tip To simplify things while you are practicing, we recommend using the same login name (for example, **saz**) and password you assigned to the first server.

6. Choose a region from the drop-down list. As we explained, you should select the same region you chose for the first server so that your subscription will not incur data-transfer charges when you synchronize between the databases on the two servers.
7. Be sure the ALLOW WINDOWS AZURE SERVICES TO ACCESS THE SERVER check box remains selected. This setting enables Microsoft Azure services like SQL Data Sync to access the server.
8. Click the checkmark icon in the lower right side of the dialog to complete the settings.
9. Wait for the new server status to change from "creating" to "started."

Next, you'll open the Microsoft Azure firewall, although this procedure is technically optional. SQL Data Sync does not require you to open the Microsoft Azure firewall to synchronize across servers. However, as explained in Chapter 1, you do need to open the firewall for your machine's IP address if you want to be able to access the server from the Silverlight-based SQL Database management portal (which you will do in upcoming procedures), and other tools (such as SQL Server Management Studio and SSDT in Visual Studio).

To open the firewall, follow these steps:

1. Click the server name.
2. Click the CONFIGURE link at the top of the page.
3. To the right of your current detected IP address, click ADD TO THE ALLOWED IP ADDRESSES.
4. Click the SAVE button at the bottom of the page.
5. Click the back icon (the large back-pointing arrow) to return to the SQL DATABASES page.

Now you'll create an empty database on the new server. To do so, follow these steps:

1. Click the DATABASES link at the top of the page.
2. Click the NEW button at the bottom of the page.
3. Click QUICK CREATE.
4. For DATABASE NAME, type **WineCloudDb**. (Because this database will run on the new server, it can be the same name as your existing database running on the first server.)

Note Conversely, if you were scaling out to separate OLTP activity from reporting activity, you could use the same server. In that case, you'd be forced to give the replica database a unique name, which might be something like *WineCloudReportingDb*.

5. Choose the server you created in the previous procedure from the SERVER drop-down list.
6. Click CREATE SQL DATABASE.

After a few more moments, the new *WineCloudDb* database is created. This database is completely empty, but it will soon contain the same tables with the same data as the existing *WineCloudDb* on the first server, once you create the sync group, configure the sync rules, and run a manual sync.

When creating the sync group, you will define the hub database and the first client database. (A client database is also often called a *reference database*.)

To create the sync group, follow these steps:

1. Click the ADD SYNC button at the bottom of the page, and then choose New Sync Group, as shown in Figure 7-5.

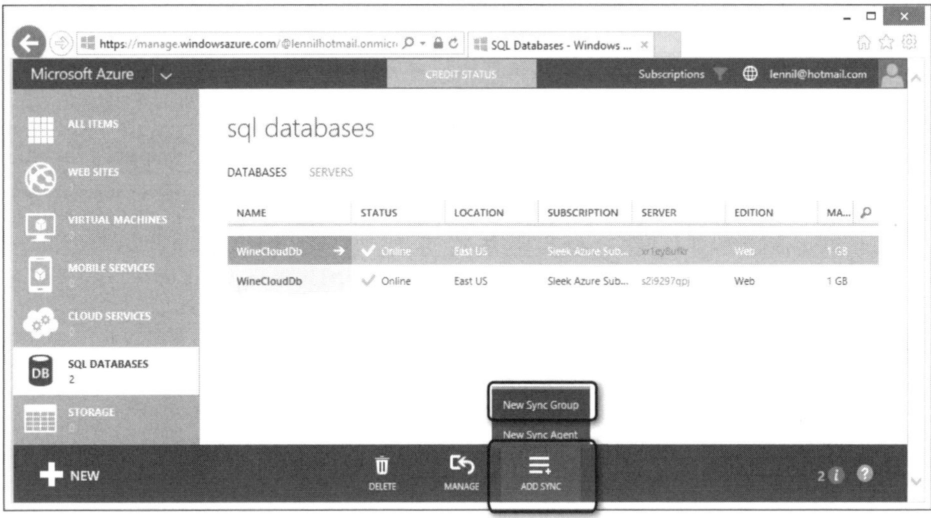

FIGURE 7-5 Creating a new sync group

2. On the Sync Group Basic Settings page, do the following:

   a. For NAME, type **WineCloudSyncGroup**.

   b. In the REGION drop-down list, choose the same region as the two servers. The page should appear similar to Figure 7-6.

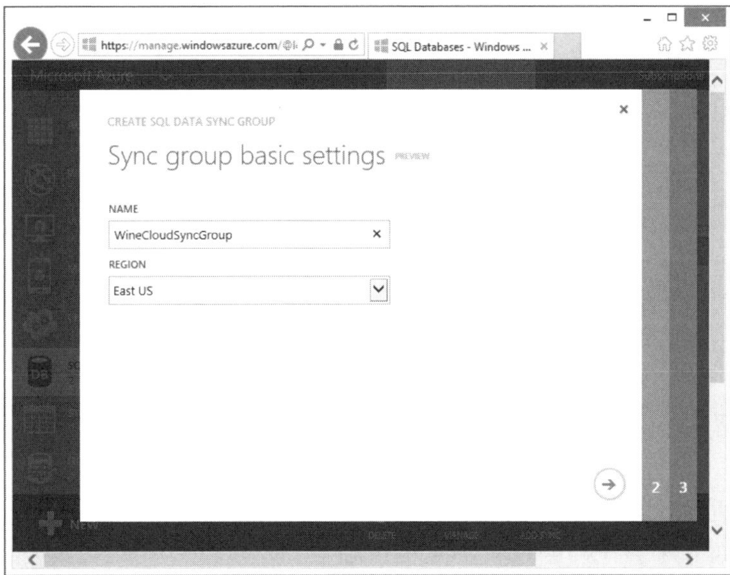

FIGURE 7-6 Naming the sync group and choosing a region to host it in

   c. Click the right-arrow Next button.

3. On the Define Sync Hub page, do the following:

   a. For HUB DATABASE, choose the *WineCloudDb* database running on the first server (the database that already has some data in it).

   b. Enter the server's administrator user name and password credentials for HUB USER NAME and HUB PASSWORD.

   c. Leave CONFLICT RESOLUTION at its default setting, Hub Wins. (We will discuss conflict resolution shortly.) The page should look similar to Figure 7-7.

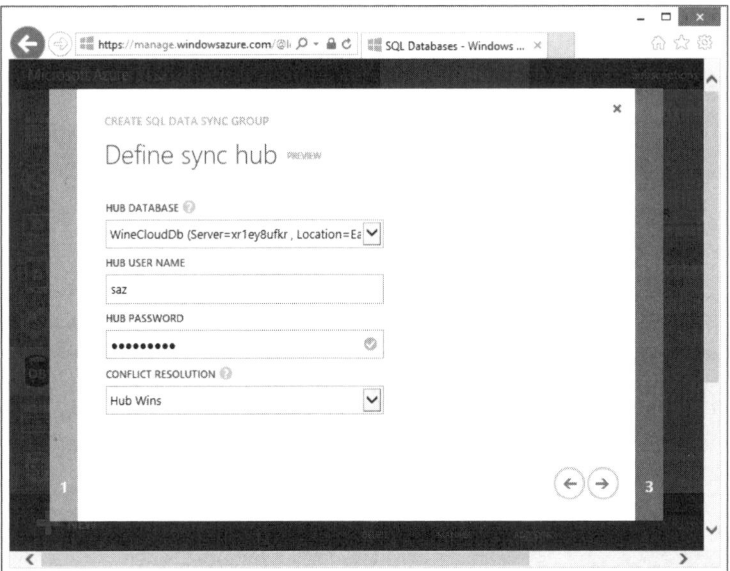

FIGURE 7-7 Configuring the hub database

Note The conflict-resolution setting cannot be changed once the sync group is created. You need to delete the sync group and re-create it if you want to change the setting.

   d. Click the right-arrow Next button. Because of the way the portal handles validation on this page, you need to wait a moment after clicking it once, and then click it again.

4. On the Add A Reference Database page, complete the following steps:

   a. For REFERENCE DATABASE, choose the *WineCloudDb* database running on the new server (the empty database you just created). You'll notice that the database selected for the hub is not even present as a choice in the drop-down list.

b. Enter the server's administrator user name and password credentials for USER NAME and PASSWORD. (If you assigned the same credentials to the new server as the original server, these are the same values you typed for the hub database on the previous page.)

c. Leave SYNC DIRECTION at its default setting, Bi-Directional. The page should look similar to Figure 7-8.

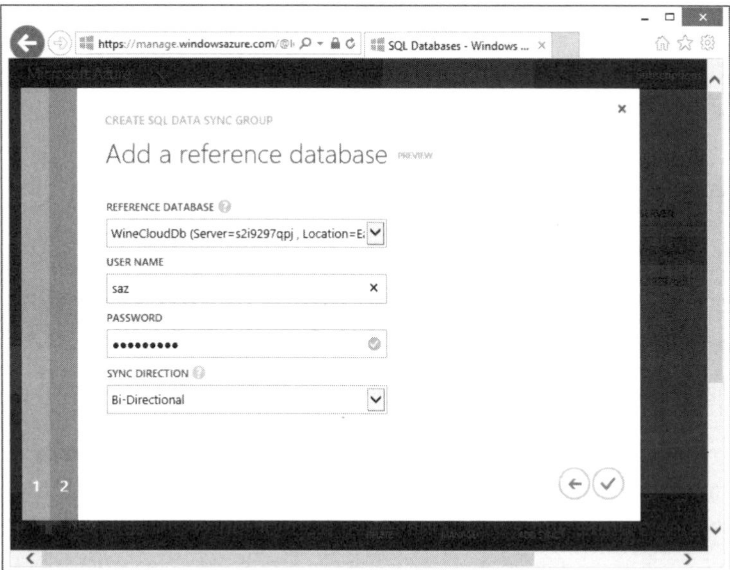

FIGURE 7-8 Configuring a reference database

Note The two other available sync direction settings are one-way from the hub to the client and one-way from the client to the hub, either of which you could choose to use rather than bi-directional, if doing so makes sense for the given scenario. (Different one-way scenarios were discussed at the beginning of this chapter.) Also note that the sync direction setting cannot be changed once the sync group is created. You need to remove a client database from the sync group and then add it again if you want to change the setting.

d. Click the checkmark "finish" button to complete the settings. Once again, you might need to wait a moment after clicking it once, and then click it again.

As shown in Figure 7-9, the sync group has been created at this point, but it is not ready. And it will remain in this Not Ready state until you further configure the sync group with *sync rules*.

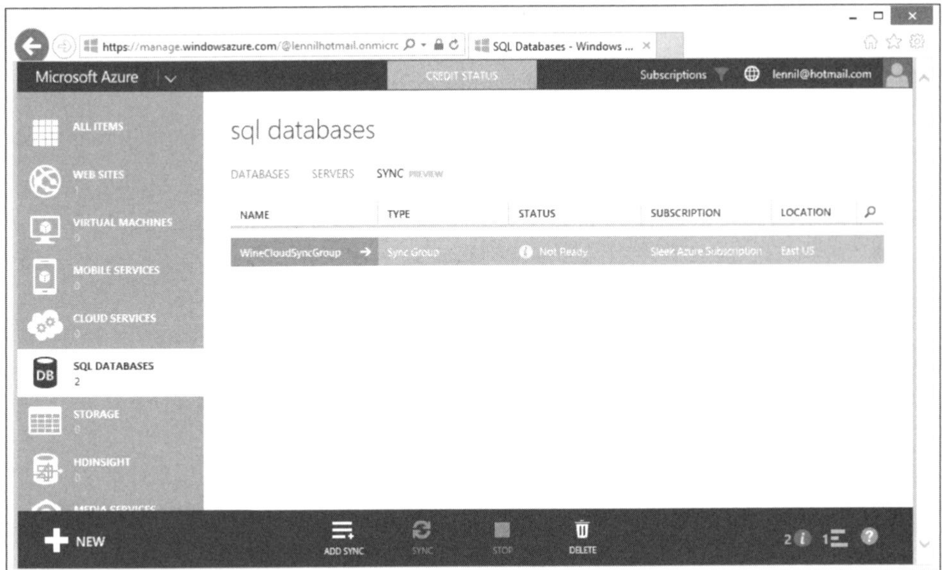

FIGURE 7-9 Viewing the newly created sync group

Also notice that the portal has added a third link (SYNC) after the standard DATABASES and SERVERS links on the SQL Databases page. When at least one sync group has been created, the SYNC link takes you to this management view of all your sync groups.

Creating sync rules

With the sync group in place, it's time to set the sync rules. Essentially, the sync rules define the *dataset*, which is to say, exactly which tables and columns you want synchronized across all reference databases in the sync group. Until at least one dataset is defined, the sync group will remain in a Not Ready state, so let's go ahead and define one now.

To configure the sync rules and define the dataset, follow these steps:

1. Click the sync group name *WineCloudSyncGroup*. This opens to the REFERENCES view that lists all the databases in the sync group, as shown in Figure 7-10. Notice that the status of each database is Not Ready, again, because no sync rules have yet been configured.

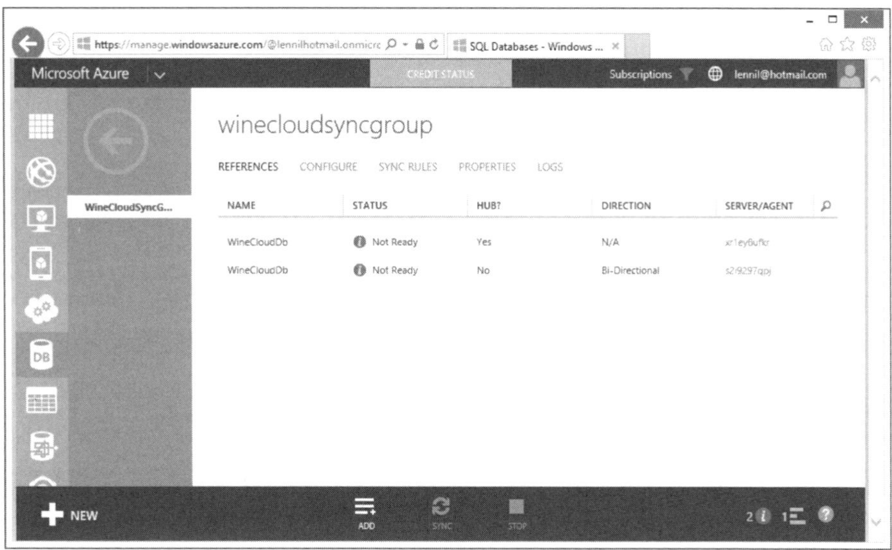

FIGURE 7-10 The REFERENCES page lists all the databases in the sync group

2. Click the SYNC RULES link at the top of the page.
3. Click DEFINE SYNC RULES beneath the message stating that you have no sync rules.
4. On the DEFINE DATASET dialog, select the *WineCloudDb* database running on the first server (the one with pre-existing tables and data, not the new empty one).
5. Click the checkmark icon to close the dialog. The SYNC RULES page now lists all the tables discovered in the *WineCloudDb* database, as shown in Figure 7-11.

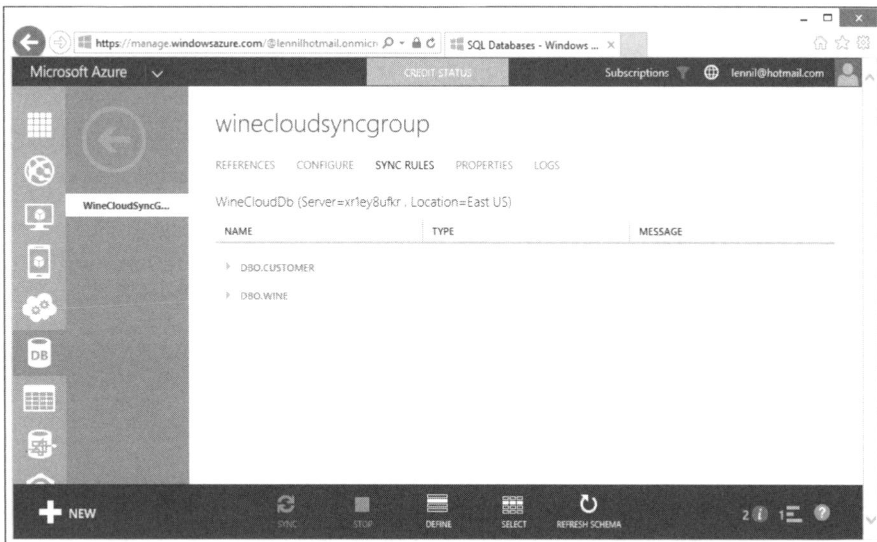

FIGURE 7-11 The SYNC RULES page listing all the tables in the database that can be synchronized

6. Click the SELECT button at the bottom of the page, and click Select All The Columns In All The Tables, as shown in Figure 7-12.

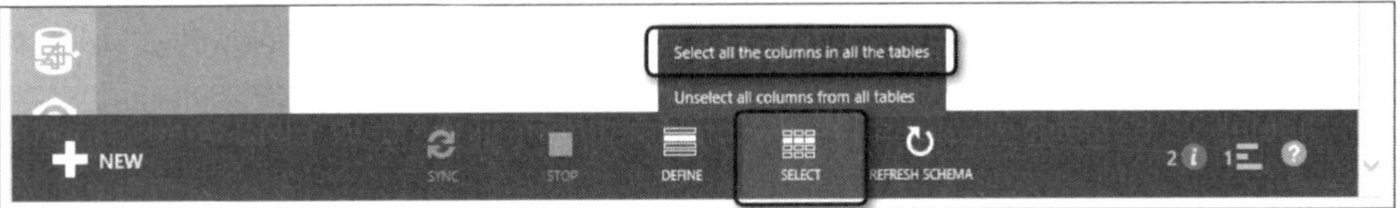

FIGURE 7-12 Selecting the entire database (all columns in all tables) for synchronization

7. Click the SAVE button at the bottom of the page, as shown in Figure 7-13.

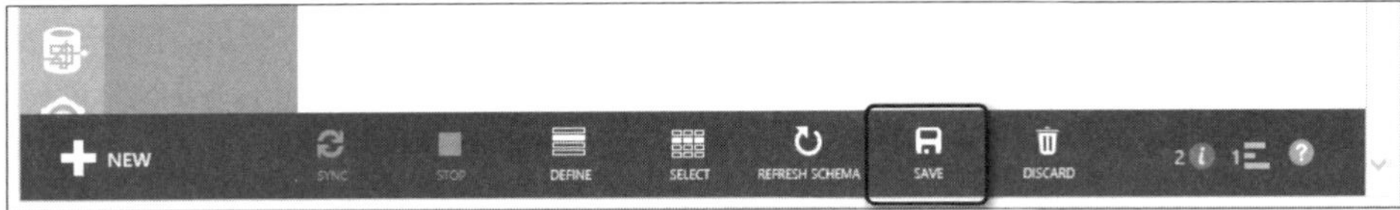

FIGURE 7-13 Saving the sync rules

8. You might need to wait a few moments for processing before the portal becomes responsive again. When processing completes, click the REFERENCES link at the top of the page. Both databases are now designated with a status of Good, as shown in Figure 7-14.

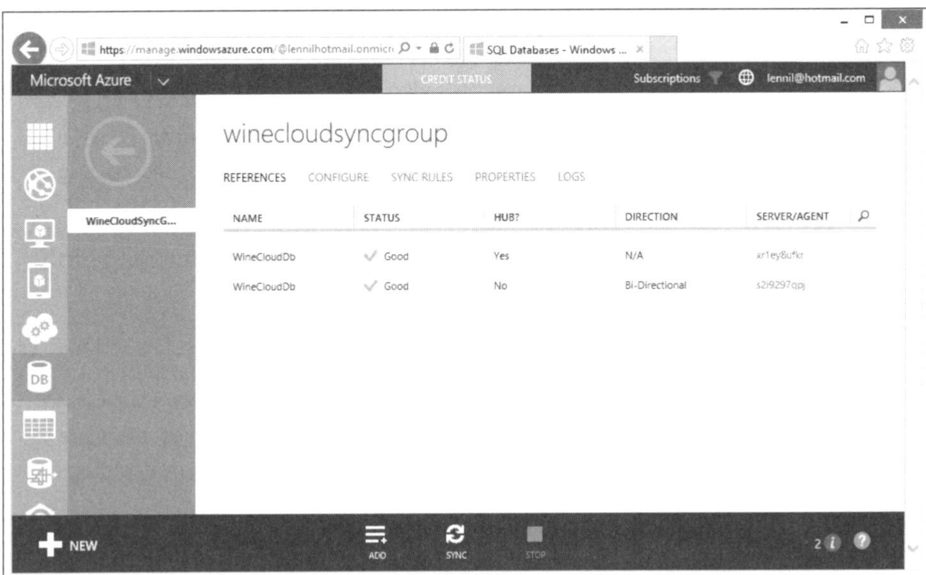

FIGURE 7-14 The REFERENCES page now showing all the databases in the sync group with a Good status

9. Click the back icon (the large back-pointing arrow) to return to the SQL DATABASES page for the new sync group. As shown in Figure 7-15, the sync group has now also transitioned to a status of Good.

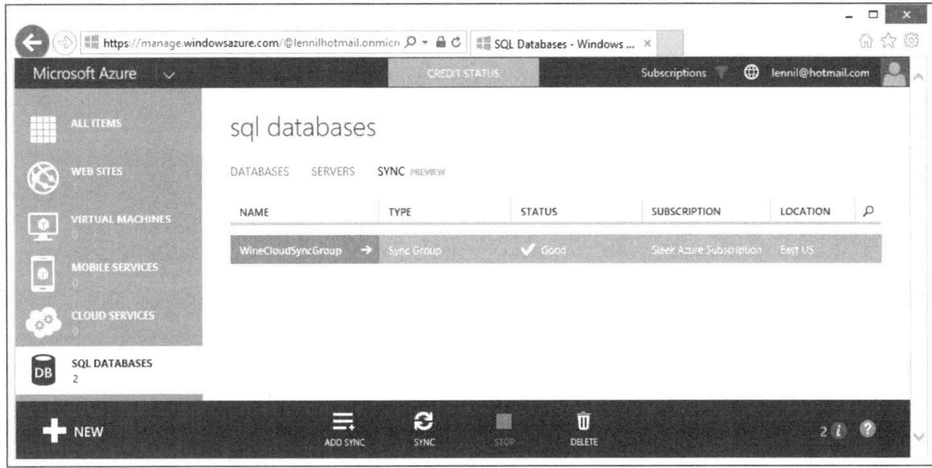

FIGURE 7-15 The SYNC page now showing the sync group with a Good status

At this point, SQL Data Sync has created tables in the new database exactly as they are defined in the existing database.

Important SQL Data Sync does more than just replicate the tables you chose to be synchronized; it also adds special objects to each database in the sync group (including on-premises SQL Server databases). To track incremental data changes, SQL Data Sync creates a change-tracking table for each table that is being synchronized, adds triggers to your base tables, and also creates some stored procedures for gathering and applying changes. Therefore, it is highly recommended that you first test SQL Data Sync in a nonproduction environment to ensure it does not have an adverse effect on your existing databases or applications.

Running a manual sync

SQL Data Sync has created tables in the new database, but it has not populated the tables with any rows yet (that is, it has copied only schema, but no data). This is because there has not yet been a synchronization pass, nor will there be until you either define an automated synchronization schedule or run a manual sync.

You'll create an automated schedule shortly, but right now you'll start by running a manual sync. To do so, follow these steps:

1. Click the SYNC button at the bottom of the page, as shown in Figure 7-16. After a few moments of processing, the sync group returns to its normal Good status. This means the synchronization was successful.

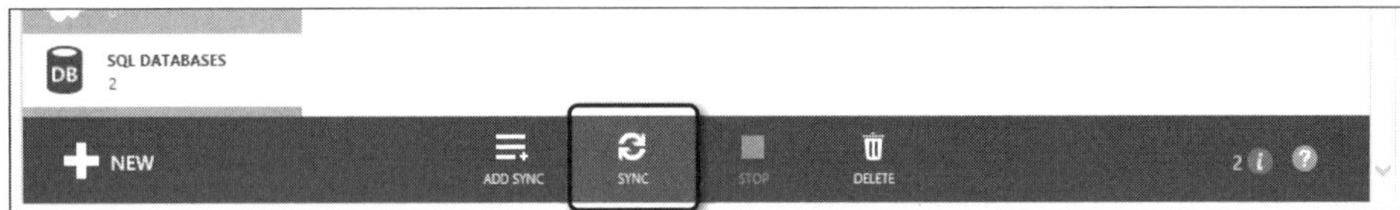

FIGURE 7-16 Running a manual sync

2. Wait a few moments for processing to complete, and click the sync group name *WineCloudSyncGroup*.
3. Click the LOGS link at the top of the page. The portal displays a message confirming that the databases synchronized successfully, as shown in Figure 7-17.

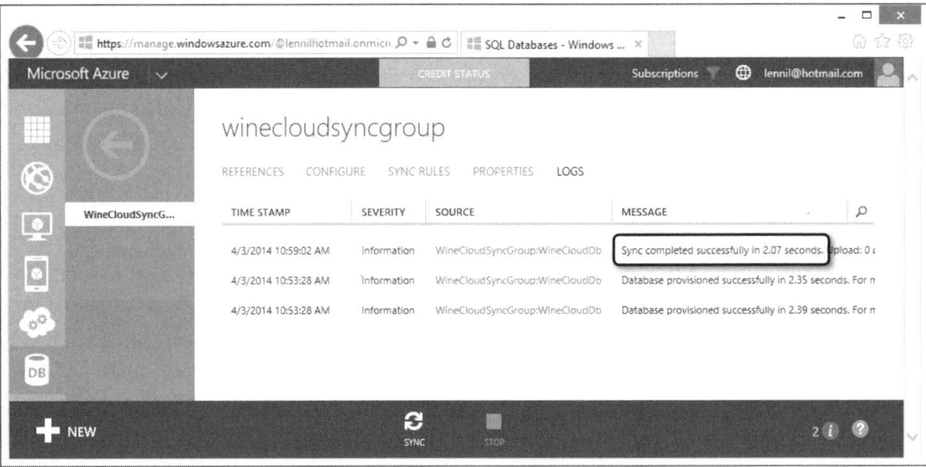

FIGURE 7-17 Viewing the sync group logs

Now you'll rely on your own two eyes to verify that, indeed, everything is working as it should. The best way to do that is to monitor both databases side by side as you change them individually, and then synchronize those changes. You can do this by opening two separate browser tabs to the SQL Database portal—one for each *WineCloudDb* database.

Note In Chapter 1, you already saw how to launch a new browser tab to the SQL Database portal. Although the following instructions are very similar to the ones we provided then, you might still want to refer to Chapter 1 because the instructions there include screen shots and details that are not repeated here.

To open the two SQL Database management portal tabs, follow these steps:

1. Click the back icon (the large back-pointing arrow) to return to the SQL DATABASES page.
2. Click the DATABASES link at the top of the page.
3. Click on the first *WineCloudDb* database.
4. Click the DASHBOARD link at the top of the page.
5. Scroll the page down a bit, and click on the MANAGE URL link in the quick glance section at the right of the page. This opens a new browser tab to the SQL Database portal's login page for the first *WineCloudDb* database.
6. On the login page, type the administrator user name and password, and click Log On. This takes you to the Summary page for the database.
7. Click the previous browser tab to return to the Microsoft Azure portal that just launched the new browser tab.
8. Click the back icon (the large back-pointing arrow) to return to the SQL DATABASES page.
9. Click on the second *WineCloudDb* database.
10. Click the DASHBOARD link at the top of the page.
11. Scroll down and click on the MANAGE URL link on the right to open another new browser tab to the SQL Database portal's login page for the second *WineCloudDb* database.
12. On the login page, type the administrator user name and password, and click Log On to go to the Summary page for the database.

Now that your environment is all set up, start by running the same simple query in each database to view and compare the contents of the *Wine* table. To run the queries, continue working in the current browser tab that's open to the SQL Database management portal for the second *WineCloudDb* database, and follow these steps:

1. Click New Query at the top of the page to open a new query window.
2. Click inside the code window, and type **SELECT * FROM Customer**.
3. Click Run at the top of the page. SQL Database executes the query and displays the results in the bottom portion of the query window, as shown in Figure 7-18.

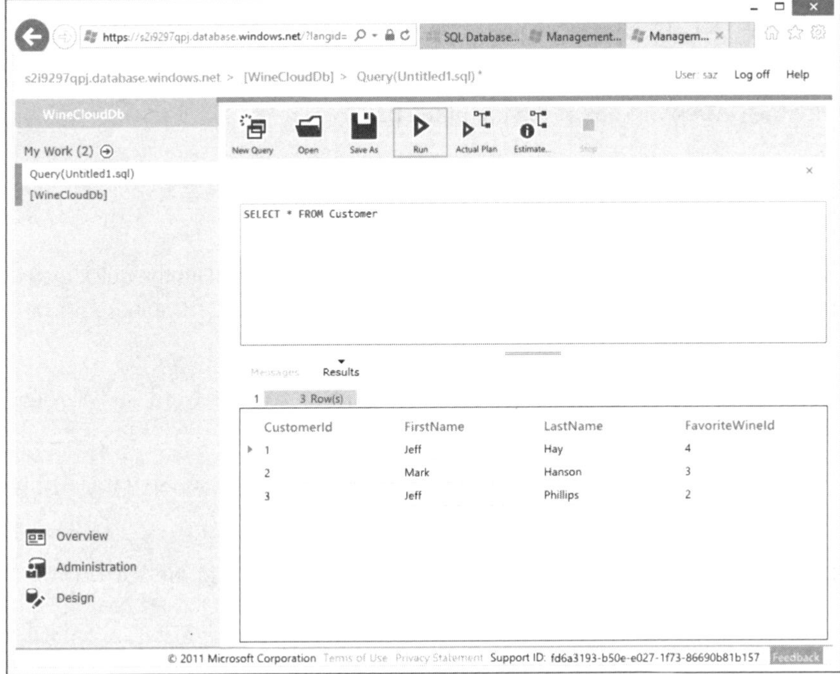

FIGURE 7-18 Querying the contents of the Customer table after the first manual sync

4. Click the browser tab that's open to the SQL Database management portal for the first *WineCloudDb* database.
5. Click New Query at the top of the page to open a new query window.
6. Click inside the code window, and type **SELECT * FROM Customer**.
7. Click Run at the top of the page. SQL Database executes the query and displays the results, which should appear identical to the results of the same query you ran in the other database, as just seen in Figure 7-18.

Receiving identical query results in both browser tabs is a clear indication that the first manual sync worked correctly and both databases are in sync. Now update some data on both sides and watch the databases sync up once again. To run the updates, continue working in the current browser tab and follow these steps:

1. On a new line below the SELECT statement you typed in the previous procedure, type **UPDATE Customer SET FavoriteWineId = 2 WHERE CustomerId = 1**.
2. Click and drag the mouse to highlight the complete UPDATE statement.

3. Click Run at the top of the page. SQL Database executes the statement and indicates that one row was affected. That is, the favorite wine ID for customer ID 1 (Jeff Hay) has changed from 4 to 2.
4. Click the browser tab that's open to the SQL Database management portal for the other *WineCloudDb* database.
5. On a new line below the SELECT statement, type **INSERT INTO Customer VALUES('Chris', 'Mayo', 3)**.
6. Click and drag the mouse to highlight the complete INSERT statement.
7. Click Run at the top of the page. SQL Database executes the statement and indicates that one row was affected. That is, a new customer row for Chris May was created with a favorite wine ID of 3.

You have now modified each database separately; one database has an updated customer, and the other has a new customer. Next, you will perform another manual sync operation and then confirm visually that each change has been synchronized properly to the other database. To do so, follow these steps:

1. Click the browser tab that's open to the Microsoft Azure portal. It should still be on the DASHBOARD page for one of the *WineCloudDb* databases from one of the earlier procedures.
2. Click the back icon (the large back-pointing arrow) to return to the SQL DATABASES page.
3. Click the SYNC link at the top of the page.
4. Click the SYNC button at the bottom of the page. After a few moments of processing, the sync group returns to its normal Good status.
5. Click the browser tab that's open to the SQL Database management portal for one of the *WineCloudDb* databases. (It doesn't matter which.)
6. Click and drag the mouse to highlight the complete SELECT statement.
7. Click Run at the top of the page. SQL Database executes the query and displays the results, which reflect both the updated and inserted customer changes, as shown in Figure 7-19.

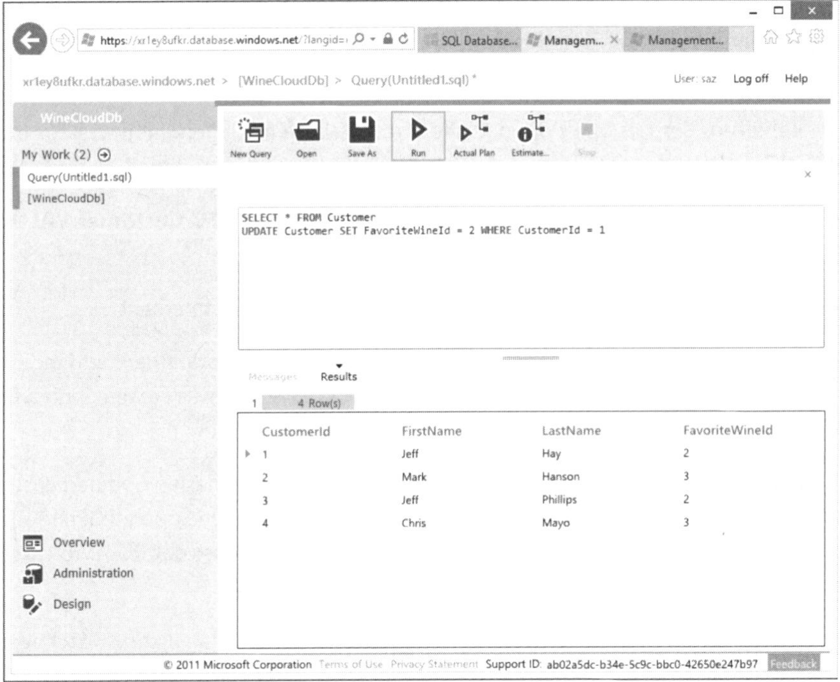

FIGURE 7-19 Querying the contents of the Customer table after a bi-directional manual sync

8. Click the browser tab that's open to the SQL Database management portal for the other *WineCloudDb* databases.

9. Click and drag the mouse to highlight the complete SELECT statement.

10. Click Run at the top of the page. SQL Database executes the query and displays the results, which should once again appear identical to the results of the same query you ran in the other database, as just seen in Figure 7-19.

Receiving identical query results again in both browser tabs now verifies that bi-directional synchronization is working. The next thing to learn about is *conflict resolution*. If the same customer row is modified differently in both databases at the same time (meaning, in between synchronizations, not necessarily simultaneously), what happens on the next synchronization?

Establishing conflict resolution

Whenever the same data is modified differently in multiple places, SQL Data Sync will always choose one version of the change to overwrite the other. Which version overwrites which is determined by the conflict resolution setting established when the sync group is created. The two available settings are Hub Wins (the default) and Client Wins.

When you created the sync group, you configured it to use a conflict resolution of Hub Wins. (You did this simply by accepting the default, as shown in Figure 7-7.) Thus, if a conflicting change is made to the same row in both the hub and the client database, the change made to the hub will override (and overwrite) the change made to the client.

When following this next procedure, you need to pay attention to which browser tab is open to the SQL Database management portal for the hub database, and which is open to the portal for the client database. You can distinguish them by the server names that appear in the upper left part of the portal page in each browser tab.

To demonstrate conflict resolution, follow these steps:

1. Click the browser tab that's open to the SQL Database management portal for the *WineCloudDb* hub database. (Check the server name in the upper left of the page.)
   a. In the code window, delete the existing INSERT or UPDATE statement (but leave the SELECT statement as-is).
   b. On a new line below the SELECT statement, type **UPDATE Customer SET LastName = 'Mayo-Hub' WHERE CustomerId = 4**.
   c. Click and drag the mouse to highlight the complete UPDATE statement.
   d. Click Run at the top of the page. SQL Database executes the statement and indicates that one row was affected.
2. Click the browser tab that's open to the SQL Database management portal for the other *WineCloudDb* database (the one on the new server).
   a. In the code window, delete the existing INSERT or UPDATE statement (but leave the SELECT statement as-is).
   b. On a new line below the SELECT statement, type **UPDATE Customer SET LastName = 'Mayo-Client' WHERE CustomerId = 4**.
   c. Click Run at the top of the page. SQL Database executes the statement and indicates that one row was affected—the same row you just modified in the hub database (with a different change).
3. Click the browser tab that's open to the Microsoft Azure portal. It should still be on the SYNC page from the manual sync you ran in the previous procedure.
4. Click the SYNC button at the bottom of the page. After a few moments of processing, the sync group returns to its normal Good status.
5. Click the browser tab that's open to the SQL Database management portal for the *WineCloudDb* hub database.
   a. Click and drag the mouse to highlight the complete SELECT statement.

b. Click Run at the top of the page. SQL Database executes the query and displays the results. As shown in Figure 7-20, the customer name change to Mayo-Hub has stuck; it has not been overwritten by the conflicting name change made to the same row in the client database.

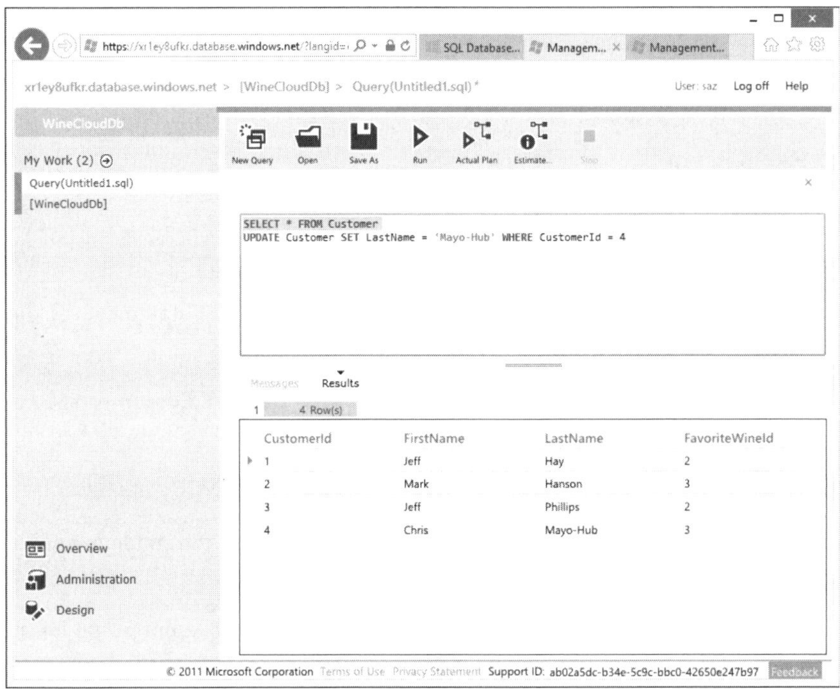

FIGURE 7-20 The hub change remains after a conflict with a client, using Hub Wins conflict resolution

6. Click the browser tab that's open to the SQL Database management portal for the other *WineCloudDb* database (the client database on the new server).

   a. Click and drag the mouse to highlight the complete SELECT statement.

   b. Click Run at the top of the page. SQL Database executes the query and displays the results. As shown in Figure 7-21, the customer name change to Mayo-Client has been overwritten by the conflicting name change (Mayo-Hub) made to the same row in the hub database.

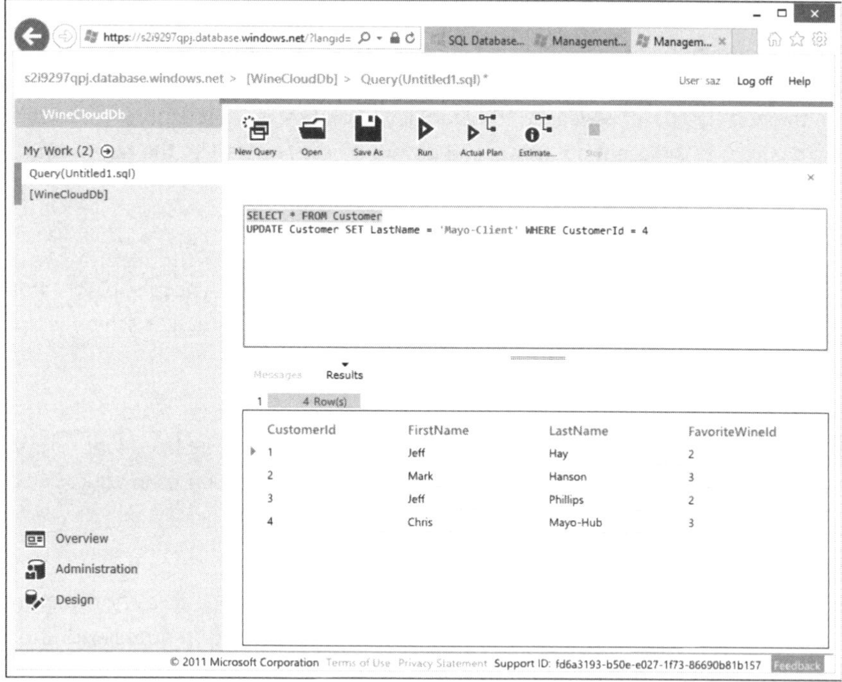

FIGURE 7-21 The client change is overwritten after a conflict with a hub, using Hub Wins conflict resolution

If the conflict resolution had been set to Client Wins, the opposite would have occurred; the change made to the client database would have remained on the client, and the change made to the hub would have been overwritten to reflect the client change (that is, the customer would have the name Mayo-Client in both databases).

When a sync group has only one client database in it, the behavior with Hub Wins or Client Wins is absolutely predictable, and it will always work as we just described. But once two or more client databases are involved, and there are conflicting changes across multiple clients (but not the hub), conflict-resolution behavior cannot be predicted, regardless of the setting:

- In the case of Hub Wins, the first client change that gets written to the hub is kept. Any conflicting data changes made in any of the other clients are discarded. Then the change written to the hub by the first client is propagated out to all the other clients.
- In the case of Client Wins, conflicting data changes made in all clients are written to the hub, each one overwriting the previous one, so that the changes written by the last client are then propagated out to all the other clients.

In either case, the winner cannot be predicted, because the order in which client changes are written to the hub is nondeterministic and can vary from one synchronization pass to another. The only predictable resolution case when multiple clients are involved is when a conflicting change is made in the hub database as well *and* the conflict resolution is set to Hub Wins. In this case, conflicting changes in the client databases will always be overwritten by the hub change.

Creating an automated sync schedule

Once you have run several manual syncs and are satisfied with your sync group, you won't want to sync manually any more. At this point, you will want to let SQL Data Sync schedule automated synchronization passes automatically.

Fortunately, SQL Data Sync supports a simple scheduling mechanism. Automation is either turned on or off. If automation is turned on, the schedule frequency can range from (approximately) five minutes to one month. This means the closest you can keep the databases in your sync group up to date by is five minutes.

Note We say *approximately* parenthetically, because the service does not guarantee precise timing. For example, you might request to run every 10 minutes and find occasionally that 11 minutes elapse between two passes.

To set an automated sync schedule that runs every 10 minutes, follow these steps:

1. Click the browser tab that's open to the Microsoft Azure portal. It should still be on the SYNC page from the manual sync you ran in previous procedures.
2. Click the sync group name *WineCloudSyncGroup*.
3. Click the CONFIGURE link at the top of the page.
4. For AUTOMATIC SYNC, click ON.
5. For SYNC FREQUENCY, type **10**.
6. Click anywhere on the page. This is necessary to shift focus away from the SYNC FREQUENCY text box, which causes the SAVE button to appear at the bottom of the page, as shown in Figure 7-22.

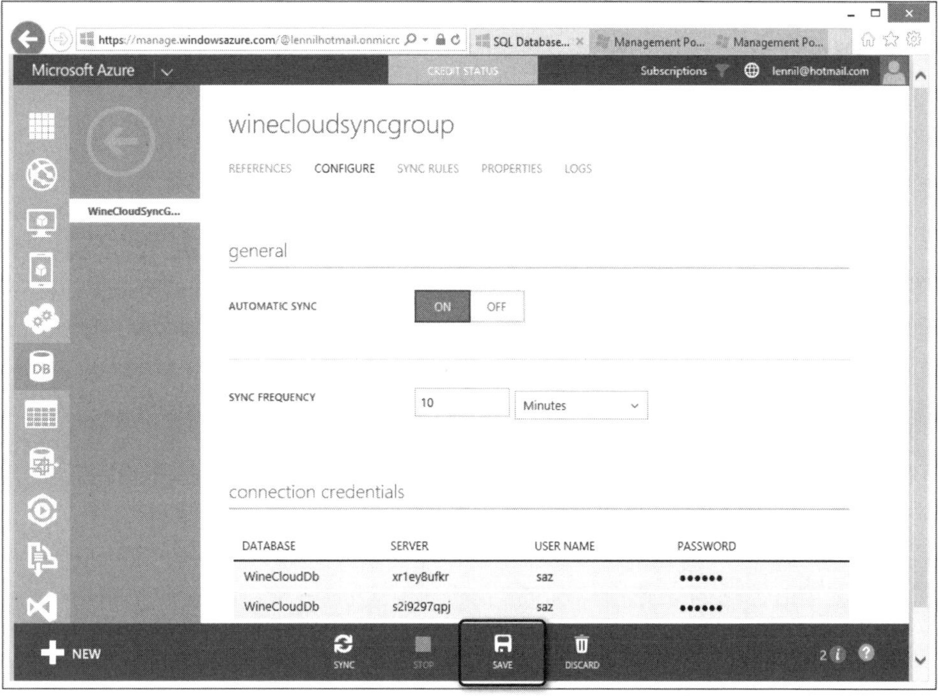

FIGURE 7-22 Configuring an automated sync schedule to run every 10 minutes

7. Click the SAVE button.

The schedule is now set. To test the schedule, follow these steps:

1. Click the browser tab that's open to the SQL Database management portal for one of the *WineCloudDb* databases. (It doesn't matter which one.)
2. In the code window, delete the existing INSERT or UPDATE statement (but leave the SELECT statement as-is).
3. On a new line below the SELECT statement, type **UPDATE Customer SET LastName = 'Mayo-Auto' WHERE CustomerId = 4**.
4. Take a break for 10 minutes (or more). Have a glass of wine (or two). You've earned it!
5. Run the SELECT statement in each of the SQL Database management portal browser tabs open to the hub and the client, and notice how the customer name is now Mayo-Auto in both databases.

During your 10-minute break, an automatic synchronization pass ran, which copied the change to the other database. At this point, you can leave things alone and let the service synchronize every 10 minutes automatically, although you can still sync manually any time you want to, of course. You can also change the interval or disable automatic synchronization as desired. Every synchronization pass (whether manual or automated) is logged and can be seen by clicking on the LOGS link (as you saw in Figure 7-17).

Creating a local SQL Server database

Now that you've got the synchronization working between two SQL Databases in the cloud, you're ready to add a local on-premises SQL Server database to the sync group. This requires the local installation of a special agent service that you can register on-premises databases with. The SQL Data Sync service in the cloud will gain access to those on-premises databases through the local agent service. Of course, this requires a local SQL Server database.

If you have access to a SQL Server instance you can create a local database on, you can use that SQL Server instance. Otherwise, you will need to install the SQL Server Express edition to host a local database so that you can continue following along. A step-by-step procedure for doing so can be found in the Introduction, in the section "Installing SQL Server Express Edition."

> **Note** This chapter assumes you are using the SQL Server Express edition for your local SQL Server database, which has an instance name of *.\sqlexpress*. If you are using another edition, you must replace the instance name *.\sqlexpress* specified in the instructions with the name of the instance you are using. For example, if you are running a primary instance of the SQL Server Developer edition on your local machine, you can simply specify the dot (.) symbol or *localhost*. If you are running a named instance on your local machine, append a backslash followed by the name of the instance (for example, *.\myinstance* or *localhost\myinstance*).

In the next procedure, you will create a new database on your local SQL Server instance called *WineLocalDb*. The local database will start out completely empty, but it will soon become a replica of the other *WineCloudDb* databases once you add it to the sync group. (This is the same approach you took earlier when you created the second *WineCloudDb* database and added it to the sync group.)

To create the local database, follow these steps:

1. Start Visual Studio 2013.
2. If the SQL Server Object Explorer is not visible, click the VIEW menu and choose SQL Server Object Explorer.
3. In the SQL Server Object Explorer, right-click SQL Server and choose Add SQL Server to display the Connect To Server dialog.
4. For Server Name, type **.\sqlexpress** (or the name of your local SQL Server instance).
5. For Authentication, choose Windows Authentication. Or, if your local SQL Server instance is configured not to support Windows Authentication, choose SQL Server Authentication and

supply valid credentials for Login and Password. The C
similar to Figure 7-23.

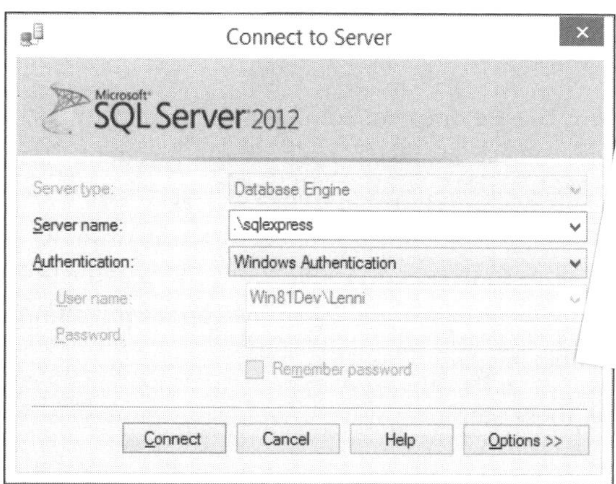

FIGURE 7-23 Connecting to a local SQL Server Express edition instance

6. Click Connect. The local instance now appears as a collapsed node in the SQL Server Object Explorer.
7. Expand the new node in the SQL Server Object Explorer.
8. Right-click Databases, and choose Add New Database.
9. Type **WineLocalDb** and press Enter. The new database now appears in the SQL Server Object Explorer, as shown in Figure 7-24.

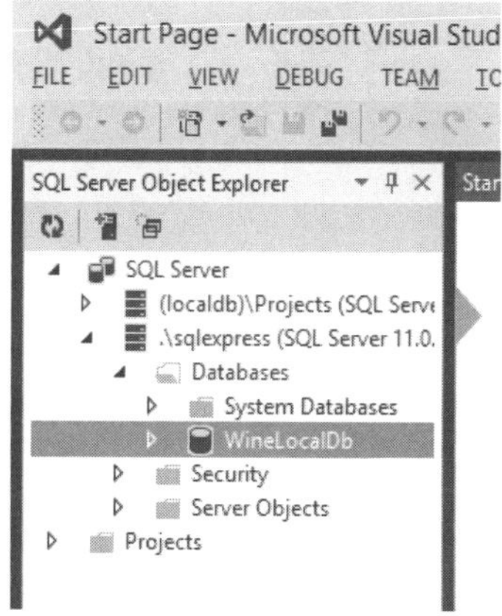

FIGURE 7-24 Creating the *WineLocalDb* database on a local SQL Server instance

You now have an empty on-premises database named *WineLocalDb*. Next, you will configure a sync agent so that this database can participate in the sync group.

c agent

mmunicates with on-premises SQL Server databases through the client agent—a vice that mediates interaction between the local database and the sync group running Azure.

his approach, the SQL Data Sync service does not communicate directly with the local ase; instead, all local-to-cloud communications take place through the agent. This means that SQL Data Sync service in the cloud can access your on-premises SQL Server databases, even if hey are located behind a firewall (which is typically the case in production environments). When the service communicates with the agent, it does so using encrypted connections and a unique token or *agent key*. The SQL Server databases authenticate the agent using the connection string and agent key, which provides a high level of security.

To install the local sync agent, follow these steps:

1. Log in to the Microsoft Azure portal (or return to the browser window where the Microsoft Azure portal is running, if it's still open).
2. Click SQL DATABASES in the vertical navigation pane on the left.
3. Click the ADD SYNC button at the bottom of the page, and then choose New Sync Agent, as shown in Figure 7-25.

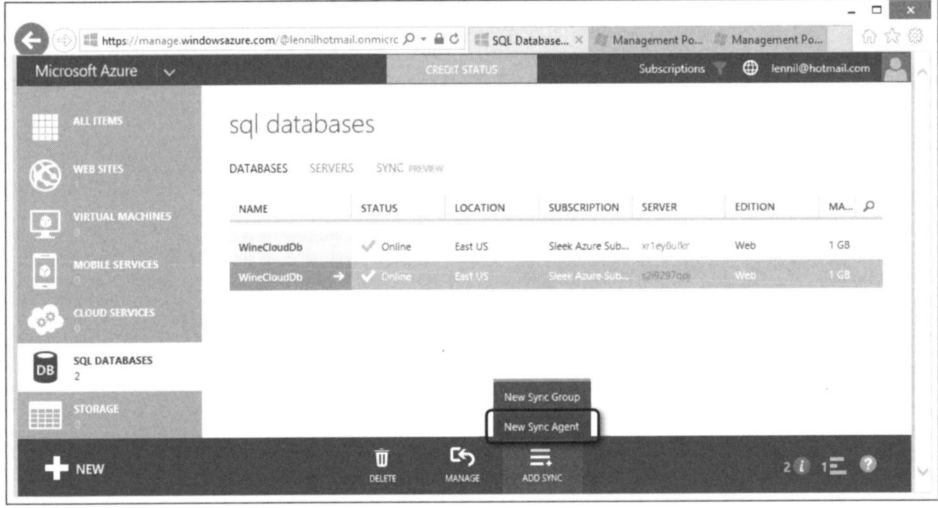

FIGURE 7-25 Creating a sync agent

4. Click the Install One Here link, as shown in Figure 7-26. This opens a new browser tab to a download page for the sync agent.

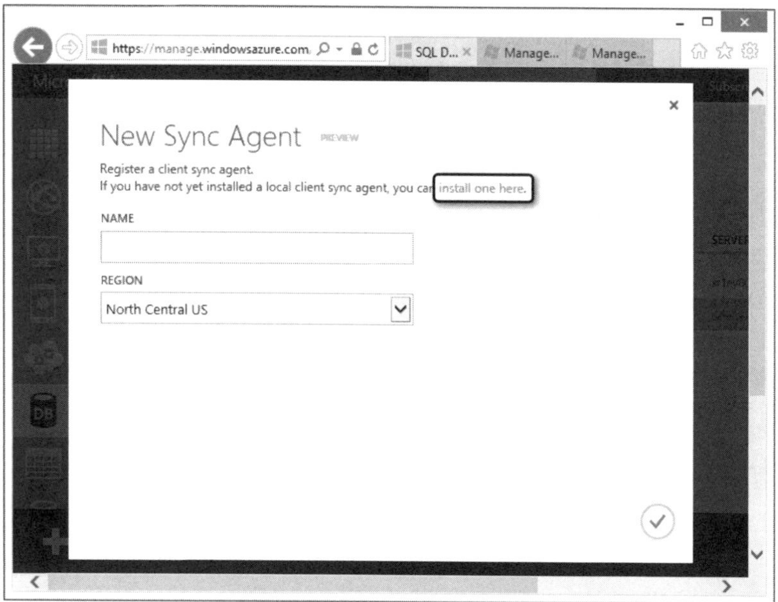

FIGURE 7-26 Using the New Sync Agent dialog link to install a new local sync agent

5. Click the large orange Download button.
6. Select *SQLDataSyncAgent-Preview-ENU.msi*, as shown in Figure 7-27.

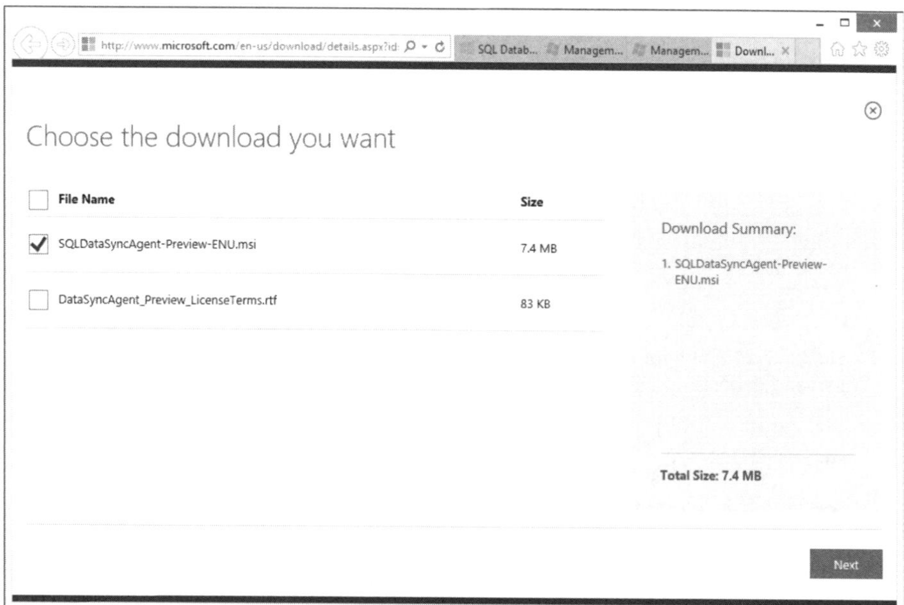

FIGURE 7-27 Selecting the SQL Data Sync Agent download

7. Click Next.

8. If you receive a pop-up warning, click Allow Once, as shown in Figure 7-28.

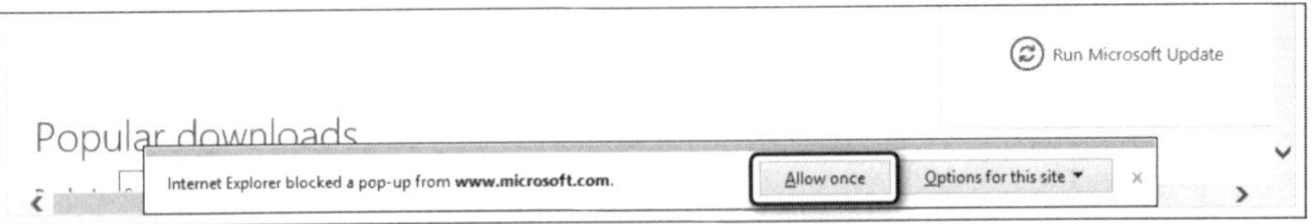

FIGURE 7-28 Temporarily allowing pop-ups to enable the download, if necessary

9. When prompted to run or save the file, choose Run. This downloads and starts the Microsoft SQL Data Sync Agent Preview Setup Wizard:

   a. On the Welcome page, click Next.

   b. On the License Agreement And Privacy Information page, click I Agree and then click Next.

   c. Type a local Windows user name and password for the account that the agent service should run under. The user name should include the local domain or machine name followed by a backslash, as shown in Figure 7-29.

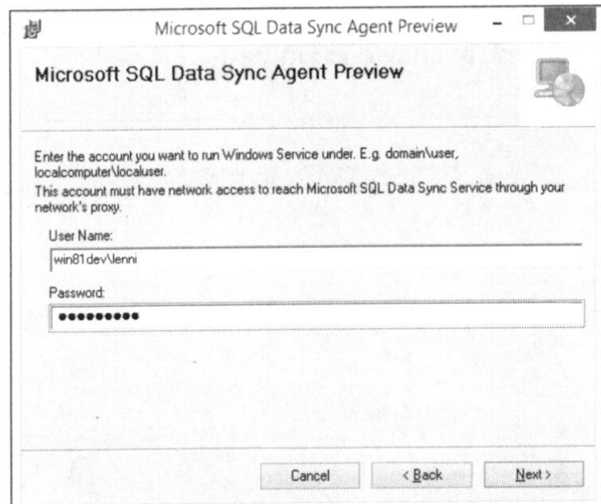

FIGURE 7-29 Configuring the Windows account that the local agent will use to access on-premises SQL Server databases.

   d. Click Next.

   e. On the Select Installation Folder page, click Next.

   f. On the Confirm Installation Page, click Next to begin the installation.

   g. If the User Account Control dialog appears, click Yes.

   h. When the installation completes, click Close.

The local agent service is now installed. In a moment, you will register the on-premises *WineLocalDb* database with the local agent. But first you need to complete the agent configuration on Microsoft Azure.

To configure the agent on Microsoft Azure, follow these steps:

1. Return to the browser tab that's still open to the Microsoft Azure portal on the New Sync Agent page.
2. For NAME, type **WineSyncAgent**.
3. In the REGION drop-down list, choose the same region as the time zone your local machine is set to. The page should appear similar to Figure 7-30.

Important You will not be able to register local databases with a sync agent located in a different region.

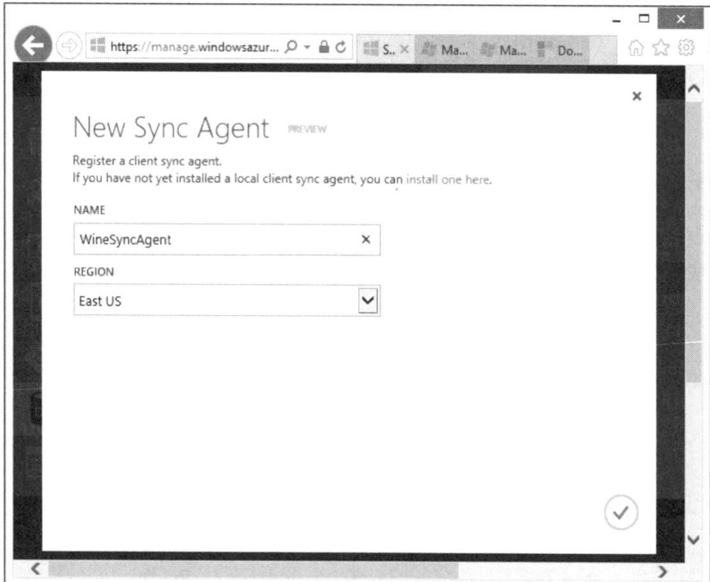

FIGURE 7-30 Configuring the sync agent on Microsoft Azure

4. Click the checkmark icon in the lower-right side of the dialog to complete the settings.
5. After a few moments, the agent is created and appears offline, as shown in Figure 7-31.

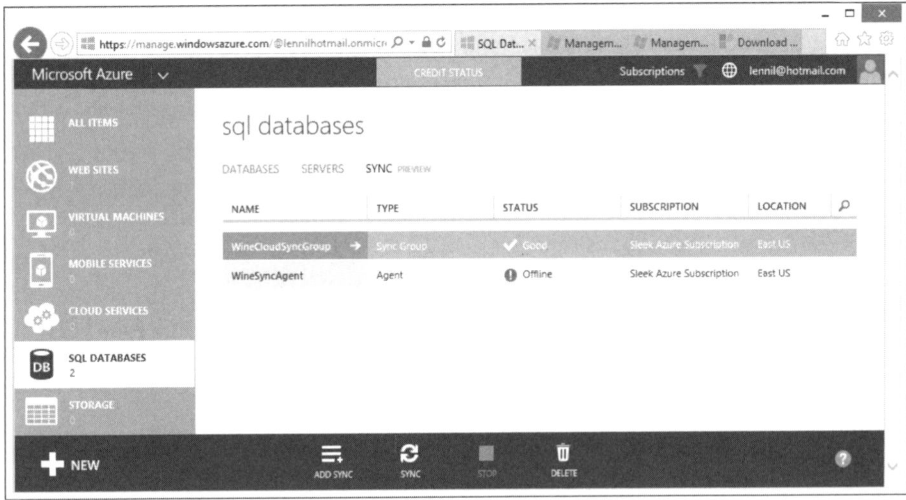

FIGURE 7-31 Viewing the new agent created on Microsoft Azure

6. Click *WineSyncAgent*. This displays the local databases registered with the agent, which is currently an empty list.
7. Click the MANAGE KEY button at the bottom of the page.
8. Click the green Generate button.
9. Click the clipboard copy button to the right of the generated key, as shown in Figure 7-32. (If you are prompted for clipboard access by Internet Explorer, click Allow Access.)

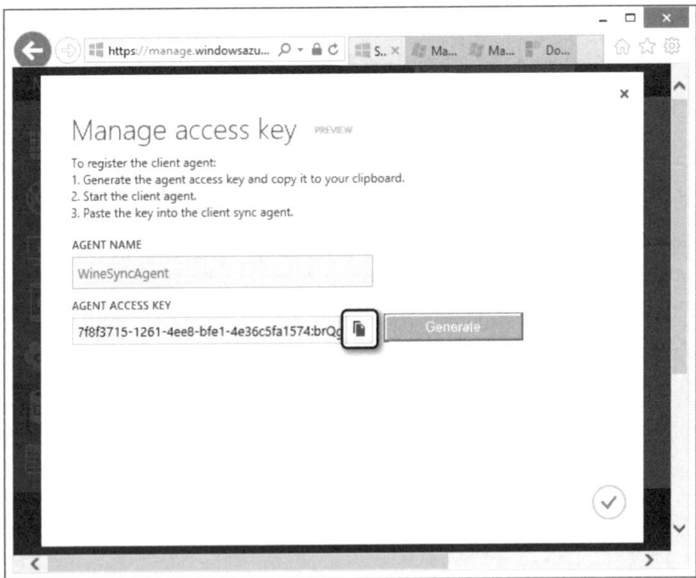

FIGURE 7-32 Generating an access key that can be used to register local SQL Server databases with the agent

Now that the agent access key has been copied to the clipboard, the last step is to register the local database with the sync agent. To do so, follow these steps:

1. From the Windows Start screen, launch Microsoft SQL Data Sync Agent Preview. You can either scroll through the tiles to find it or just type **data sync agent** to run an app search, and then click on the Microsoft SQL Data Sync Agent Preview tile, as shown in Figure 7-33.

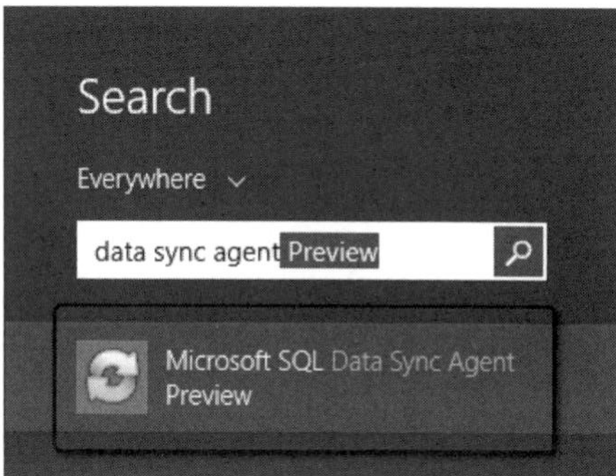

FIGURE 7-33 Launching the SQL Data Sync agent from the Windows 8 Start screen.

2. If the User Account Control dialog appears, click Yes.
3. Click the Submit Agent Key button .
4. Right-click in the Agent Key text box, and choose Paste. This pastes the key generated on the portal, as shown in Figure 7-34.

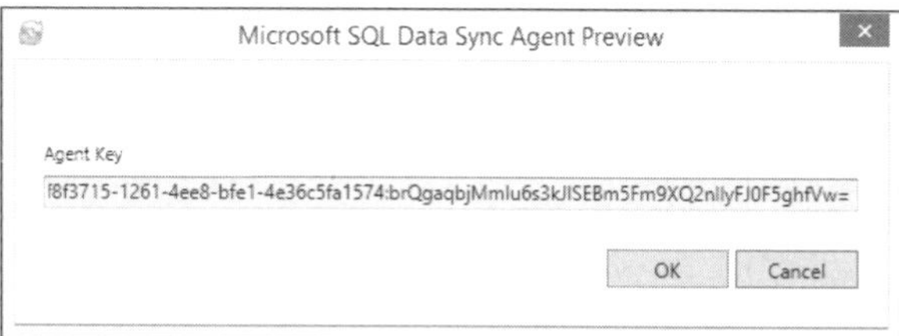

FIGURE 7-34 Providing the service-generated access key to the local agent service

5. Click OK.
6. Click the Ping Sync Service button. You should receive a message dialog stating that the agent successfully pinged SQL Data Sync, which you can close by clicking OK.
7. Click Register to display the SQL Server Configuration dialog.
   a. For Authentication, choose Windows Authentication. Or, if your local SQL Server instance does not support Windows Authentication, choose SQL Server Authentication and supply valid credentials for Login and Password.
   b. For Server Name, type **.\sqlexpress** (or the name of your local SQL Server instance).

c. For Database, type **WineLocalDb**. The SQL Server Configuration dialog should appear similar to Figure 7-35.

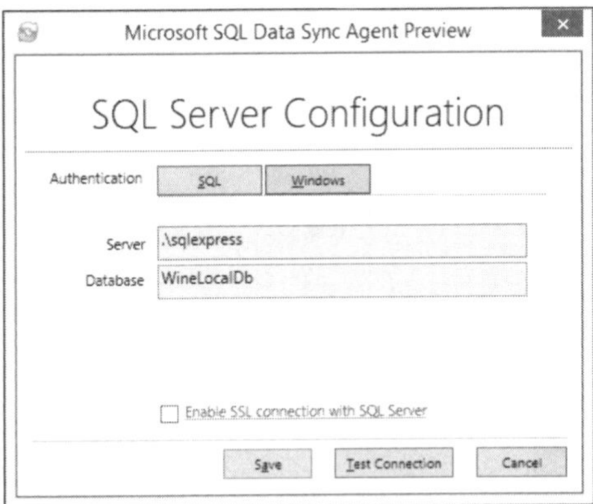

FIGURE 7-35 The SQL Server Configuration dialog, which is used to register a local SQL Server database with Microsoft Azure SQL Data Sync

d. Click Save. The database is registered with the local agent service, as shown in Figure 7-36.

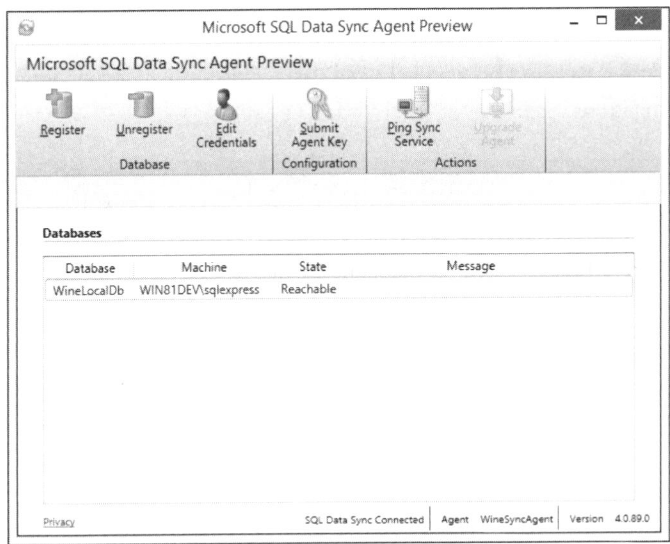

FIGURE 7-36 Registering an on-premises SQL Server database with the local SQL Data Sync agent service

8. Return to the browser tab that's still open to the Microsoft Azure portal on the Manage Access Key page.

9. Click the checkmark icon in the lower-right side of the dialog to close the Manage Access Key page.

10. On the *WineSyncAgent* page, the portal now displays the *WineLocalDb* databases registered with the agent, as shown in Figure 7-37.

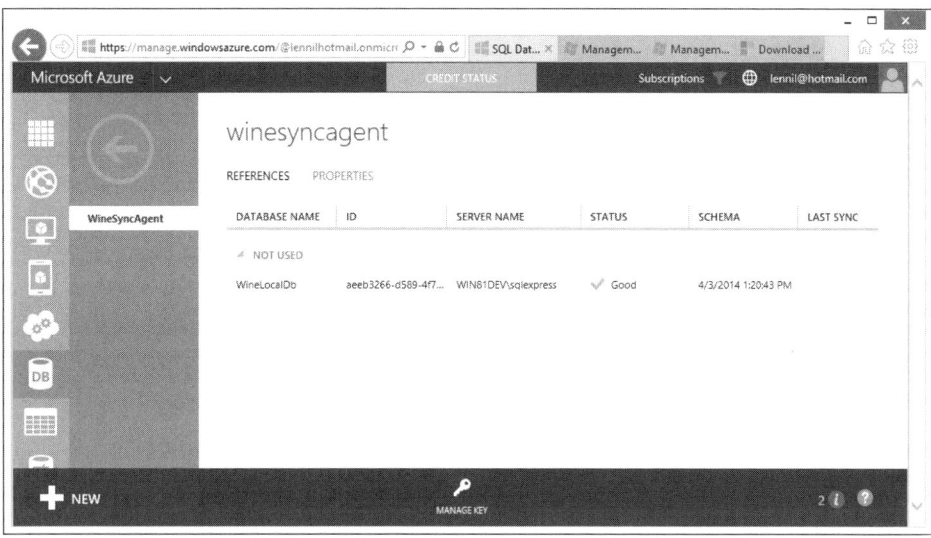

FIGURE 7-37 Viewing on-premises SQL Server databases registered with the agent

Now that the on-premises *WineLocalDb* database is registered with the agent, it's easy to add it to the sync group. To do so, follow these steps:

1. Click the back icon (the large back-pointing arrow) to return to the SYNC page. As shown in Figure 7-38, the sync agent status has now transitioned from Offline to Online. (It might be necessary to refresh the page by pressing F5 to see the transitioned status.)

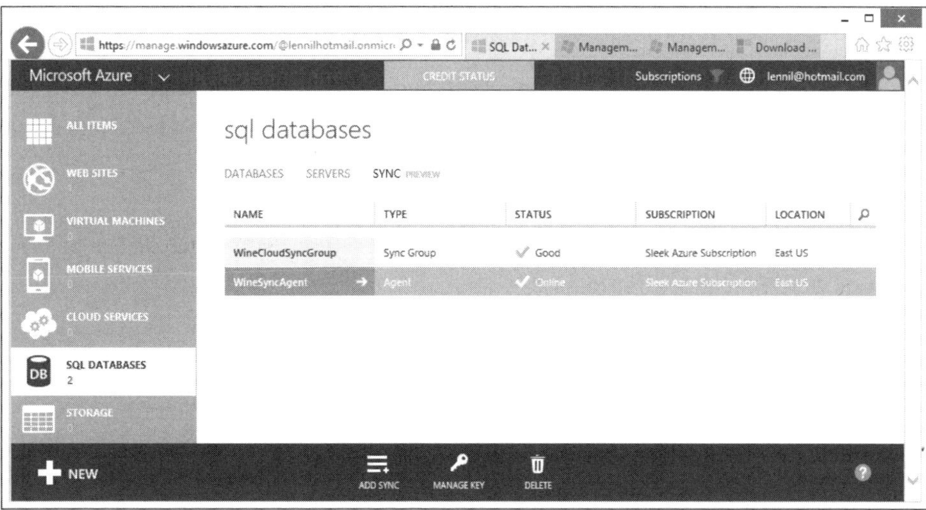

FIGURE 7-38 The *WineSyncAgent* now appears online in the Microsoft Azure portal

2. Click *WineCloudSyncGroup*. This displays the reference databases of the sync group, which still currently includes just the two *WineCloudDb* databases in the cloud.

3. Click the ADD button at the bottom of the page to display the Add A Reference Database dialog.

4. On the Add A Reference Database page, do the following:

    a. For REFERENCE DATABASE, choose the *WineLocalDb* database that appears beneath SQL Server Databases - WineSyncAgent, as shown in Figure 7-39.

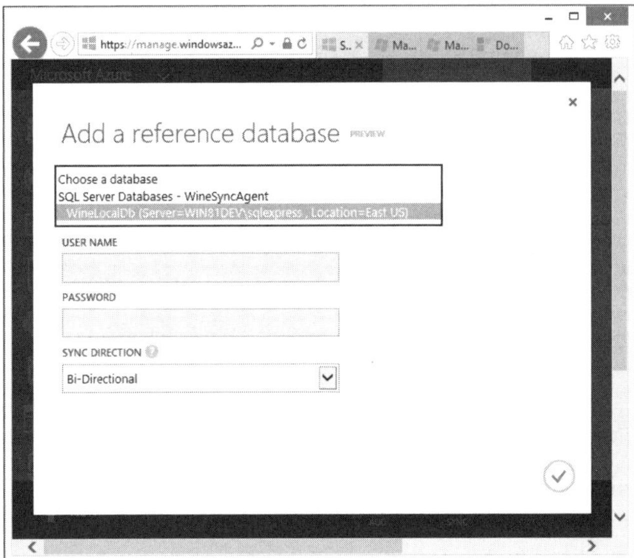

FIGURE 7-39 Selecting the on-premises database registered with the agent for inclusion in the sync group.

    b. If the local database was registered using Windows Authentication, no credentials are required and the USER NAME and PASSWORD text boxes will be disabled. Otherwise, enter the user name and password you supplied when you registered the local database in the previous procedure's step 7.

    c. Leave the SYNC DIRECTION at its default setting, Bi-Directional. The page should look similar to Figure 7-40.

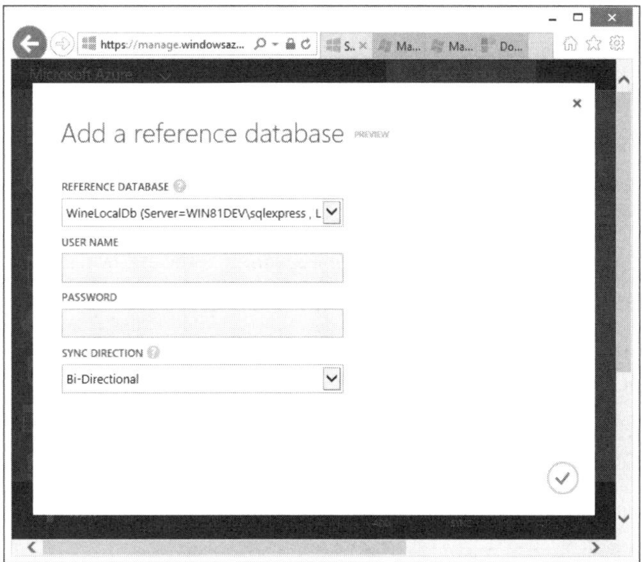

FIGURE 7-40 Adding the on-premises database to the sync group

   d. Click the checkmark "finish" button to complete the settings.

5. Click the SAVE button at the bottom of the page. After a few moments of processing, the database is added to the sync group, and all three databases (the two *WineCloudDb* databases and the one on-premises *WineLocalDb* database) are designated with a status of Good, as shown in Figure 7-41.

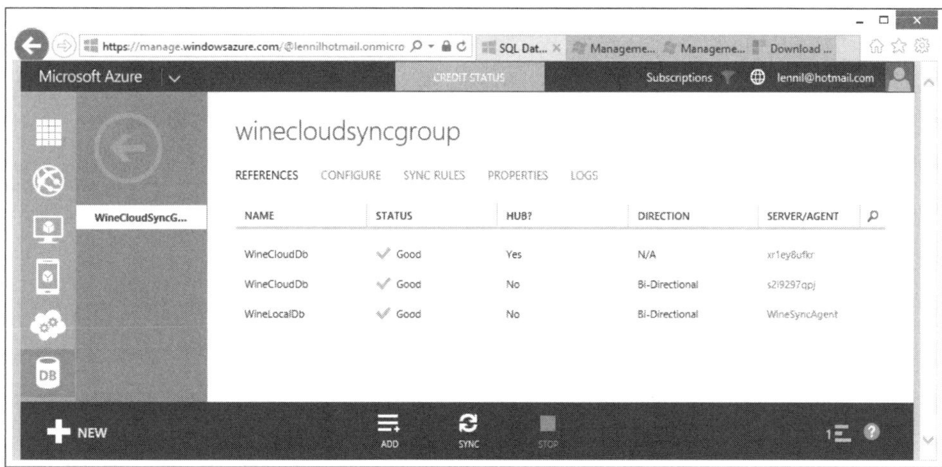

FIGURE 7-41 The sync group configured with two Microsoft Azure SQL Databases and one on-premises SQL Server database

6. Now either wait approximately 10 minutes (the automatic sync interval you configured for the sync group) or click the SYNC button at the bottom of the page if you'd rather not wait. This updates the entire sync group, which includes the local SQL Server database you just added to the sync group.

7. Switch back to Visual Studio, which should still be open from when you created the empty *WineLocalDb* database in a previous step.

8. In the SQL Server Object Explorer, expand the *WineLocalDb* database node, and then expand the *Tables* node nested beneath the database node.

9. Right-click the *dbo.Customer* table, and choose View Data. As shown in Figure 7-42, the table now contains all the customer data pulled in from the *WineCloudDb* hub database.

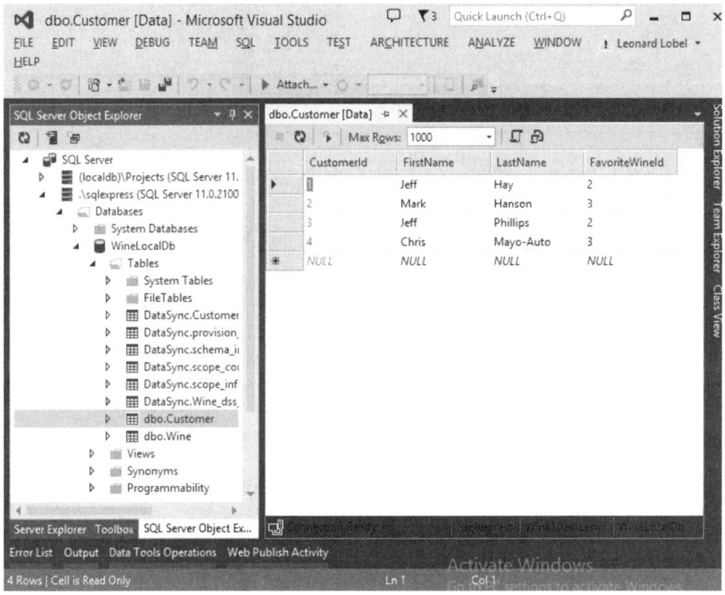

FIGURE 7-42 The on-premises SQL Server database now containing the customer data synchronized from the *WineCloudDb* hub database

Congratulations! You just created a fully functional sync group that synchronizes data bi-directionally between multiple SQL Databases on Microsoft Azure and an on-premises SQL Server database running locally. The client databases (the second *WineCloudDb* database and the on-premises *WineLocalDb* database) are both configured for bi-directional synchronization, so any changes made in any of the databases in the sync group (including the hub) will be replicated automatically across all the other databases.

Furthermore, because the sync group's conflict resolution is set to Hub Wins, changes made to rows in the hub database will overwrite changes made to the same rows in any of the client databases if those changes are made within the same sync interval. And, as explained in the section "Establishing Conflict Resolution," if conflicting changes are made across only client databases but not the hub database, the first client change that gets written to the hub is the one that will be used to update the rest of the sync group; conflicting data changes made in any of the other clients will be discarded. Take some time now to experiment with the sync group by making changes to the hub and client databases (including conflicting changes), and then view the effects of synchronization (either by waiting approximately 10 minutes or forcing a manual sync between changes).

Pitfalls and best practices

We conclude this chapter by discussing a few points to keep in mind when working with SQL Data Sync. There are several things you can do to ensure you gain the best possible performance, starting with choosing the location of your cloud databases. The geographic location where your SQL Databases are hosted can impact both the efficiency and cost of the otherwise free SQL Data Sync service. To minimize latency, locate your SQL Database servers in data centers as physically close as possible to your on-premises SQL Server database locations.

Next, limit your synchronization to include just the items you need to sync. As you saw, SQL Data Sync doesn't require the entire database to participate in a sync group, so you should always select the fewest tables and columns possible when you configure your dataset. This practice improves performance by reducing the overall payload of a synchronization pass.

Another consideration to bear in mind is the frequency with which a synchronization pass occurs. If a pass attempts to synchronize a sync group that has not yet completed a prior synchronization, the attempt will fail. When planning a schedule, take care that you set the interval sufficiently large enough to ensure that synchronization completes before the next synchronization pass starts. Also, remember that the intervals are approximate, and that the finest automation schedule you can implement is once every five minutes.

The sync schedule can affect your SQL Database costs as well. Although at the time of this writing Microsoft offers SQL Data Sync as a free service, SQL Database fees are charged according to the amount of data moved out of a data center. To minimize costs, you should consider dividing data into separate sync groups according to the frequency with which the data changes. Volatile data should be synchronized at a higher frequency than static or lookup data. Partitioning sync groups in this way allows you to configure an optimal schedule that helps reduce costs by sending data less frequently.

One pitfall to avoid when setting up multiple sync groups is a condition known as a *sync loop*. A sync loop occurs when a change in a record in one sync group is rewritten to the same record by a second sync group, similar to a circular reference. This highly undesirable condition can potentially enter an infinite loop and consume enough resources to significantly degrade performance. Furthermore, you will pay fees for moving data into and out of SQL Database unnecessarily. You can avoid sync loops in a few ways:

- Design your sync groups such that a loop cannot occur; that is, don't let the same table be synchronized by two different sync groups.
- Specify a sync direction such that a loop condition cannot exist.

Finally, be aware of the standard security measures taken by the SQL Data Sync service:

- Data is encrypted whenever it is transmitted.
- All SQL Database connection points use SQL authentication.
- SQL Database and SQL Server connections are always encrypted.
- Encrypted SQL Server connections are further secured using an agent key.

Summary

This chapter taught you all about SQL Data Sync, a Microsoft Azure service that provides automatic data replication across any number of SQL Databases hosted on Microsoft Azure as well as local SQL Server databases hosted on-premises.

We began by explaining the *hub-and-spoke* architecture upon which SQL Data Sync is based, and then described the variety of scenarios in which the service can be configured. This includes one-way replication from data mastered in SQL Server on-premises to SQL Databases on Microsoft Azure, one-way replication in the reverse direction to pull data populated in Microsoft Azure SQL Database down to an on-premises SQL Server database, and full bi-directional synchronization across SQL Databases hosted in multiple Microsoft Azure data centers and local SQL Server databases hosted in multiple on-premises locations.

With that foundation laid, you then created a sync group to synchronize between two Microsoft Azure SQL Databases in the cloud, learned about the two different conflict-resolution strategies (Hub Wins and Client Wins), and set up an automated schedule to keep the databases in sync on a regular basis. Finally, you installed and configured a sync agent and registered a local on-premises SQL Server database with the sync group to achieve complete two-way synchronization between the local SQL Server database and the SQL Databases in the cloud.

CHAPTER 8

Designing and tuning for scalability and high performance

—Eric Boyd

When developing applications and systems intended for real use, performance is an important consideration. Today's users have short attention spans and need immediate results, which means their applications must be responsive and deliver results quickly. Data lies at the core of many systems, and often that data is stored in relational databases like SQL Database. Optimizing data access can often provide significant improvements and benefits to application performance.

In this chapter, you will optimize and tune database performance for Microsoft Azure SQL Database. This includes optimizing execution speed and performance, as well as reliability. To demonstrate these concepts throughout this chapter, a reference application is needed. In the second section, "Creating a RESTful Web API," you will create an ASP.NET Web API that works with data from SQL Database using both ADO.NET and Entity Framework (EF). Then you will improve the reliability and performance of this Web API by managing database connections and connection errors, reducing latency and considering other optimizations like using the most appropriate storage service for your data. Later in the chapter, you learn how to scale up SQL Database using SQL Database Premium. The last sections of the chapter guide you through scaling your SQL Database out with a partitioning strategy known as *sharding*.

Entity Framework is a Microsoft data access framework that simplifies mapping database objects to .NET objects. EF uses ADO.NET internally for data access, but the additional object relational mapping that EF performs adds performance overhead. When optimizing data access performance, one common technique is to reduce the number of abstractions between your application code and databases. Using lower-level data access technologies like ADO.NET directly often improves data access performance. In addition to performance optimization, many existing applications use ADO.NET for data access. Therefore, both ADO.NET and EF are discussed in this chapter.

Note This chapter uses EF and Web API to demonstrate performance concepts. Chapter 10, "Building cloud solutions," delves into much more detail on both of these important technologies.

Achieving high performance in the cloud

Virtually infinite amounts of hardware and computing resources is one of the major value propositions for moving to the cloud. While the quantity of computing resources owned and managed by a cloud vendor is ultimately finite, at peak loads, most organizations would demand only a small fraction of the available resources. However, most applications, especially typical enterprise applications, are not designed in a way that can make use of this large pool of hardware. Most applications are not designed to scale horizontally (often called *scaling out*)—that is, to chunk up and distribute the load across many servers and storage nodes. Instead, most applications depend on having control of the hardware and scaling vertically (often called *scaling up*)—that is, to increase the capacity and performance of centralized computing resources by purchasing larger and more powerful servers and storage devices.

Cloud vendors such as Microsoft provide some ability to scale up. At the time of this writing, Microsoft Azure compute instances range in size from a shared 1-GHz CPU with 768 MB of RAM to a 16-by-2.6 GHz CPU instance with 112 GB of RAM. The Microsoft Azure Platform as a Service (PaaS) services, such as SQL Database, also have some ability to scale up. For example, a single SQL Database can range in size from a 100-MB database to 150 GB, and with the Preview availability of SQL Database Premium, the computing resources for a single SQL Database server can be scaled. (You will learn more about SQL Database Premium in the section "Scaling up SQL Database.")

Microsoft Azure provides some capability to scale computing resources up; unfortunately, there will always be a physical limit and upper bound to the amount of computing capacity you can get from a single resource, whether that's a server, storage device, or service. To scale big, you must scale out. And to scale out, your applications must be architected in a way that allows them to be distributed across multiple instances of computing hardware.

In addition to scalability, because you don't control the hardware configuration that SQL Database is running on, you can't scale the server hardware up with the same control as you could in your own data center, and because SQL Database is a multitenant service with multiple customers sharing the same physical compute resources, the performance characteristics will quite likely be different than that of your own private data center. As a result, you might have to tune database performance differently than you would in your own data center.

Creating a RESTful web API

To get started, you'll create the *WineCloudDb* database with a *Wine* table and a *Customer* table. You will then create a new ASP.NET Web Application project. The ASP.NET Web Application will contain ASP.NET Web APIs using ADO.NET for the *Customer Web API* and Entity Framework for the *Wine Web API*. Throughout the chapter, you will build upon this project as you learn how to design and optimize for performance, reliability, and scalability.

Creating the sample database

For the Web APIs in this chapter, you will use the script shown in Listing 8-1 to create *WineCloudDb* and populate it with a few wines and customers. Then you will create ASP.NET Web APIs that return wines and customers.

Note In other chapters, the *WineCloudDb* database included *Wine*, *Customer*, and *Order* tables. This chapter does not make use of the *Order* table, which is why it is omitted here.

LISTING 8-1 Script to create the sample *WineCloudDb* database for the Web APIs

```
CREATE TABLE Wine (
 WineId int PRIMARY KEY,
 Name nvarchar (50),
 Category nvarchar (15),
 Year int,
 Price money)

CREATE TABLE Customer (
 CustomerId int PRIMARY KEY,
 FirstName nvarchar(50),
 LastName nvarchar(15),
 FavoriteWineId int,
 CONSTRAINT FK_Customer_Wine FOREIGN KEY (FavoriteWineId) REFERENCES Wine (WineId))

INSERT INTO Wine VALUES
 (1, 'Chateau Penin', 'Bordeaux', 2008, 34.90),
 (2, 'McLaren Valley', 'Cabernet', 2005, 48.50),
 (3, 'Mendoza', 'Merlot', 2010, 42.00),
 (4, 'Valle Central', 'Merlot', 2009, 52.00)

INSERT INTO Customer VALUES
 (1, 'Jeff', 'Hay', 4),
 (2, 'Mark', 'Hanson', 3),
 (3, 'Jeff', 'Phillips', 2)
```

This script creates the *WineCloudDb* tables and loads some sample data into them. Once you create this sample data, you will build Web APIs that return the wine and customer data.

To create the *WineCloudDb* database, follow these steps:

1. From the Windows Start screen, launch SQL Server Management Studio (SSMS). You can either scroll through the app tiles to find it (in the Microsoft SQL Server 2012 category) or just type **sql server management studio** to run a search, and then click on the tile. After a brief moment, the Connect To Server dialog appears.

2. In the Connect To Server dialog, do the following:

    a. For Server Name, type **<*servername*>.database.windows.net**. This is the fully qualified name to the SQL Database server, where <*servername*> should be replaced by the name assigned to your server.

    b. For Authentication, select SQL Server Authentication from the drop-down list. (SQL Database does not support Windows Authentication.)

    c. For Login and Password, type the user name and password you assigned the server when you created it.

    d. Click the Connect button.

3. In the Object Explorer, expand the Databases node.

4. If the *WineCloudDb* database exists from a previous chapter, delete it now by doing the following:

    a. Right-click the *WineCloudDb* database, and choose Delete.

    b. In the Delete Object dialog, click OK.

5. Create the database by completing the following steps:

    a. In the Object Explorer, right-click the server name and choose New Query to open a new query window connected to the *master* database.

    b. In the query window, type **CREATE DATABASE WineCloudDb**.

    c. Press F5 (or click the Execute button in the toolbar) to create the database.

    d. Close the query window without saving the script.

6. In the Object Explorer, right-click the Databases node and choose Refresh. The *WineCloudDb* database you just created should now appear.

7. Right-click the *WineCloudDb* database, and choose New Query to open a new query window connected to the *WineCloudDb* database.

8. Type the code shown in Listing 8-1 into the query window (or paste it in from the listing file downloaded from the book's companion website).

9. Press F5 (or click the Execute button in the toolbar) to create the database schema and populate some data.

You now have a new *WineCloudDb* database that will serve as the data source for your Web APIs.

Note You needed to create the database and populate it in two separate query windows because SQL Database does not support the *USE* statement found in SQL Server for switching the connection from the *master* database to the *WineCloudDb* database. See Chapter 3, "Differences between SQL Server and Microsoft Azure SQL Database," for more information on differences between SQL Database and SQL Server.

Creating a new solution

Visual Studio projects are contained inside a Microsoft Visual Studio solution, so you'll start by creating an empty solution. Then you'll add an ASP.NET Web Application project. The ASP.NET Web Application project will contain your ASP.NET Web APIs. This solution will contain only one project, but Visual Studio requires the project to be in a solution, and it will implicitly create one if it doesn't already exist. So you'll be proactive and create one from the beginning.

To create the new solution, follow these steps:

1. Start Visual Studio 2013.
2. Click the FILE menu, and then choose New | Project to display the New Project dialog.
3. On the left of the New Project dialog, expand Templates, Other Project Types, and choose Visual Studio Solutions.
4. Select the Blank Solution template, name the solution **WineSolution**, and choose any desired location for the solution, as shown in Figure 8-1.

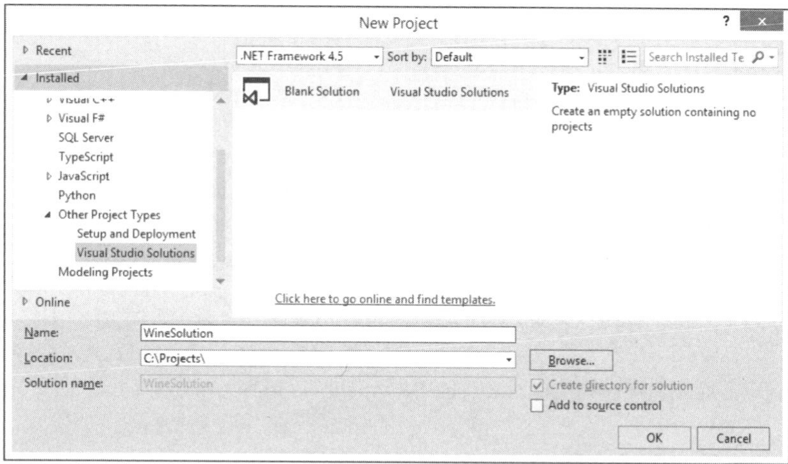

FIGURE 8-1 The New Project dialog for creating the Blank Solution

5. Click OK to create the solution.

The Solution Explorer now shows the new *WineSolution*. (If the Solution Explorer is not visible, click the VIEW menu and choose Solution Explorer.) Now that you have an empty solution, you're ready to create a new ASP.NET Web API project.

Creating an ASP.NET Web API project

When creating new ASP.NET projects using Visual Studio, it is recommended that you use the ASP.NET Web Application project type. This type of project can contain Model-View-Controller (MVC), Web Forms, and Web API project items. In the following procedures, you will create ASP.NET Web APIs in an ASP.NET Web Application project.

To create a new ASP.NET Web API project, follow these steps:

1. Right-click *WineSolution* in Solution Explorer, and choose Add | New Project to display the Add New Project dialog.
2. On the left of the New Project dialog, expand Installed, expand Visual C#, and choose Web.
3. Choose the ASP.NET Web Application template, which is typically selected by default.
4. Name the project **WineCloudWebApi** and click OK, as shown in Figure 8-2, to display the New ASP.NET Project dialog.

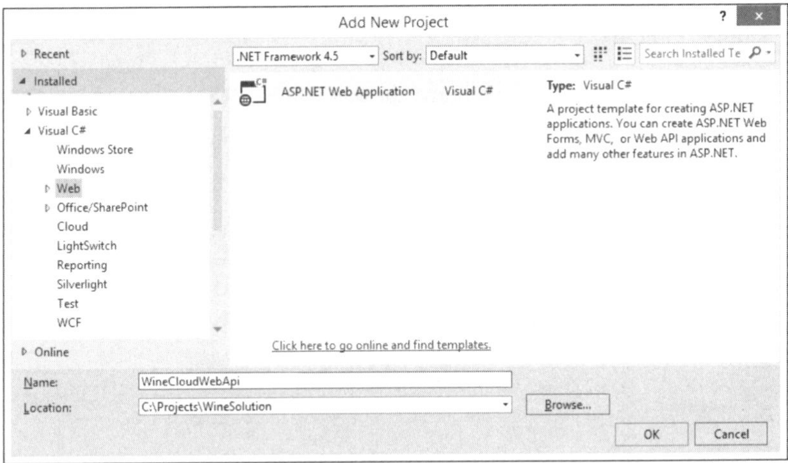

FIGURE 8-2 Creating a new ASP.NET Web Application project

5. Choose the Web API template and click OK, as shown in Figure 8-3.

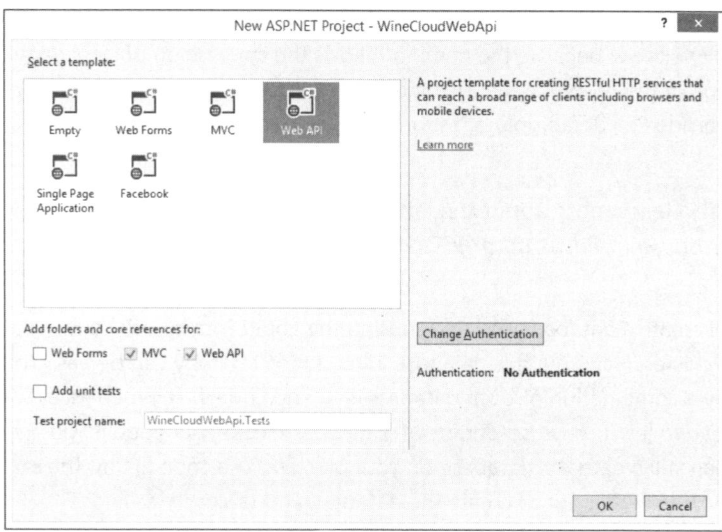

FIGURE 8-3 Creating a new ASP.NET Web API project

You have now created an empty ASP.NET Web Application project with references to the ASP.NET Web API assemblies. The project also references the ASP.NET MVC assemblies, which makes it possible to run both Web API and MVC applications in the same ASP.NET Web Application project.

Adding an Entity Framework Code First Web API controller

Now that you have created an ASP.NET Web Application project for your *WineCloudDb* Web APIs, you are ready to add Web API controllers. Web API controllers are similar to MVC controllers in that they respond to HTTP requests with HTTP responses. The first Web API Controller you'll add will use Entity Framework Code First for data access to the *WineCloudDb* database.

In earlier versions of Entity Framework, the entity model and database mappings could be configured only in an EDMX file, typically using the graphical Entity Data Model (EDM) designer in Visual Studio. With the Code First feature added in EF 4, you can choose instead to create your own Plain Old CLR Object (POCO) classes and configure the database conventions and mapping in code. This approach provides a number of advantages over using EDMX files. One of the most significant advantages is loose coupling of models from the persistence framework. This makes it easier to test your entity models in isolation from your database, add additional properties and methods, and use them across multiple application layers.

Creating a POCO class for use with Entity Framework is quite simple, and there are just a few rules you must follow. First, the class needs to be public. Second, the properties need to be public. And last, the data types of the model need to match the columns in your table. Entity Framework Code First is convention based, which means a number of patterns are built into Entity Framework. If these patterns are followed in your entity model and database design, Entity Framework can automatically map your entity model to the database without any manual configuration. The entity model for the *Wine* table, as shown in Listing 8-2, contains properties that match the columns in the *Wine* table, but there are no dependencies on Entity Framework. Entity Framework knows the *WineId* property maps to the primary key of the *Wine* table, because the naming follows the convention of class name followed by "Id" and the data type of the property is numeric or a GUID. Listing 8-3 contains the context class you will customize to override EF's default pluralization naming strategy.

More Info You can learn more about the Entity Framework conventions at *http://msdn.microsoft.com/en-us/data/jj679962.aspx.*

By default, EF will create a database and tables using the Entity Framework conventions and the POCO entity model classes. However, this database initialization strategy can be easily disabled so that you get to enjoy a combination of both database-first and code-first experiences with EF. That is, you don't *need* to let EF "reverse-engineer" a database from your code if you want to use code first; you can still create the database on your own and use code first at the same time. It's easy to tell Entity Framework not to create the database and tables by calling *Database.SetInitializer<WineDbContext>(null)* at the end of the *Application_Start* method in the *Global.asax.cs.*

One of the default Entity Framework Code First conventions is to pluralize table names. This means that, by default, Entity Framework expects that *Wine* entities are stored in a table named *Wines* (plural). However, the *WineCloudDb* database has a *Wine* table (singular), not a *Wines* table. Again, it's easy to override this default behavior by overriding the EF context's *OnModelCreating* method and calling *modelBuilder.Conventions.Remove<PluralizingTableNameConvention>()*. Removing this default convention will match the entity class name to a table name, which will map the *Wine* entity POCO class to the same-named *Wine* table in the database.

LISTING 8-2 The *Wine.cs* model class

```
using System;

namespace WineCloudWebApi.Models
{
  public class Wine
  {
    public int WineId { get; set; }
    public string Name { get; set; }
    public string Category { get; set; }
    public int? Year { get; set; }
    public Decimal? Price { get; set; }
  }
}
```

LISTING 8-3 The *WineDbContext.cs* Entity Framework context class

```
using System.Data.Entity;
using System.Data.Entity.ModelConfiguration.Conventions;

namespace WineCloudWebApi.Models
{
  public class WineDbContext : DbContext
  {
    public WineDbContext() : base(“name=WineDbContext”) {}

    public DbSet<Wine> Wines { get; set; }

    protected override void OnModelCreating(DbModelBuilder modelBuilder)
    {
        base.OnModelCreating(modelBuilder);
        modelBuilder.Conventions.Remove<PluralizingTableNameConvention>();
    }
  }
}
```

To create a Web API using Entity Framework for the *Wine* table, follow these steps:

1. Right-click the *Models* folder beneath the *WineCloudWebApi* project in the Solution Explorer, and choose Add | Class to display the Add New Item dialog.
2. Name the class **Wine.cs** and click Add, as shown in Figure 8-4.

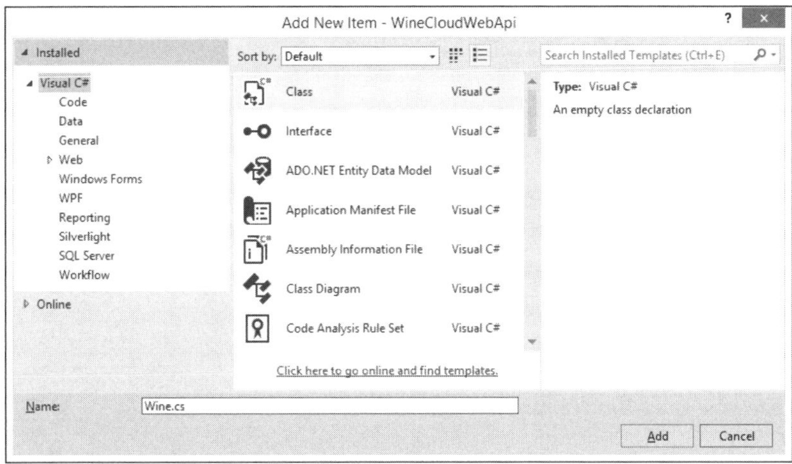

FIGURE 8-4 Adding a *Wine.cs* model class

3. Replace the template code generated automatically by Visual Studio with the code shown in Listing 8-2.

4. Build the *WineSolution* by selecting Build | Build Solution in the menu at the top or pressing Ctrl+Shift+B.

Note The next step in this procedure is to add a new Web API controller using the Wine model class you just created. Visual Studio finds the model classes using the built assemblies within the solution. This requires you to build the solution now so that Visual Studio can find the model class in the next step.

5. Right-click the Controllers folder in the *WineCloudWebApi* project in the Solution Explorer, and choose Add | Controller to display the Add Scaffold dialog.

6. Choose the Web API 2 Controller With Actions, Using Entity Framework controller, and click Add, as shown in Figure 8-5. This scaffold automatically creates Web API methods in the new controller class that retrieve (GET) and update (PUT, POST, DELETE) entities.

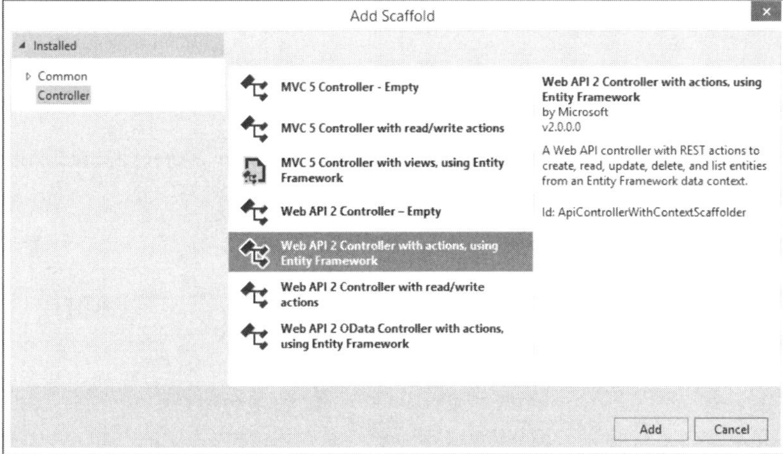

FIGURE 8-5 Adding the Entity Framework Web API 2 controller

7. In the Add Controller dialog, supply the information for the new Wine controller by doing the following:

   a. For the Controller name, type **WineController**.

   b. Leave the Use Async Controller Actions check box unselected.

   c. For the Model class, select Wine (WineCloudWebApi.Models) from the drop-down list.

   d. For the Data context class, click the New Data Context button and type **WineCloudWebApi.Models.WineDbContext** in the New Data Context Type text box and click Add, as shown in Figure 8-6.

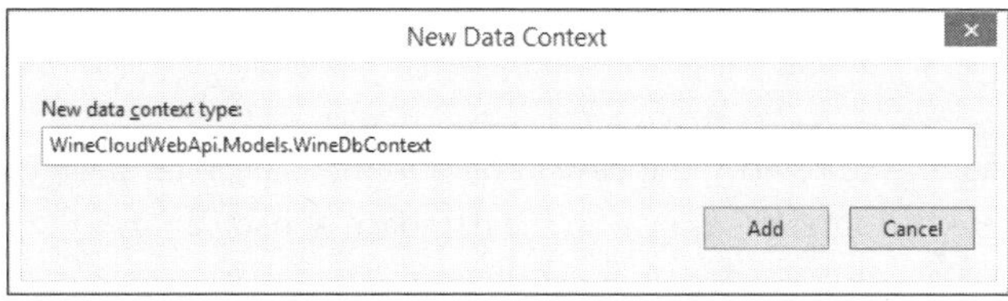

FIGURE 8-6 Creating the Entity Framework data context

e. The Add Controller dialog should now appear as shown in Figure 8-7. Click Add to create the controller.

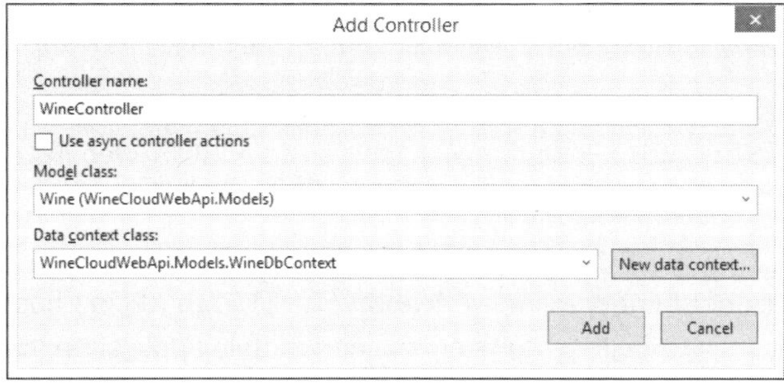

FIGURE 8-7 Adding and configuring the *WineController* class with Entity Framework

8. Double-click the *Web.config* file beneath the *WineCloudWebApi* project in the Solution Explorer, and locate the *WineDbContext* connection string setting in the *connectionStrings* section.

9. Change the *WineDbContext* connection string to **Server=tcp:<*servername*>.database.windows.net,1433; Database=WineCloudDb; User ID=<*username*>@<*servername*>; Password=<*password*>; Trusted_Connection=False; Encrypt=True; Connection Timeout=30;**.

   a. Replace <*servername*> with the name of the SQL Database server that contains the *WineCloudDb* database.

   b. Replace <*username*> and <*password*> with the user name and password you assigned the server when you created it.

10. Double-click the *WineDbContext.cs* file beneath the Models folder in the Solution Explorer and replace the template code with the code in Listing 8-3. The code adds an override of the *OnModelCreating* method that removes the default pluralizing table convention. This tells EF to look for a table named *Wine* (singular) and not *Wines* (plural) for storing rows of *Wine* entities in the database.

11. Double-click the *Global.asax.cs* file beneath the WineCloudWebApi project in the Solution Explorer.

12. Make the following changes to remove the default database initialization strategy, and tell EF not to attempt to create the database (because the database already exists):

    a. Add the following two *using* statements at the top of the file:
    using System.Data.Entity;
    using WineCloudWebApi.Models;

    b. Add the following line of code at the end of the *Application_Start* method:
    Database.SetInitializer<WineDbContext>(null);

13. Build the *WineSolution* by selecting Build | Build Solution in the menu at the top or pressing Ctrl+Shift+B.

You have now created a RESTful Web API for the *Wine* table using ASP.NET Web API and Entity Framework, and you're ready to test it.

Note You can learn more about Entity Framework and ASP.NET Web API in Chapter 10. In Chapter 10, you will learn how to build a multitier web and mobile application in Microsoft Azure using SQL Database.

Testing the Wine Web API

Now that you have created the Wine Web API, you should test it to verify that it returns the correct data from the *Wine* table in the *WineCloudDb*.

To test the Wine Web API, follow these steps:

1. Select the *WineSolution* in the Solution Explorer, and press F5 or click Debug | Start Debugging. This opens Internet Explorer (or your default debugging web browser) at the default page of the *WineCloudWebApi* project, as shown in Figure 8-8.

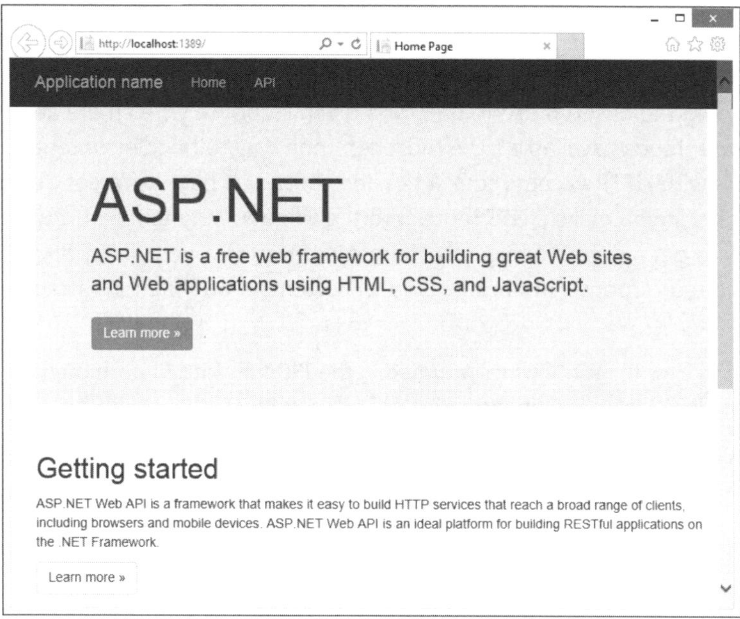

FIGURE 8-8 The default page from the *WineCloudWebApi* project

2. Append the URL in the browser's address bar with **api/Wine**, and press Enter. This executes the *GetWines* method on the *WineController* and responds with the list of wines from the *WineCloudDb* database. Internet Explorer's default behavior asks if you would like to save or open the results from the Web API call, as shown in Figure 8-9.

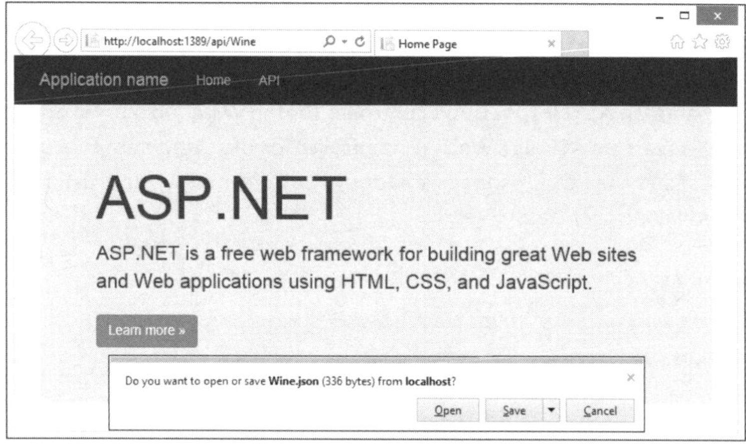

FIGURE 8-9 The *Wine.json* file returned by the Wine API

Note ASP.NET Web API implements a feature called *content negotiation*. The HTTP specification (RFC 2616) defines content negotiation as "the process of selecting the best representation for a given response when there are multiple representations available." The most common way to handle content negotiation is with HTTP Accept request headers. Browsers have different default Accept headers. If you make a GET request to the Wine API in multiple browsers, you are likely to get a different response. In Internet Explorer, you will often get a JSON-formatted response; in Chrome, you will often get an XML-formatted response.

3. Click Open to view the list of wines returned in the JSON results. (If prompted for how to open this type of file, click More Options and choose Notepad.)
4. Append the URL in the browser's address bar with **/2**, and press Enter. This executes the *GetWine* method on the *WineController* and responds with the Wine record for *WineId* 2.
5. Click Open to view the results.

You have now created a Wine Web API using ASP.NET Web API and Entity Framework Code First. You have also tested it in the browser and verified that it returns results from the *WineCloudDb* database. Next you will add a Web API Controller for the *Customer* table using raw ADO.NET rather than Entity Framework. It is common to have enterprise applications that use ADO.NET because they were developed prior to the introduction of Entity Framework. Raw ADO.NET is also commonly used when trying to boost data-access performance. As a result, in the following section you will use ADO.NET to build a Web API controller for the *Customer* table.

Adding an ADO.NET Web API controller

Thus far, you created a Visual Studio solution and added an ASP.NET Web Application project to that solution. You then created an ASP.NET Web API controller for the *Wine* table using Entity Framework Code First. Now, you'll create an ASP.NET Web API controller for the *Customer* table using raw ADO.NET. Listing 8-4 shows the POCO model class for the *Customer* entity, and Listing 8-5 shows its corresponding Web API controller class.

LISTING 8-4 The *Customer.cs* model class

```
namespace WineCloudWebApi.Models
{
  public class Customer
  {
    public int CustomerId { get; set; }
    public string FirstName { get; set; }
    public string LastName { get; set; }
    public int? FavoriteWineId { get; set; }
  }
}
```

LISTING 8-5 The *CustomerController.cs* Web API controller class

```
using System;
using System.Collections.Generic;
using System.Configuration;
using System.Data.SqlClient;
using System.Web.Http;
using System.Web.Http.Description;
using WineCloudWebApi.Models;

namespace WineCloudWebApi.Controllers
{
  public class CustomerController : ApiController
  {
    // GET api/Customer
    public IList<Customer> GetCustomers()
    {
      IList<Customer> customers = new List<Customer>();
      var connectionString =
       ConfigurationManager.ConnectionStrings["WineDbContext"].ConnectionString;

      using (var connection = new SqlConnection(connectionString))
      {
        var commandText = "SELECT * FROM Customer";
        using (var command = new SqlCommand(commandText, connection))
        {
          connection.Open();
          using (var reader = command.ExecuteReader())
          {
            while (reader.Read())
            {
              var customer = new Customer
              {
                CustomerId = Convert.ToInt32(reader["CustomerId"]),
                FirstName = reader["FirstName"].ToString(),
                LastName = reader["LastName"].ToString(),
                FavoriteWineId = reader["FavoriteWineId"] as int?
              };
              customers.Add(customer);
            }
          }
        }
      }
      return customers;
    }

    // GET api/Customer/5
    [ResponseType(typeof(Customer))]
    public IHttpActionResult GetCustomer(int id)
    {
      Customer customer = null;
      var connectionString =
       ConfigurationManager.ConnectionStrings["WineDbContext"].ConnectionString;
```

```
            using (var connection = new SqlConnection(connectionString))
            {
              var commandText = "SELECT * FROM Customer WHERE CustomerId = @CustomerId";
              using (var command = new SqlCommand(commandText, connection))
              {
                command.Parameters.AddWithValue("@CustomerId", id);
                connection.Open();
                using (var reader = command.ExecuteReader())
                {
                  if (reader.Read())
                  {
                    customer = new Customer
                    {
                      CustomerId = Convert.ToInt32(reader["CustomerId"]),
                      FirstName = reader["FirstName"].ToString(),
                      LastName = reader["LastName"].ToString(),
                      FavoriteWineId = reader["FavoriteWineId"] as int?
                    };
                  }
                }
              }
            }

            if (customer == null)
            {
              return NotFound();
            }
            return Ok(customer);
          }
        }
      }
```

To create a Customer Web API using ADO.NET, follow these steps:

1. Right-click the Models folder in the *WineCloudWebApi* project in the Solution Explorer, and choose Add | Class to display the Add New Item dialog.
2. Name the class **Customer.cs**, and click Add.
3. Replace the template code generated automatically by Visual Studio with the code shown in Listing 8-4 earlier, and build the *WineSolution* by selecting Build | Build Solution in the menu at the top or pressing Ctrl+Shift+B.
4. Right-click the Controllers folder in the *WineCloudWebApi* project in the Solution Explorer, and choose Add | Controller to display the Add Scaffold dialog.
5. Choose the **Web API 2 Controller - Empty** controller, and click Add. This displays the Add Controller dialog.

6. Type **CustomerController** for Controller name, and click Add.

7. Replace the template code with the code shown in Listing 8-5 earlier, and build the *WineSolution* by selecting Build | Build Solution in the menu at the top or pressing Ctrl+Shift+B.

You have now added a new ASP.NET Web API controller for the *Customer* table using ADO.NET instead of Entity Framework. The Customer Web API provides methods to get customer data, but it doesn't provide methods for adding or updating customers. Similar to the *Wine* entity model, the *Customer* entity model, as shown in Listing 8-4, doesn't have any data-access dependencies and is a simple POCO class. The *Customer* controller, as shown in Listing 8-5, queries the Customer table using the ADO.NET *SqlConnection*, *SqlCommand*, and *SqlDataReader* classes. It creates and populates instances of the *Customer* entity model class and returns the *Customer* objects. ASP.NET Web API then serializes the *Customer* objects into the appropriate response formats and sends them back to the requestor.

Testing the Customer Web API

Now that you have created a Customer Web API, you should test it to verify that it returns the correct data from the *Customer* table in the *WineCloudDb* database:

1. Select the *WineSolution* in the Solution Explorer, and press F5 or click Debug | Start Debugging. This opens Internet Explorer or your default debugging web browser at the default page of the *WineCloudWebApi* project.

2. Append the URL in the browser's address bar with **api/Customer**, and press Enter. This executes the *GetCustomers* method on the *WineController* and responds with the list of Customers from the *WineCloudDb* database. Internet Explorer's default behavior asks if you would like to save or open the results from the Web API call.

3. Click Open to view the results.

4. Append the URL in the browser's address bar with **/3**, and press Enter. This executes the *GetCustomer* method on the *CustomerController* and responds with the *Customer* record for *CustomerId* 3.

5. Click Open to view the results.

You have now set up an ASP.NET Web API project to get data from the *Wine* and *Customer* tables in the *WineCloudDb* database. Your project has Web APIs that use both Entity Framework Code First and raw ADO.NET. With this project now in place, we will build upon it in the following sections of this chapter to demonstrate performance tuning and scalability with SQL Database.

Managing SQL Database connections

Database connections in Microsoft Azure SQL Database can have different characteristics and behaviors than you've likely experienced with SQL Server on-premises. To provide reliability and great user experiences, these behaviors must be accounted for in your applications that use SQL Database. In addition to these different connection behaviors, you should also implement general best practices for interacting with databases, regardless of whether they are on-premises or in the cloud.

Opening late, closing early

There are limits on most compute resources, both in the cloud and on-premises. In SQL Database, one aspect that is limited is the number of database connections you can have open at any given time. To be a well-behaved consumer of SQL Database resources and connections, you should open database connections only when you need to interact with a SQL Database and as late as possible. When you are finished interacting with the database, you should close and release the connection. Entity Framework abstracts away the database connections, and you expect Entity Framework to be a good consumer of database resources. But when you are explicitly opening database connections using raw ADO.NET, you should open the database connections as close to the database interactions as possible. In Listing 8-5, you can see the call to *connection.Open()* occurs immediately before the *SqlCommand* is executed. Because the connection is wrapped in a *using* statement, as soon as the body of the *using* statement is exited, the connection will be disposed of, which closes the connection and releases its resources.

Pooling connections

There is overhead and a performance penalty when establishing new database connections. To help minimize this performance penalty, ADO.NET can pool connections. Connection pooling works by keeping a client's connections open in a pool of managed connections. When the client needs to open a connection, ADO.NET checks for an existing connection in the pool with a connection string that matches. If a connection already exists, it returns that connection to the client to interact with the database. If a connection doesn't exist, a new connection is established. When the client is finished with the connection and closes the connection, instead of destroying the connection, it is returned to the pool. Only connections with the exact same configuration and connection strings can be pooled, and the connection pool is scoped to an *AppDomain*. By default, ADO.NET uses connection pooling, and it is a generally recommended best practice to dramatically reduce the cost of opening connections.

Recovering from connection faults

SQL Database connections can be unexpectedly terminated for many reasons. The network architecture of SQL Database includes firewalls, load balancers, gateways, and database nodes. There are many components between the client and the database. Errors in these components can cause connections to terminate unexpectedly. SQL Database might also terminate connections when failing over to another node in the three-node clusters. In addition to errors and failover, SQL Database analyzes the activity of connections and the resource-consumption metrics of the database node. If SQL Database determines that it needs to throttle a connection to keep the overall service healthy, and to avoid negatively affecting other tenants of SQL Database, it may throttle and terminate the connection. These types of connection terminations are referred to as *transient faults*. Transient faults are temporary issues or errors that are expected to recover quickly. If your application is aware of these transient faults, it can try to reconnect over a short period of time and the connection loss might not even be noticeable to the user. If not, the application will throw an exception and the user will likely be presented with an error.

Not all terminated connections are caused by transient errors. However, errors raised by SQL Database return an error number you can use to determine what type of error occurred. Your application can compare the error number to the known transient error numbers. If there's a match, your application can try to reconnect and retry the transaction; if there's not a match, the error is not temporary and will need to be handled differently. If that sounds like a lot of work, don't worry—the Microsoft Azure Customer Advisory Team, in conjunction with Microsoft Patterns & Practices, has simplified this by creating the Transient Fault Handling Application Block. This library is part of the Enterprise Library family of application blocks, and it can be integrated into your application to simplify the recovery during transient faults. It can be used with SQL Database and other Microsoft Azure services that might have transient errors, including Service Bus and Storage.

In the following sections, you will integrate the Transient Fault Handling Application Block into the *WineCloudWebApi* project. Specifically, you'll modify the Wine and Customer Web APIs to recover gracefully from transient fault conditions.

Adding the Transient Fault Handling Application Block

To get started with the Transient Fault Handling Application Block, you must add a reference to it and integrate it into your project. In the following steps, you will add a reference to the Transient Fault Handling Application Block using NuGet. If you've not used NuGet before, there are a few basic facts we should tell you. It is a package manager that simplifies adding references to your projects with all of their associated dependencies. NuGet also makes it easy to update your dependencies and libraries when new versions are released. Documentation about NuGet and a repository of the publicly available NuGet packages are available at *www.nuget.org*.

Follow these steps to add a reference to the Transient Fault Handling Application Block:

1. Right-click the *WineCloudWebApi* project in the Solution Explorer, and choose Manage NuGet Packages to display the Manage NuGet Packages dialog.
2. Choose Online on the left, type **transient fault sql database** in the search box in the upper right corner, and press Enter.
3. Select Enterprise Library - Transient Fault Handling Application Block - Microsoft Azure SQL Database Integration from the search results, and click Install as shown in Figure 8-10.

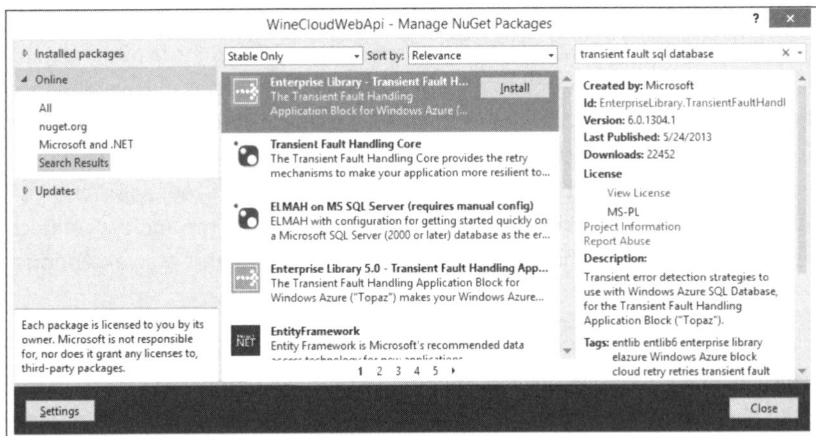

FIGURE 8-10 Installing the Transient Fault Handling Application Block using the Manage NuGet Packages dialog

4. In the License Acceptance dialog, click I Accept as shown in Figure 8-11. This downloads and adds a reference to *Microsoft.Practices.EnterpriseLibrary.TransientFaultHandling.Data.dll* and its dependencies.

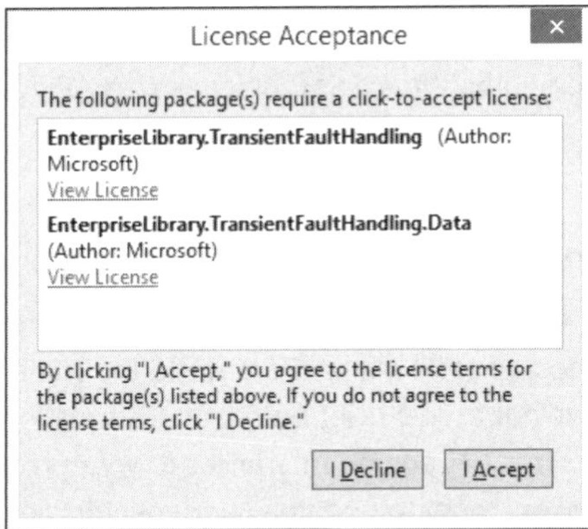

FIGURE 8-11 Accepting the license for the Transient Fault Handling Application Block

5. When installation completes, click Close.

You have now added a reference to the Transient Fault Handling Application Block using NuGet and are now ready to get started integrating it into the *WineCloudWebApi* project. In the next two sections, you will modify the Wine and Customer Web APIs to recover from transient errors.

Using the Transient Fault Handling Application Block with ADO.NET

The Transient Fault Handling Application Block provides components and classes you can use to configure how transient faults are detected and handled in your application. Table 8-1 shows the major components of the Transient Fault Handling Application Block.

TABLE 8-1 Major components of the Transient Fault Handling Application Block

Component	Description
Detection strategy	Determines when an exception is a transient fault condition
Retry strategy	Defines how often and how many times to retry when a fault is identified as a transient fault
Retry policy	Combines a detection strategy and a retry strategy, and is used to call services that might encounter transient faults

Detection strategies are used by the Transient Fault Handling Application Block to determine if an error is transient and whether the failed service call should be retried. Detection strategies are classes that implement the *ITransientErrorDetectionStrategy* interface, and the Transient Fault Handling Application Block has implementations for SQL Database, Service Bus, Storage, and Caching. The procedures in this chapter use the *SqlDatabaseTransientErrorDetectionStrategy* class to detect SQL Database transient error conditions, but you can implement your own detection strategy using the *ITransientErrorDetectionStrategy* interface.

Retry strategies are used to define the frequency and number of times the Transient Fault Handling Application Block will retry and attempt to automatically recover from a transient error. Retry strategies are classes that derive from the *RetryStrategy* class. Table 8-2 shows the retry strategies that are implemented in the Transient Fault Handling Application Block.

TABLE 8-2 Retry strategies in the Transient Fault Handling Application Block

Class	Description
ExponentialBackoff	Retries a specified number of times, exponentially delaying retries based on specified back-off parameters
FixedInterval	Retries a specified number of times with a fixed interval between each retry
Incremental	Retries a specified number of times with an incrementing interval between each retry

Using a detection strategy and a retry strategy, you create a retry policy using the *RetryPolicy* class. The retry policy will inspect errors that occur using the detection strategy and execute the retry strategy if an error is identified as a transient error. The Transient Fault Handling Application Block provides multiple ways for you to integrate it into your applications. You can use new classes that encapsulate existing classes to make them transient-fault and retry aware. *ReliableSqlConnection* is a class that encapsulates *SqlConnection*. You can use it in place of *SqlConnection* to automatically handle retrying when transient faults occur. There are also extension methods for existing classes, including the *SqlConnection* and *SqlCommand* classes. These extension methods can be used to utilize retry policies, as shown in the following procedures.

To handle transient faults in the *GetCustomers* method, follow these steps:

1. Expand the *Controllers* folder beneath the *WineCloudWebApi* project in Solution Explorer.
2. Double-click CustomerController.cs, and add the following *using* statement to the list of *using* statements at the top:
   using Microsoft.Practices.EnterpriseLibrary.TransientFaultHandling;
3. Locate the *GetCustomers* method, and type the following two lines of code just below the assignment of the *connectionString* variable:
   var retryStrategy =
   new Incremental(5, TimeSpan.FromSeconds(1), TimeSpan.FromSeconds(2));
   var retryPolicy =
   new RetryPolicy<SqlDatabaseTransientErrorDetectionStrategy>(retryStrategy);
4. Replace `connection.Open();` with **connection.OpenWithRetry(retryPolicy);**
5. Replace `command.ExecuteReader()` with **command.ExecuteReaderWithRetry(retryPolicy)**

To handle transient faults in the *GetCustomer* method, follow these steps:

1. Locate the *GetCustomer* method, and type the following two lines of code just below the assignment of the *connectionString* variable:
   var retryStrategy =
   new Incremental(5, TimeSpan.FromSeconds(1), TimeSpan.FromSeconds(2));
   var retryPolicy =
   new RetryPolicy<SqlDatabaseTransientErrorDetectionStrategy>(retryStrategy);
2. Replace `connection.Open();` with **connection.OpenWithRetry(retryPolicy);**
3. Replace `command.ExecuteReader()` with **command.ExecuteReaderWithRetry(retryPolicy)**

You are now handling transient fault conditions that might occur when using SQL Database using the *Incremental* retry strategy in the Customer Web API. The Incremental retry strategy works with three parameters.

The first parameter defines the number of times to retry. In the preceding procedure, you configured the Incremental retry strategy to retry five times. The second and third parameters together define the amount of time between each retry attempt. The second parameter defines the time to wait before the first retry, and the third parameter defines the amount of time to add to each subsequent retry attempt. In the preceding procedure, you set the second parameter to one second and the third parameter to two seconds. This will retry after one second, three seconds, five seconds, seven seconds, and nine seconds.

By defining a retry policy using the Transient Fault Handling Application Block, and by using extension methods on the *SqlConnection* and *SqlCommand* classes provided by the Transient Fault Handling Application Block, the Customer Web API is now resilient to transient error conditions, and minimal code changes were needed. In the next section, you will handle transient error conditions with Entity Framework.

Using the Transient Fault Handling Application Block with Entity Framework

In the previous section, you implemented retry logic when transient error conditions occurred using the Transient Fault Handling Application Block. You did that using extension methods on the *SqlConnection* and *SqlCommand* classes provided by the Transient Fault Handling Application Block. For the Customer Web API, that solution works really well because the data-access code is raw ADO.NET that uses these classes. The Wine Web API uses Entity Framework for data access, and the ADO.NET *SqlConnection* and *SqlCommand* classes are not exposed. Therefore, handling transient error conditions using Entity Framework requires a slightly different solution.

In the following procedure, you will use the same *RetryPolicy* class you used earlier with the extension methods on the *SqlConnection* and *SqlCommand* classes. The *RetryPolicy* class has an *ExecuteAction* method that is designed to execute code that encapsulates ADO.NET. This is useful when working with object relational mapping (ORM) and data-access platforms such as Entity Framework. Listing 8-6 shows a modified *WineController* class with Entity Framework calls that result in queries to SQL Database surrounded by the *ExecuteAction* method. The manual changes you need to apply to the code generated automatically by the scaffolding is indicated in bold type. Any exceptions that bubble up to the *RetryPolicy* will be inspected for transient error conditions and retried appropriately.

LISTING 8-6 The *WineController.cs* class using the Transient Fault Handling Application Block to handle transient error conditions

```
using Microsoft.Practices.EnterpriseLibrary.TransientFaultHandling;
using System;
using System.Collections.Generic;
using System.Data;
using System.Data.Entity;
using System.Data.Entity.Infrastructure;
using System.Linq;
using System.Net;
using System.Net.Http;
using System.Web.Http;
using System.Web.Http.Description;
using WineCloudWebApi.Models;

namespace WineCloudWebApi.Controllers
{
  public class WineController : ApiController
  {
    private WineDbContext db = new WineDbContext();
    private RetryPolicy<SqlDatabaseTransientErrorDetectionStrategy> _retryPolicy;
```

```
public WineController()
{
  var retryStrategy =
   new Incremental(5, TimeSpan.FromSeconds(1), TimeSpan.FromSeconds(2));
  _retryPolicy =
   new RetryPolicy<SqlDatabaseTransientErrorDetectionStrategy>(retryStrategy);
}

// GET api/Wine
public IQueryable<Wine> GetWines()
{
  IQueryable<Wine> wines = null;
  _retryPolicy.ExecuteAction(() =>
  {
    wines = db.Wines;
  });
  return wines;
}

// GET api/Wine/5
[ResponseType(typeof(Wine))]
public IHttpActionResult GetWine(int id)
{
  Wine wine = null;
  _retryPolicy.ExecuteAction(() =>
  {
    wine = db.Wines.Find(id);
  });

  if (wine == null)
  {
    return NotFound();
  }
  return Ok(wine);
}

// PUT api/Wine/5
public IHttpActionResult PutWine(int id, Wine wine)
{
  if (!ModelState.IsValid)
  {
    return BadRequest(ModelState);
  }

  if (id != wine.WineId)
  {
    return BadRequest();
  }

  db.Entry(wine).State = EntityState.Modified;
  try
  {
    _retryPolicy.ExecuteAction(() =>
```

```
    {
      db.SaveChanges();
    });
  }
  catch (DbUpdateConcurrencyException)
  {
    if (!WineExists(id))
    {
      return NotFound();
    }
    else
    {
      throw;
    }
  }

  return StatusCode(HttpStatusCode.NoContent);
}

// POST api/Wine
[ResponseType(typeof(Wine))]
public IHttpActionResult PostWine(Wine wine)
{
  if (!ModelState.IsValid)
  {
    return BadRequest(ModelState);
  }

  db.Wines.Add(wine);
  _retryPolicy.ExecuteAction(() =>
  {
    db.SaveChanges();
  });

  return CreatedAtRoute("DefaultApi", new { id = wine.WineId }, wine);
}

// DELETE api/Wine/5
[ResponseType(typeof(Wine))]
public IHttpActionResult DeleteWine(int id)
{
  Wine wine = null;
  _retryPolicy.ExecuteAction(() =>
  {
    wine = db.Wines.Find(id);
  });

  if (wine == null)
  {
    return NotFound();
  }
```

```
      db.Wines.Remove(wine);
      _retryPolicy.ExecuteAction(() =>
      {
        db.SaveChanges();
      });

      return Ok(wine);
    }

    protected override void Dispose(bool disposing)
    {
      if (disposing)
      {
        db.Dispose();
      }
      base.Dispose(disposing);
    }

    private bool WineExists(int id)
    {
      bool wineExists = false;
      _retryPolicy.ExecuteAction(() =>
      {
        wineExists = db.Wines.Count(e => e.WineId == id) > 0;
      });

      return wineExists;
    }
  }
}
```

To handle transient faults in the Wine controller class, follow these steps:

1. Expand the *Controllers* folder beneath the *WineCloudWebApi* project in Solution Explorer.
2. Double-click the *WineController.cs* file.
3. Update the code as indicated by the bolded sections of Listing 8-6. Specifically:
    a. Add a using statement for *Microsoft.Practices.EnterpriseLibrary.TransientFaultHandling*.
    b. Add a private field to store the retry policy.
    c. Add a constructor that creates the retry policy.
    d. Wrap each line of code that invokes a query or calls *SaveChanges* inside the retry policy's *ExecuteAction* method.

You have now handled transient error conditions using both ADO.NET and Entity Framework. The Transient Fault Handling Application Block is a huge help in doing this in a simple, quick, and succinct way. Without it, you would have to write the code to identify when an error is transient and temporary by comparing error numbers from SQL exceptions to a list of known transient errors. You would then have to write the code to retry a specified number of times at specified intervals, before implementing all of it in your application's data-access code. Using the Transient Fault Handling Application Block instead will greatly accelerate your development.

Transient error conditions are not something you should ignore. If your application does not account for these conditions, your application could experience dropped connections and throttling, resulting in errors and bad experiences for your users, when it could be avoided by retrying and continuing on. This is a common area of frustration and source of reliability issues for new users of SQL Database, and it can be avoided at the outset by integrating the Transient Fault Handling Application Block into your applications from the start.

Reducing network latency

In addition to differences in connection management, as discussed in the previous section, latency can also be a big performance and reliability challenge for SQL Database users. *Latency* can be defined as the time delay between cause and effect. With SQL Database, the time it takes for a query to get from a client to SQL Database, and to get the computed results from SQL Database back to the client, is known as *latency*. In on-premises data centers, a common way to reduce latency between web servers and database servers is to directly connect these servers using high-speed gigabit and fiber optic network connections. However, in the public cloud, you don't have control over the infrastructure and cannot make those hardware and network tweaks. But you can still optimize your services and applications to minimize latency.

Keeping services close

One way to reduce network latency is to minimize the distance between services that communicate with each other. In Microsoft Azure, you choose which data center regions you provision and deploy your services in. To reduce latency, it is best to deploy your SQL Database servers and the applications that interact with your SQL Database servers in the same data center region. You may not be able to keep the physical distance short in all cases. If you have applications running in your on-premises data center that need to interact with SQL Database, you have a physical distance between the services that you cannot reduce. In these cases, if latency becomes an issue, you might need to consider techniques like caching and batching to reduce the latency.

Minimizing round trips

Whenever there is a distance between services and the potential for latency, even in your own on-premises data center, you want to reduce the "chattiness" and network round trips in your applications.

These are some things you can do to reduce network round trips to SQL Database:

- **Encapsulate complex data access in stored procedures** if the data access results in multiple round trips and queries to SQL Database. For example, if a query depends on results from a previous query, instead of making multiple rounds trips to the database from the client, combining those in a single stored procedure will reduce the network latency.

- **Batch using table-valued parameters** by passing in a table-valued parameter to a stored procedure instead of making multiple calls with single parameters to the same stored procedure.
- **Use client-side storage and caching** to reduce network traffic when retrieving lookup data and data that changes infrequently. In addition to client-side storage, you can also use distributed caching services like Microsoft Azure Cache to keep data in memory and share the cached data across multiple nodes.
- **Avoid retrieving metadata at runtime** to reduce roundtrips. This includes using classes like *SqlCommandBuilder* that query metadata at runtime.

Effectively using SQL Database

You'll often find nonrelational and binary data stored in relational databases like SQL Server. This is common in enterprise applications, where developers view SQL Server as a managed data-storage platform for all data. Storing everything in SQL Server simplifies application development because developers need to understand only a single platform and learn a single set of client libraries. In addition to development experience, another reason SQL Server is often used for all kinds of data is because it is commonly architected to be always highly available, and that makes it easy to build a system with multiple distributed clients or multiple load-balanced web servers connected back to the single SQL Server platform. However, to achieve this level of availability, significant infrastructure and hardware investments are made, and much time is invested into the architecture and design of the SQL Server installation.

When you consider performance, scalability, and cost, relational databases are usually not the best places to store unstructured, nonrelational, and binary data. (The FILESTREAM feature in SQL Server represents an exception to this rule of thumb, but FILESTREAM, unfortunately, is not supported in SQL Database.) One of the ways you can increase the performance of SQL Database is to use it to store and serve relational data and only relational data, and use one of the alternative storage services to manage unstructured or semistructured nonrelational data.

Using the best storage service

There are multiple data services available in Microsoft Azure that are better suited for managing nonrelational and binary data than SQL Database. Microsoft Azure Storage has three storage services for other types of data: Table, Blob, and Queue. These services are all intended for nonrelational data. This type of data is not the best fit for relational databases like SQL Database.

Table storage works well for large quantities of structured, nonrelational data. Table storage is a schema-less, entity store where you can store an object with multiple key-value pairs. Logging and telemetry data is typically nonrelational and not analyzed in same structure as it was stored in initially. With this in mind, this kind of data is a good fit for Table storage.

Blob storage is a massively scalable file server service in Microsoft Azure. It is intended to store binary files, including documents and media. If you are storing binary large objects (BLOBs) in a database using the *varbinary(max)* data type (again, FILESTREAM is not supported), Blob storage is a good alternative solution for storing that data. Using Blob storage will reduce the load on SQL Database and will also reduce the amount of data stored in SQL Database. In addition to having performance benefits, Blob storage is significantly cheaper than SQL Database.

Queue storage is a service designed for queuing messages for asynchronous processing. This is often done using a database table with status columns. You can reduce load and contention on SQL Database by using Queue storage for these scenarios.

When data is accessed frequently and changed infrequently, that data is a great candidate for caching. Microsoft Azure provides a Cache service that can be deployed to your own compute instances in Microsoft Azure, or you can consume a managed Cache service. In simple cases, storing and accessing data from the local file system might meet your needs.

Optimizing queries

Many performance-tuning techniques and principles for SQL Database are the same as SQL Server in your own data center. In SQL Database, queries must be optimized and tuned just like in SQL Server on-premises. Query tuning is a very big topic and is outside the scope of this book; however, there is already a lot of good content written on this topic in other books. The basic principles of analyzing execution plans, optimizing queries to reduce disk I/O and wait time, and tuning indexes are the same as in SQL Server. However, identifying slow queries and queries that are good candidates for optimization is a little different than it is in SQL Server. SQL Database does not contain SQL Server functionality that requires elevated permissions or has the potential to impact the performance and reliability of other tenants; therefore, SQL Profiler cannot be used with SQL Database. Knowing how to identify queries that are slow and can be improved in SQL Database is very valuable and is discussed in Chapter 9, "Monitoring and managing SQL Database."

Scaling up SQL Database

SQL Database is a shared, multitenant, relational database service that can have variable performance characteristics. At the time of this writing, a new service named *SQL Database Premium* is in Preview. You can use it to attain consistent and predictable performance by reserving compute resources exclusively for your database. SQL Database Premium has the two service levels shown in Table 8-3.

TABLE 8-3 Service levels of SQL Database Premium

Service Level	Description
P1	1 CPU core, 8 GB of memory and 150 disk input/output operations per second (IOPS).
P2	2 CPU cores, 16 GB of memory and 300 IOPS.

Note Microsoft regularly releases new features for Microsoft Azure. These features often begin as Preview services, which don't come with service level agreements (SLAs) or warranties, and they are typically not supported by Microsoft customer support. While in Preview, services often have reduced pricing (and sometimes are free). When a service progresses from Preview to General Availability (GA), the service gets service level agreements, warranties, support, and full pricing. For more information about Microsoft Azure preview services, visit *http://azure.microsoft.com/en-us/services/preview/.*

To sign up for the SQL Database Premium Preview, follow these steps:

1. Log in to the Microsoft Azure Account management portal at *https://account.windowsazure.com.*
2. Click the Preview Features button as shown in Figure 8-12 to display the Microsoft Azure preview features.

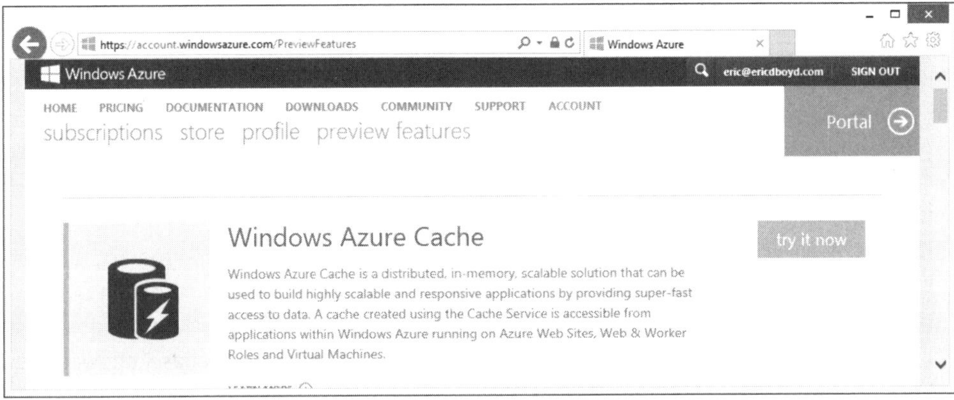

FIGURE 8-12 The Preview Features link in the Microsoft Azure account portal

3. Click the Try It Now button to the right of Premium For SQL Database, as shown in Figure 8-13, to activate the SQL Database Premium preview.

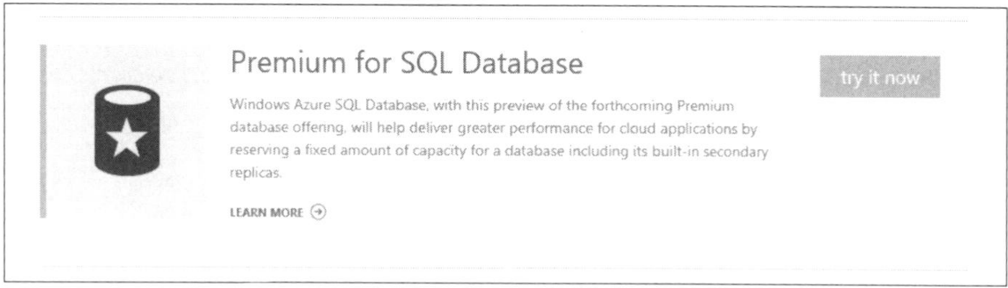

FIGURE 8-13 Activating the SQL Database Premium preview feature in the Microsoft Azure account portal

4. Choose the subscription you want to use with SQL Database Premium in the Add Preview Feature dialog, as shown in Figure 8-14, and click the check mark in the bottom right corner.

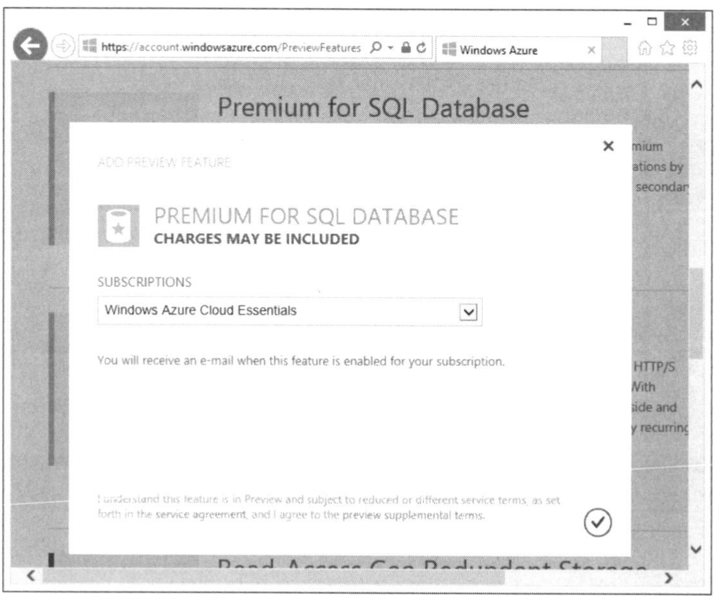

FIGURE 8-14 Selecting the subscription in the Add Preview Feature dialog

You have now requested to be signed up for the SQL Database Premium preview. Requests are queued and approved based on current capacity and demand. You will receive an email informing you when your request has been approved and SQL Database Premium preview has been activated in your subscription. Once the preview has been activated, you can then request a SQL Database Premium quota for your SQL Database servers.

To request a SQL Database Premium quota, follow these steps:

1. Log in to the Microsoft Azure portal at *https://manage.windowsazure.com*. This brings you to the main portal page showing ALL ITEMS.
2. Click SQL DATABASES in the vertical navigation pane on the left.
3. Click the SERVERS link at the top of the page. This displays a list of your Microsoft Azure SQL Database servers.
4. In the NAME column, click the server that you want to request a Premium database quota for.
5. Navigate to the server home screen by clicking on the cloud with the lightning bolt icon.
6. Click Request Premium Database Quota in the Premium Database section as shown in Figure 8-15.

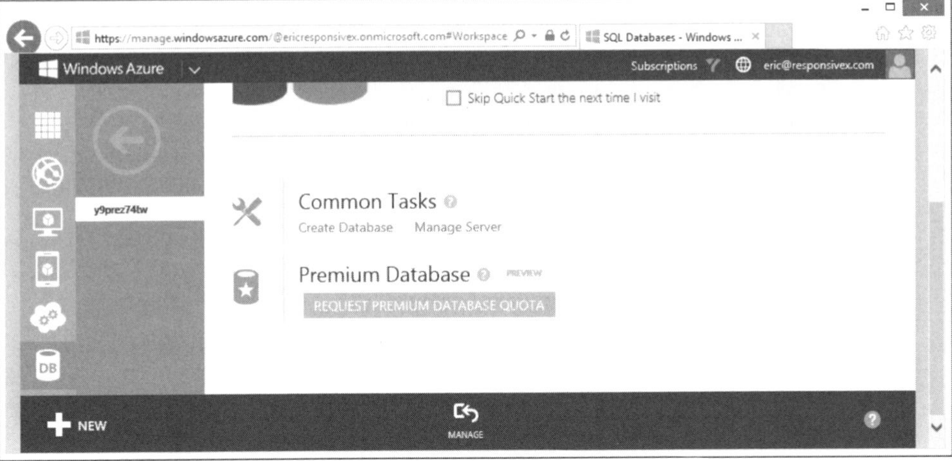

FIGURE 8-15 Requesting a SQL Database Premium quota in the Microsoft Azure management portal

You have now requested to have a SQL Database Premium quota added to your SQL Database server. Requests are queued and approved based on current capacity and demand. The status of a Premium Database Quota request is displayed in the Premium Database section of the server home screen where you initiated the request. After you initiate the request and prior to it being approved, a Pending Approval message will be displayed, as shown in Figure 8-16. You can cancel the request by clicking the Cancel Request link. When your request is approved and you have a SQL Database Premium quota on your server, you will also receive an email notification. Once you have a SQL Database Premium quota, you can create a new database or associate an existing database with your SQL Database Premium quota.

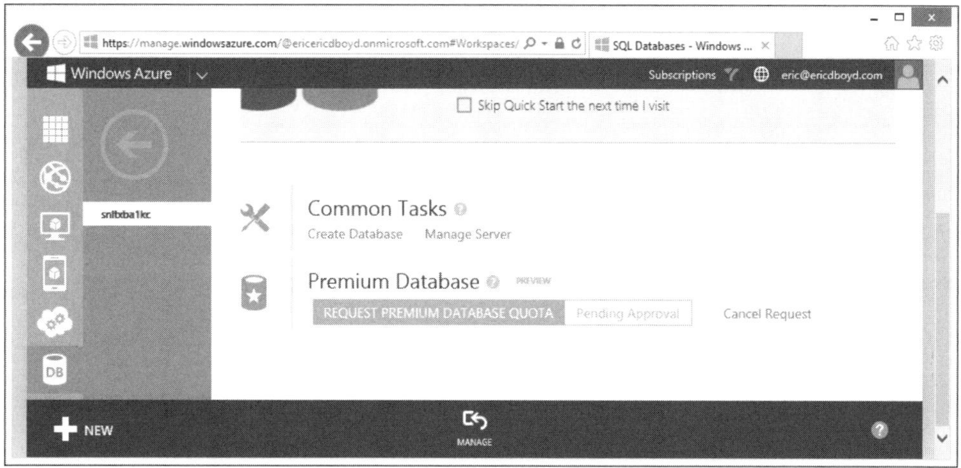

FIGURE 8-16 Finding the status of a SQL Database Premium quota request in the Microsoft Azure management portal

To upgrade an existing database to SQL Database Premium, follow these steps:

1. Log in to the Microsoft Azure portal at *https://manage.windowsazure.com*, and click SQL Databases in the vertical navigation pane on the left.
2. In the NAME column, click the database you want to upgrade to SQL Database Premium. This database must be in your SQL Database server with an approved SQL Database Premium quota.
3. Click the SCALE link at the top of the page, and configure SQL Database Premium:
   a. For Edition, select Premium. This upgrades your database from the Web and Business editions to the SQL Database Premium edition.
   b. For Reservation Size, you can select either P1 or P2. P1 is 1 core, 8 GB of memory and 150 IOPS. P2 is equivalent to two P1s. The page should appear similar to Figure 8-17.

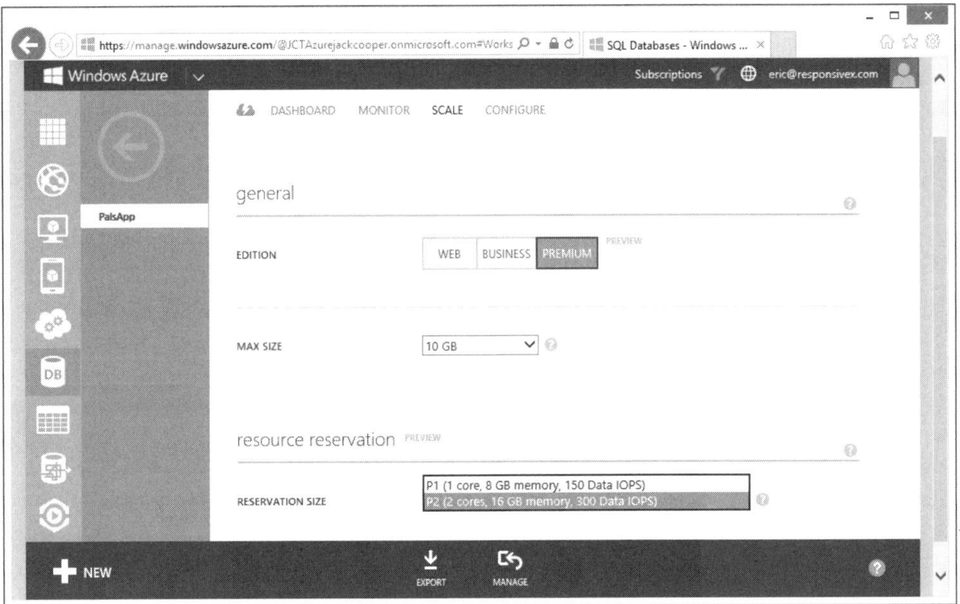

FIGURE 8-17 Selecting the SQL Database Premium reservation size

4. Click the SAVE button at the bottom of the page.

You have now scaled up your SQL Database using the preview of SQL Database Premium. With SQL Database Premium, you reserve a portion of the SQL Database server compute resources just for your database. This resource reservation provides consistent and predictable performance characteristics for a SQL Database.

Partitioning data

Scaling relational databases is not a trivial task. Stateless application and web servers are typically simple to scale. By deploying a new server and adding it to a load balancer, you instantly add capacity and scale your application. But the relationship characteristic and the ACID (Atomic, Consistent, Isolated, and Durable) properties of relational databases make it difficult to distribute a database across multiple compute nodes. If you need to scale a relational database across multiple compute nodes, you must partition the data. The following sections will describe approaches and techniques for partitioning databases.

Scaling out with functional partitions

One of the most common ways databases get partitioned is by function. Partitioning by function splits up data into multiple databases that each have closely related tables. Using the *WineCloudDb* database as an example, if you partitioned that database by function, you might split it into a *Customer* database and a *Catalog* database. The *Customer* database would contain the *Customer* table and the *Catalog* database would contain the *Wine* table. If you also had an eCommerce application to sell the wine, you might have an *Order* database with *Order* and *OrderDetail* tables. Functional partitioning is also referred to as *vertical partitioning*. It is generally easier to implement and use than horizontal partitioning, which will be described in the next section.

To partition your data functionally, you need to remove database-enforced relationships and foreign keys between tables that will be in different databases. You can then split your tables into multiple databases, but without the database-level constraints, your applications will need to enforce the relationships between the tables that span databases. Any queries that join data across the tables that have been split into multiple databases need to be split, and the database-connection strings need to be updated to direct the application to the appropriate database. Splitting databases into functional partitions can get complex and time consuming if there are lots of relationships between tables, and lots of queries and applications that need to be updated.

One of the goals when partitioning data is to balance and equally distribute load across multiple compute nodes. Although partitioning data by function can help split up the load across multiple compute nodes, it is unlikely that your load will be distributed evenly across functional partitions. In the next section, you'll explore another data-partitioning technique call *sharding*. Sharding is a technique that makes it easier to achieve an even load distribution.

Scaling out with shards

To equally distribute the load on relational databases across multiple compute nodes, you need to consider partitioning data within a single table. Partitioning a single table across multiple databases is referred to as *horizontal partitioning* or *sharding*. In the following procedure, you will partition the *WineCloudDb* into multiple shards based on customers. The *WineCloudDb* data set is small, but it will be sufficient to demonstrate sharding. You will split the database into two databases: the first with one customer record, and the second one with two customer records. When sharding databases, you must have an algorithm that determines what records will go in each database shard. You can partition customers into multiple shards in a number of ways. You can partition customers by the first letter of their last name, and that would result in 26 databases shards. But remember that the goal is to distribute load as evenly as possible, and using the first letter of last names is unlikely to be an even distribution, because some letters are more common than others.

In our *WineCloudDb* example, you will partition by a range of *CustomerId* values. The customer with a *CustomerId* of 1 will go into one database shard, the customers with a *CustomerId* ranging from 2 to 3 will go into another database shard. When sharding databases, you also need to have an index or map of how your data is partitioned so that, first, you can find your records and, second, you have a way to rearrange your records within the database shards if you find that your distribution is not equal and needs to be rebalanced. In the following example, the shard map is implemented in code for simplicity and readability. Typically, though, you implement the shard map in a persistent data store separate from your code.

Similar to functional partitions, it can be challenging to shard data when you have relationship constraints and foreign keys. Often, reference and lookup data will get duplicated and stored in each shard. (The Microsoft Azure SQL Data Sync service can help you maintain multiple copies of reference data tables across multiple shards; see Chapter 7, "Microsoft Azure SQL Data Sync," for more information.) In the *WineCloudDb* example, you will store the *Wine* table in each shard. If the customer table has relationships to other customer-related tables, you typically partition those tables and store those related records in the same database shard as the customer record. In the *WineCloudDb* example, the *Customer* table doesn't have additional customer-related tables, which makes sharding this database a lot simpler.

Creating the shard databases

For the Web APIs in this chapter, you will use the script shown in Listing 8-7 to create two *WineCloudDb* database shards and populate them each with the same set of wines. Then you will populate them each with *different* customers, and create ASP.NET Web APIs that return customers from the sharded databases.

LISTING 8-7 Script to create sharded databases

```
CREATE TABLE Wine (
 WineId int PRIMARY KEY,
 Name nvarchar (50),
 Category nvarchar (15),
 Year int,
 Price money)

CREATE TABLE Customer (
 CustomerId int PRIMARY KEY,
 FirstName nvarchar(50),
 LastName nvarchar(15),
 FavoriteWineId int,
 CONSTRAINT FK_Customer_Wine FOREIGN KEY (FavoriteWineId) REFERENCES Wine (WineId))

INSERT INTO Wine VALUES
 (1, 'Chateau Penin', 'Bordeaux', 2008, 34.90),
 (2, 'McLaren Valley', 'Cabernet', 2005, 48.50),
 (3, 'Mendoza', 'Merlot', 2010, 42.00),
 (4, 'Valle Central', 'Merlot', 2009, 52.00)
```

To create the *WineCloudDb* database shards, follow these steps:

1. From the Windows Start screen, launch SSMS. You can either scroll through the app tiles to find it (in the Microsoft SQL Server 2012 category) or just type **sql server management studio** to run a search, and then click on the tile. After a brief moment, the Connect To Server dialog appears.
2. In the Connect To Server dialog, do the following:
    a. For Server Name, type ***<servername>*.database.windows.net**. This is the fully qualified name to the SQL Database server, where *<servername>* should be replaced by the name assigned to your server.

b. For Authentication, select SQL Server Authentication from the drop-down list. (SQL Database does not support Windows Authentication.)

c. For Login and Password, type the user name and password you assigned the server when you created it.

d. Click the Connect button.

3. Create the databases.

   a. In the Object Explorer, right-click the server name and choose New Query to open a new query window connected to the *master* database.

   b. In the query window, type:
   CREATE DATABASE WineCloudDbShard1
   GO
   CREATE DATABASE WineCloudDbShard2
   GO

   c. Press F5 (or click the Execute button in the toolbar) to create the two databases.

   d. Close the query window without saving the script.

4. In the Object Explorer, right-click the Databases node and choose Refresh. The *WineCloudDbShard1* and *WineCloudDbShard2* databases you just created should now appear.

5. Right-click the *WineCloudDbShard1* database, and choose New Query to open a new query window connected to the *WineCloudDbShard1* database.

6. Type the code shown in Listing 8-7 into the query window (or paste it in from the listing file downloaded from the book's companion website).

7. Press F5 (or click the Execute button in the toolbar) to create the database objects for the first shard, and then close the query window without saving the script.

8. Right-click the *WineCloudDbShard1* database, and choose New Query to open a new query window connected to the *WineCloudDbShard1* database.

9. Type the following code into the query window:

```
INSERT INTO Customer VALUES (1, 'Jeff', 'Hay', 4)
```

10. Press F5 (or click the Execute button in the toolbar) to add a customer row for Jeff Hay to the *WineCloudDbShard1* database, and then close the query window without saving the script.

11. Right-click the *WineCloudDbShard2* database, and choose New Query to open a new query window connected to the *WineCloudDbShard2* database.

12. Type the code shown in Listing 8-7 into the query window (or paste it from the listing file downloaded from the book's companion website).

13. Press F5 (or click the Execute button in the toolbar) to create the database objects for the second shard, and then close the query window without saving the script.

14. Right-click the *WineCloudDbShard2* database, and choose New Query to open a new query window connected to the *WineCloudDbShard2* database.

15. Type the following code into the query window:

```
INSERT INTO Customer VALUES
 (2, 'Mark', 'Hanson', 3),
 (3, 'Jeff', 'Phillips', 2)
```

16. Press F5 (or click the Execute button in the toolbar) to add two customer rows for Mark Hanson and Jeff Phillips to the *WineCloudDbShard2* database, and then close the query window without saving the script.

You now have two new databases named *WineCloudDbShard1* and *WineCloudDbShard2* that will serve as the data source for your customer Web APIs. Each database has the same reference data in the *Wine* table, but the *Customer* table is partitioned horizontally between them.

Using shards with ADO.NET and ASP.NET Web API

Now that you have two database shards set up for the *WineCloudDb* database, you are ready to modify the Customer Web API you created earlier in this chapter to retrieve data from these multiple databases.

Listing 8-8 shows the classes used for working with the individual shard databases. The *Shard* class defines a shard database with the range of IDs that it will contain using the *BeginId* and the *EndId* properties. The *Shard* class also has a *ConnectionString* property that has a connection string for the database shard. The *ShardRoot* class represents the logical root that tracks the multiple shard databases that collectively form the single logical database. The *CustomerShard* class is the logical root implementation for the *WineCloudDb* database shards. It uses the *Shard* and *ShardRoot* classes to collect the multiple customer databases into one logical container. The *GetShard* method on the *CustomerShard* class makes it easy to retrieve the database shard for a specified customer.

LISTING 8-8 Customer data sharding classes

```
using System.Collections.Generic;
using System.Linq;

namespace WineCloudWebApi.Data
{
  public class Shard
  {
    public int Id { get; set; }
    public int BeginId { get; set; }
    public int EndId { get; set; }
    public string ConnectionString { get; set; }
  }
```

```
public class ShardRoot
{
  public ShardRoot() { Shards = new List<Shard>(); }
  public IList<Shard> Shards { get; private set; }
}

public class CustomerShard
{
  private static CustomerShard _instance;
  private static object _lockObj = new object();

  public static CustomerShard Instance
  {
    get
    {
      if (_instance == null)
      {
        lock (_lockObj)
        {
          if (_instance == null)
          {
            _instance = new CustomerShard();
          }
        }
      }
      return _instance;
    }
  }

  public ShardRoot ShardRoot { get; private set; }

  public CustomerShard()
  {
    ShardRoot = new ShardRoot();
    ShardRoot.Shards.Add(new Shard
    {
      Id = 1,
      BeginId = 1,
      EndId = 1,
      ConnectionString =
          "Server=tcp:<ServerName>.database.windows.net,1433;" +
          "Database=WineCloudDbShard1;User ID=<UserName>@<ServerName>;" +
          "Password=<Password>;Trusted_Connection=False;" +
          "Encrypt=True;Connection Timeout=30;"
    });
    ShardRoot.Shards.Add(new Shard
    {
      Id = 2,
      BeginId = 2,
      EndId = 3,
      ConnectionString =
          "Server=tcp:<ServerName>.database.windows.net,1433;" +
          "Database=WineCloudDbShard2;User ID=<UserName>@<ServerName>;" +
          "Password=<Password>;Trusted_Connection=False;" +
```

```
                "Encrypt=True;Connection Timeout=30;"
        });
    }

    public Shard GetShard(int id)
    {
      return ShardRoot.Shards
        .FirstOrDefault(shard => shard.BeginId <= id && shard.EndId >= id);
    }
  }
}
```

The *CustomerController* shown in Listing 8-9 has been modified to retrieve customers from the multiple databases using the *CustomerShard* class. The changes to the *GetCustomer* method are simple. Using the ID passed into the *GetCustomer* method, the database where that customer exists is returned by the *GetShard* method on the *CustomerShard* class. Then, using the same logic as in the previous *CustomerController* examples in this chapter, the customer table is queried and the Customer is returned. The changes required to get a single record as needed for the *GetCustomer* method are minimal.

However, the changes required for the *GetCustomers* method are a little more complex. Whenever a database is sharded into multiple databases, querying data that spans the multiple databases can be challenging. To query across the databases, you must query each database and merge the results. This approach is commonly referred to as *fan-out* querying. If you have many databases, you do not want to execute those queries in a series, waiting for the previous query to return, because that increases response time and provides a slower experience for users. Instead, you want to execute those queries simultaneously and aggregate the results as they are returned in parallel. The *GetCustomers* method in Listing 8-9 shows a simple fan-out query implementation using the Task Parallel Library. In this example, each database shard is queried for customers in parallel and the results from each query are merged and returned as one list of customers.

LISTING 8-9 *CustomerController* with support for *Customer* shards

```
using System;
using System.Collections.Generic;
using System.Data.SqlClient;
using System.Threading.Tasks;
using System.Web.Http;
using System.Web.Http.Description;
using Microsoft.Practices.EnterpriseLibrary.TransientFaultHandling;
using WineCloudWebApi.Data;
using WineCloudWebApi.Models;

namespace WineCloudWebApi.Controllers
{
  public class CustomerController : ApiController
```

```
{
  // GET api/Customer
  public IList<Customer> GetCustomers()
  {
    var customers = new List<Customer>();

    Parallel.ForEach(CustomerShard.Instance.ShardRoot.Shards,
        new ParallelOptions
         { MaxDegreeOfParallelism = CustomerShard.Instance.ShardRoot.Shards.Count },
        shard =>
        {
          var shardCustomers = new List<Customer>();
          var connectionString = shard.ConnectionString;
          var retryStrategy =
           new Incremental(5, TimeSpan.FromSeconds(1), TimeSpan.FromSeconds(2));
          var retryPolicy =
           new RetryPolicy<SqlDatabaseTransientErrorDetectionStrategy>(retryStrategy);

          using (var connection = new SqlConnection(connectionString))
          {
            var commandText = "SELECT * FROM Customer";
            using (var command = new SqlCommand(commandText, connection))
            {
              connection.OpenWithRetry(retryPolicy);
              using (var reader = command.ExecuteReaderWithRetry(retryPolicy))
              {
                while (reader.Read())
                {
                  var customer = new Customer
                  {
                    CustomerId = Convert.ToInt32(reader["CustomerId"]),
                    FirstName = reader["FirstName"].ToString(),
                    LastName = reader["LastName"].ToString(),
                    FavoriteWineId = reader["FavoriteWineId"] as int?
                  };
                  shardCustomers.Add(customer);
                }
              }
            }
          }
          customers.AddRange(shardCustomers);
        });

    return customers;
  }

  // GET api/Customer/5
  [ResponseType(typeof(Customer))]
  public IHttpActionResult GetCustomer(int id)
  {
    Customer customer = null;

    Shard customerShard = CustomerShard.Instance.GetShard(id);
    if (customerShard != null)
```

```
{
  var connectionString = customerShard.ConnectionString;
  var retryStrategy =
   new Incremental(5, TimeSpan.FromSeconds(1), TimeSpan.FromSeconds(2));
  var retryPolicy =
   new RetryPolicy<SqlDatabaseTransientErrorDetectionStrategy>(retryStrategy);

  using (var connection = new SqlConnection(connectionString))
  {
    var commandText = "SELECT * FROM Customer WHERE CustomerId = @CustomerId";
    using (var command = new SqlCommand(commandText, connection))
    {
      command.Parameters.AddWithValue("@CustomerId", id);
      connection.OpenWithRetry(retryPolicy);
      using (var reader = command.ExecuteReaderWithRetry(retryPolicy))
      {
        if (reader.Read())
        {
          customer = new Customer
          {
            CustomerId = Convert.ToInt32(reader["CustomerId"]),
            FirstName = reader["FirstName"].ToString(),
            LastName = reader["LastName"].ToString(),
            FavoriteWineId = reader["FavoriteWineId"] as int?
          };
        }
      }
    }
  }
}

if (customer == null)
{
  return NotFound();
}
return Ok(customer);
    }
  }
}
```

To use the database shards with the customer Web API, follow these steps:

1. Open the *WineSolution* in Visual Studio 2013.
2. Right-click the *WineCloudWebApi* project in Solution Explorer, and choose Add | New Folder.
3. Name the new folder **Data**, and press Enter.
4. Right-click on the newly created *Data* folder, and choose Add | Class to display the Add New Item dialog.
5. Name the new class **CustomerShard.cs**, and click Add.

6. Replace the template code with the code shown earlier in Listing 8-8. In the connection strings contained in the code, do the following:

    a. Replace *<ServerName>* with the name of the SQL Database server that contains the shard databases.

    b. Replace *<UserName>* and *<Password>* with the user name and password you assigned the server when you created it.

7. Expand the *Controllers* folder beneath the *WineCloudWebApi* project in Solution Explorer.

8. Double-click the *CustomerController.cs*, and replace the code with the code shown earlier in Listing 8-9.

9. Build the *WineSolution* by selecting Build | Build Solution in the menu at the top or pressing Ctrl+Shift+B.

You have now split the *WineCloudDb* database into multiple database shards, splitting on customer records. You can test the customer API using the same steps from the "Testing the Customer Web API" section.

Listing 8-8 and Listing 8-9 show a simple implementation of integrating database sharding into your application. In Listing 8-8, there are classes to manage and group the sharded databases; in Listing 8-9, the *CustomerController* has a simple implementation of fan-out querying using the Task Parallel Library. This implementation works for scenarios that are small and not overly complex, but in larger and more complex scenarios you will likely need additional capabilities to track database shards and update data across shards. There are existing libraries you can use to help with these additional capabilities. The Microsoft Azure Customer Advisory Team creates guidance, frameworks, and reference applications based on what they have learned from real-world customer engagements. Microsoft Azure CAT has developed a reference application called *Cloud Service Fundamentals in Windows Azure* that includes a library named *Microsoft.AzureCat.Patterns.Data.SqlAzureDalSharded* that contains classes that will help you when sharding relational databases. You can reuse this library in your applications, and it is available at *http://code.msdn.microsoft.com/windowsazure/Cloud-Service-Fundamentals-4ca72649.*

Note EF can also be used when sharding databases. Using the same approach shown in Listing 8-9, you can use the Task Parallel Library to execute queries across multiple databases in parallel. However, instead of using raw ADO.NET objects to access your database, you use EF objects. You construct an EF *DbContext* for each database, instead of opening a new *SqlConnection*. Using the *DbContext* object, you then query the appropriate *DbSet* property using LINQ To Entities. Sharding with EF is possible, but if you are trying to boost performance, the performance overhead that comes with using EF may encourage you to use raw ADO.NET instead.

Summary

This chapter introduced you to optimizing performance and scaling Microsoft Azure SQL Database. You created an ASP.NET Web API that was used as a reference application throughout the chapter, and you improved the reliability and performance of this Web API by managing database connections and connection errors and reducing latency in Microsoft Azure. You then considered other optimizations, like using the most appropriate storage service for your data and query optimization. Later in the chapter, you scaled up SQL Database using SQL Database Premium. And in the last section, you scaled your SQL Database with partitioning and sharding strategies.

Designing highly available, high-performance, scalable systems is a very large topic. This chapter provided an understanding of the most important concepts, principles, and techniques for achieving high performance and scale with SQL Database, but there is a lot more for you to learn on your own.

CHAPTER 9

Monitoring and management

—Eric Boyd

Any service you intend to use in a production application must provide monitoring and management capabilities. Monitoring should provide insight into the health of the service and, ultimately, the health of your application. So, in the first half of this chapter, you will learn how to monitor SQL Database using the management portal, the Service Dashboard, and built-in dynamic management views and functions.

In previous chapters, you managed SQL Database using graphical user interface (GUI) tools such as the Microsoft Azure management portal, SQL Database management portal, SQL Server Management Studio (SSMS), and SQL Server Data Tools (SSDT). These GUI tools are convenient when you are getting started, but as your applications mature and you move toward production, you identify processes that are frequently repeated and GUIs become inconvenient. To save time and reduce human error, you need to automate these processes. Thus, the second half of this chapter teaches you how to manage SQL Database using the Microsoft Azure Service Management Application Programming Interface (API).

Creating the sample database

The procedures throughout this chapter work with a server that already has a database on it, such as the *WineCloudDb* database you worked with in other chapters. If you haven't created this database, or you deleted it, you can create it by following the steps in this section. If you already have a *WineCloudDb* database created from work in any other chapter, you can skip the steps in this section and proceed to the "Monitoring" section.

For the exercises in this chapter, use the script shown in Listing 9-1 to create *WineCloudDb* and populate it with a few wines and customers.

LISTING 9-1 Script to create the sample *WineCloudDb* database

```
CREATE TABLE Wine (
 WineId int PRIMARY KEY,
 Name nvarchar (50),
 Category nvarchar (15),
 Year int,
 Price money)

CREATE TABLE Customer (
 CustomerId int PRIMARY KEY,
 FirstName nvarchar(50),
 LastName nvarchar(15),
 FavoriteWineId int,
 CONSTRAINT FK_Customer_Wine FOREIGN KEY (FavoriteWineId) REFERENCES Wine (WineId))

INSERT INTO Wine VALUES
 (1, 'Chateau Penin', 'Bordeaux', 2008, 34.90),
 (2, 'McLaren Valley', 'Cabernet', 2005, 48.50),
 (3, 'Mendoza', 'Merlot', 2010, 42.00),
 (4, 'Valle Central', 'Merlot', 2009, 52.00)

INSERT INTO Customer VALUES
 (1, 'Jeff', 'Hay', 4),
 (2, 'Mark', 'Hanson', 3),
 (3, 'Jeff', 'Phillips', 2)
```

To create the *WineCloudDb* database, follow these steps:

1. From the Windows Start screen, launch SSMS. You can either scroll through the app tiles to find it (in the Microsoft SQL Server 2012 category) or just type **sql server management studio** to run a search, and then click on the tile. After a brief moment, the Connect To Server dialog appears.
2. In the Connect To Server dialog, do the following:
   a. For Server Name, type **<*servername*>.database.windows.net**. This is the fully qualified name to the SQL Database server, where <*servername*> should be replaced by the name assigned to your server.
   b. For Authentication, select SQL Server Authentication from the drop-down list. (SQL Database does not support Windows Authentication.)
   c. For Login and Password, type the user name and password you assigned the server when you created it.
   d. Click the Connect button.
3. In the Object Explorer, expand the Databases node.

4. If the *WineCloudDb* database exists from a previous chapter, delete it now.
   a. Right-click the *WineCloudDb* database, and choose Delete.
   b. In the Delete Object dialog, click OK.
5. Create the database.
   a. In the Object Explorer, right-click the server name and choose New Query to open a new query window connected to the *master* database.
   b. In the query window, type **CREATE DATABASE WineCloudDb**.
   c. Press F5 (or click the Execute button in the toolbar) to create the database.
   d. Close the query window without saving the script.
6. In the Object Explorer, right-click the Databases node and choose Refresh. The *WineCloudDb* database you just created should now appear.
7. Right-click the *WineCloudDb* database, and choose New Query to open a new query window connected to the *WineCloudDb* database.
8. Type the code shown in Listing 9-1 into the query window (or paste it in from the listing file downloaded from the book's companion website).
9. Press F5 (or click the Execute button in the toolbar) to create the database schema and populate some data.

You now have a new *WineCloudDb* database you can use for the exercises in this chapter.

Note It was necessary to create the database and populate it in two separate query windows because SQL Database does not support the USE statement found in SQL Server for switching the connection from the *master* database to the *WineCloudDb* database. See Chapter 3, "Differences between SQL Server and Microsoft Azure SQL Database," for more information on differences between SQL Database and SQL Server.

Monitoring

SQL Database provides multiple options for monitoring the health and operations of your servers and databases. In this section, you will learn how to monitor SQL Database using the Microsoft Azure management portal, Microsoft Azure Service Dashboard, SQL Database management portal, and dynamic management views and functions. Using a combination of the tools described in this section, you will be able to get a comprehensive view of the health of your servers and databases in SQL Database.

Using the management portal

The Microsoft Azure management portal is the centralized place to manage all your Microsoft Azure services, including SQL Database. Using the management portal, you can create and delete SQL Database servers, create and delete databases, and manage your servers and databases, just as you've seen throughout this book. In addition, the management portal also provides monitoring and dashboard capabilities that help you understand the usage and health of your servers and databases. If you are managing multiple databases in SQL Database, you might want to quickly view how many databases you have deployed and how many databases you have remaining in your SQL Database quota. Just as with database size limits, SQL Database has limits on the number of databases each server can contain. At the time of this writing, the quota is 150 databases per server.

Follow these steps to view SQL Database server usage:

1. Log in to the Microsoft Azure management portal at **https://manage.windowsazure.com**. This brings you to the main portal page showing ALL ITEMS.
2. Click SQL DATABASES in the vertical navigation pane on the left.
3. Click the SERVERS link at the top of the page. This displays a list of your Microsoft Azure SQL Database servers.
4. In the NAME column, click the server that contains the *WineCloudDb* database. This opens a page with links for the selected server.
5. Click the DASHBOARD link at the top of the page. This displays the SQL Database server usage overview as shown in Figure 9-1.

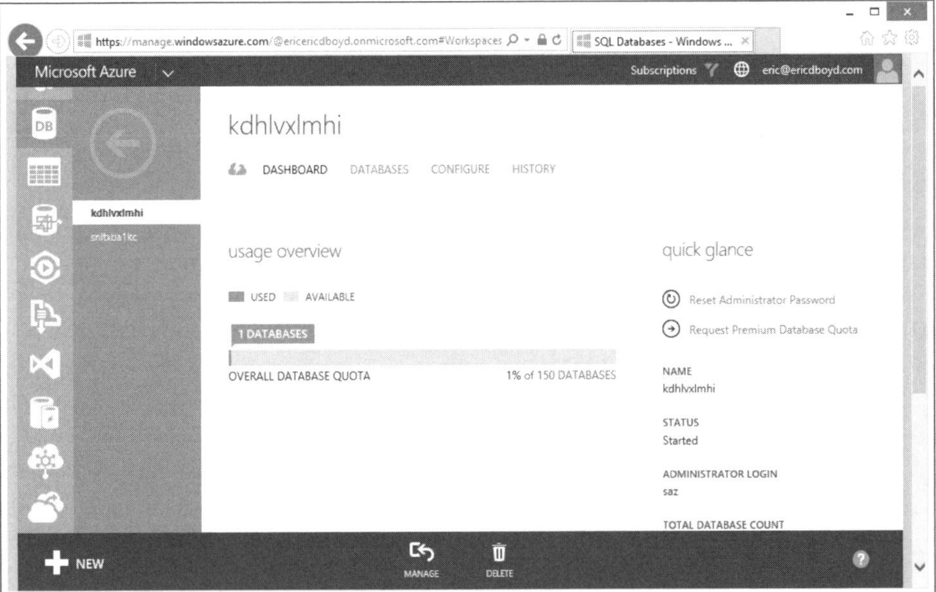

FIGURE 9-1 Viewing SQL Database server usage

The SQL Database server usage overview displays a bar that shows you the number of databases that are currently in use and the number of databases remaining in your server's quota. Figure 9-1 is showing the usage overview for a SQL Database server named *kdhlvxlmhi*. The server has one database in use out of the 150-database quota.

In addition to showing server usage and quotas, the Microsoft Azure management portal displays usage and operational metrics for each database. The database dashboard in the management portal displays the allocated size of a database, the space that is currently used, and the remaining free space.

To view database usage metrics, follow these steps:

1. If you closed the Microsoft Azure management portal since the last procedure, log in to the Microsoft Azure management portal at **https://manage.windowsazure.com**. This brings you to the main portal page showing ALL ITEMS.
2. Click SQL DATABASES in the vertical navigation pane on the left. This displays a list of your databases.
3. Click the *WineCloudDb* database.
4. Click the DASHBOARD link at the top of the page.
5. Scroll the page down a bit, and find the "Usage Overview" section as shown in Figure 9-2. This displays the used and available storage for your database.

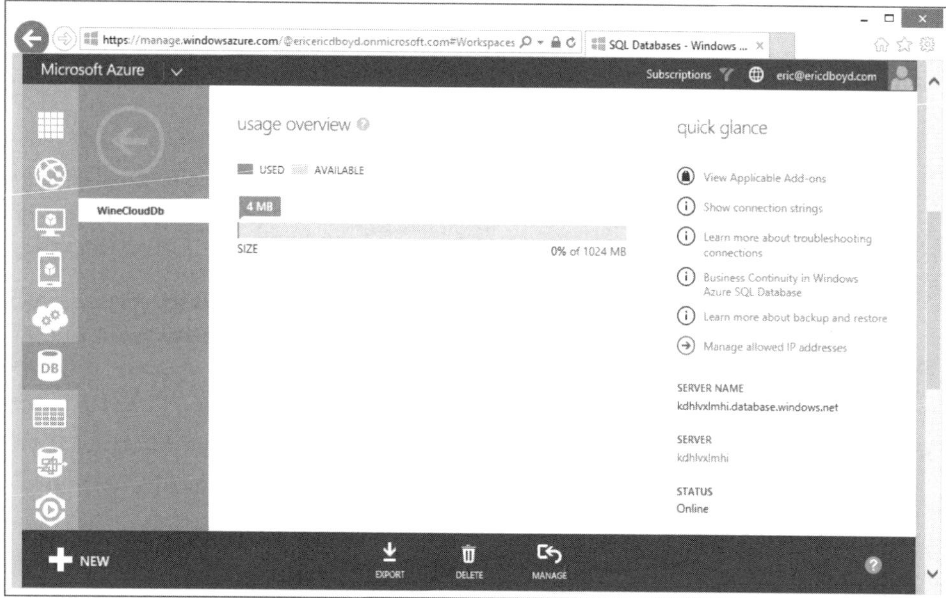

FIGURE 9-2 Viewing SQL Database size usage

A chart of select operational metrics is also displayed at the top of the dashboard page, as shown in Figure 9-3.

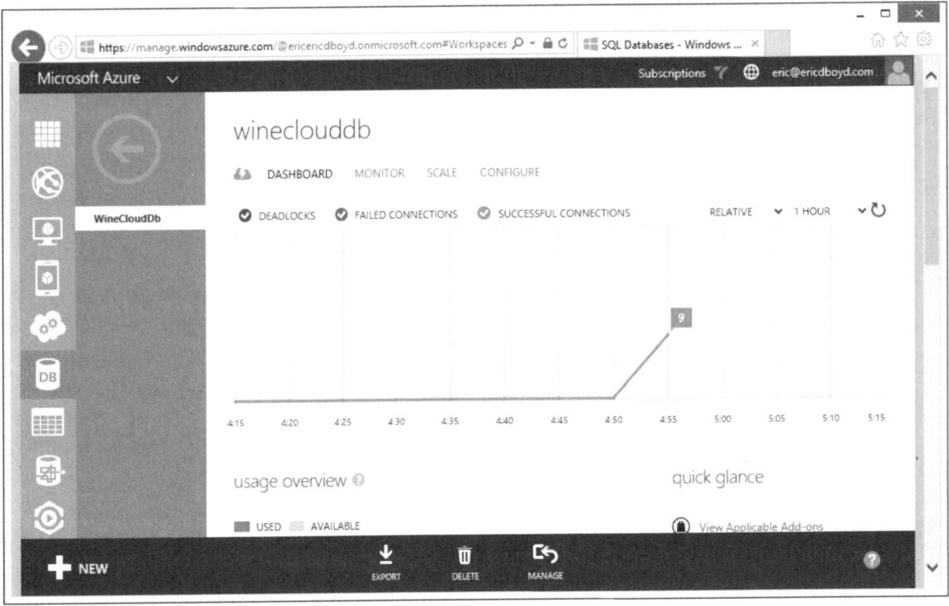

FIGURE 9-3 The metrics chart on the dashboard of a SQL Database

By default, deadlocks, failed connections, and successful connections are displayed for the past hour. You can change the reporting period from one hour to 24 hours, 7 days, or 14 days. You can also toggle the chart between showing relative values, which display the actual values relative to each other, or absolute values, which display the actual values relative to zero as displayed on the Y axis. Both can be configured using the drop-down lists above the chart on the right side. By clicking the check mark to the left of each named metric above the chart, you can also show and hide the metrics plotted on the chart. When you click the refresh button in the upper-right corner above the chart, the metrics displayed on the chart are updated.

The monitor page displays the details for each metric and allows you to customize which metrics are displayed in the details list and on the chart. In addition to the deadlocks, failed connections, and successful connections (which are displayed by default), you can choose to display metrics for connections that were blocked by the firewall, current database size, and throttled connections.

More Info For more information on the SQL Database firewall, see Chapter 2, "Configuration and pricing," and Chapter 5, "Security and backup." For more information on connection management and throttled connections, see Chapter 8, "Designing and tuning for scalability and high performance."

Follow these steps to display additional metrics:

1. If you closed the Microsoft Azure management portal since the last procedure, log in to the Microsoft Azure management portal at **https://manage.windowsazure.com**. This brings you to the main portal page showing ALL ITEMS.
2. Click SQL DATABASES in the vertical navigation pane on the left. This displays a list of your databases.
3. Click the *WineCloudDb* database.
4. Click the MONITOR link at the top of the page. This displays the metrics chart at the top and the list of metrics with their minimum, maximum, average, and total values in the list below, as shown in Figure 9-4.

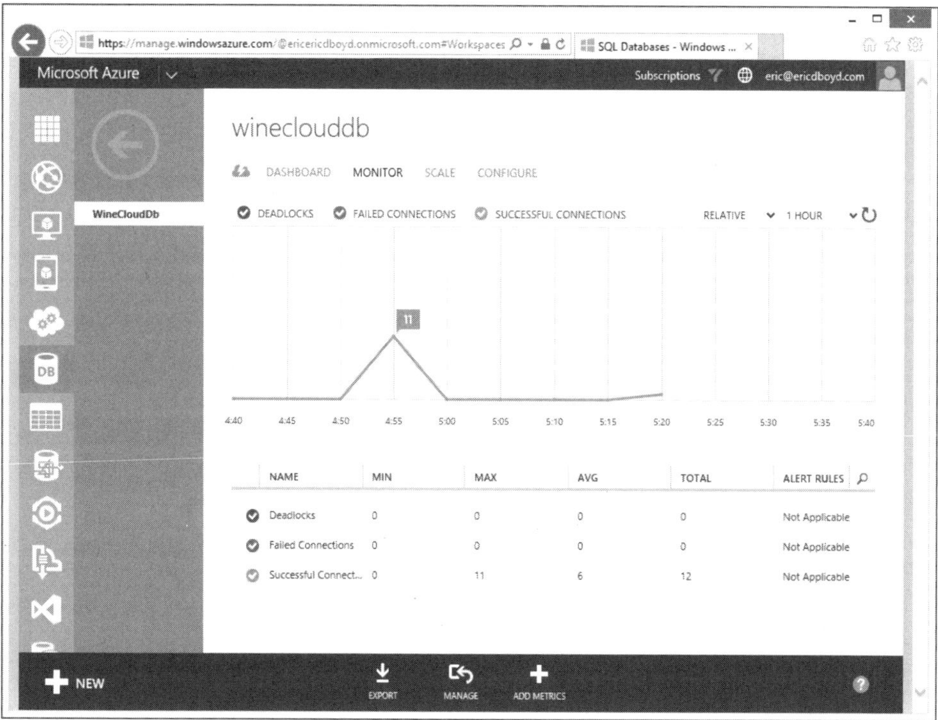

FIGURE 9-4 SQL Database Monitor page, with the chart and details for the configured metrics

5. Click the ADD METRICS button at the bottom of the page to display the CHOOSE METRICS dialog.
6. Select the Blocked By Firewall check box at the top of the list as shown in Figure 9-5.

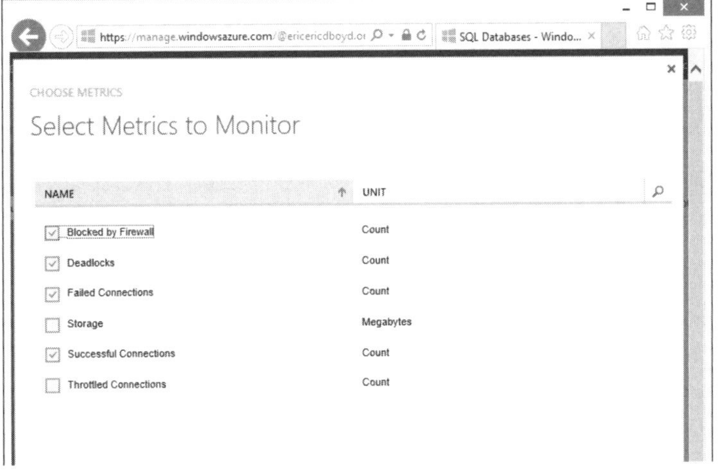

FIGURE 9-5 The Choose Metrics dialog of the Monitor page for a SQL Database

7. Click the check mark in the lower-right corner to close the dialog.

You have now added the Blocked By Firewall metric to the list of metrics displayed at the bottom of the Monitor page. By default, the newly added metrics are not added to the chart at the top. To display the metric on the chart, click the gray circle to the left of the metric name in the list of metrics. After you click the gray circle icon, the icon will be changed to a colored circle with a check mark and the metric will be displayed in the chart, as shown in Figure 9-6.

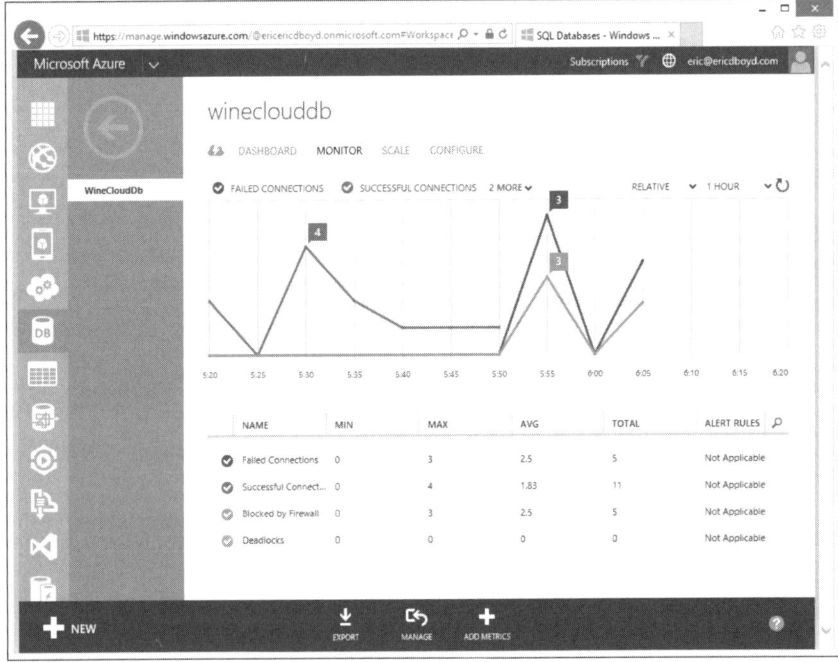

FIGURE 9-6 A newly added metric in the list of metrics on the Monitor page of a SQL Database

To delete a metric from the list of displayed metrics and the chart, select the metric in the list. This displays a DELETE METRIC button at the bottom of the page to the right of the ADD METRICS button. Click the DELETE METRIC button, and the metric will be removed from the list and the chart.

Microsoft Azure Service Dashboard

The health of your SQL Database servers and databases depend on the health of the overall Microsoft Azure SQL Database service. Data centers, servers, and cloud services can experience health issues and service outages for various reasons. Knowing when there's an issue with the overall service can save you a lot of time and frustration when troubleshooting your application issues. The Microsoft Azure Service Dashboard (shown in Figure 9-7), is a website that shows the current and historical health of all the services in Microsoft Azure. Browse to *http://azure.microsoft.com/en-us/support/service-dashboard/* to display the Microsoft Azure Service Dashboard.

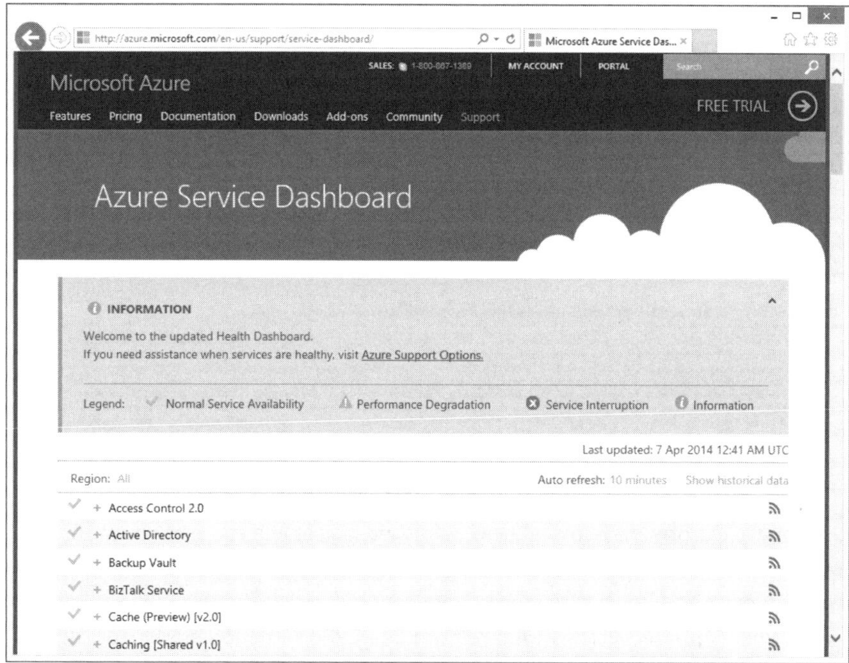

FIGURE 9-7 The Microsoft Azure Service Dashboard

Each Microsoft Azure service is listed on the Service Dashboard page. To the left of each service name is an icon that represents the current state of each service. If the service has a green check mark next to it, the service is operating normally. If it has an orange triangle warning icon, the performance of the service is not normal and is currently running with degraded performance. If a red circle error icon is displayed, the service is experiencing an outage. Clicking the plus sign to the left of the service name expands the list of regions where the service is deployed, and you can view the health of the service in each region. Clicking the RSS icon on the right side of each row displays an RSS feed with a descriptive status history, as shown in Figure 9-8. You can subscribe to the Service Dashboard RSS feeds with an RSS reader, and you can also create a custom operations dashboard using the RSS feeds as an API.

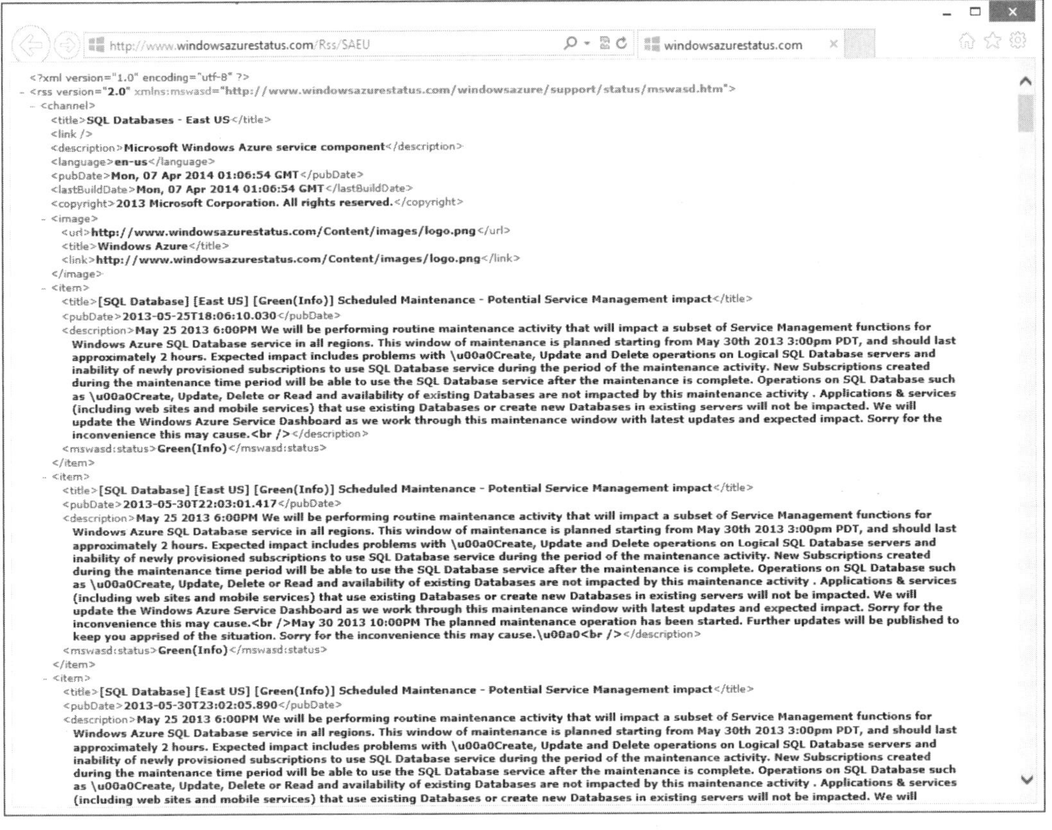

FIGURE 9-8 The SQL Database Service Dashboard RSS feed

By default, the Service Dashboard automatically refreshes the service statuses every 10 minutes. The refresh interval can be set to 1 minute, 2 minutes, 5 minutes, 10 minutes, or Off to disable the automatic refresh. You can also filter the displayed data center regions to show only the regions that are relevant to you. When you use Microsoft Azure for managed production workloads, the Service Dashboard is a website that can be displayed on a monitor in your operations center so that you can stay informed of any service interruptions in Microsoft Azure.

SQL Database management portal

The SQL Database management portal (which was introduced in Chapter 1, "Getting started with Microsoft Azure SQL Database") is another useful tool when monitoring SQL Database usage and performance. Allocated database capacity, current database size, and available free space are displayed on the database summary page, along with active users and connections, as shown in Figure 9-9.

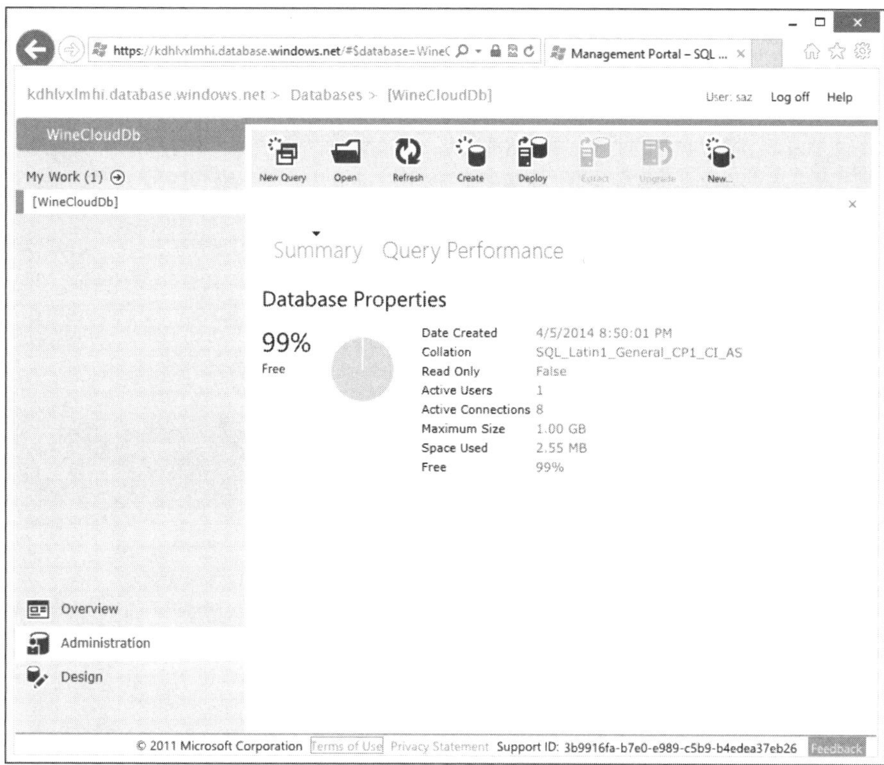

FIGURE 9-9 The SQL Database management portal database summary page

Monitoring and troubleshooting query performance can be a difficult task. Tools that help you identify bottlenecks and pinpoint improvement opportunities can help you be more effective when optimizing queries. The SQL Database management portal provides tools to help you identity inefficient queries.

To view performance of recent queries, follow these steps:

1. If you closed the Microsoft Azure management portal since the last procedure, log in to the Microsoft Azure management portal at **https://manage.windowsazure.com**. This brings you to the main portal page showing ALL ITEMS.
2. Click SQL DATABASES in the vertical navigation pane on the left. This displays a list of your databases.
3. Click the *WineCloudDb* database.
4. Click the MANAGE button at the bottom of the page to open the SQL Database management portal.
5. Type the username (for example, **saz**) and password you assigned when you created the server, and click Log On. This displays the Summary page for the database, as shown earlier in Figure 9-9.

6. Click the Query Performance link at the top of the page to display the list of high-cost queries, as shown in Figure 9-10. You can sort the table of queries by clicking on the headers at the top.

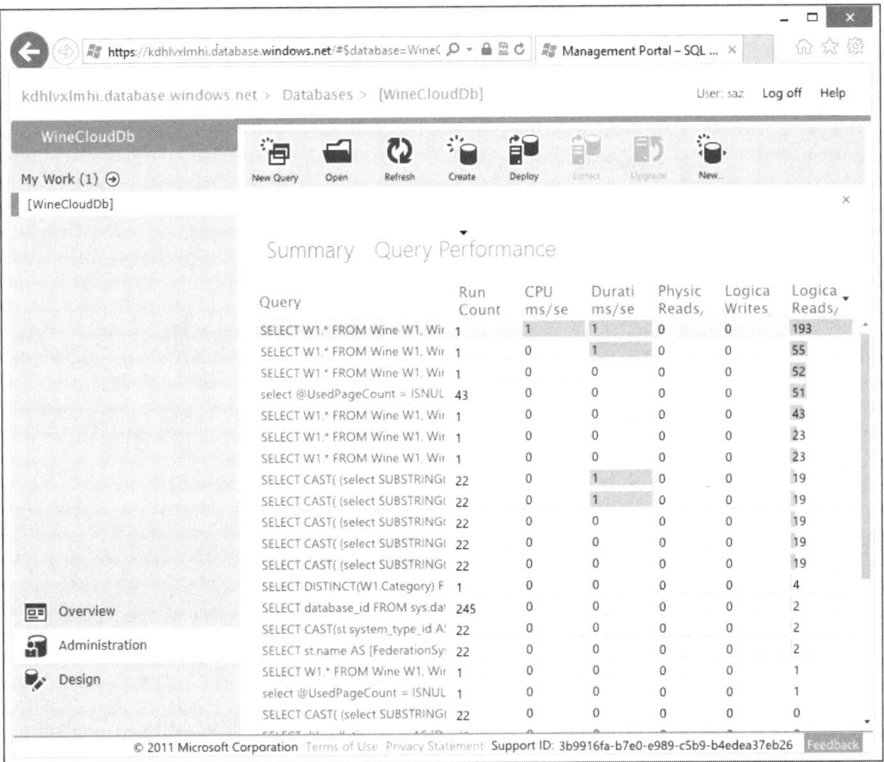

FIGURE 9-10 The Query Performance page in the SQL Database management portal

7. Click on one of the queries in the list to display the Query Plan Details. The portal displays the query, the resources used by the query, and the details of the query's execution plan, as shown in Figure 9-11.

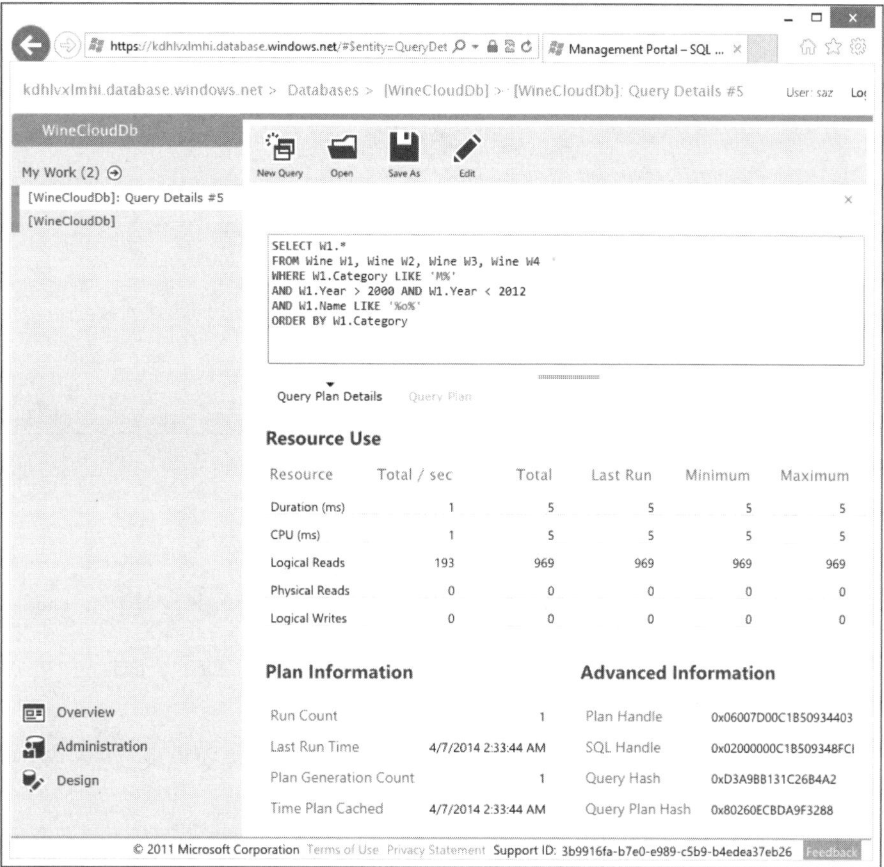

FIGURE 9-11 The Query Plan Details area in the SQL Database management portal.

Note The query displayed on the Query Plan Details page is read-only. To edit the query, click the Edit button in the ribbon at the top of the page.

8. Click the Query Plan link below the query to display the execution plan, as shown in Figure 9-12. Using the buttons on the right, above the graphical query plan, you can toggle the display of the execution plan display between the graphical, grid, and tree views. The icons on the left side enable you to highlight the operations of the execution plan based on CPU or IO cost and the types of operations.

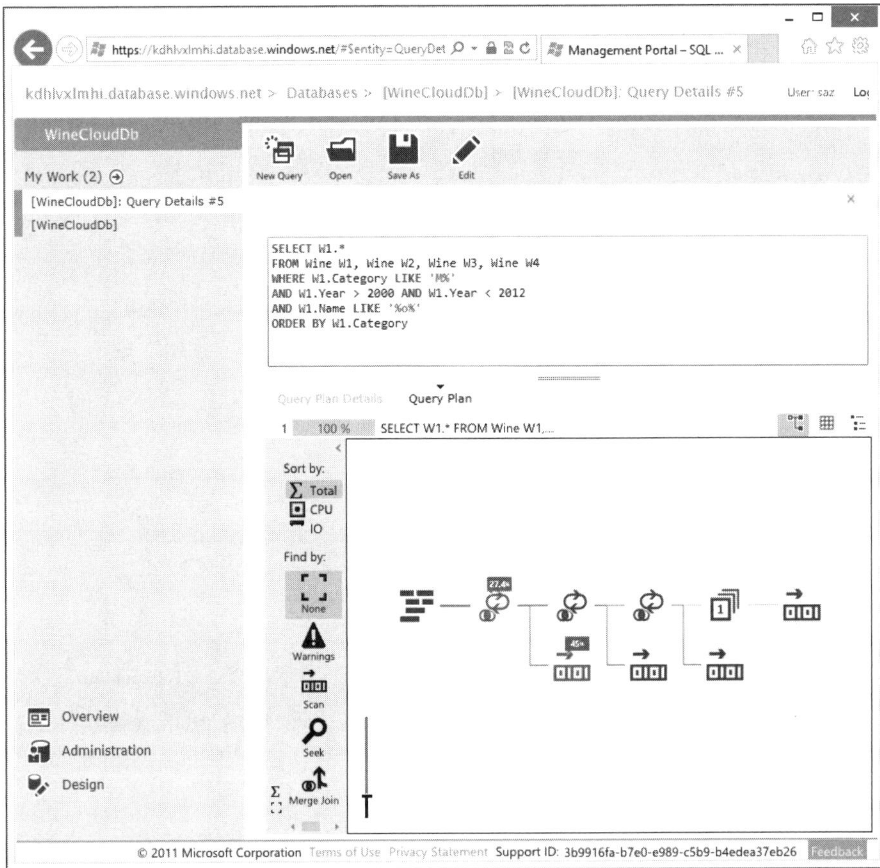

FIGURE 9-12 The Graphical Query Plan in the SQL Database management portal

9. Click an operation in the execution plan to view the details and performance cost of the operation, as shown in Figure 9-13. If you are viewing a large execution plan with many operations, the graphical execution plan can be zoomed in and out.

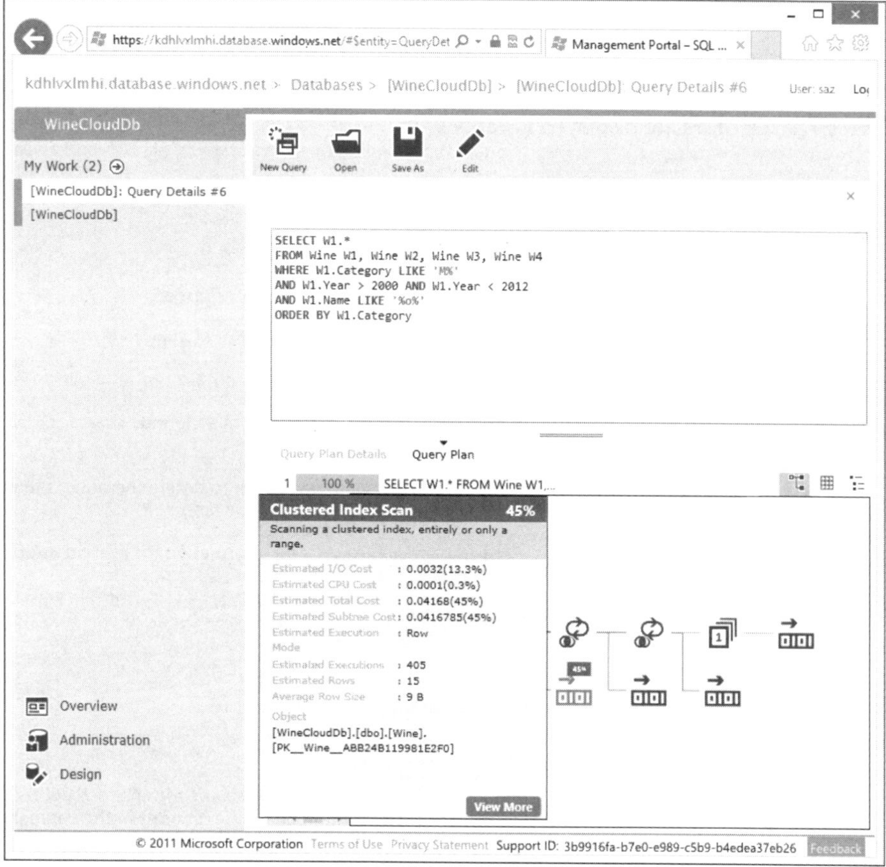

FIGURE 9-13 The Operation details in the SQL Database management portal graphical execution plan

You have now used SQL Database management portal to identify queries in your database with a high performance cost. Using this portal, you can drill into a query's execution plan, identify expensive operations, and review the details of a specific operation. The SQL Database management portal gets the expensive queries displayed in the Query Performance page from SQL Database dynamic management views, which are explained in the next section.

Dynamic management views and functions

Dynamic management views (DMV) and dynamic management functions (DMF) give insight into operations and resource consumption inside Microsoft Azure SQL Database. DMVs were first introduced in SQL Server 2005 and are designed to provide an alternative to using system tables and functions to monitor SQL Server. SQL Database includes a subset of these SQL Server dynamic management views that help monitor servers and databases, and that help diagnose performance problems caused by blocked or long-running queries, inefficient execution plans, and resource bottlenecks. SQL Database includes support for three categories of DMVs: database DMVs, execution DMVs, and transaction DMVs. All DMVs are defined in the *sys* schema.

Database

Database-related dynamic management views and functions provide database focused insight and metrics. The database-related DMVs included in SQL Database are displayed in Table 9-1. The database-related DMFs are displayed in Table 9-2.

TABLE 9-1 Database-related dynamic management views

Name	Description
dm_db_index_usage_stats	Returns counts of different types of index operations and the time each type of operation was last performed
dm_db_missing_index_details	Returns detailed information about missing indexes
dm_db_missing_index_group_stats	Returns summary information about groups of missing indexes
dm_db_missing_index_groups	Returns information about what missing indexes are contained in a specific missing index group
dm_db_objects_impacted_on_version_change	Provides an early warning system to determine objects that will be impacted by major release upgrades
dm_db_partition_stats	Returns page and row-count information for every partition in the database
dm_db_wait_stats	Returns information about all the waits encountered by threads that executed during operation

TABLE 9-2 Database-related dynamic management functions

Name	Description
dm_db_index_operational_stats	Returns current low-level I/O, locking, latching, and access method activity for each partition of a table or index in the database
dm_db_index_physical_stats	Returns size and fragmentation information for the data and indexes of the specified table or view
dm_db_missing_index_columns	Returns information about database table columns that are missing and index

One database metric that is particularly important to monitor is database size. If the size of your database reaches the size quota, your queries will return error code 40544. (See Chapter 2 for more information about the database size quota.) When you reach your size quota, you cannot insert or update data or create new database objects until you increase the maximum size of your database or delete data. Using DMVs, you can monitor the size of your database proactively and take the appropriate actions before your applications receive errors resulting from a database that has reached its size quota.

More Info SQL Database raises errors unique to SQL Database, and each error is identified with an error code or error number. These errors include general errors for features, objects, and syntax not supported by SQL Database, errors that occur when copying databases, and connection errors. For more information and a list of the SQL Database error codes, visit *http://msdn.microsoft.com/en-us/library/ff394106.aspx*.

To calculate the size of your database using database DMVs, follow these steps:

1. If you closed the Microsoft Azure management portal since the last procedure, log in to the Microsoft Azure management portal at **https://manage.windowsazure.com**. This brings you to the main portal page showing ALL ITEMS.
2. Click SQL DATABASES in the vertical navigation pane on the left. This displays a list of your databases.
3. Click the *WineCloudDb* database.
4. Click the MANAGE button at the bottom of the page to open the SQL Database management portal.
5. Type the user name (for example, **saz**) and password you assigned when you created the server, and click Log On. This displays the Summary page for the database.
6. Click New Query in the ribbon at the top.
7. Type **SELECT SUM(reserved_page_count) * 8.0 / 1024 AS 'MBs Used' FROM sys.dm_db_partition_stats**, and click Run in the ribbon at the top. This executes the query and displays the current database size, as shown in Figure 9-14.

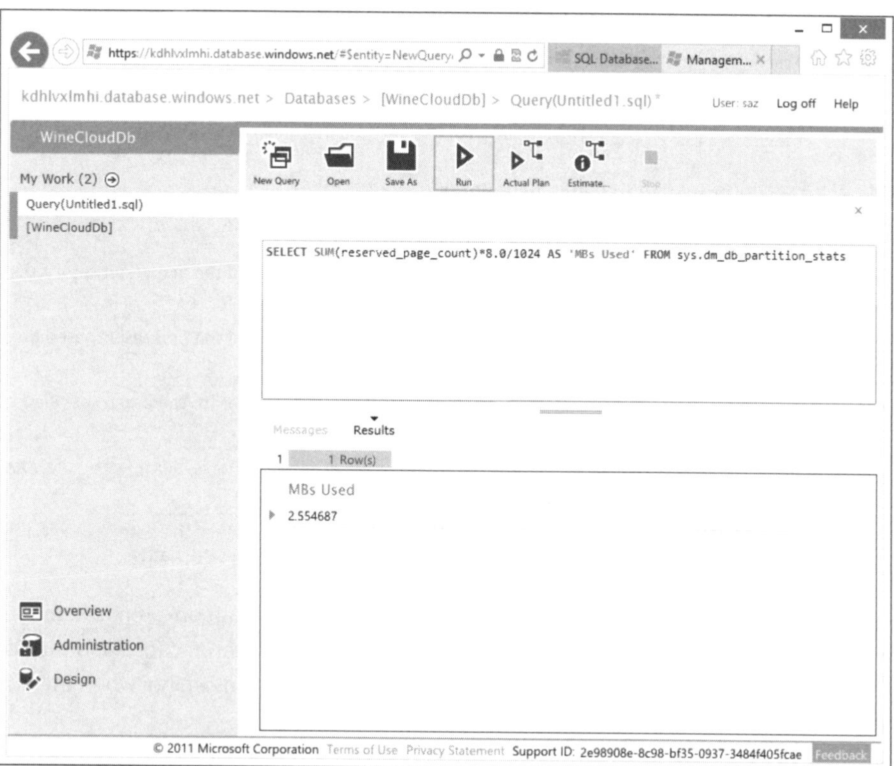

FIGURE 9-14 Getting database size using DMVs in the SQL Database management portal

Obtaining the current database size, as you did in the preceding steps, is an example of using database DMVs. The other database DMVs can be used to get insight into index usage, indexes that are needed, and wait time encountered during query execution.

Execution

Execution-related DMVs provide insight into connections, sessions, and the requests that your SQL Database servers receive. The execution-related DMVs that are included in SQL Database are listed in Table 9-3. Execution-related DMFs are listed in Table 9-4.

TABLE 9-3 Execution-related dynamic management views

Name	Description
dm_exec_cached_plans	Returns a row for each query plan that is cached by SQL Database
dm_exec_connections	Returns information about the connections established to SQL Database
dm_exec_procedure_stats	Returns aggregate performance statistics for cached stored procedures
dm_exec_query_memory_grants	Returns information about the queries that have acquired a memory grant or that still require a memory grant to execute
dm_exec_query_stats	Returns aggregate performance statistics for cached query plans
dm_exec_requests	Returns information about each request that executes
dm_exec_sessions	Returns information about all active user connections and internal tasks
dm_exec_trigger_stats	Returns aggregate performance statistics for cached triggers

TABLE 9-4 Execution-related dynamic management functions

Name	Description
dm_exec_describe_first_result_set	Returns the metadata description of the first result set for the statement
dm_exec_describe_first_result_set_for_object	Returns the metadata description of the first result based on an object Id
dm_exec_query_plan	Returns the Showplan in XML format for the batch specified by the plan handle
dm_exec_sql_text	Returns the text of the SQL batch that is identified by the specified sql handle
dm_exec_text_query_plan	Returns the Showplan in text format for the batch specified by the plan handle or a specific statement within the batch

Database connections are finite resources that get managed both on-premises and in the cloud. Using execution DMVs, you can view all the active SQL Database connections and see connection properties such as the login, how much CPU time the session is consuming, when the last request occurred, and more.

To view the active SQL Database connections and sessions using execution DMVs, follow these steps:

1. If you closed the Microsoft Azure management portal since the last procedure, log in to the Microsoft Azure management portal at **https://manage.windowsazure.com**. This brings you to the main portal page showing ALL ITEMS.
2. Click SQL DATABASES in the vertical navigation pane on the left. This displays a list of your databases.
3. Click the *WineCloudDb* database.
4. Click the MANAGE button at the bottom of the page to open the SQL Database management portal.
5. Type the user name (for example, **saz**) and password you assigned when you created the server, and click Log On. This displays the Summary page for the database.
6. Click New Query in the ribbon at the top.
7. Type **SELECT e.connection_id, s.session_id, s.login_name, s.cpu_time, s.last_request_end_time FROM sys.dm_exec_sessions s INNER JOIN sys.dm_exec_connections e ON s.session_id = e.session_id**, and click Run in the ribbon at the top. This executes the query and displays the connection and session results, as shown in Figure 9-15.

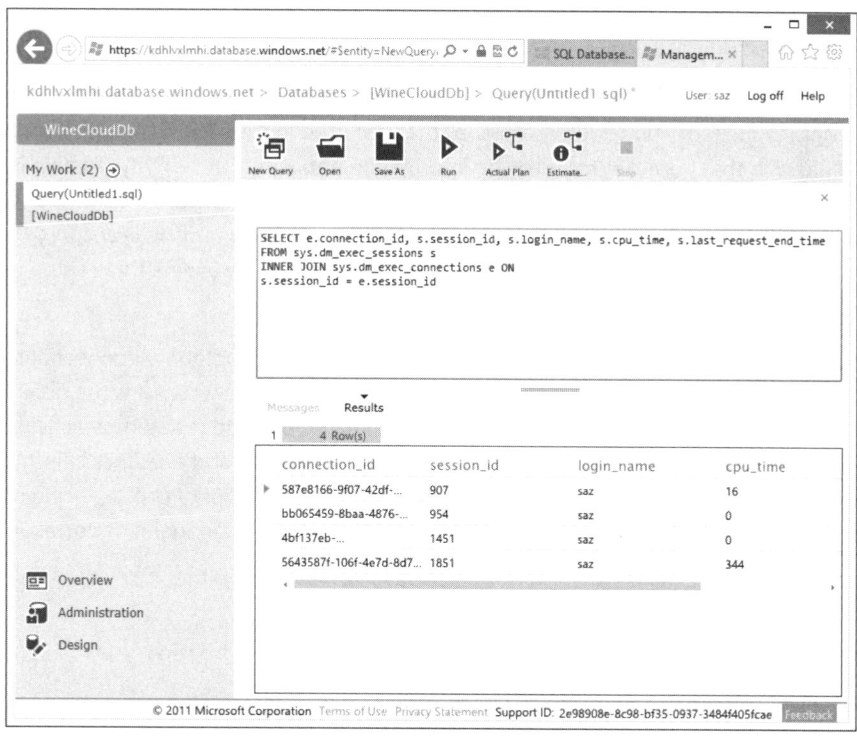

FIGURE 9-15 Viewing SQL Database connections and sessions using execution DMVs in the SQL Database management portal

Execution-related DMVs and DMFs provide information about connections, sessions, requests, and execution performance. These DMVs and DMFs are useful when troubleshooting connection problems and poor query performance.

Transaction

Transaction-related DMVs provide information about database transactions and locks. The transaction-related DMVs included in SQL Database are listed in Table 9-5. SQL Database does not contain transaction-related DMFs.

TABLE 9-5 Transaction-related dynamic management views

Name	Description
dm_tran_active_transactions	Returns information about transactions for your current database
dm_tran_database_transactions	Returns information about transactions at the database level
dm_tran_locks	Returns information about currently active lock manager resources
dm_tran_session_transactions	Returns correlation information for associated transactions and sessions

Database contention, locking and deadlocks can cause application unresponsiveness, hangs, and errors. You can use transaction-related DMVs to view current locking activity and blocking in your SQL Database.

Event tables

Dynamic management views are very helpful tools when monitoring and troubleshooting current activity, but if you are trying to research issues that occurred in the past, dynamic management views cannot help with that because they provide information about current activity. To help investigate issues that occurred in the past and are no longer occurring, SQL Database introduced two catalog views in the master database, named *sys.database_connection_stats* and *sys.event_log*. These *event tables*, as they are commonly referred to, collect and store database events that can be used to troubleshoot past behavior.

The *sys.database_connection_stats* view provides a summary of database connections, both successful connections and failed connections. The *sys.event_log* view contains the details of connectivity-related events. Together these views can be used to troubleshoot database activity, including failed connections, terminated connections, throttled connections, and deadlocks. Both of these views exist in the *master* database and can be queried using your tool of choice, including SQL Server Management Studio, SQL Server Data Tools, or the SQL Database management portal.

Programming the Service Management REST API

The ability to monitor the health of services like SQL Database is essential when using them for production workloads. In the previous section, you monitored SQL Database using the Microsoft Azure management portal, Microsoft Azure Service Dashboard, SQL Database management portal, and the SQL Database dynamic management views. Using these GUIs to manage SQL Database can be easy to get started, but automating the management of frequently repeated tasks becomes important as you get more comfortable with SQL Database and your applications mature. In this section, you will learn how to automate management of repeated SQL Database tasks using the Service Management REST API.

Note The Azure PowerShell cmdlets can also be used to effectively automate the management of SQL Database. See Chapter 2 for detailed information on downloading, installing, and using the PowerShell cmdlets for Microsoft Azure SQL Database.

The Service Management API lies at the core of all the services in Microsoft Azure. The Service Management API can be used to create new SQL Database servers and databases, manage the SQL Database firewall rules, and even reset the administrator password. This API is based on HTTP and REST, is publicly accessible, and can be used by any device or platform that can issue HTTP requests. SQL Database APIs can be grouped into three major categories: APIs for managing SQL Database servers, APIs for managing databases, and APIs for managing server-level firewall rules.

To use the Service Management API, you must authenticate and be authorized to manage the Microsoft Azure subscription. You can authenticate using an X.509 v3 certificate (referred to as a *management certificate*) or using OAuth 2.0 with Microsoft Azure Active Directory. To authenticate with a management certificate, you must either have a management certificate that is already added to your Microsoft Azure subscription or create a new X.509 v3 certificate to use as a management certificate.

Follow these steps to create a new management certificate:

1. Launch the Developer Command Prompt as an administrator. An easy way to do this is to press the Windows key, type **Developer Command Prompt**, right-click on the Developer Command Prompt result that is displayed, and click Run As Administrator in the toolbar at the bottom of the screen. This will launch the Developer Command Prompt as an administrator.
2. Type **makecert -sky exchange -r -n "CN=Microsoft Azure Service Management Certificate" -pe -a sha1 -len 2048 -ss My "<*file-path*>\MicrosoftAzureService-ManagementCertificate.cer"**, and press Enter. This will create a new X.509 v3 certificate, add it to your personal certificate store, and save your certificate in a file named *MicrosoftAzureServiceManagmentCertificate.cer* in the folder you specified.

Note Replace <*file-path*> with the path to the folder where you want your new X.509 certificate saved.

Now that you have created a new X.509 v3 certificate to use for your Microsoft Azure management certificate, you need to upload it to your Microsoft Azure subscription.

To upload your management certificate to Microsoft Azure, follow these steps:

1. If you closed the Microsoft Azure management portal since the last procedure, log in to the Microsoft Azure management portal at **https://manage.windowsazure.com**. This brings you to the main portal page showing ALL ITEMS.
2. Click SETTINGS at the bottom of the vertical navigation pane on the left.
3. Click the Management Certificates link at the top of the page to display your management certificates.
4. Click the Upload button at the bottom of the page to display the Upload A Management Certificate dialog, as shown in Figure 9-16.

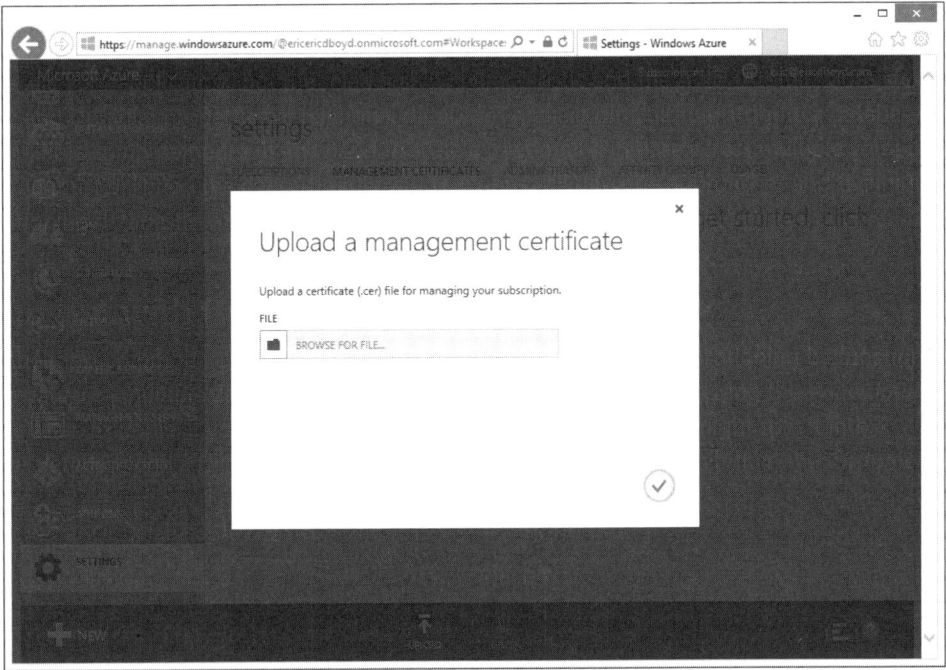

FIGURE 9-16 The Upload A Management Certificate dialog in the Microsoft Azure management portal

5. Click the folder icon, and locate the *MicrosoftAzureServiceManagementCertificate.cer* file you created in the previous procedure.

6. Click the check mark in the lower right corner to upload your management certificate. Once the upload is finished, your management certificate will be displayed in the list of management certificates, as shown in Figure 9-17.

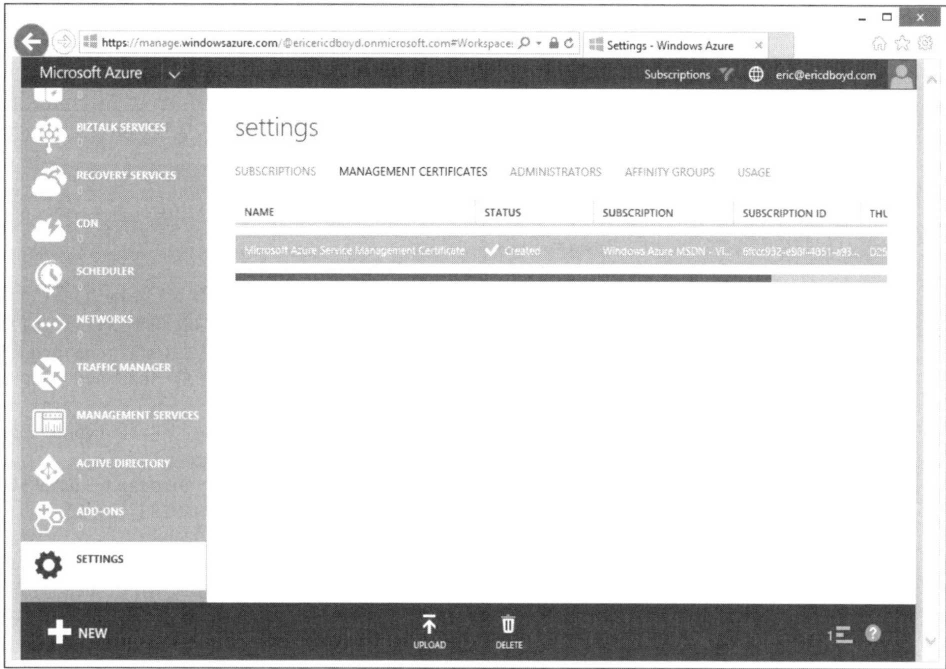

FIGURE 9-17 The list of management certificates in the Microsoft Azure management portal

You have now created an X.509 v3 certificate and uploaded it to your Microsoft Azure subscription's management certificates. With the certificate in place, you can authenticate to the Microsoft Azure Service Management API and use the API to manage SQL Database.

In the following procedure, you will create a console application that makes HTTP requests to the Service Management API to create a database. The console application code shown in Listing 9-2 retrieves your management certificate from your local certificate store by the thumbprint of the certificate. It then builds an *HttpWebRequest* for the Service Management REST API, adds the management certificate to the request, and executes the request asynchronously. The results and response for the request are written to the console once the request has completed.

LISTING 9-2 The console application code using the Microsoft Azure Service Management REST API

```
using System;
using System.IO;
using System.Net;
using System.Security.Cryptography.X509Certificates;
using System.Text;
```

```
namespace AzureServiceManagementApi
{
  class Program
  {
    static void Main()
    {
      var subscriptionId = "<subscription-id>";
      var certThumbprint = "<certificate-thumbprint>";
      var serverName = "<server-name>";
      var databaseName = "<database-name>";

      var certificateStore = new X509Store(StoreName.My, StoreLocation.CurrentUser);
      certificateStore.Open(OpenFlags.ReadOnly);
      X509Certificate2Collection certs = certificateStore.Certificates.Find
       (X509FindType.FindByThumbprint, certThumbprint, false);

      if (certs.Count == 0)
      {
        Console.WriteLine
         ("Couldn't find the certificate with thumbprint:" + certThumbprint);
        return;
      }

      certificateStore.Close();

      var request = (HttpWebRequest)HttpWebRequest.Create(new Uri(
        "https://management.core.windows.net:8443/" +
        subscriptionId +
        "/services/sqlservers/servers/" + serverName + "/databases"));

      request.Method = "POST";
      request.ClientCertificates.Add(certs[0]);
      request.ContentType = "application/xml";
      request.Headers.Add("x-ms-version", "2012-03-01");

      var sb = new StringBuilder("<?xml version=\"1.0\" encoding=\"utf-8\"?>");
      sb.Append("<ServiceResource xmlns=\"http://schemas.microsoft.com/windowsazure\">");
      sb.AppendFormat("<Name>{0}</Name>", databaseName);
      sb.Append("<Edition>Web</Edition>");
      sb.Append("<MaxSizeGB>1</MaxSizeGB>");
      sb.Append("<CollationName>SQL_Latin1_General_CP1_CI_AS</CollationName>");
      sb.Append("</ServiceResource>");

      var formData = UTF8Encoding.UTF8.GetBytes(sb.ToString());
      request.ContentLength = formData.Length;

      using (var postStream = request.GetRequestStream())
      {
        postStream.Write(formData, 0, formData.Length);
      }

      Console.WriteLine("Creating Database: " + databaseName);
```

```
        try
        {
          RequestState state = new RequestState();
          state.Request = request;
          IAsyncResult result = request.BeginGetResponse(RespCallback, state);
        }
        catch (WebException ex)
        {
          var error = new StreamReader(ex.Response.GetResponseStream()).ReadToEnd();
          Console.WriteLine("Error: " + error);
        }
        catch (Exception ex)
        {
          Console.WriteLine("Error: " + ex.Message);
        }
        Console.ReadKey();
      }

      public static string EncodeToBase64String(string original)
      {
        return Convert.ToBase64String(Encoding.UTF8.GetBytes(original));
      }

      private static void RespCallback(IAsyncResult result)
      {
        var state = (RequestState)result.AsyncState;
        var request = state.Request;

        var response = (HttpWebResponse)request.EndGetResponse(result);

        var statusCode = response.StatusCode.ToString();
        var reqId = response.GetResponseHeader("x-ms-request-id");

        Console.WriteLine("Creation Return Value: " + statusCode);
        Console.WriteLine("RequestId: " + reqId);
      }
    }

    public class RequestState
    {
      const int BufferSize = 4096;
      public StringBuilder RequestData;
      public byte[] BufferRead;
      public WebRequest Request;
      public Stream ResponseStream;
      public Decoder StreamDecode = Encoding.UTF8.GetDecoder();

      public RequestState()
      {
        BufferRead = new byte[BufferSize];
        RequestData = new StringBuilder(String.Empty);
        Request = null;
        ResponseStream = null;
      }
    }
  }
```

To create a console application that creates a new SQL Database using the Service Management API, follow these steps:

1. Launch Visual Studio 2013 as an administrator. From the Windows start screen, you can either scroll through the tiles to find it or just type **visual studio 2013** to run an app search. Right-click on the Visual Studio 2013 tile or result, and click Run As Administrator in the toolbar at the bottom of the screen. This will launch Visual Studio 2013 as an administrator.

Note Running Visual Studio 2013 as an administrator is required because the console application needs to get a certificate from the local certificate store to authenticate with the Microsoft Azure Service Management API. To debug the console application as an administrator, you need to run Visual Studio as an administrator.

2. Click the FILE menu, and then choose New | Project to display the New Project dialog.
3. On the left of the New Project dialog, expand Templates, Visual C# and choose Console Application.
4. Name the solution and project **AzureServiceManagementApi**, and choose any desired location, as shown in Figure 9-18.

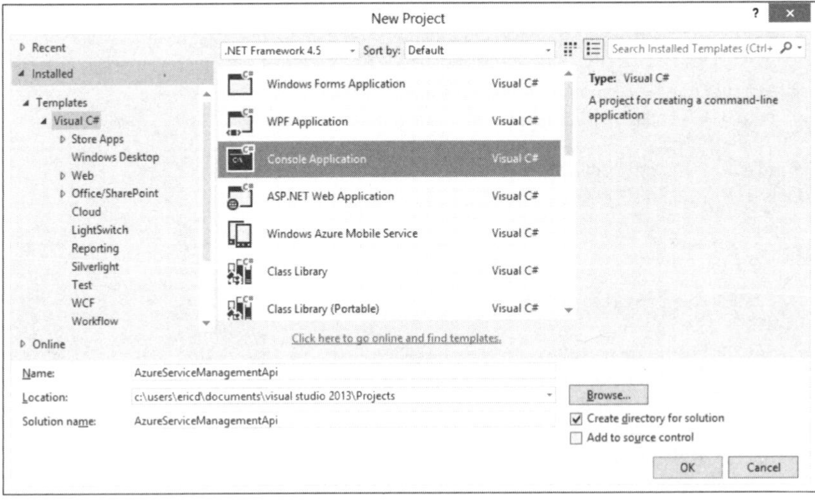

FIGURE 9-18 Creating a new console application in Visual Studio 2013

5. Replace the template code in the *Program.cs* with the code shown earlier in Listing 9-2, and change the values of the variables at the top as follows:

   a. Replace *<subscription-id>* with your Microsoft Azure subscription Id. This can be found under Settings | Subscriptions in the Microsoft Azure management portal.

   b. Replace *<certificate-thumbprint>* with the thumbprint of your management certificate. This can found under Settings | Management Certificates in the Microsoft Azure management portal.

   c. Replace *<server-name>* with the name of the server that was assigned when you created your SQL Database server.

   d. Replace *<database-name>* with **WineCloudDbMgmtApi**. This is the name of the database that will be created by the console application using the Service Management API.

6. Press F5 or click Debug | Start Debugging. This opens the console application and creates the database, as shown in Figure 9-19.

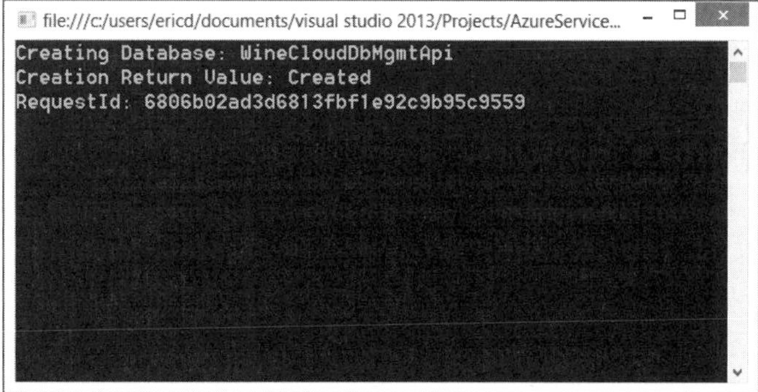

FIGURE 9-19 Creating a database in SQL Database using the Service Management API

You have successfully created a SQL Database using the REST-based Microsoft Azure Service Management API in a console application. You can verify your database was created using the Microsoft Azure management portal by finding your new database in the SQL Database server that you used in the previous procedure. In addition to creating databases, you can create, update, delete, and view SQL Database resources, including servers, databases, and firewall rules. For more information on the available Service Management APIs for SQL Database, visit *http://msdn.microsoft.com/en-us/library/gg715283.aspx*.

Summary

This chapter introduced you to monitoring SQL Database using graphical user interfaces and tools like the Microsoft Azure management portal, Microsoft Azure Service Dashboard, and SQL Database management portal. You also peeked inside the operations and performance of your SQL Database using dynamic management views and functions, and SQL Database event tables. Services you intend to use in production applications must provide monitoring capabilities, and Microsoft Azure SQL Database provides numerous monitoring options.

You then automated the management of your SQL Database using the Service Management APIs. The Service Management APIs are a collection of REST web APIs that enable you to programmatically manage your services in Microsoft Azure. These REST APIs are central to Microsoft Azure management and provide the foundation for graphical management tools like the Microsoft Azure management portal, and even command-line interfaces like the Microsoft Azure PowerShell cmdlets. As your applications mature and you move toward production, you identify frequently repeated operations that are great candidates for automating using the Service Management API (or PowerShell). It's important to automate these processes to save time and reduce human error.

This chapter introduced you to SQL Database monitoring and management capabilities, and it provided a foundation for you to build upon. Now you can dig deeper into monitoring SQL Database by creating your own monitoring queries using DMVs and DMFs. You can also further explore Service Management REST APIs (as well as the PowerShell cmdlets covered in Chapter 2) that enable you to automate management of SQL Database servers, database, firewall rules, and more.

CHAPTER 10

Building cloud solutions

—Leonard Lobel

At the very beginning of this book, back in Chapter 1, we introduced you to the concept of cloud computing. We began by describing the Infrastructure as a Service (IaaS), Platform as a Service (PaaS), and Software as a Service (SaaS) acronyms. We also explained that Microsoft Azure SQL Database in particular, is delivered as a platform—that is, it is a PaaS offering. With each successive chapter, you then explored different focus areas of the SQL Database platform. And now that you have arrived at the last chapter of the book, we present you with an end-to-end treatment for building a cloud solution on top of SQL Database. By "end-to-end," we mean a stack of layered components, where each layer is concerned with its own area of responsibility, and collectively, they work together to furnish a feature-complete application.

In this chapter, we show you how to combine SQL Database with other components to produce your own complete SaaS solution. In other words, you will learn how to build layers on top of SQL Database to deliver a ready-to-use application that runs completely in the cloud on Microsoft Azure. The solution you will create in this chapter builds on the sample *WineCloudDb* database we've been using to demonstrate throughout this book, and it includes a website that allows users to place orders through their browser, and a mobile app that allows users to manage the wines in the database from their Microsoft Windows Phone device.

You will build the application layer by layer, from the bottom up, starting from the database level and working your way up to the user interface (UI). The complete solution stack is shown in Figure 10-1.

Here is a high-level overview of the tasks you will perform in this chapter:

- Start with an existing Microsoft Azure SQL Database.
    - Create a *WineCloudDb* database with *Wine* and *Customer* data.
- Create a new SQL Server Database project.
    - Import the database schema from *WineCloudDb* into a new SQL Server database project. This will enable you to use SQL Server Data Tools (SSDT) to work in offline mode, disconnected from SQL Database.

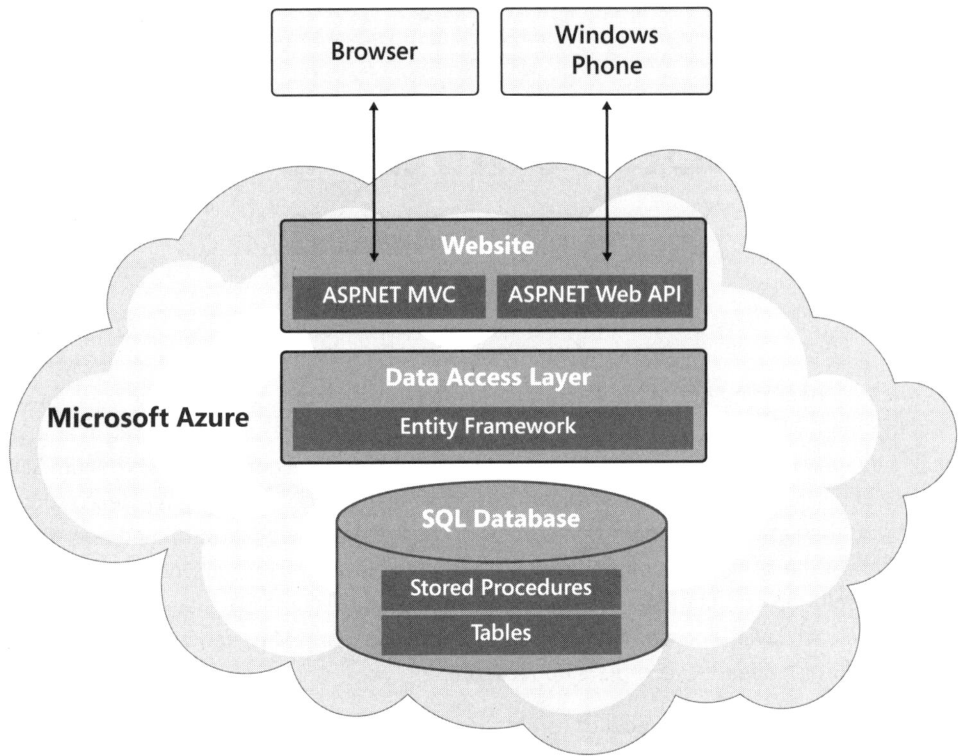

FIGURE 10-1 The complete solution is composed of these distinct application layers.

- Extend the database design in the database project.
  - Add a new column to the *Wine* table.
  - Create a new *Order* table.
  - Create stored procedures to control how data in the *Order* table can be inserted, updated, or deleted.
  - Deploy the offline database project changes back to Microsoft Azure SQL Database.
- Create a data access layer (DAL).
  - Use the Entity Framework (EF) to manage all database connections and commands.
  - Design an Entity Data Model (EDM) to configure how EF interacts with the tables and stored procedures in the database.

- Create an ASP.NET website:
  - Build a Model-View-Controller (MVC) Web application, which users can access with any browser to place orders.
  - Create a Web API to expose create, retrieve, update, and delete (CRUD) operations for wines in the database.
- Create a Windows Phone 8 app with the Windows Phone Software Development Kit (SDK).
  - Build a mobile app that communicates with the Web API to implement a wine catalog, which users can use to view, add, modify, and delete wines with their Windows Phone 8 device.

You will build all of these pieces as separate but related projects inside a single Microsoft Visual Studio solution.

So many choices

This chapter presents a complete, multitiered cloud solution, using SQL Database on the back end. Several Microsoft technologies are readily available to achieve this—it is by no means necessary to implement your cloud solution using the particular technologies we chose to use here.

You will create a data access layer using the Entity Framework, but another .NET data-access technology (such as traditional ADO.NET) might be a perfectly suitable alternative, depending on the scenario. Although you will create the website with the ASP.NET Model-View-Controller (MVC) framework, you can certainly choose to do so using standard ASP.NET web forms with .aspx pages. And for the web service, you will use the increasingly popular ASP.NET Web API to implement Representational State Transfer (REST) protocol services, although other service platforms such as Simple Object Access Protocol (SOAP) with Windows Communication Foundation (WCF), WCF Data Services (which also offers quick and easy REST services over EF), or WCF RIA (Rich Internet Application) Services, and others can be used as well.

The reason we chose these particular technologies is to keep a potentially overwhelming scenario as simple as possible. Our goal with this single chapter is for you to learn the basic layered architecture of a finished solution, using technologies that can be leveraged as quickly and easily as possible. The Entity Framework manages all database connections, commands, and readers for you automatically, and it provides ready-to-use data-access objects instantaneously. For the website, ASP.NET MVC can help you build more maintainable and testable applications than traditional web forms development with .aspx pages. And with Web API, Visual Studio *scaffolding* features make it virtually effortless to expose a REST-based web service over EF with full CRUD support.

That said, we strongly encourage you to explore alternatives for creating your own cloud solutions over SQL Database. The MVC framework has emerged as an extremely popular platform for building websites, but traditional ASP.NET web forms (using .aspx files) is by no means obsolete, and still carries several notable advantages over MVC that should not be overlooked. Likewise, the Web API has been rapidly gaining popularity for creating lightweight REST-based web services, but you can also consider building your own Microsoft Azure cloud service to host full-fledged WCF, WCF Data Services, or WCF RIA Services. To create your own cloud service in Visual Studio, you need to download and install the Microsoft Azure SDK for .NET from *http://www.windowsazure.com/en-us/downloads*.

Regardless of which particular technologies you choose, however, the core concepts of multiple tiers and layered design presented in this chapter are the same.

Creating the SQL Database

To get started, you will use SSDT inside Visual Studio to quickly create a *WineCloudDb* database similar to the one you've used throughout this book. As shown in Listing 10-1, the database will just contain a *Wine* and *Customer* table and a few rows of data, but you will soon extend this design with additional columns, tables, and stored procedures to fully support the solution.

LISTING 10-1 Script to create the *WineCloudDb* database

```
CREATE TABLE Wine(
  WineId int IDENTITY PRIMARY KEY,
  Name nvarchar(50) NOT NULL,
  Category nvarchar(15) NOT NULL,
  Year int);

CREATE TABLE Customer(
  CustomerId int IDENTITY PRIMARY KEY,
  FirstName nvarchar(50) NOT NULL,
  LastName nvarchar(50) NOT NULL,
  FavoriteWineId int,
  CONSTRAINT FK_Customer_Wine FOREIGN KEY (FavoriteWineId) REFERENCES Wine(WineId));

SET IDENTITY_INSERT Wine ON;
INSERT Wine (WineId, Name, Category, Year) VALUES
 (1, 'Chateau Penin', 'Bordeaux', 2008),
 (2, 'McLaren Valley', 'Cabernet', 2005),
 (3, 'Mendoza', 'Merlot', 2010),
 (4, 'Valle Central', 'Merlot', 2009);
SET IDENTITY_INSERT Wine OFF;

SET IDENTITY_INSERT Customer ON;
INSERT Customer (CustomerId, FirstName, LastName, FavoriteWineId) VALUES
 (1, 'Jeff', 'Hay', 4),
 (2, 'Mark', 'Hanson', 3),
 (3, 'Jeff', 'Phillips', 2);
SET IDENTITY_INSERT Customer OFF;
```

To create the *WineCloudDb* database, follow these steps:

1. Start Visual Studio 2013.
2. If the SQL Server Object Explorer is not visible, click the VIEW menu and choose SQL Server Object Explorer.
3. In the SQL Server Object Explorer, right-click SQL Server and choose Add SQL Server to display the familiar Connect To Server dialog.
4. In the Connect To Server dialog, do the following:
    a. For Server Name, type **<*servername*>.database.windows.net**. This is the fully qualified name to the SQL Database server, where <*servername*> should be replaced by the name assigned to your server.
    b. For Authentication, select SQL Server Authentication from the drop-down list. (SQL Database does not support Windows Authentication.)
    c. For Login and Password, type the user name and password you assigned the server when you created it.
    d. Click the Connect button. The server now appears as a collapsed node in the SQL Server Object Explorer.
5. Expand the server node in the SQL Server Object Explorer.
6. Expand the server's Databases node.
7. If a previous version of *WineCloudDb* is present from work you did in an earlier chapter, delete it now by doing the following:
    a. Right-click the existing *WineCloudDb* database, and choose Delete.
    b. Click OK to confirm.
9. Right-click the Databases node, and choose Add New Database.
10. Type **WineCloudDb**, and press Enter. The new database now appears in the SQL Server Object Explorer.
11. Right-click the *WineCloudDb* database, and choose New Query to open a new query window.
12. Type the code shown in Listing 10-1 into the query window (or paste it in from the listing file downloaded from the book's companion website).
13. Press Ctrl+Shift+E to execute the script (or press the play button icon in the query window's toolbar).
14. Close the query window. (It isn't necessary to save the changes.)

Extending the SQL Database

Until now, you've used SQL Server Data Tools (SSDT) inside of Visual Studio 2013 to work with SQL Database in a connected fashion. Using SSDT for connected development is similar to using SQL Server Management Studio (SSMS), and working connected certainly carries a convenience factor when all you need to do is query or tweak something quickly on a live server. However, this is not the preferred way to develop databases using SSDT. The proper way to build databases with SSDT is by working offline in a disconnected fashion, using SQL Server Database projects. With this approach, you can rely on the definition of the database living inside of a Visual Studio project (rather than the database itself) where it can be preserved, protected, and versioned using source code control (SCC).

In this chapter, you will start with the pre-existing SQL Database in the cloud that you just created using *connected SSDT*, and import its schema definition into a new SQL Server database project. Then you will continue developing the database using *disconnected SSDT*—that is, by working with the offline project and deploying changes incrementally to the live SQL Database.

Creating a new solution

Visual Studio projects are contained inside a Visual Studio solution, so you'll start by creating an empty solution. Then you'll import the database design from SQL Database into a new SQL Server Database project, the first of several projects that you will create for the solution. Once the project is created, you will extend the *WineCloudDb* database design it by adding more columns, tables, and stored procedures. Then you will deploy the updated design by publishing the project back SQL Database in the cloud.

To create the new solution, follow these steps:

1. In Visual Studio 2013, click the FILE menu, then choose New | Project to display the New Project dialog.
2. On the left of the New Project dialog, expand Templates, Other Project Types, and choose Visual Studio Solutions.
3. Select the Blank Solution template, name the solution **WineCloudSolution**, and choose any desired location for the solution as shown in Figure 10-2.
4. Click OK to create the solution.

The Solution Explorer now shows the new *WineCloudSolution*. (If the Solution Explorer is not visible, click the VIEW menu and choose Solution Explorer.) Now that you have an empty solution, you're ready to create a new SQL Server Database project.

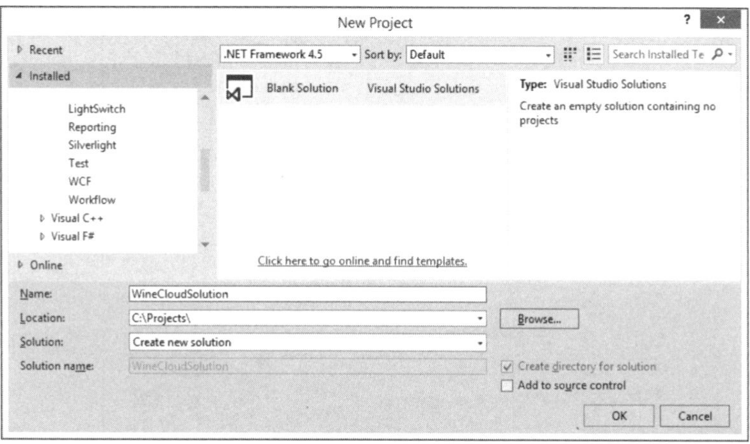

FIGURE 10-2 Creating a new blank solution

Creating a SQL Server Database project

With a SQL Server Database project, you can develop your database with no connection whatsoever to SQL Server, SQL Database, or the Internet. A SQL Server Database project is a Visual Studio project that contains individual declarative Transact SQL (T-SQL) source-code files that collectively define the complete structure of a database. Because the database definition is maintained this way inside a Visual Studio project, it can be preserved and protected with a source-code control (SCC) system (such as Team Foundation Server or Git), just like the artifacts in any other type of Visual Studio project. Furthermore, SSDT provides the (localdb) SQL Server instance that can be used to test your database project before deploying it back to a live server.

There are several ways to create a SQL Server Database project. You can start with an empty project, design a database structure from the ground up inside the project, and then publish the entire structure to a new SQL Database. Or, if you already have an existing SQL Database (such as the *WineCloudDb* database in our scenario), you can import the database into the project. In the next several procedures, you will create a new project and then import the *WineCloudDb* database structure into the project.

To create the SQL Server Database project, follow these steps:

1. Right-click *WineCloudSolution* in Solution Explorer, and choose Add | New Project to display the Add New Project dialog.
2. On the left side of the New Project dialog, expand Installed and choose SQL Server.
3. Select the SQL Server Database Project template, and name the project **WineCloudDb** (it's usually a good idea to name the project after the database), as shown in Figure 10-3.

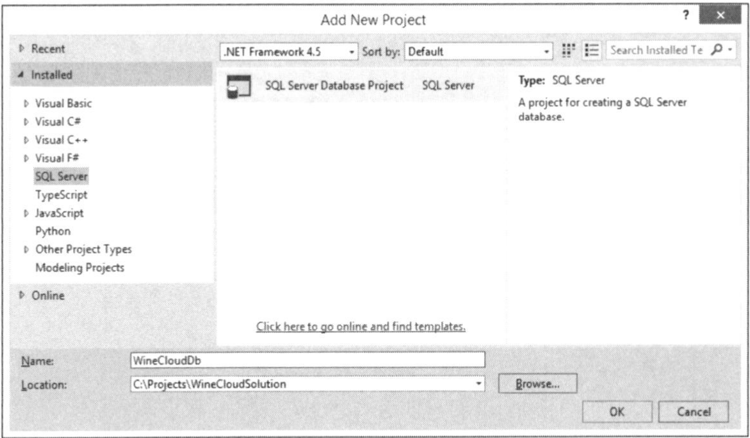

FIGURE 10-3 Creating a new SQL Server Database project

4. Click OK to create the project and add it to the solution.

Your solution now has a single database project, but there are no items defined in the project yet.

Setting the target platform

One of the advantages of SQL Server Database Projects is that you can design databases that work with different versions of SQL Server (including SQL Server 2005, 2008, 2008 R2, and 2012) and Microsoft Azure SQL Database. In the project properties, you can set the target platform to specify the particular version of SQL Server you intend to deploy the project to.

By choosing a target platform, you are directing Visual Studio to validate the project and verify that the database design is compatible with that particular version. The validation occurs in real time—as you modify the project, Visual Studio constantly checks your design in the background and raises errors if you attempt to do something that is not supported by the specified target platform. (Chapter 3 discusses important differences between Microsoft Azure SQL Database and on-premises versions of SQL Server.)

When you create a new SQL Server Database project, the target platform is set to SQL Server 2012 by default. So before making any changes to the database project, it is a good idea to set the target platform to let Visual Studio know that you intend to deploy the project to Microsoft Azure SQL Database rather than on-premises SQL Server 2012.

To set the project's target platform switch to SQL Database, follow these steps:

1. Right-click the *WineCloudDb* project in Solution Explorer, and choose Properties. At the top of the Project Settings tab, notice that the Target Platform is set to SQL Server 2012.

2. Click the Target Platform drop-down list, and choose Windows Azure SQL Database, as shown in Figure 10-4. (Note that this is the old name for what has since been rebranded as Microsoft Azure SQL Database.)

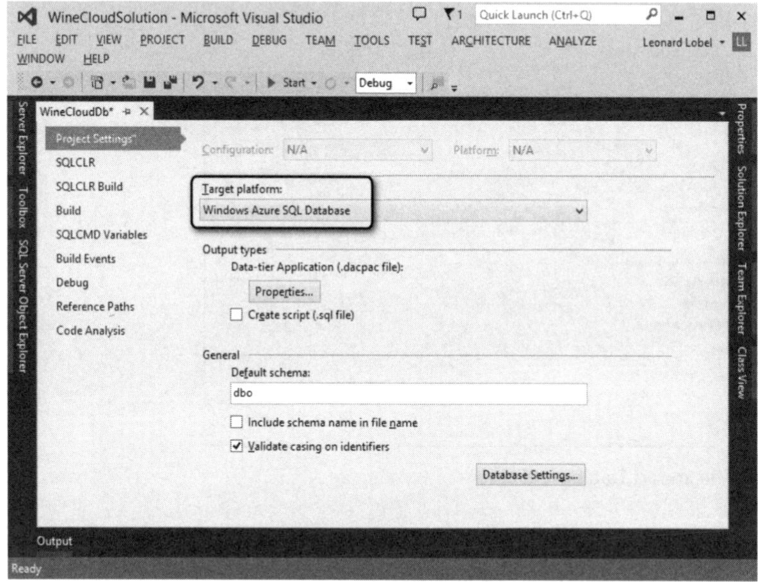

FIGURE 10-4 Changing the database project's target platform

3. Click the FILE menu, and choose Save Selected Items (or press Ctrl+S).

With this setting in place, you can work with the project secure in the knowledge that Visual Studio will alert you if you attempt to do something that is not compatible with SQL Database specifically. Now it's time to import the *WineCloudDb* database into the project.

Importing from SQL Database into the project

Importing the database populates the project with all the T-SQL source files that completely define the existing *WineCloudDb* database structure—in this case, the *Wine* and *Customer* tables you created with the code in Listing 10-1. It's easy to do this with the Import Database dialog.

To import the *WineCloudDb* database from SQL Database into the project, follow these steps:

1. Right-click the *WineCloudDb* project in Solution Explorer, and choose Import | Database to display the Import Database dialog, as shown in Figure 10-5.

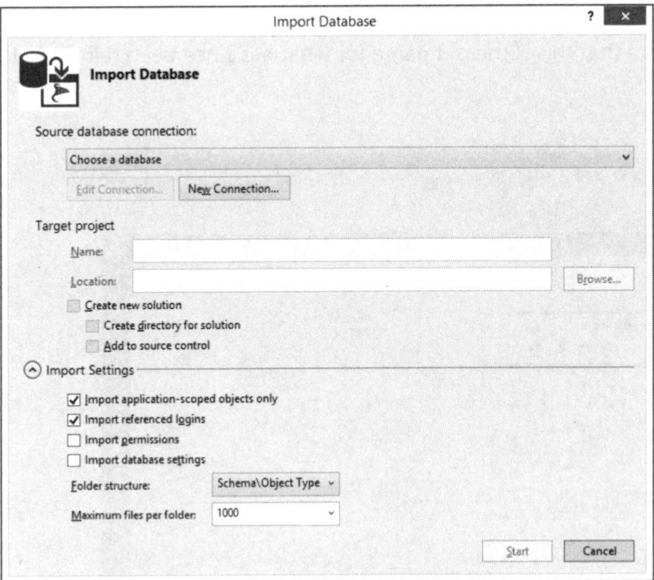

FIGURE 10-5 The Import Database dialog

2. Beneath Source Database Connection, click the New Connection button to display the Connection Properties dialog.
3. For Server Name, type the complete host name for the SQL Database server. As usual, this is the server name randomly assigned when you created the server, followed by *.database.windows.net*.
4. Choose Use SQL Server Authentication, and type the user name and password you previously assigned to the server.
5. Click the drop-down list beneath the Select Or Enter A Database Name radio button, and select the *WineCloudDb* database. The Connection Properties dialog should now appear as shown in Figure 10-6.
6. Click OK to close the Connection Properties dialog and return to the Import Database dialog.
7. Click Start. It takes just a few moments for Visual Studio to examine the database and discover all the objects it contains, as shown in Figure 10-7.

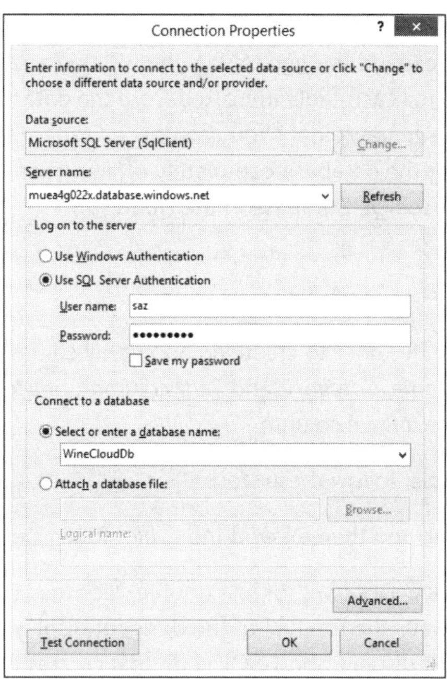

FIGURE 10-6 The Connection Properties dialog

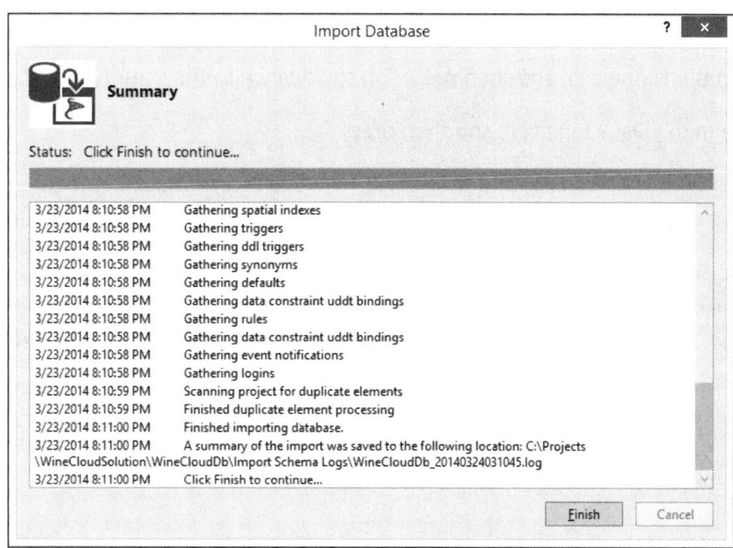

FIGURE 10-7 Importing the *WineCloudDb* SQL Database into the *WineCloudDb* SQL Server Database project

8. Click Finish.

In the Solution Explorer, notice that the project now has a *dbo* folder, which is the schema under which the imported objects are contained. If you expand the *dbo* folder, you will find a *Tables* folder, and beneath that folder, you will find one *.sql* file for each table imported from the database. (You should see a *Customer.sql* and *Wine.sql* files in the *Tables* folder.) You can now edit these files, which essentially means that you can continue designing the database completely offline. Then, whenever you wish, you can deploy the revised design back to SQL Database in the cloud.

Adding a new column to the *Wine* table

In the next procedure, you will use the SSDT table designer to create an additional column in the *Wine* table. The *Wine* table already has *WineId, Name, Category,* and *Year* columns, but to use it as a catalog for placing orders, it will also need to have a *Price* column.

To create the new *Price* column in the *Wine* table, follow these steps:

1. In Solution Explorer, expand the *dbo* folder, and then expand the *Tables* folder beneath *dbo.*
2. Right-click the *Wine.sql* file, and choose View Designer (or just double-click the *Wine.sql* file). This opens the designer in a split-screen view; the top half of the designer displays a grid that shows all the columns, and the bottom half displays the T-SQL code that creates the table with those columns.
3. In the grid at the top of the designer, click in the Name cell in the empty row at the bottom of the grid.
4. Type **Price** in the Name cell, and then press Tab to advance to the Data Type cell.
5. Type **money** in the Data Type cell, and then press Tab.
6. Clear the Allow Nulls check box, and then press Tab. This means that SQL Database will not permit null values when storing rows in the table; each wine will have to have a price.
7. Type **0** in the Default cell. This is necessary because the *Wine* table already contains rows of data. Because null values are not permitted in the *Price* column, this default value will assign a price of 0 to each existing row in the table when you deploy the new design back to SQL Database.
8. Click the FILE menu, and choose Save Wine.sql (or press Ctrl+S).

The table designer should now appear as shown in Figure 10-8.

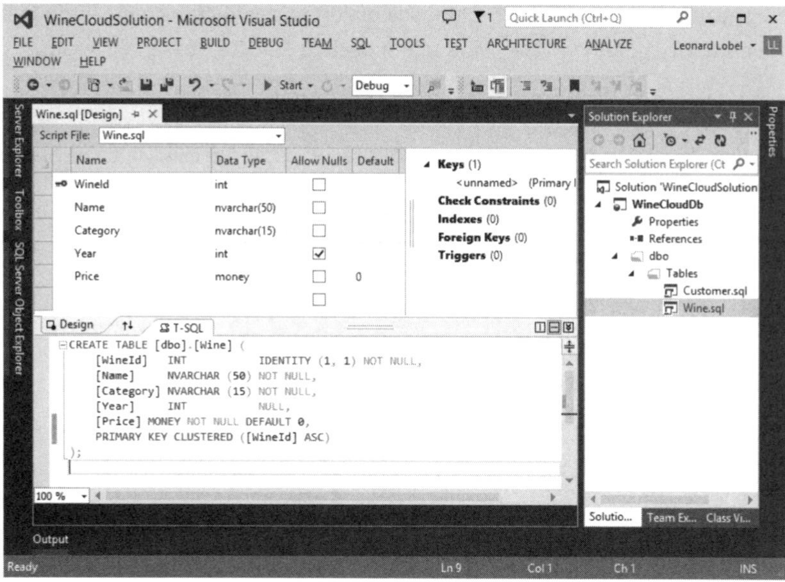

FIGURE 10-8 Adding new columns to the *Wine* table using the table designer

Tip In this procedure, you applied a change to the design grid on top, and Visual Studio automatically updated the T-SQL code on the bottom. However, the table designer supports bi-directional editing. So you can also apply your changes by editing the T-SQL code directly on the bottom, and Visual Studio will automatically update the design grid on the top. You will use this technique shortly when you add the *Order* table to the database in an upcoming procedure.

You had to assign default values for the *Price* column because the *Wine* table already contains data, and the table has been designed not to permit null values in this new column. Thus, a default must be established at this point because *some* value needs to be assigned to the *Price* column in the existing rows. However, once the new table is deployed and the existing rows are updated with the default values, you might want to remove the default value assignment from the table design so that new rows added in the future would be required to supply non-*NULL* values for *Price*.

Deploying the project to Microsoft Azure SQL Database

The Publish Database dialog lets you deploy a SQL Server Database project to a real database. The publish process invokes a *schema compare* operation, which examines the structure of both the source project and target database and generates a change script—a set of T-SQL statements that modifies the database to match the project.

In the next procedure, you will use the Publish Database dialog to deploy the change you made to the project (adding the new *Price* column in the *Wine* table) back to SQL Database in the cloud.

To deploy the project, follow these steps:

1. Right-click the *WineCloudDb* project in Solution Explorer, and choose Publish to display the Publish Database dialog, as shown in Figure 10-9.

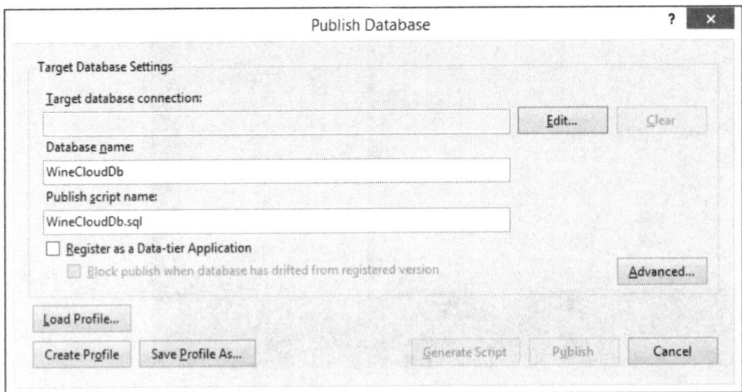

FIGURE 10-9 The Publish Database dialog

2. Click the Edit button to the right of the Target Database Connection to display the familiar Connection Properties dialog. Supply the connection information to the *WineCloudDb* database as you've done before:

   a. For Server Name, type the complete host name for the SQL Database server (the server name followed by *database.windows.net*).

   b. Choose Use SQL Server Authentication.

   c. Type the user name and password you previously assigned to the server.

   d. Click the drop-down list beneath the Select Or Enter A Database Name radio button, and select the *WineCloudDb* database (if not already selected by default).

3. Click OK to close the Connection Properties dialog. The Publish Database dialog should now appear as shown in Figure 10-10.

4. Click the Save Profile As button, type **WineCloudDb**, and click Save. This saves the connection information you just entered to a file named *WineCloudDb.publish.xml* so that you won't need to reenter it every time you deploy again in the future.

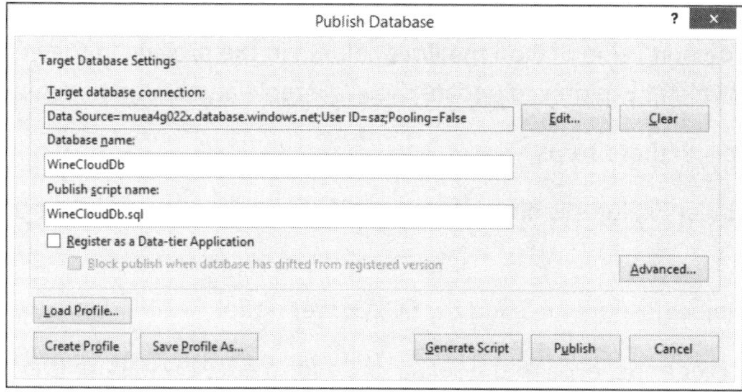

FIGURE 10-10 The Publish Database dialog after supplying target database connection information

5. Click the Publish button to start the deployment process.

> **Tip** You can click the Generate Script button instead of clicking Publish. This will also invoke the schema compare operation and generate the change script for the deployment. But rather than executing the change script, Visual Studio will open it in a new query window. This gives you the opportunity to view the script so that you can see exactly what actions will be taken. Then you can choose to execute the script as-is, edit it, or save it to be executed later.

During the deployment process, Visual Studio displays the progress and status in the Data Tools Operations window. Figure 10-11 shows the Data Tools Operations window once the deployment completes successfully.

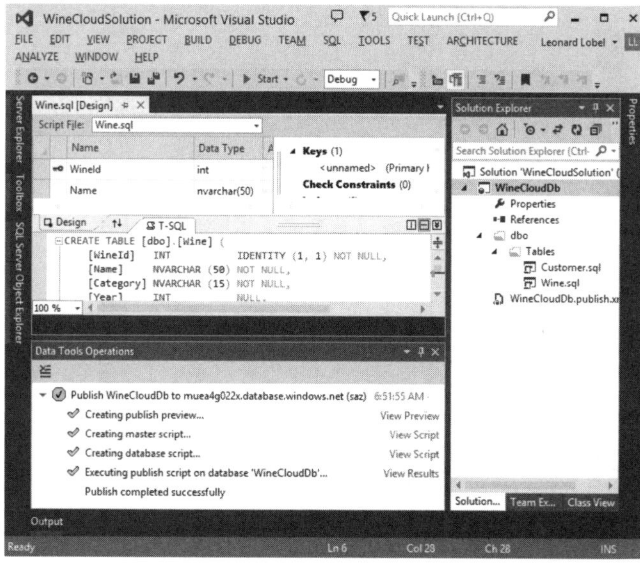

FIGURE 10-11 Deployment status is displayed in the Data Tools Operations pane

The *Wine* table in the database now includes the new *Price* column, but all the wine prices are 0 because you established a default value of 0 on the *Price* column in the project. In the next procedure, you will use the SQL Server Object Explorer to update the *Wine* table and assign prices in each row.

To set the wine prices, follow these steps:

1. If the SQL Server Object Explorer is not visible, click the VIEW menu and choose SQL Server Object Explorer.
2. In the SQL Server Object Explorer, expand the SQL Server node.
3. Beneath the SQL Server node, expand the server node for the SQL Database (the one with your server name followed by *.database.windows.net*).
4. Expand the Database node.
5. Expand the *WineCloudDb* database node.
6. Expand the Tables node.
7. Right-click the *dbo.Wine* table node, and choose View Data. This opens a new window to four rows for the wines added in Listing 10-1, all of which have a price of 0 because of the default value you assigned to the *Price* column when you added it to the table.
8. Click in the *Price* cell on the first row, and change the value from 0 to **34.90** (or just make up any price).
9. Repeat the previous step for each of the three remaining rows, changing the Price column in those rows from 0 to **48.50**, **42.00**, and **52.00** (or, again, assign any fictitious values). Your screen should appear similar to the one shown in Figure 10-12.

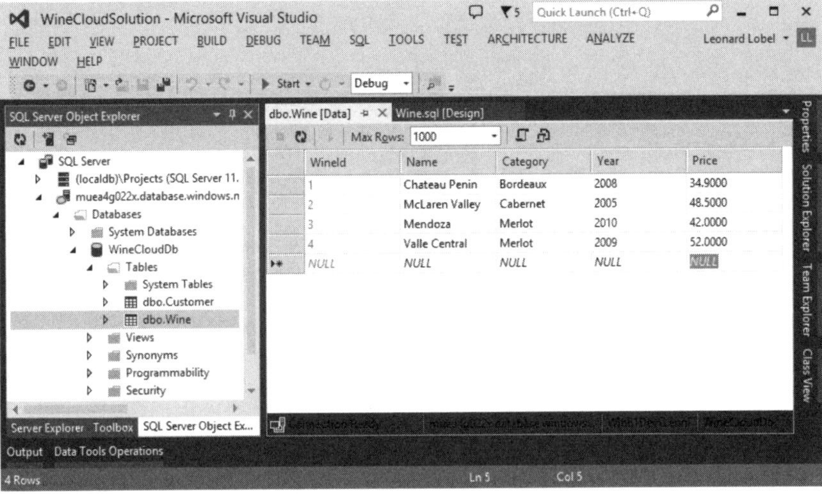

FIGURE 10-12 Using the SQL Server Object Explorer to edit prices in the *Wine* table

Creating the *Order* table

The next thing to do is create an *Order* table so that users can place orders to purchase wine. Typically, you would also have an order detail table so that a single order can be placed for multiple wines. However, you will stop with the *Order* table to keep the scenario as simple as possible; in this application, only one type of wine (in any quantity) can be purchased with each order.

In the next procedure, you will return to the database project to create the *Order* table, and then deploy the project once again to SQL Database. This demonstrates the iterative development cycle you follow when designing databases with a SQL Server Database project in Visual Studio:

- Make the database changes offline in a SQL Server Database project.
- Deploy the changes to SQL Database via a publish process. This generates and executes a change script based on a schema compare operation between the project and the database.

To create the *Order* table, follow these steps:

1. In Solution Explorer, expand the *dbo* folder.
2. Beneath the *dbo* folder, right-click the *Tables* folder and choose Add | Table.
3. Name the table **Order.sql**, and click Add to open the table designer. The designer starts with a single integer column named *Id* that is already defined as the table's primary key.
4. Add the *OrderId* column:
    a. Click in the Name cell, and change the *Id* column to **OrderId**.
    b. In the Properties window, expand Identity Specification and change the (Is Identity) property from False to True. (If the Properties window is not visible, click the VIEW menu and choose Properties Window.) When you insert new orders into the table, this tells SQL Database to automatically assign incrementing integer values for this column in each new row.
5. Add the *OrderedOn* column by doing the following:
    a. Type **OrderedOn** in the Name cell beneath *OrderId*, and press Tab to advance to the Data Type cell.
    b. Type **datetime2(7)** in the Data Type cell.
    c. Deselect Allow Nulls.
6. Add the remaining columns using the code window instead of the table schema grid by completing the following steps:
    a. Click in the code window beneath the table schema grid to place the text cursor immediately before the closing parenthesis character.

b. Type the following code for the remaining columns (and notice how the designer updates the table schema grid as you type):

```
,CustomerId int NOT NULL
,WineId int NOT NULL
,Quantity int NOT NULL
,UnitPrice money NOT NULL
,Price money NOT NULL
,AddedOn datetime2 NOT NULL DEFAULT SYSDATETIME()
,UpdatedOn datetime2 NULL
```

The *CustomerId* and *WineId* columns are foreign keys to the *Customer* and *Wine* tables, respectively, so the last step in designing the *Order* table is to establish foreign-key relationships on these columns. Doing so will ensure that an order cannot be placed for customers or wines that don't actually exist.

To create the foreign-key relationship between the *Order* and *Customer* tables, follow these steps:

1. In the upper right area of the table designer, right-click Foreign Keys and choose Add New Foreign Key.
2. Name the new foreign key **FK_Order_Customer**. (It is best practice to assign foreign-key names that indicate which tables participate in the relationship.) This generates an incomplete *FOREIGN KEY* clause in the T-SQL code window at the bottom of the designer.
3. Edit the *FOREIGN KEY* clause in the T-SQL code window to read **FOREIGN KEY (CustomerId) REFERENCES Customer(CustomerId)**.

Next, repeat the same steps to create the foreign-key relationship between the *Order* and *Wine* tables:

1. In the upper right area of the table designer, right-click Foreign Keys and choose Add New Foreign Key.
2. Name the new foreign key **FK_Order_Wine**.
3. Edit the second *FOREIGN KEY* clause added in the T-SQL code window at the bottom of the designer to read **FOREIGN KEY (WineId) REFERENCES Wine(WineId)**.
4. Click the FILE menu, and choose Save Order.sql (or press Ctrl+S).

The completed design for the *Order* table should now appear as shown in Figure 10-13.

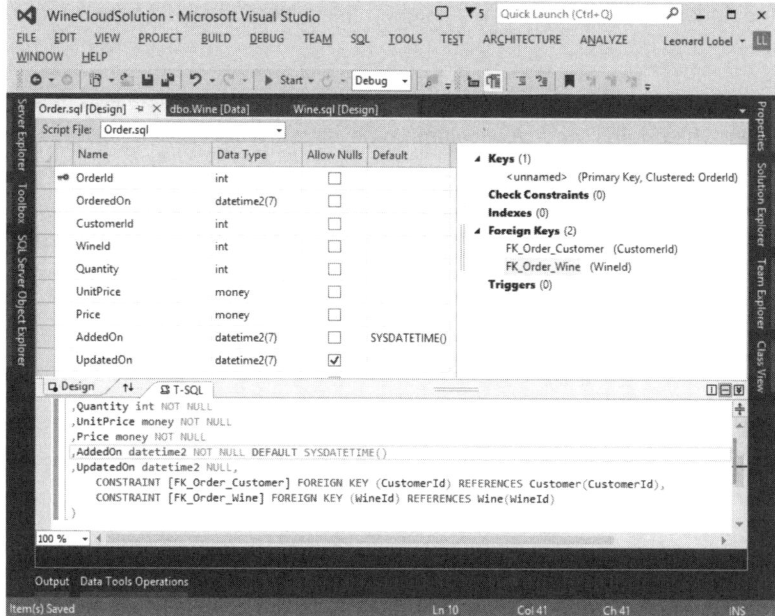

FIGURE 10-13 The completed *Order* table design

Creating stored procedures for the *Order* table

The *Order* table design is complete. But you won't want to allow applications to insert, update, or delete rows directly in the table. Instead, you will want to create stored procedures to control access to the table. This approach lets you protect the table against storing data that is invalid according to custom business rules. For example, there is nothing preventing a row in this table from storing a negative number in the *Quantity* column or an invalid amount in the *UnitPrice* and *Price* columns. Nor is there any assurance that new rows added to the table will be assigned the current date and time in the *AddedOn* column, or that existing rows updated in the table will be assigned the current date and time in the *UpdatedOn* column.

Creating stored procedures to facilitate access to the table protects the database against storing invalid data and ensures that critical business calculations and validation rules cannot be bypassed. So rather than allowing direct access to the table, client applications will be given indirect access to the tables via stored procedures that apply whatever rules you choose to enforce. In a sense, this establishes a "service layer" over the tables in the database. In the next several procedures, you will create three stored procedures for the *Order* table to ensure that the following rules are in place:

- The *Quantity* column in every row is always assigned a positive number greater than zero.
- The *UnitPrice* column in every row is always derived from the current price of the wine specified by the *WineId* column.
- The *Price* column in every row is always calculated as the result of multiplying *Quantity* and *Price*.

- For new rows, the *AddedOn* column is always assigned the current date and time on the database server.
- For updated rows, the *UpdatedOn* column is always assigned the current date and time on the database server, and the original *AddedOn* column is never overwritten.
- Orders less than one year old cannot be deleted.

The stored procedures that enforce these rules are shown in Listing 10-2 (insert), Listing 10-3 (update), and Listing 10-4 (delete):

LISTING 10-2 The *InsertOrder* stored procedure

```
CREATE PROCEDURE InsertOrder
  @OrderedOn datetime2,
  @CustomerId int,
  @WineId int,
  @Quantity int
AS

  -- Don't permit zero or negative numbers for Quantity
  IF @Quantity < 1
   THROW 50000, 'Quantity must be 1 or more', 1;

  -- Derive unit price from Wine table
  DECLARE @UnitPrice money = (SELECT Price FROM Wine WHERE WineId = @WineId);

  -- Ensure the specified Wine ID exists
  IF @@ROWCOUNT = 0
   THROW 50000, 'The specified wine was not found', 1;

  -- Calculate total price
  DECLARE @Price money = @Quantity * @UnitPrice;

  -- Use the current date and time for AddedOn
  DECLARE @AddedOn datetime2 = SYSDATETIME();

  INSERT INTO [Order]
    (OrderedOn, CustomerId, WineId, Quantity, UnitPrice, Price, AddedOn)
   VALUES
    (@OrderedOn, @CustomerId, @WineId, @Quantity, @UnitPrice, @Price, @AddedOn);

  -- Return the new OrderId
  SELECT OrderId = SCOPE_IDENTITY();
```

LISTING 10-3 The *UpdateOrder* stored procedure

```
CREATE PROCEDURE UpdateOrder
  @OrderId int,
  @OrderedOn datetime2,
  @CustomerId int,
```

```
  @WineId int,
  @Quantity int
AS

  -- Don't permit zero or negative numbers for Quantity
  IF @Quantity < 1
   THROW 50000, 'Quantity must be 1 or more', 1;

  -- Derive unit price from Wine table
  DECLARE @UnitPrice money = (SELECT Price FROM Wine WHERE WineId = @WineId);

  -- Ensure the specified Wine ID exists
  IF @@ROWCOUNT = 0
   THROW 50000, 'The specified wine was not found', 1;

  -- Calculate total price
  DECLARE @Price money = @Quantity * @UnitPrice;

  -- Use the current date and time for UpdatedOn
  DECLARE @UpdatedOn datetime2 = SYSDATETIME();

  -- Update the row
  UPDATE [Order]
   SET
    OrderedOn = @OrderedOn,
    WineId = @WineId,
    Quantity = @Quantity,
    UnitPrice = @UnitPrice,
    Price = @Price,
    UpdatedOn = @UpdatedOn
   WHERE
    OrderId = @OrderId;
```

LISTING 10-4 The *DeleteOrder* stored procedure

```
CREATE PROCEDURE DeleteOrder
  @OrderId int
AS

  -- Don't permit orders less than one year old to be deleted
  DECLARE @DaysOld int =
   (SELECT DATEDIFF(DAY, OrderedOn, SYSDATETIME()) FROM [Order] WHERE OrderId = @OrderId);

  -- Ensure the specified Order ID exists
  IF @@ROWCOUNT = 0
   THROW 50000, 'The specified order was not found', 1;

  -- Ensure orders less than one year old are never deleted
  IF @DaysOld < 365
   THROW 50000, 'Orders less than one year old cannot be deleted', 1;

  -- Delete the row
  DELETE FROM [Order]
   WHERE OrderId = @OrderId;
```

In the *InsertOrder* stored procedure, the incoming *@Quantity* parameter is validated to ensure that a number greater than zero is supplied. The *@UnitPrice* variable is then assigned the unit price of the specified wine by querying the *Wine* table against the *@WineId* parameter. After testing *@@ROWCOUNT* to ensure that the specified wine exists, the *@Price* variable is calculated by multiplying *@Quantity* with *@UnitPrice*. The *@AddedOn* variable is then declared and assigned the current date and time by the SYSDATETIME function. An INSERT statement then inserts the new row with a combination of values supplied by input parameters and established by logic in the stored procedure. Finally, a SELECT statement returns the new primary key value assigned for the *OrderId* of the new row, which is obtained with the SCOPE_IDENTITY function.

The *UpdateOrder* stored procedure performs the same validation on the incoming *@Quantity* parameter to ensure that an existing order's quantity is not changed to a zero or negative number. It also repeats the same pricing logic to recalculate *@UnitPrice* and *@Price* if an existing order's quantity or wine selection is changed. (Certainly, the common pricing code can be maintained in a single user-defined function that is shared by both the *InsertOrder* and *UpdateOrder* stored procedures.) The *@UpdatedOn* variable is then declared and assigned the current date and time by the SYSDATETIME function. An UPDATE statement then updates the row (using the current date and time in *@UpdatedOn* for the *UpdatedOn* column). Notice that the *AddedOn* column is not affected by the UPDATE statement, which ensures that the date and time stored in *AddedOn* at the time the row was created can never be modified.

In the *DeleteOrder* stored procedure, the number of elapsed days since *OrderDate* is calculated and stored in the *@DaysOld* variable. The *@@ROWCOUNT* function is then tested to verify that the specified order actually exists, and then the *@DaysOld* variable is tested to ensure that the date of the existing order is at least one year (365 days) ago. Finally, a DELETE statement deletes the specified order from the table.

More Info There are other techniques besides stored procedures that can protect tables from invalid data. For example, you can define a *check constraint* on the *Quantity* column to ensure that negative numbers are not permitted, instead of testing for that condition in a stored procedure. You can also create a *trigger* to check that an order is at least one year old before permitting its row to be deleted. In general however, triggers are best avoided, because they introduce nondeterministic behavior. (That is, when multiple triggers are defined, the order in which they fire is not guaranteed, which can lead to subtle bugs that are difficult to troubleshoot.) Using stored procedures is often the best approach, because they provide a clean layer over tables in which you can consolidate all your custom logic (such as calculating prices, and controlling the date and time values assigned to the *AddedOn* and *UpdatedOn* columns, as shown here).

To create the three stored procedures, follow these steps:

1. In Solution Explorer, right-click the *dbo* folder and choose Add | New Folder.
2. Name the new folder **Stored Procedures**, and press Enter.

> **Note** This folder would have been created automatically earlier just like the *Tables* folder was, if there had been at least one stored procedure in the database at the time you imported it into the project.

3. Right-click the *Stored Procedures* folder, and choose Add | Stored Procedure.
4. Name the new file for the stored procedure **InsertOrder.sql**, and click Add.
5. Replace the template code generated automatically by Visual Studio with the code shown earlier in Listing 10-2. Your screen should appear similar to Figure 10-14.

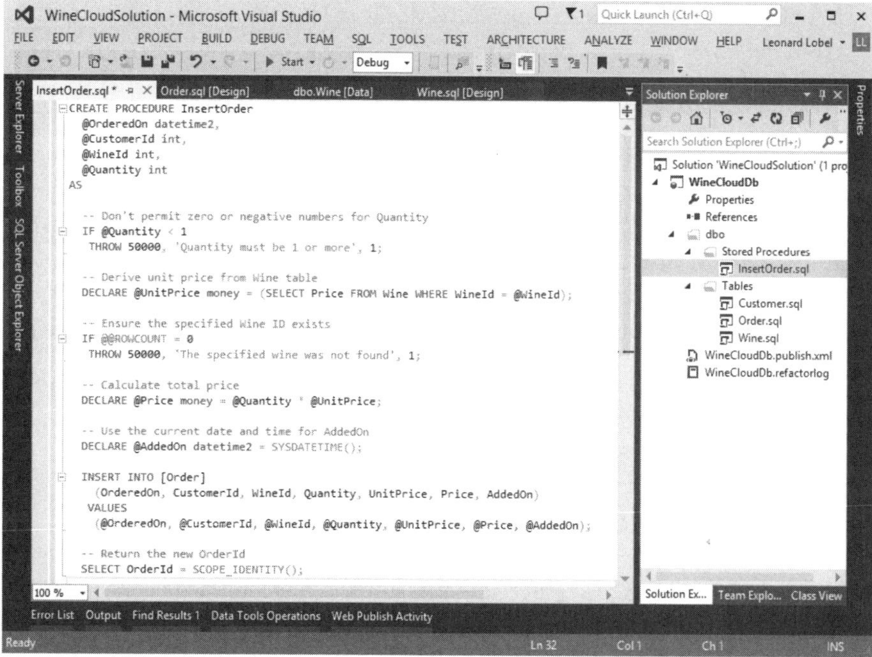

FIGURE 10-14 Adding a new stored procedure to the SQL Server Database project

6. Right-click the Stored Procedures folder, and choose Add | Stored Procedure.
7. Name the new file for the stored procedure **UpdateOrder.sql**, click Add, and replace the template code with the code shown earlier in Listing 10-3.
8. Right-click the Stored Procedures folder, and choose Add | Stored Procedure.
9. Name the new file for the stored procedure **DeleteOrder.sql**, click Add, and replace the template code with the code shown earlier in Listing 10-4.
10. Click the FILE menu, and choose Save All (or press Ctrl+Shift+S).

Now that you have added a new table and three new stored procedures in the project, you are ready to deploy those changes back to SQL Database in the cloud. You will do this using the same publish procedure you followed for the previous deployment. This time, however, you won't need to re-enter all the connection information, because you saved that information to a profile when you deployed the last time.

To redeploy the project, follow these steps:

1. Right-click the *WineCloudDb* project in Solution Explorer, and choose Publish to display the Publish Database dialog. (See Figure 10-10 earlier in the chapter.)
2. Click the Load Profile button toward the bottom of the dialog.
3. Double-click the *WineCloudDb.publish* XML file to load the connection information that you saved during the previous deployment.
4. Click the Publish button to start the deployment process.

As when you deployed the first time, Visual Studio generates and executes the change script that updates the database in the cloud to match the database design in the project. This time, that means the *WineCloudDb* SQL Database is updated with the new *Order* table and its foreign-key relationships to the *Customer* and *Wine* tables, as well as the three new stored procedures for inserting, updating, and deleting rows in the *Order* table. Refresh the *WineCloudDb* database node in SQL Server Object Explorer to verify that the database now contains the new objects published from the project.

The database design is complete, and you are now ready to start working on the solution's data access layer.

Creating the data access layer

The data access layer (DAL) is the component that serves as the interface between the back-end database and the rest of an application. You have many options for building a DAL, and in the upcoming sections, you will build a DAL using the Entity Framework (EF). Today, EF has emerged as Microsoft's recommended technology for implementing a data access layer. EF, which was first released as part of .NET 3.5 SP1 in 2008, raises the level of abstraction far beyond that which is offered by ADO.NET. Entity Framework is an object relational mapper (ORM) that can dramatically boost your developer productivity in many scenarios, but it is by no means the only viable choice for a DAL.

Of course, the Microsoft .NET Framework includes ADO.NET, which provides a set of classes you can use to build a data access layer. Since the very first version of .NET released in 2002, developers have had two choices for working with ADO.NET. One option is to use the raw ADO.NET objects, which include connections, commands, and readers. This approach requires a lot of manual effort, because you need to write explicit code to connect to the database, issue commands to request data, transfer the requested data from readers into objects, track changes made to those objects, and then finally issue commands to send the modified objects back to the database. Although somewhat antiquated and primitive, this technique is by no means obsolete. Indeed, despite its power and popularity, Entity Framework does carry a substantial amount of overhead, which can result in degraded performance in large-scale scenarios, compared to the speed of direct database access with raw ADO.NET.

The second conventional ADO.NET choice is to use the *Dataset* object in conjunction with data adapters. Visual Studio provides a graphical *Dataset* designer that automatically generates a lot of code for you. The generated code configures the connection and command objects, and it maps individual data elements (tables and columns) between the database and the strongly typed in-memory *Dataset* object. Once populated, a *Dataset* can track its own changes, making it relatively easy for you to push updated data back to the database. This approach provides a layer of abstraction that relieves you from a great deal of the manual effort required to achieve the same result using the raw ADO.NET classes. However, the *Dataset* is not a true business object or entity. Today, therefore, you won't find many scenarios where it makes sense to use the *Dataset* rather than EF when building the DAL in a new .NET application.

The overriding point is that it's far more important that you *have* a properly implemented DAL in place than which approach you actually decide to take. Certainly, every case is different, but in many common line-of-business (LOB) scenarios, you will find EF more than well suited for the task. EF dramatically simplifies data access by abstracting away the underlying database connection, command, and reader objects and providing a robust set of object services capable of materializing objects retrieved from querying the database, tracking them in memory, and pushing their changes back to the database. EF can also dynamically generate SELECT statements to query the database and INSERT, UPDATE, and DELETE statements to update the database, or it can provide the same object services equally well by invoking stored procedures that let you maintain total control over how queries are executed and updates are processed. There are also many more advanced mapping possibilities in EF that are far beyond the scope of this chapter, such as the ability to model inheritance, entity-splitting, table-splitting, and many-to-many relationships.

Introducing the Entity Data Model

At the heart of the Entity Framework lies the Entity Data Model (EDM), and Visual Studio provides a rich graphical designer that makes it easy to manage and maintain the EDM. In Chapter 8, "Designing and tuning for scalability and high performance," you built an application using the "code-first" approach. With code-first EF, the EDM is present, but not visible. Instead, the code-first approach infers the EDM from the entity classes that you write yourself in code, but the EDM is still there. In this section, you will use the database-first approach to create an *.edmx* file in Visual Studio from the *WineCloudDb* database. This will introduce you to the EDM designer in Visual Studio, which makes it easy to customize the model in many ways, particularly for mapping stored procedures.

The EDM consists of three parts. First there is the *storage schema*, which describes the physical structure of the database. Then there is the *conceptual schema*, which describes classes for the business entities used in the application. Finally, you have the *mapping* schema, which defines how the storage and conceptual schemas relate to one another. These three pieces (collectively called the model's *metadata*) are self-contained in a single *.edmx* file inside your project.

Once you create the EDM, your applications and services concern themselves only with the conceptual schema, while EF handles all the data access for you dynamically at runtime. This means that when you need to retrieve data into objects, EF figures out and executes the appropriate T-SQL SELECT queries (or stored procedures) and populates ready-to-use objects from the results automatically. Then, when it comes time to save modified objects, EF similarly figures out and executes the appropriate T-SQL INSERT, UPDATE, and DELETE statements (or stored procedures) needed to persist the changes back to the database. EF is able to perform this magic because it knows how the conceptual business entities map to the physical database structure from the metadata in the EDM.

The EDM you will create in the next section defines a simple one-to-one mapping between the conceptual and storage schemas. However, you should be aware that much more complex mappings are possible. For example, a single entity in the conceptual schema might be mapped to multiple tables in the database, in which case EF will join the tables together at query time and split the updates across them when saving changes. Conversely, multiple entity types might be mapped to a single table in the database, in which case EF distinguishes each row in the table based on a designated column that identifies the entity type. This type of mapping can also be used to define inheritance in the conceptual schema.

Creating the Data Access Layer project

For quick-and-dirty prototyping, it's quite common to create the EDM right inside of the application that consumes it. In production scenarios, however, the proper practice is to contain the EDM file in its own class library (DLL) project so that it can be easily shared by multiple applications. All you need to do is reference the DLL assembly containing the EDM and add the appropriate database connection string to the application's configuration file (either *web.config* or *app.config*).

In this section, you will create the EDM in its own class library project for an easily shareable DAL. Then you will reference the DAL class library from a separate ASP.NET MVC project. As you will soon see, it is easy to copy the connection string from the class library's *app.config* file into the MVC project's *web.config* file to access the database.

More Info Another commonly recommended practice is to implement the *repository pattern*. The repository is another layer you can add to your solution that manages the DAL directly, while the entire rest of the application interacts only with the repository. In this manner, only the repository layer knows that you are using EF (or something else) as the DAL, and consequently, only the repository layer needs to be changed if you ever decided to switch between using EF, raw ADO.NET, or any other DAL option. Although you will not also be implementing a repository pattern in this solution, keep in mind that doing so in your production applications will make it extremely easy to switch between different DAL options with minimal disruption to the rest of the solution, if the need ever arises.

To create the DAL class library project, follow these steps:

1. Right-click *WineSolution* in Solution Explorer, and choose Add | New Project to display the Add New Project dialog.
2. On the left side of the New Project dialog, expand Installed and choose Visual C#.
3. Select the Class Library template, and name the project **WineCloudModel**.
4. Click OK to create the project and add it to the solution.
5. The *Class1.cs* file created automatically by Visual Studio can be deleted, so right-click it, choose Delete, and click OK.

You are now ready to create the Entity Data Model in the *WineCloudModel* project.

Creating an Entity Data Model

To create the Entity Data Model (EDM), follow these steps:

1. Right-click the *WineCloudModel* project in Solution Explorer, and choose Add | New Item to display the Add New Item dialog.
2. On the left side of the Add New Item dialog, expand Installed, Visual C#, and choose Data.
3. Click the ADO.NET Entity Data Model item, and name the file **WineModel.edmx**, as shown in Figure 10-15.

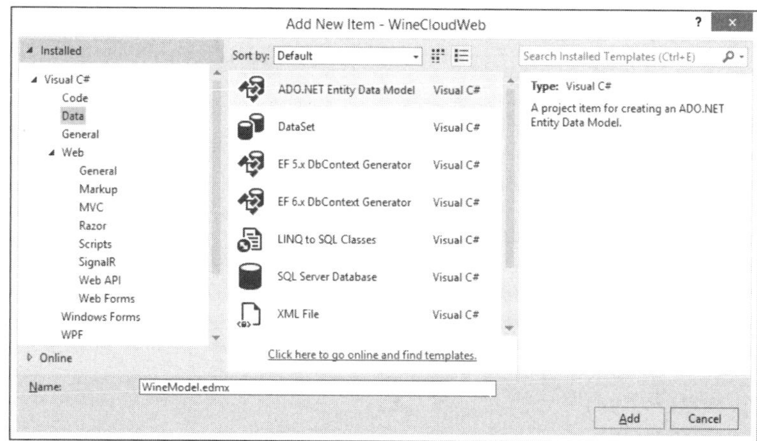

FIGURE 10-15 Creating a new Entity Data Model

4. Click Add to start the Entity Data Model Wizard.
5. On the Choose Model Contents page, the Generate From Database option is already selected by default, so just click Next.
6. On the Choose Your Data Connection page, click the New Connection button.

7. If the Choose Data Source dialog appears, click Microsoft SQL Server, and then click Continue.

8. In the familiar Connection Properties dialog, supply the same connection information to connect to the *WineCloudDb* database that you've used throughout this chapter:

   a. For Server Name, type **<*servername*>.database.windows.net** (replacing *<servername>* with the server name that was assigned when you created your server).

   b. Choose Use SQL Server Authentication, and type the user name and password you assigned to the server.

   c. This time, be sure and select the Save My Password check box. Otherwise, the password will not be saved for the connection string at runtime in step 9.

   d. In the drop-down list beneath the Select Or Enter A Database Name radio button, select the *WineCloudDb* database.

   e. Click OK to close the Connection Properties dialog.

9. Choose Yes to include sensitive data (namely, the password) in the connection string. The Entity Data Model Wizard should now appear as shown in Figure 10-16.

Important In production applications, it is not acceptable to include the password in the connection string (which gets stored in the application's configuration file). Instead, you should choose No and then assign the password in C# code at runtime.

FIGURE 10-16 Setting the data connection in the Entity Data Model Wizard

10. Click Next to display the Choose Your Version page.

11. The desired version, Entity Framework 6.0 should already be selected by default, so just click Next to display the Choose Your Database Objects And Settings page.

12. Expand Tables, dbo, and then select the check boxes for the *Customer*, *Order*, and *Wine* tables. (Don't include the *_RefactorLog* table in the model; this table was generated automatically and is used only by the refactoring features of the SQL Server Database Project.)

13. Expand Stored Procedures and Functions, dbo, and then select the dbo check box to select the *InsertOrder*, *UpdateOrder*, and *DeleteOrder* stored procedures in the database.

14. Deselect the last check box in the dialog, Import Selected Stored Procedures And Functions Into The Entity Data Model. The Entity Data Model Wizard should now appear as shown in Figure 10-17.

More Info This step isn't strictly necessary, but it does prevent needless overhead in the EDM. Deselecting this check box means that you never intend to call the *InsertOrder*, *UpdateOrder*, and *DeleteOrder* stored procedures directly via EF, and it's therefore not necessary for the wizard to create function imports and complex types (these are essentially strongly-typed wrappers around stored procedure calls and the schema results returned by those stored procedure calls). Instead, you will shortly map these stored procedures to the *Order* entity so that EF calls them automatically whenever it needs to save changes to the *Order* table in the database.

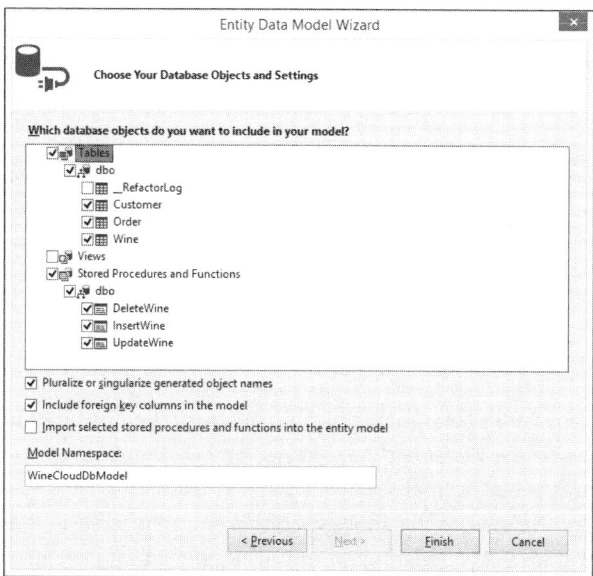

FIGURE 10-17 Selecting tables and stored procedures to be imported into the Entity Data Model

15. Click Finish.

> **Note** After clicking Finish, you might receive multiple Security Warning messages for running the template. (This refers to the special template used internally by the EDM designer to automatically generate code.) If you receive this warning, just click OK. (You can also select the check box to prevent the template security warning from appearing again repeatedly.)

Visual Studio adds the necessary EF references to the project, generates the Entity Data Model, and then displays it in the EDM designer as shown in Figure 10-18.

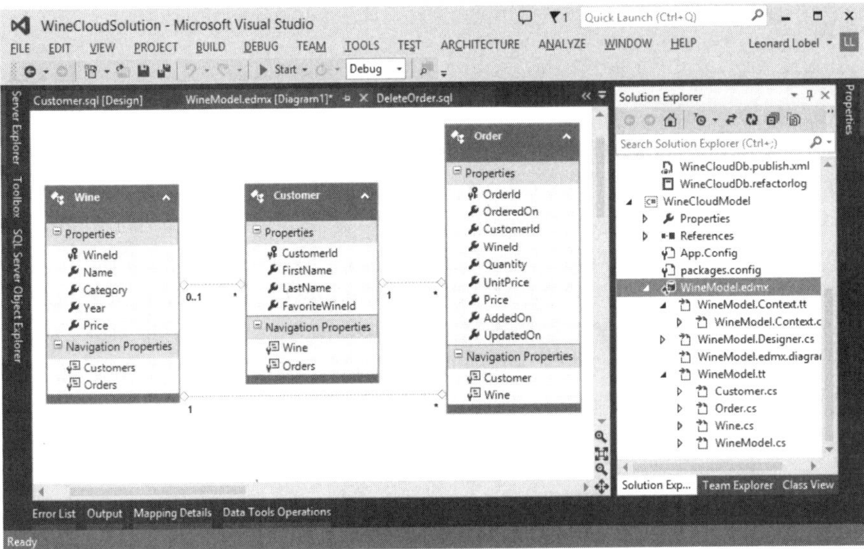

FIGURE 10-18 The generated Entity Data Model displayed in the EDM designer

The *Wine*, *Customer*, and *Order* entities displayed in the EDM designer represent classes that correspond to tables of the same name that were discovered in the database. Similarly, each of the entity classes has properties that are mapped to columns of the same name in each table. Furthermore, notice that each entity has *navigation* properties and associations that are based on foreign-key relationships discovered between the tables in the database:

- The *Wine* entity has the navigation properties *Customers* and *Orders* (both plural).
  - In Listing 10-1, you established a foreign relationship between the *Customer* table's *FavoriteWineId* column and the *WineId* primary-key column in the *Wine* table. You defined this column to allow nulls, meaning that some customers might not have a *FavoriteWineId* value. Thus, the association between the entities is displayed graphically in the designer by a connecting line, with a "0..1" appearing on the *Wine* side (which indicates zero or one favorite wines) and an asterisk (*) symbol (which indicates many) on the *Customer* side. The *Customers* navigation property is on the "many" side of this relationship, so all the

customers for a given favorite wine are accessible through that *Wine* entity's *Customers* navigation property.

    - Later, you established a foreign-key relationship between the *Order* table's *WineId* column and the *WineId* primary-key column in the *Wine* table. You defined this column not to permit nulls, meaning that every *Order* row must have a *WineId* value identifying the wine that was ordered. Thus, the association between the entities is displayed graphically in the designer by a connecting line, with a "1" appearing on the *Wine* side (which indicates one and only one wine) and an asterisk (*) symbol (indicating many) on the *Order* side. The *Orders* navigation property is on the "many" side of this relationship, so all the orders for a given wine are accessible through that *Wine* entity's *Orders* navigation property.

- The *Customer* entity has navigation properties *Wine* (singular) and *Orders* (plural).

    - The *Wine* property is on the "zero or one" side of the customer's favorite wine relationship, so each customer's favorite wine (if that customer has one) can be accessed through the *Customer* entity's *Wine* navigation property.

    - You also established a foreign-key relationship between the *Customer* table's *OrderId* column and the *OrderId* primary-key column in the *Order* table. You defined this column not to permit nulls, meaning that every *Order* row must have a *CustomerId* value identifying the customer that placed the order. Thus, the association between the entities is displayed graphically in the designer by a connecting line, with a "1" appearing on the *Customer* side and an asterisk (*) symbol (indicating many) on the *Order* side. The *Orders* navigation property is on the "many" side of this relationship, so all the orders for a given customer can be accessed through the *Customer* entity's *Orders* navigation property.

- The *Order* entity has the navigation properties *Customer* and *Order* (both singular).

    - The *Customer* property is on the "one" side of the order's customer relationship, so each order's customer can be accessed through the *Order* entity's *Customer* navigation property.

    - Similarly, the *Wine* property is on the "one" side of the order's wine relationship, so each order's wine can be accessed through the *Order* entity's *Wine* navigation property.

The Entity Data Model Wizard imported both tables and stored procedures. But unlike the tables, which the wizard also maps to same-named entities in the conceptual model, stored procedures do not get mapped automatically. So it's still your job to map the three stored procedures (*InsertOrder*, *UpdateOrder*, and *DeleteOrder*) to the *Order* entity in the model. By default (that is, if you don't do this), EF will simply generate direct T-SQL INSERT, UPDATE, and DELETE statements when you save changes to the *Wine* table, and you won't get the added functionality (such as custom validation and pricing logic) that is programmed into the stored procedures.

Recall that *InsertOrder* returns a single-row resultset with the new *OrderId* value assigned to the new *Order* row. (See the SELECT statement at the bottom of Listing 10-2.) When you map this stored procedure to the *Order* entity, you inform the EDM of the value it returns by defining *result bindings*. This instructs EF to refresh new *Order* entity objects by "shoving" the return value back into the *OrderId* property of the memory-resident instance after performing an insert.

To map the *InsertOrder*, *UpdateOrder*, and *DeleteOrder* stored procedures to the *Order* table, follow these steps:

1. Right-click on the *Order* entity, and choose Stored Procedure Mapping. This displays the Mapping Details window.
2. In the Mapping Details window, click <Select Insert Function>, expand the drop-down list, and choose the *InsertOrder* stored procedure. The designer automatically maps the stored procedure input parameters to the same-named entity properties, but you need to map the *OrderId* value returned by the stored procedure back into the entity manually in the next step.
3. Beneath Result Column Bindings, click <Add Result Binding>, type **OrderId**, and press Enter. The designer correctly maps this result column to the *OrderId* property.
4. Click <Select Update Function>, expand the drop-down list, and choose the *UpdateOrder* stored procedure. Again, the stored procedure parameters get mapped automatically to the same-named entity properties of the *Order* entity.
5. Click <Select Delete Function>, expand the drop-down list, and choose the *DeleteOrder* stored procedure.
6. Click the FILE menu, and choose Save All (or press Ctrl+Shift+S).

Note Once again, click OK on any template Security Warning dialogs that appear.

After completing this procedure, the Mapping Details window should appear as shown in Figure 10-19.

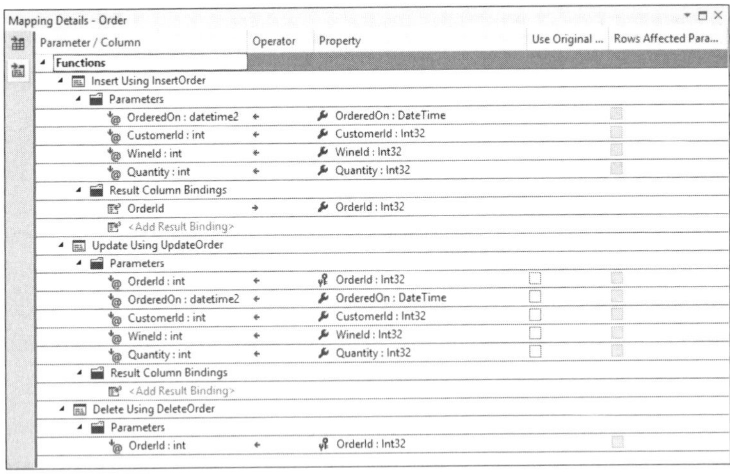

FIGURE 10-19 The EDM designer Mapping Details window with stored procedures mapped to the *Order* entity

With the EDM design complete, the solution has a functioning EF-based data access layer. EF will automatically handle database connections, generate queries, materialize and track objects, and call stored procedures, and you don't have to write any code to make it work!

Creating the website

With a functioning DAL in place, you're ready to create the ASP.NET MVC website. This site will let users place orders over the web using any browser. After building and testing the site locally in an ASP.NET Web Application Project, you will deploy it to Microsoft Azure to run as a website in the cloud.

Note This chapter presents a very simple application, which is just enough to demonstrate how multiple components in a layered solution interact. In real-world scenarios, authentication and authorization must also be implemented; however, those details lie beyond the scope of this chapter.

An MVC website works by examining the requested URL and determining which controller, and which action on that controller, the request should be directed to. A controller is really just a class, and an action is really just a method of that class. When the action method runs, it returns the view that gets rendered as Hypertext Markup Language (HTML) and JavaScript in the client browser. MVC binds the view to a model that defines the data that gets supplied to the view.

The rules that govern how a URL maps to specific controllers and actions are specified in the MVC application's routing table. Default behavior (such as which controller and action is invoked when none is specified in the URL) is also configured in the routing table. The default routing table for a new MVC application specifies a default controller named Home with a default action named Index, which means that the *Index* method of the *HomeController* class will be invoked for a URL that does not specify a controller and action.

You will also use the "scaffolding" template feature in Visual Studio to create the *HomeController* class. This code-generation feature automatically creates several actions in the controller class, along with individual views that correspond to each action. When used with Entity Framework, these scaffolded actions and views fully implement standard select, insert, update, and delete functionality for any entity in the EDM.

Creating an ASP.NET web application project

To create the web application project, follow these steps:

1. Right-click *WineSolution* in Solution Explorer, and choose Add | New Project to display the Add New Project dialog.
2. On the left side of the New Project dialog, expand Installed, Visual C#, and choose Web.

3. Choose the ASP.NET Web Application template.

4. Name the project **WineCloudWeb** (as shown in Figure 10-20), and click OK.

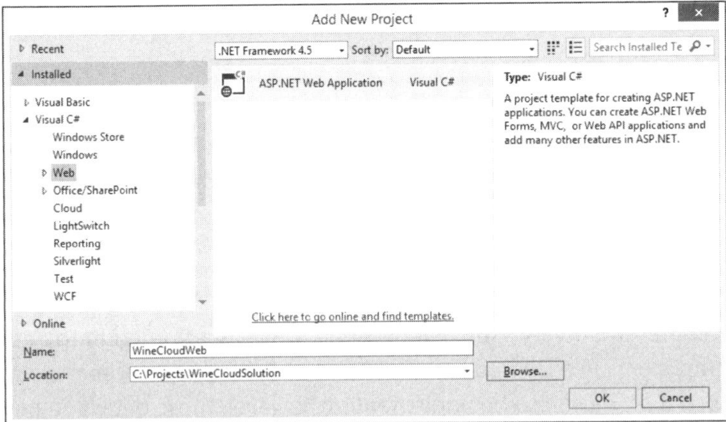

FIGURE 10-20 Creating a new ASP.NET web application project

5. In the New ASP.NET Project dialog, choose the Empty template.

6. Select the MVC and Web API check boxes, as shown in Figure 10-21. This adds project references to the MVC assemblies to support the website, as well as references to the Web API assemblies for the REST services you will add later to support the mobile Windows Phone 8 app.

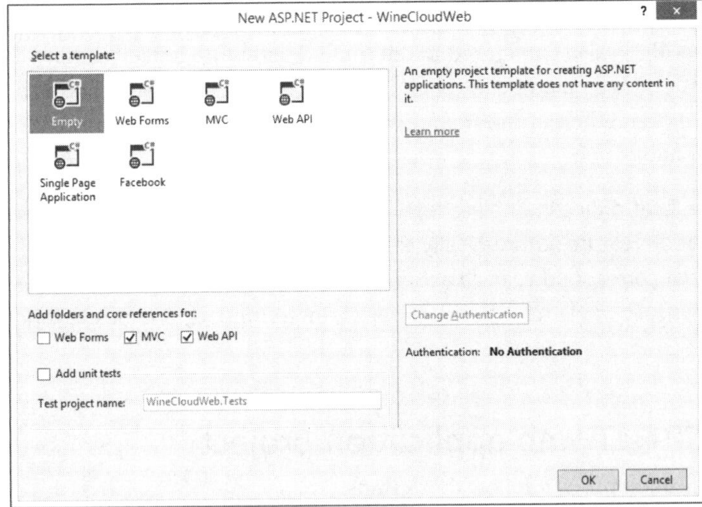

FIGURE 10-21 Selecting core references for MVC and Web API in a new empty ASP.NET web application project

7. Click OK.

By choosing a combination of the Empty template with core MVC and Web API references, you ensure the new project starts out completely fresh (without the extra sample-code baggage injected by the other templates), but still references all the necessary assemblies to support the building of the MVC website now and the Web API services (to support the Windows Phone 8 app) a bit later.

Referencing the data access layer

The "M" in MVC stands for *model*. In this particular solution, the EDM in the *WineCloudModel* project serves as the model for the MVC application. This means that the entity classes defined in the data access layer are equally suitable as model classes in the user interface (UI) layer, which is a huge convenience factor when using MVC together with EF because it basically means you don't need to worry about the model at all. Instead, you can focus more on the "VC" in MVC—that is, on designing views and writing controller classes around the model.

Before the *WineCloudWeb* MVC application can use the EDM in the *WineCloudModel* project as the model for the UI, two things need to be done:

- The *WineCloudWeb* project must establish a reference to the *WineCloudModel* project.
- The entity connection string must be copied from the *WineCloudModel* project to the *WineCloudWeb* application.

You will perform both these tasks in the next two procedures. First, to reference the *WineCloudModel* project from the *WineCloudWeb* project, follow these steps:

1. Expand the *WineCloudWeb* project in Solution Explorer to reveal its References node.
2. Right-click the References node, and choose Add Reference to display the Reference Manager dialog.
3. Expand the Solution item on the left, and click the Projects tab beneath Solution. This allows you to select from other projects in the solution to reference.
4. Select the *WineCloudModel* project check box, as shown in Figure 10-22.

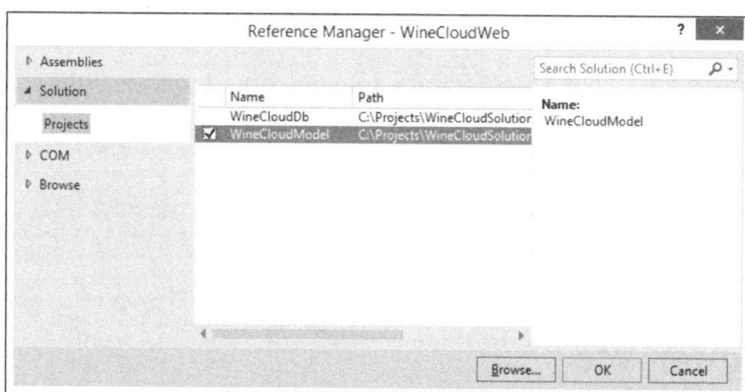

FIGURE 10-22 Adding a reference from the ASP.NET Web application project to the DAL project

5. Click OK.

Even though the EDM and DAL are in the *WineCloudDb* project, EF always looks in the configuration file of the launching executable application or website at runtime to find the entity connection string, which in turn, contains the actual database connection string. When the EDM is created in a class library project, as is the case here, the connection string is contained in the class library project's *App.Config* file. However, the connection string in *App.Config* will never be found at runtime, because a class library is a DLL file with no entry point (that is, it can never be the launching executable application).

In this solution, *WineCloudWeb* is the launching application, so EF will look inside its *Web.config* file for the entity connection string whenever data access is required. If the connection string is not present in *Web.config*, EF won't find it at runtime and will throw an exception as a result. So you need to perform a simple copy/paste operation to resolve the situation.

To copy the entity connection string and paste it into *Web.config*, follow these steps:

1. Copy the connection string from *App.Config* in the *WineCloudModel* project by doing the following:
    a. Expand the *WineCloudModel* project in Solution Explorer to reveal its *App.Config* file.
    b. Double-click the *App.Config* file to open it.
    c. Select the entire *<connectionStrings>* section. This should contain a single connection named *WineCloudDbEntities* and include the surrounding *<connectionStrings>* and *</connectionStrings>* tags.
    d. Press Ctrl+C to copy the selected code to the clipboard.
2. Paste the connection string to *Web.config* in the *WineCloudWeb* project by doing the following:
    a. Expand the *WineCloudWeb* project in Solution Explorer to reveal its *Web.config* file.
    b. Double-click the *Web.config* file to open it.
    c. Click to position the text cursor just after the *<configuration>* element and just before the *<appSettings>* element at the top of the file.
    d. Press Ctrl+V to paste the *<connectionStrings>* section copied to the clipboard.
3. Click FILE and choose Save Web.config (or press Ctrl+S) to save the changes.

The *WineCloudWeb* project is now all set up to use the EDM defined in the *WineCloudModel* project as the model in the MVC application.

Creating the user interface

In an MVC application, a user request gets routed to a particular action of a particular controller. The action then returns the appropriate view for the request, which is rendered by the browser. When you are building an MVC application together with Entity Framework, a special feature called *scaffolding* provides a big head start by generating a controller with actions and corresponding views to facilitate maintenance (select, insert, update, and delete) of any entity in the EDM.

In the next procedure, you will scaffold a new controller with views and actions for the *Order* entity. As we mentioned earlier, the Home controller is the default controller if one is not specified on the URL. Therefore, you will name the controller *HomeController* (even though *OrderController* is arguably a better name, given the controller's purpose). By naming it *HomeController*, you won't need to specify anything in the URL to get to the Home controller's *Index* action, and the default MVC routing rules won't need to be modified.

To create the scaffolding for a new Home MVC controller with actions and views for the *Order* entity, follow these steps:

1. Right-click the *WineCloudModel* project in Solution Explorer, and choose Build.

> **Important** This project must be built before it can be used by other projects that reference it. If you don't first build this project, you will encounter errors when attempting to add the scaffolded views in this procedure, because they are based on the EDM in the *WineCloudModel* project.

2. Right-click the *Controllers* folder in the *WineCloudWeb* project in Solution Explorer, and choose Add | New Scaffolded Item.
3. In the Add Scaffold dialog, select MVC 5 Controller With Views, Using Entity Framework, as shown in Figure 10-23.

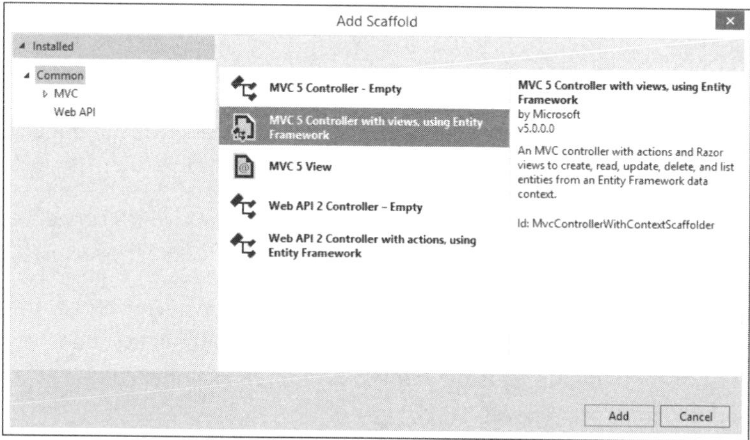

FIGURE 10-23 The Add Scaffold dialog has several choices for creating a new MVC controller class.

4. Click Add.

5. In the Add Controller dialog, do the following:

   a. Change *Default1* to **Home** so that the controller name is *HomeController.*

   b. For Model Class, choose Order (WineCloudModel) from the drop-down list.

   c. For Data Context Class, choose WineCloudDbEntities (WineCloudModel) from the drop-down list.

   d. Deselect the Reference Script Libraries and Use A Layout Page check boxes. The Add Controller dialog should appear similar to Figure 10-24.

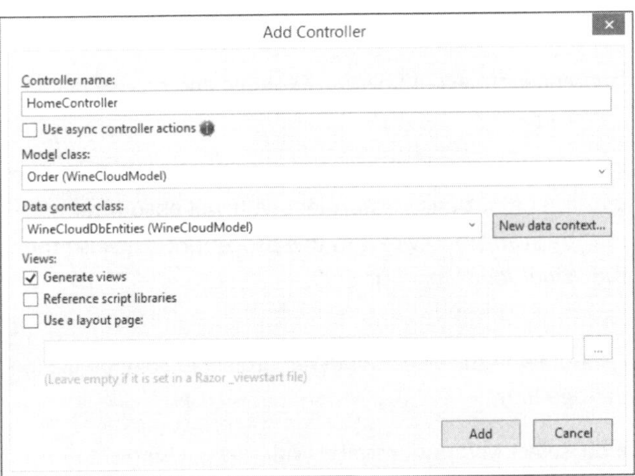

FIGURE 10-24 Adding an MVC 5 controller class, with automatically generated views for EF

   e. Click Add.

Look at the *WineCloudWeb* project in the Solution Explorer, and take a moment to review what Visual Studio just created for you. First open the *HomeController.cs* class that was added to the *Controllers* folder. If you examine the code, you will notice several things:

- The class inherits from the *System.Web.Mvc.Controller* base class, which is what makes this an MVC controller class.
- Several public methods that return an *ActionResult* object have been created. These are the controller's action methods. Based on a combination of the URL syntax of an incoming request and the HTTP method used to issue the request (GET or POST), one of these action methods will be called to handle the request.
- Each action method is preceded by a comment line that indicates the type of HTTP request (GET or POST) and URL syntax that the action method will handle:
  - A GET request responds by selecting an order or list of orders.
  - A POST request responds by creating a new order, modifying an existing order, confirming the deletion of an existing order, or deleting an existing order.

- The action method signatures (their names and parameters) are expressed in a slash-delimited format on the URL, following the controller name.
- Each action method returns a view to satisfy the request. The actual view that gets returned is based on the action and the model object returned in the action method's *ActionResult*.
- The first action method is named *Index*, which matches the default action of Index when no action is specified in the URL with a GET request. Because the Home controller is also the default controller, this *Index* method is the one that will be called if no controller and action is specified in the URL. This method retrieves all the orders in the database, along with each order's related customer and wine objects. It then returns a view that matches the action name and a model object for the list of orders, which is the (same-named) *Index* view.

You can (and probably will) modify or extend the controller class to accommodate specific requirements of your application. For example, you can add and remove actions, or you can change their behavior. For this project, the scaffolding has generated all the actions needed to support viewing, adding, modifying, and deleting orders with the website, so the generated code is ready to be used.

Next have a look at the *Views* folder in Solution Explorer. Expand the *Views* folder, and notice that it now contains a *Home* subfolder. This is more of the convention-based approach that MVC takes: things are found by name. Thus, views that serve the actions of a specific controller are contained in a subfolder beneath *Views* that is named after the controller. Expand the *Home* subfolder and you will see several *.cshtml* files. These are the view files generated by the scaffolding, and there is one for each of the Home controller actions. Again, by MVC naming convention, the view files are named after the action method of the controller:

- *Create.cshtml*
- *Delete.cshtml*
- *Details.cshtml*
- *Edit.cshtml*
- *Index.cshtml*

With the model coming from the EDM in the *WineCloudModel* DAL project, and the views and controllers generated by scaffolding, there is just a small amount of manual work needed to get this MVC website up and running. Specifically, the generated Create and Edit views include HTML input controls for every property of the *Order* entity, including properties you actually don't want the user to provide values for. Recall that logic in the *InsertOrder* (shown in Listing 10-2) and *UpdateOrder* (shown in Listing 10-3) stored procedures are responsible for setting the *AddedOn* and *UpdatedOn* properties to the current date and time, and that they calculate the *UnitPrice* and *Price* properties based on the particular wine and quantity being ordered. The scaffolding logic is smart, but it's not smart enough to understand that you don't want input fields for these four properties present in the Create and Edit views. So it's up to you to remove them yourself.

To remove the undesired fields from the Create and Edit views, follow these steps:

1. Expand the *Home* folder beneath the *Views* folder of the *WineCloudModel* project in Solution Explorer.
2. Double-click the *Create.cshtml* file to open it.
3. Among the *<div>* elements for each *Order* property, find and delete the four *<div>* elements for the *UnitPrice*, *Price*, *AddedOn*, and *UpdatedOn* properties.
4. Double-click the *Edit.cshtml* file to open it.
5. Repeat the same edit you just performed for *Create.cshtml* to delete the *<div>* elements for *UnitPrice*, *Price*, *AddedOn*, and *UpdatedOn*.
6. Click the FILE menu, and choose Save All (or press Ctrl+Shift+S).

The MVC website is now ready for testing.

Testing the website locally

Get some satisfaction now, and try out the website. To run the application locally and enter a few test orders, follow these steps:

1. Right-click the *WineCloudWeb* project in Solution Explorer, and choose Set As Startup Project.
2. Press F5 (or click the Internet Explorer play button in the toolbar) to launch the website in Internet Explorer. As already explained, with no controller or action specified in the URL, this navigates to the Index view of the Home controller by default. This view displays a list of all the orders in the system, which is empty at this time. The view also provides a Create New link, which navigates to the Create view.
3. Click the Create New link to navigate to the Create view of the Home controller. The data entry screen appears as shown in Figure 10-25.

FIGURE 10-25 Placing an order on the website

4. Type any date in the OrderedOn text box.
5. Select any customer from the CustomerId drop-down list.
6. Select Mendoza from the WineId drop-down list.
7. In the Quantity text box, type **2**.
8. Click the Create button.
9. After the order is saved to the database, the browser redirects to the Index action of the Home controller. This displays the list of orders, including the order you just placed, as shown in Figure 10-26.

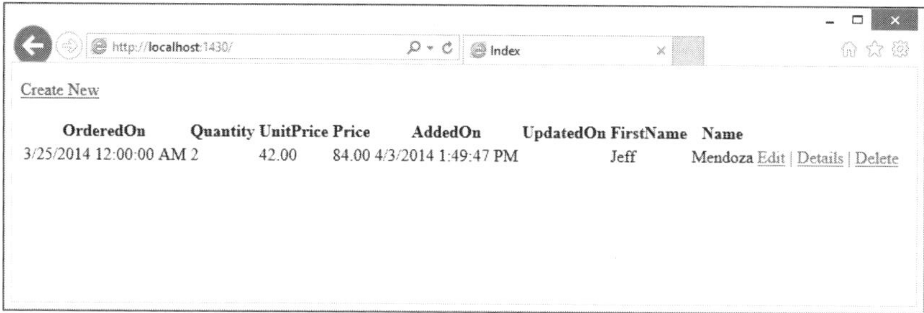

FIGURE 10-26 The confirmation page after placing the order

10. Just to get the feel for it, click Create New to enter another order or two. Also try out the Edit, Details, and Delete links.
11. Close the browser when you're done testing.

To suit your needs in a production scenario, you surely need to take this project much further. Beyond obvious aesthetics, one of the many things you would still need to do on your own to customize this project for a production application is to implement proper exception handling. If an error occurs in SQL Database when you attempt to save an order, a *DbUpdateException* gets thrown on the EF call to the *SaveChanges* method in the *HomeController* class. Because you haven't written any exception-handling code, Visual Studio will break on the error. When you press F5 to continue, the browser will display the default (and rather unfriendly) unhandled error page, because you haven't designed a friendlier unhandled error page customized for your own application. The default error page shows the underlying *SqlException* that was thrown by SQL Database. If the *SqlException* was thrown because of a THROW statement in one of the validation checks inside the stored procedures, the error page also shows the message text of the validation rule.

With no exception handling or client-side validations in place, it's easy to prove that the validations in the stored procedures embedded in the EDM are working as expected. You should simply encounter an unhandled exception if you attempt to enter an invalid order. Again, of course, for a production application, you need to implement a far more robust exception-handling strategy that can distinguish between different types of errors, determine whether an error message is safe or unsafe to display, and might also include additional logging, notification, and navigation logic. You would also implement client-side validations so that the error never gets the chance to occur in the first place. But right here and now, you can just try and "crash" the site to test the validations in the stored procedures.

For example, if you try to create or update an order with a quantity value lower than 1, the quantity validation in either the *InsertOrder* or *UpdateOrder* stored procedure will THROW an error. In turn, you will receive an error page as shown in Figure 10-27.

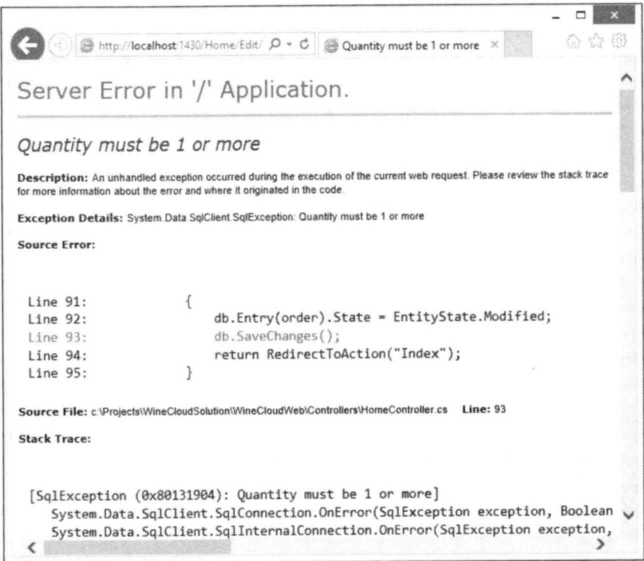

FIGURE 10-27 The unhandled exception page for an error thrown by the stored procedure's quantity validation

You can also test the logic in the *DeleteOrder* stored procedure that protects orders less than a year old from being deleted. If you create a new order with an *OrderedOn* date more than one year old, you will have no problem deleting it. But if you try to delete an order less than a year old, you will receive an error page as shown in Figure 10-28.

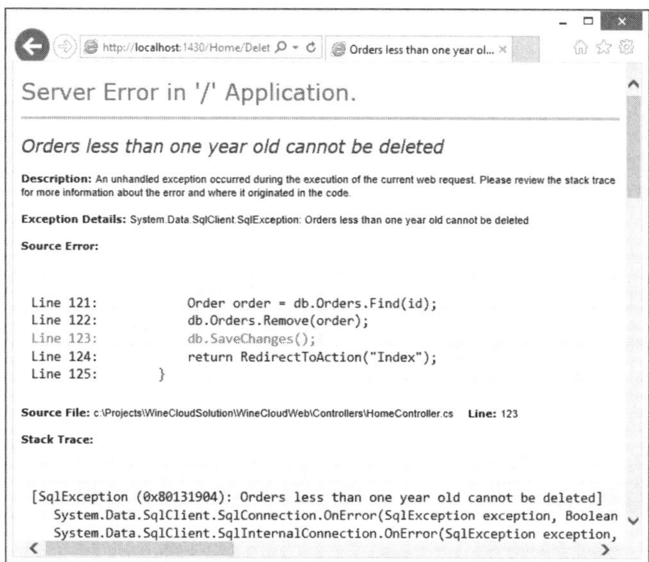

FIGURE 10-28 The unhandled exception page for an error thrown by the stored procedure's delete validation

Up to this point, you have been running the website locally, even though the local website has been interacting with the live Azure SQL Database in the cloud. In the next section, you will deploy the website to Microsoft Azure so that both the website and the database are running in the cloud.

Deploying the website to Microsoft Azure

After testing the website locally, you can deploy it to the cloud very easily. All you do is create a Website on Microsoft Azure using the Microsoft Azure management portal and download the new website's publish settings. Then, any time and as often you wish, you can publish the project to the website from right inside Visual Studio.

To create the website, follow these steps:

1. Log in to the Microsoft Azure portal at *https://manage.windowsazure.com*. This brings you to the main portal page showing ALL ITEMS.
2. Click WEB SITES in the vertical navigation pane on the left.
3. Click the NEW button at the bottom of the page.
4. Click QUICK CREATE.
5. In the URL text box, type **winecloudweb**. This specifies that the website will be accessible at *http://winecloudweb.azurewebsites.net*.

Note This must be a globally unique name. Although we released the name *winecloudweb* prior to publishing this book, there is still a good chance that someone else might be using it at the time you are following along with this procedure. In this case, just append something like your initials or choose some other name that nobody else has chosen.

6. In the REGION drop-down list, choose the same (or nearest) region you selected for the SQL Database. Keeping all the application components hosted in the same region maximizes performance and avoids billing fees. (See Chapter 2, "Configuration and pricing," for more information on pricing.) Your screen should appear similar to Figure 10-29.

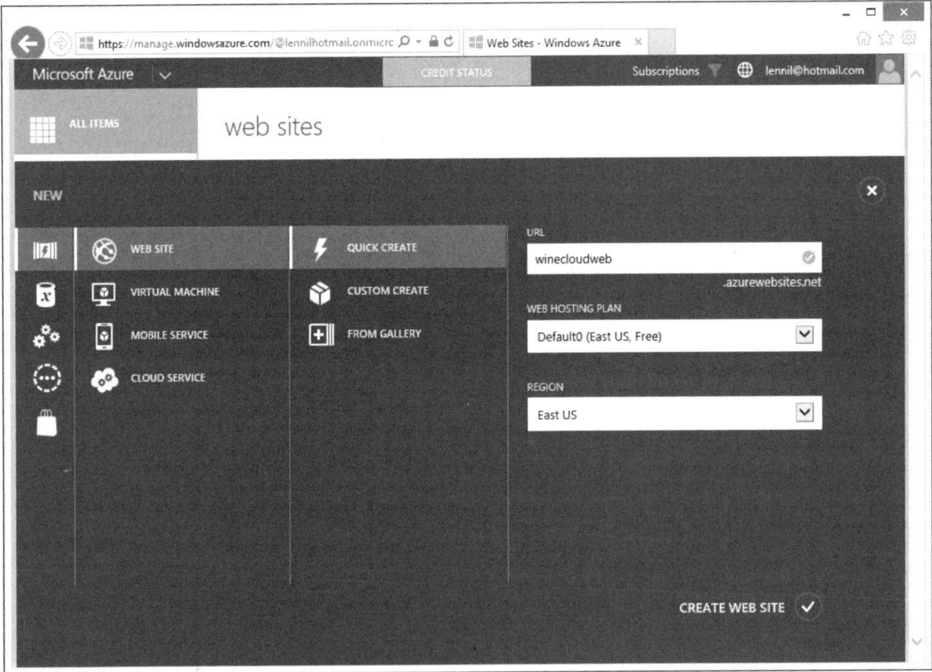

FIGURE 10-29 Creating a new website on Microsoft Azure

7. Click CREATE WEB SITE. It takes just a few moments to create the website, and the portal indicates that the website is running, as shown in Figure 10-30.

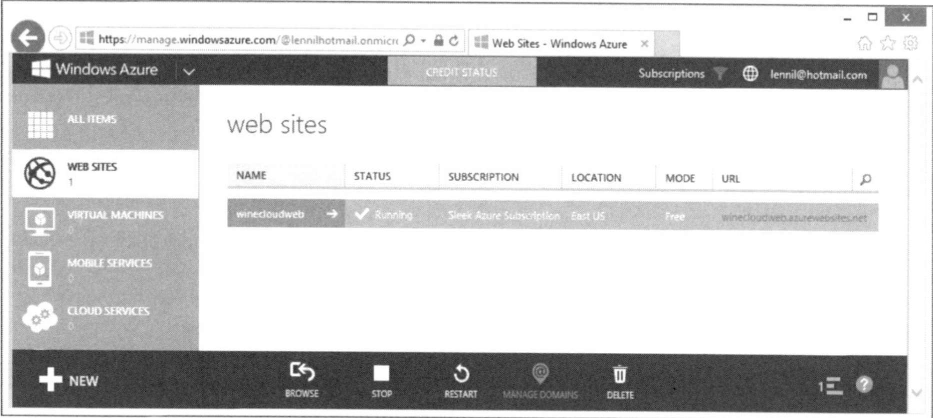

FIGURE 10-30 The Microsoft Azure portal shows that the *winecloudweb* website is up and running.

8. Click *winecloudweb* in the NAME column to display the dashboard page for the website.
9. Beneath Publish Your App, click the Download The Publish Profile link.
10. After a brief moment, the publish settings file is generated and you are prompted to open or save it, as shown in Figure 10-31.

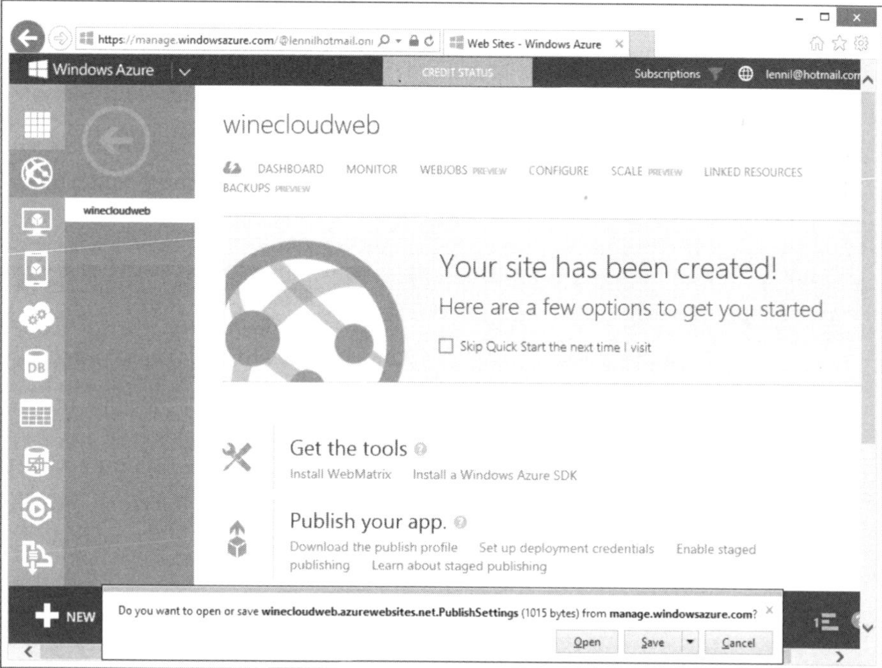

FIGURE 10-31 Generating a publish profile for deploying a Microsoft Azure website

11. Click the drop-down portion of the Save button, and choose Save As.

12. In the Save As dialog, navigate to the top-level folder of the *WineCloudWeb* project, and click Save.

Using the profile you just downloaded, you can now deploy the project to the website from Visual Studio. To do so, follow these steps:

1. Switch back to Visual Studio.
2. Right-click the *WineCloudWeb* project in Solution Explorer, and choose Publish to display the Publish Web dialog, as shown in Figure 10-32.

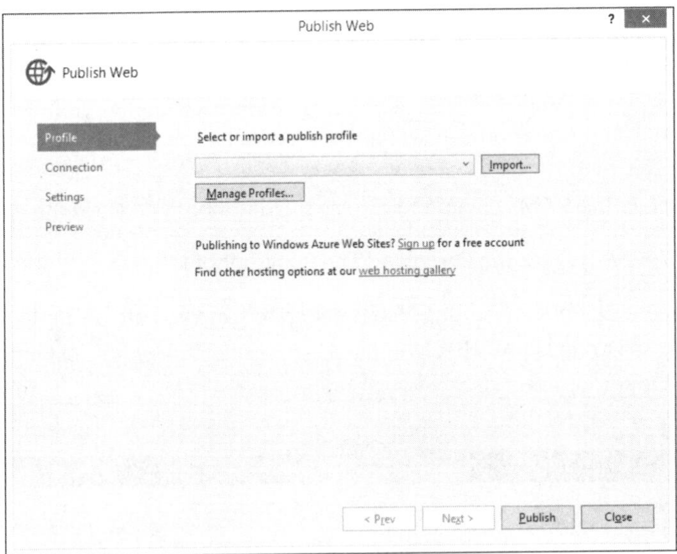

FIGURE 10-32 The Publish Web dialog

3. Click Import.
4. In the Import Publish Profile dialog, click Browse.
5. Navigate to the top-level folder of the *WineCloudOrderWeb* project where you saved the publish profile in the previous procedure.
6. Double-click the *winecloudweb.azurewebsites.net.PublishSettings* file.
7. Click OK. This advances to the Connection page, which gets populated automatically with information loaded from the profile, as shown in Figure 10-33.

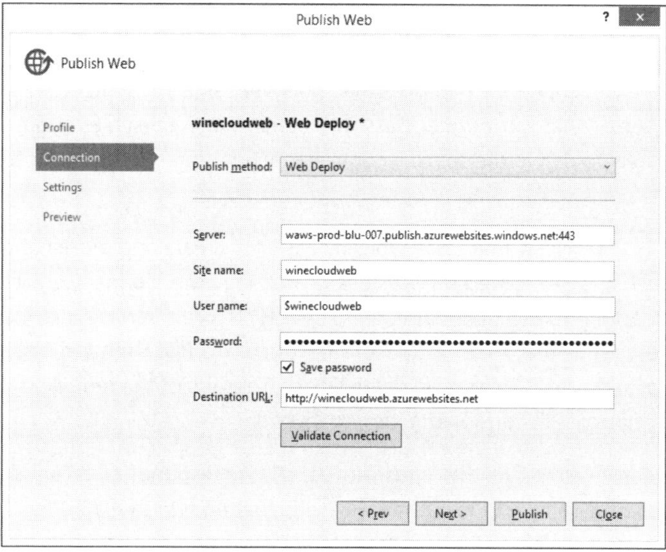

FIGURE 10-33 The Connection page is automatically populated with information from the profile.

8. Click Next to advance to the Settings page.
9. Click Next to advance to the Preview page.
10. Click Publish. Because of all the assemblies used by the project, it can take several minutes to deploy the first time. However, subsequent deployments will typically take only a few seconds.

Everything is now running in the cloud—not just the website, but the DAL, and SQL Database as well. All of that is running on hardware you never need to manage, worry about, touch, or see. Go and enjoy the benefits of having a complete multitiered solution hosted on Microsoft Azure. You can reach it from any browser, anywhere, anytime.

Once deployed, Visual Studio automatically launches the browser to the website. By default, it displays the Index view of the Home controller, which should show the same data you entered while testing the website locally. This is because the local website used the *WineCloudDb* SQL Database deployed on Microsoft Azure, and that's the same database that the deployed website is now using.

To run the application from any browser on any machine, just navigate to *http://winecloudweb.azurewebsites.net* (of course, you need to adjust this URL for the name you supplied when you created the website, which will be different if the name *winecloudweb* has already been taken). Take some time now and use the website to enter a few more orders, as you did earlier when you were testing the site locally.

Creating the ASP.NET Web API services

With ASP.NET Web API, you can create web services that work very similarly to MVC web applications. Just like MVC, a Web API service has a controller class with actions, and a flexible routing engine that defines the rules and defaults to derive the specific controller action that is invoked in response to a URL request over HTTP.

Web API implements REST services, which are typically easier to create and more lightweight than other types of services, such as SOAP-based services using WCF. (See the "So many choices" sidebar at the beginning of this chapter.) To facilitate data access over HTTP, REST services are mapped to standard HTTP request verbs such that a GET request retrieves data, a POST request inserts data, a PUT request updates data, and a DELETE request deletes data. The URL of the request is parsed by the Web API runtime to determine which controller action to invoke.

For example, a GET request with a URL that ends with */api/Wine* responds by returning all the wines in the database, while the same GET request with a URL that ends with */api/Wine/5* returns only a single wine with the *WineId* value of 5. The other HTTP verbs package additional information for the request in the HTTP request header. This is information that is either impractical or impossible to encode in the URL. For example, a PUT request with a URL that ends with */api/Wine/3* means that a single wine with the *WineId* value of 3 is to be updated, while the actual data for the updated wine (the updated name, category, year, and price) is embedded into the HTTP request header as a simple dictionary of key value pairs.

Data is returned by Web API services as a string in JavaScript Object Notation (JSON) format. Recall that when you create the project, you also chose to include the core assemblies for Web API. (See Figure 10-21.) One of those assemblies is *Newtonsoft.Json*, which is a popular library for serializing objects into JSON strings and deserializing JSON strings back into object instances. For a GET request, the Web API calls into this library to serialize objects into a JSON-formatted string to return to the client. The client, in turn, can also call into this library to deserialize the JSON-formatted string received from the GET request into a live object on the client.

Like MVC website applications, Web API services are defined inside an ASP.NET Web Application project, and you can certainly create another ASP.NET Web Application project to be used only for Web API services. For simplicity, however, you will add the Web API services to the same ASP.NET Web Application project you just created for the MVC website. The project already includes the core assemblies for Web API (as you can see in Figure 10-21), so it is all ready to host Web API services in addition to the MVC website; all you need to do is add a Web API controller class to the project.

Visual Studio provides a scaffolding feature similar to the one you used earlier to generate the MVC controller with actions and views. In the case of a new Web API controller, the scaffolding fully supports CRUD operations against any entity in the EDM. As you will see, the default routing engine rules maintain separation between MVC and Web API controllers based on the presence or absence of */api* in the URL. Requests without */api* in the URL are directed to MVC controllers, and those with */api* in the URL are routed to Web API controllers.

Adding a Web API controller

In the next procedure, you will scaffold a new controller with CRUD actions for the *Wine* entity. Then, in the final section of the chapter, you will consume this controller's Web API services from a Windows Phone 8 app.

Note If you experience déjà vu as you create and test the Web API controller, it might be because you recently completed Chapter 8. You created and tested the very same Wine Web API controller in Chapter 8 while learning how to handle transient SQL Database errors with Entity Framework.

To create the scaffolding for a new Wine Web API controller with CRUD actions for the *Wine* entity, follow these steps:

1. Right-click the *Controllers* folder in the *WineCloudWeb* project in Solution Explorer, and choose Add | New Scaffolded Item.
2. In the Add Scaffold dialog, select Web API 2 Controller With Actions, Using Entity Framework, as shown in Figure 10-34.

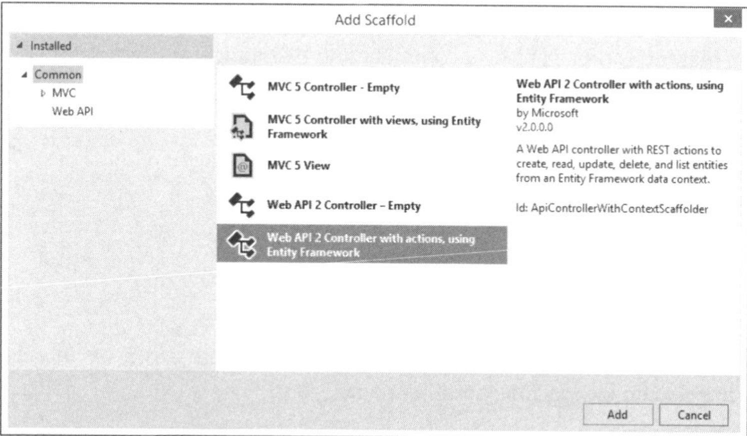

FIGURE 10-34 The Add Scaffold dialog has several choices for creating a new Web API controller class.

3. Click Add.
4. In the Add Controller dialog, do the following:
   a. Change *Default1* to **Wine** so that the controller name is *WineController*.
   b. For Model Class, choose Wine (WineCloudModel) from the drop-down list.
   c. For Data Context Class, choose WineCloudDbEntities (WineCloudModel) from the drop-down list. The Add Controller dialog should appear similar to Figure 10-35.

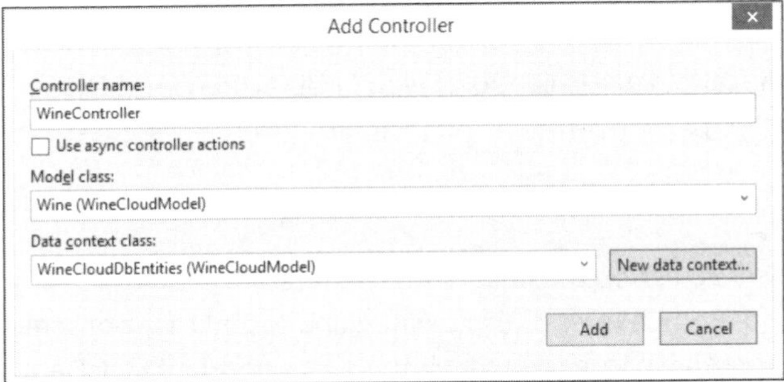

FIGURE 10-35 Adding a Web API 2 controller class, with automatically generated actions for EF

d. Click Add.

Now take a look at what has been created for you. Open the *WineController.cs* class, and examine the code that was generated. Notice the following:

- The class inherits from *System.Web.Http.ApiController*, which is what makes this a Web API controller class.
- Several public action methods have been created. Based on the URL of an incoming request, and the type of the incoming request, one of these action methods will be called.
- Each action method is preceded by a comment line that indicates the type of HTTP request and URL syntax that the action method will handle:
  - A GET request responds by selecting a wine or list of wines.
  - A POST request responds by inserting a new wine.
  - A PUT request responds by updating an existing wine.
  - A DELETE request responds by deleting an existing wine.
- The action method signatures (their names and parameters) are expressed in a slash-delimited format on the URL, following the controller name.
- As indicated in the comment line above each method, the Web API routing engine prepends */api* to the action name in the URL. As we mentioned, this ensures isolation between HTTP requests for an MVC controller (without */api* in the URL) and HTTP requests for a Web API control (with */api* present in the URL).

There is one small additional step you need to take before you can start using this new Web API controller. When the JSON result is received from the service, the JSON serializer attempts to serialize all related entities that it discovers, which can result in circular references that cause errors. To avoid this problem, the JSON serializer must be told to ignore circular references.

If you followed along with the procedures in Chapter 8, you might be wondering why this extra measure must be taken, because it wasn't necessary in that chapter when you created a *Wine* controller just as you did now. The answer is the *Order* table, which is present in this chapter's *WineCloudDb* database but was not present in the database for Chapter 8. With the *Order* table present and related to both the *Wine* and *Customer* tables, the possibility exists for Wine A to reference Order B, which references Customer C, which then in turn references Wine A as Customer C's favorite wine. Following the references from that point results in an infinite loop that is short-circuited by telling the JSON serializer not to attempt serializing the same object instance more than once.

To instruct the JSON serializer that circular references should be ignored, follow these steps:

1. Expand the *App_Start* folder of the *WineCloudWeb* project in Solution Explorer to reveal the *WebApiConfig.cs* file.
2. Double-click the *WebApiConfig.cs* file to open it.
3. Add the following line of code to the bottom of the *Register* method:

```
config.Formatters.JsonFormatter.SerializerSettings.ReferenceLoopHandling =
 Newtonsoft.Json.ReferenceLoopHandling.Ignore;
```

4. Click the FILE menu, and choose Save App_Start\WebApiConfig.cs (or press Ctrl+S).

The Web API controller is now ready for testing.

Testing the Web API

To test out a few Web API service calls, follow these steps:

1. Press F5 (or click the Internet Explorer play button in the toolbar) to launch the website in Internet Explorer. As usual, this displays the Index view of the Home controller.
2. Append the URL in the browser's address bar with **api/Wine**, and press Enter. This executes the *GetWines* action method in the *WineController* class and responds with the list of wines from the *WineCloudDb* database. Internet Explorer's default behavior asks if you would like to save or open the results from the Web API call, as shown in Figure 10-36.

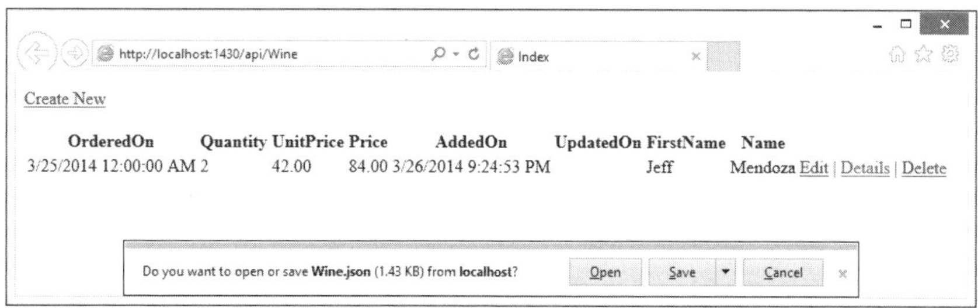

FIGURE 10-36 The browser prompts to open or save the *Wine.json* file returned by the Wine API

3. Click Open to view the list of wines returned in the JSON results, as shown in Figure 10-37. (If prompted for how to open this type of file, click More Options and choose Notepad.)

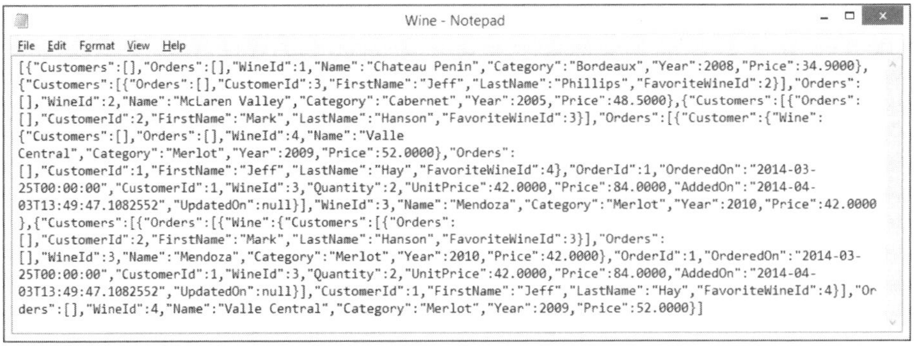

Wine - Notepad

File Edit Format View Help


```
[{"Customers":[],"Orders":[],"WineId":1,"Name":"Chateau Penin","Category":"Bordeaux","Year":2008,"Price":34.9000},
{"Customers":[{"Orders":[],"CustomerId":3,"FirstName":"Jeff","LastName":"Phillips","FavoriteWineId":2}],"Orders":
[],"WineId":2,"Name":"McLaren Valley","Category":"Cabernet","Year":2005,"Price":48.5000},{"Customers":[{"Orders":
[],"CustomerId":2,"FirstName":"Mark","LastName":"Hanson","FavoriteWineId":3}],"Orders":[{"Customer":{"Wine":
{"Customers":[],"Orders":[],"WineId":4,"Name":"Valle
Central","Category":"Merlot","Year":2009,"Price":52.0000},"Orders":
[],"CustomerId":1,"FirstName":"Jeff","LastName":"Hay","FavoriteWineId":4},"OrderId":1,"OrderedOn":"2014-03-
25T00:00:00","CustomerId":1,"WineId":3,"Quantity":2,"UnitPrice":42.0000,"Price":84.0000,"AddedOn":"2014-04-
03T13:49:47.1082552","UpdatedOn":null}],"WineId":3,"Name":"Mendoza","Category":"Merlot","Year":2010,"Price":42.0000
},{"Customers":[{"Orders":[{"Wine":{"Customers":[{"Orders":
[],"CustomerId":2,"FirstName":"Mark","LastName":"Hanson","FavoriteWineId":3}],"Orders":
[],"WineId":3,"Name":"Mendoza","Category":"Merlot","Year":2010,"Price":42.0000},"OrderId":1,"OrderedOn":"2014-03-
25T00:00:00","CustomerId":1,"WineId":3,"Quantity":2,"UnitPrice":42.0000,"Price":84.0000,"AddedOn":"2014-04-
03T13:49:47.1082552","UpdatedOn":null}],"CustomerId":1,"FirstName":"Jeff","LastName":"Hay","FavoriteWineId":4}],"Or
ders":[],"WineId":4,"Name":"Valle Central","Category":"Merlot","Year":2009,"Price":52.0000}]
```


FIGURE 10-37 Viewing the *Wine.json* file returned by the Wine API in Notepad

4. Back in the browser, append the URL in the browser's address bar with **api/Wine/2**, and press Enter. This executes the *GetWine* method on the *WineController* and responds with the record for *WineId* 2.

5. Click Open to view the JSON response in Notepad. This time, the response includes just the single requested wine.

At this point, you are running the Web API services locally, even though the local services are interacting with the live Azure SQL Database in the cloud. In the next section, you will deploy *WineCloudWeb* again so that the MVC website, Web API services, and the database are all running in the cloud.

Deploying the Web API

With the new Web API controller class added to the project and tested, you are ready to deploy the project to Microsoft Azure once again. Doing so will make the Web API accessible to the Windows Phone 8 app that you will be building next. This is the same procedure you already performed earlier in this chapter when you initially deployed the MVC website. But because the project has already been previously deployed, this deployment is relatively much quicker than it was the first time.

To deploy the updated project with the new Web API controller to Microsoft Azure, follow these steps:

1. Right-click the *WineCloudWeb* project in Solution Explorer, and choose Publish to display the Publish Web dialog. Because you already deployed this project earlier, the dialog opens directly to the Preview page, ready to publish using the previous settings, as shown in Figure 10-38.

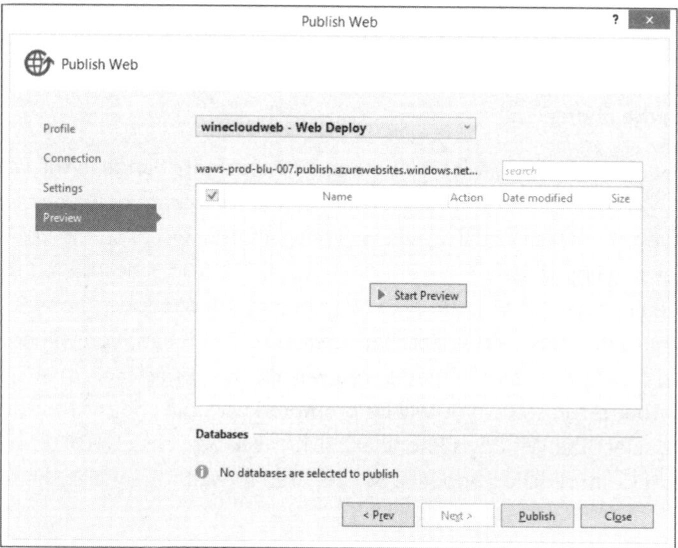

FIGURE 10-38 The Publish Web dialog

2. Click Publish. Within just a few moments, the project is deployed, and Visual Studio opens a new browser window to the site on Microsoft Azure.
3. Verify that the deployed Web API services work properly by testing them just as you did locally. Simply tweak the URL in the browser's address bar with different */api/Wine* requests, and ensure the correct JSON results are returned in response.

Everything is now in place to support the Windows Phone 8 app, which will call into the Web API services you just created.

Creating the Windows Phone application

The next and last piece of this solution is to build a native Windows Phone 8 app. This app will consume the Web API services you created in the previous section to provide a wine catalog that allows the user to view, create, edit, and delete wines in the database.

Installing the Windows Phone SDK 8.0

The first step before building any Windows Phone 8 app is to install the Windows Phone SDK, if you haven't done so already.

The Windows Phone SDK contains everything you need to build Windows Phone 8 apps, including a number of Visual Studio project templates designed specifically for a Windows Phone device. The programming model is essentially Silverlight, meaning that if you have any Silverlight (or Windows Presentation Foundation [WPF]) experience, you already possess the essential skills needed to quickly build useful Windows Phone apps. (If not, worry not; we'll explain all the important parts of the code.) The SDK also provides a phone emulator that integrates with Visual Studio to provide you with the standard debugging experience, allowing you to set breakpoints, watch values, and single-step through code running on the phone.

With the release of Visual Studio 2013, Microsoft made an important change in the way it ships this SDK. Previously, the SDK was not included with Visual Studio, and a separate download was always required. This remains true with earlier Visual Studio versions, but now Visual Studio 2013 includes the SDK. However, as shown in Figure 10-39, the option to install the SDK is deselected by default. So unless you have overridden this default at setup time by selecting the Windows Phone 8.0 SDK check box, you will need to re-run setup now and select that check box. This means you will need access to the original Visual Studio 2013 distribution media. You will also need to close Visual Studio before installing the SDK. When you re-run setup, you will be prompted with the choices Modify, Repair, and Uninstall. Choose Modify, select the Windows Phone 8.0 SDK check box, click UPDATE, and then click Yes when the User Account Control dialog appears. Be prepared to wait for a while; the SDK has a lengthy installation process.

> **Important** If you are running Visual Studio 2013, it will *not* be sufficient to find and download the SDK from Microsoft's website. Doing so will install the SDK, but only for Visual Studio 2012. If you don't have Visual Studio 2012, the SDK will include the Visual Studio 2012 shell with project templates for Windows Phone, but you still won't have Windows Phone templates in Visual Studio 2013. The *only* way to add the SDK to Visual Studio 2013 is to re-run setup and select the check box.

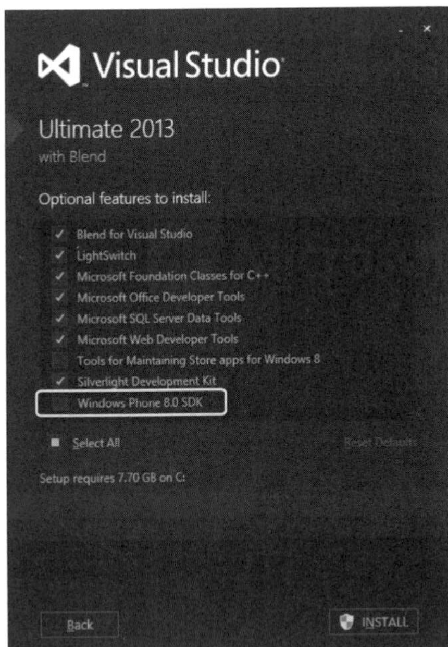

FIGURE 10-39 By default, the Visual Studio 2013 Setup dialog does not select the Windows Phone 8.0 SDK

Creating the Windows Phone Project

With the SDK installed, you're ready to create the Windows Phone project. As we mentioned already, this is essentially a Silverlight application designed to run on the phone.

To create the Windows Phone project, follow these steps:

1. If you closed Visual Studio 2013 to install the Windows Phone 8.0 SDK, restart it now and reopen *WineCloudSolution*.
2. Right-click *WineCloudSolution* in Solution Explorer, and choose Add | New Project to display the Add New Project dialog.
3. On the left of the New Project dialog, expand Installed, Visual C#, and choose Windows Phone.
4. Choose the Windows Phone App template, which is typically selected by default.
5. Name the project **WineCloudPhone**, and click OK, as shown in Figure 10-40.

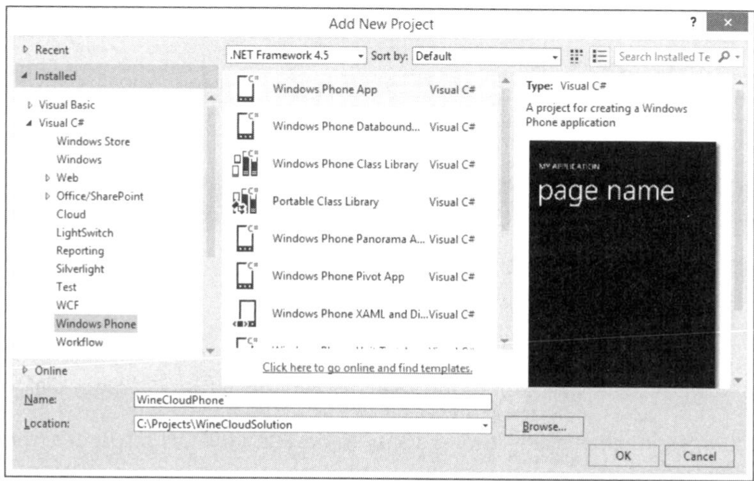

FIGURE 10-40 Creating a new Windows Phone application project

6. Click OK.

Visual Studio creates the project, and you're ready to start building the phone app.

Adding Json.NET

As we began explaining, this phone app will call the Web API services you recently created in the *WineCloudWeb* ASP.NET Web Application project. Those services will return *Wine* entities on the server as JSON-formatted strings to the client, so you will want to be able to access Json.NET (the Newtonsoft.Json library) on the Windows Phone. This will let you easily deserialize the JSON responses received from the service into *Wine* object instances on the phone.

There is a special version of Json.NET available specifically for the Windows Phone. It can be downloaded and referenced by the phone app very easily by using the NuGet Package Manager in Visual Studio. To download and reference Json.NET, follow these steps:

1. Right-click the *WineCloudPhone* project in Solution Explorer, and choose Manage NuGet Packages.
2. On the left, expand the Online tab and select nuget.org.
3. In the Search Online text box in the upper-right, type **json.net** (as shown in Figure 10-41) and press Enter.

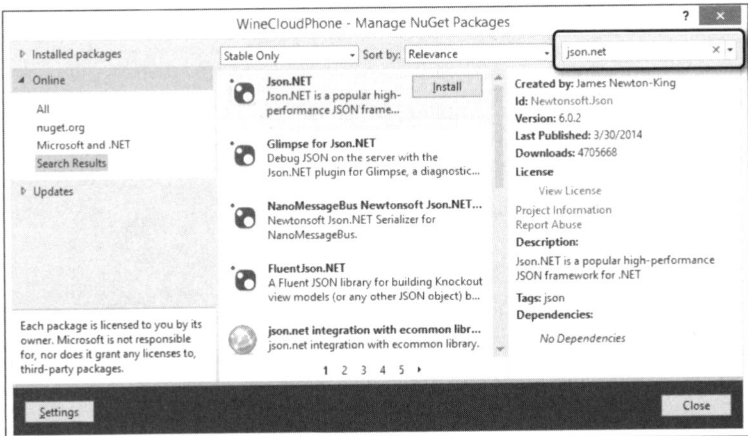

FIGURE 10-41 Downloading and adding a reference to Json.NET using the NuGet Package Manager

4. Click the Install button for Json.NET.
5. After Json.NET is installed, click Close to close the Manage NuGet Packages dialog.

With the Json.NET reference in place, it will be easy to deserialize JSON responses from the Web API service in the phone app.

Creating the App's main page

The Windows Phone SDK provides multiple templates for creating Windows Phone apps. Among them is the Windows Phone Databound App template, which starts your new project off with all the elements in place to support the Model-View-ViewModel (MVVM) pattern. MVVM has similarities with MVC, where one of its differences is that it is stateful (MVVM retains state between requests) rather than stateless (MVC does not retain state). MVVM certainly has its benefits, but this project will use the basic Windows Phone App template. This is a minimal template that contains nothing more than a basic main page that you will customize for the wine catalog.

The main page will have two panels, only one of which shall be made visible at any time, programmatically. The app will present the complete list of wines in the first panel and enable data entry in controls laid out in the second panel.

Windows Phone apps have two files per page: Extensible Application Markup Language (XAML), and .NET (C# or Visual Basic) code-behind. As you will see, XAML has powerful binding capabilities. XAML binding features greatly reduce the amount of code-behind you need to write. This is particularly significant, because there are no scaffolding features in Visual Studio to build out the XAML as there is to build out the HTML views in an MVC application. Listing 10-5 shows the *Wine* model class, Listing 10-6 shows the XAML markup for the main page of the wine phone app, and Listing 10-7 shows the code-behind for the main page.

LISTING 10-5 The *Wine.cs* Windows Phone app model class

```
namespace WineCloudPhone
{
  public class Wine
  {
    public int WineId { get; set; }
    public string Name { get; set; }
    public string Category { get; set; }
    public int? Year { get; set; }
    public decimal Price { get; set; }
  }
}
```

LISTING 10-6 The *MainPage.xaml* Windows Phone app markup

```
<phone:PhoneApplicationPage
  x:Class="WineCloudPhone.MainPage"
  xmlns="http://schemas.microsoft.com/winfx/2006/xaml/presentation"
  xmlns:x="http://schemas.microsoft.com/winfx/2006/xaml"
  xmlns:phone="clr-namespace:Microsoft.Phone.Controls;assembly=Microsoft.Phone"
  xmlns:shell="clr-namespace:Microsoft.Phone.Shell;assembly=Microsoft.Phone"
  xmlns:d="http://schemas.microsoft.com/expression/blend/2008"
  xmlns:mc="http://schemas.openxmlformats.org/markup-compatibility/2006"
  mc:Ignorable="d"
  FontFamily="{StaticResource PhoneFontFamilyNormal}"
  FontSize="{StaticResource PhoneFontSizeNormal}"
  Foreground="{StaticResource PhoneForegroundBrush}"
  SupportedOrientations="Portrait" Orientation="Portrait"
  shell:SystemTray.IsVisible="True"
  Loaded="PhoneApplicationPage_Loaded">
  <Grid x:Name="LayoutRoot" Background="Transparent">
    <Grid.RowDefinitions>
      <RowDefinition Height="Auto"/>
      <RowDefinition Height="*"/>
    </Grid.RowDefinitions>
```

```
    <StackPanel x:Name="TitlePanel" Grid.Row="0">
      <TextBlock Text="WINE CLOUD CATALOG" Style="{StaticResource PhoneTextNormalStyle}" />
      <TextBlock Text="wines" Style="{StaticResource PhoneTextTitle1Style}" />
    </StackPanel>
    <Grid x:Name="ContentPanel" Grid.Row="1">
      <StackPanel x:Name="WineListPanel">
        <ListBox Height="500" x:Name="WineListBox" ItemsSource="{Binding}"
         SelectionChanged="WineListBox_SelectionChanged">
          <ListBox.ItemTemplate>
            <DataTemplate>
              <StackPanel>
                <TextBlock Text="{Binding Path=Name}" TextWrapping="NoWrap"
                 Style="{StaticResource PhoneTextExtraLargeStyle}"/>
                <TextBlock Text="{Binding Path=Year}" TextWrapping="NoWrap"
                 Style="{StaticResource PhoneTextSubtleStyle}"/>
                <TextBlock Text="{Binding Path=Category}" TextWrapping="NoWrap"
                 Style="{StaticResource PhoneTextSubtleStyle}"/>
              </StackPanel>
            </DataTemplate>
          </ListBox.ItemTemplate>
        </ListBox>
        <Button x:Name="NewWineButton" Content="New" Width="120"
         Click="NewWineButton_Click" />
      </StackPanel>
      <StackPanel x:Name="WineDetailPanel" Visibility="Collapsed">
        <TextBlock Text="NAME" />
        <TextBox Text="{Binding Path=Name, Mode=TwoWay}" />
        <TextBlock Text="YEAR" />
        <TextBox Text="{Binding Path=Year, Mode=TwoWay}" />
        <TextBlock Text="CATEGORY" />
        <TextBox Text="{Binding Path=Category, Mode=TwoWay}" />
        <TextBlock Text="PRICE" />
        <TextBox Text="{Binding Path=Price, Mode=TwoWay}" />
        <StackPanel Orientation="Horizontal" HorizontalAlignment="Center">
          <Button x:Name="DeleteButton" Content="Delete" Width="120"
           Click="DeleteButton_Click" />
          <Button x:Name="SaveButton" Content="Save" Width="120"
           Click="SaveButton_Click" />
          <Button x:Name="CancelButton" Content="Cancel" Width="120"
           Click="CancelButton_Click" />
        </StackPanel>
      </StackPanel>
    </Grid>
  </Grid>
</phone:PhoneApplicationPage>
```

LISTING 10-7 The *MainPage.xaml.cs* Windows Phone app code-behind

```
using Microsoft.Phone.Controls;
using Newtonsoft.Json;
using System;
using System.Net;
```

```
using System.Windows;
using System.Windows.Controls;

namespace WineCloudPhone
{
  public partial class MainPage : PhoneApplicationPage
  {
    private const string WebApiUrl = @"http://winecloudweb.azurewebsites.net/api/Wine";

    private Wine _wine;

    public MainPage()
    {
      InitializeComponent();
    }

    private void PhoneApplicationPage_Loaded(object sender, RoutedEventArgs e)
    {
      LoadWines();
    }

    private void LoadWines()
    {
      var wc = new WebClient();
      wc.Headers["Accept"] = "application/json";
      wc.DownloadStringCompleted += new DownloadStringCompletedEventHandler(WinesLoaded);

      // GET api/Wine
      wc.DownloadStringAsync(new Uri(WebApiUrl));
    }

    private void WinesLoaded(object sender, DownloadStringCompletedEventArgs e)
    {
      if (e.Error != null)
      {
        MessageBox.Show("Error: " + e.Error.Message);
        return;
      }

      var wines = JsonConvert.DeserializeObject<Wine[]>(e.Result);

      WineListPanel.Visibility = Visibility.Visible;
      WineDetailPanel.Visibility = Visibility.Collapsed;
      LayoutRoot.DataContext = wines;
    }

    private void NewWineButton_Click(object sender, RoutedEventArgs e)
    {
      _wine = new Wine()
      {
        Name = "New Wine",
        Year = 2004,
        Category = "New Category",
        Price = 19.99M
      };
```

```
    DeleteButton.Visibility = Visibility.Collapsed;
    WineListPanel.Visibility = Visibility.Collapsed;
    WineDetailPanel.Visibility = Visibility.Visible;
    LayoutRoot.DataContext = _wine;
  }

  private void WineListBox_SelectionChanged(object sender, SelectionChangedEventArgs e)
  {
    var addedItems = e.AddedItems as object[];
    if ((addedItems == null) || (addedItems.Length != 1))
    {
      return;
    }

    _wine = (Wine)e.AddedItems[0];

    DeleteButton.Visibility = Visibility.Visible;
    WineListPanel.Visibility = Visibility.Collapsed;
    WineDetailPanel.Visibility = Visibility.Visible;
    LayoutRoot.DataContext = _wine;
  }

  private void SaveButton_Click(object sender, RoutedEventArgs e)
  {
    var wc = new WebClient();
    wc.Headers[HttpRequestHeader.ContentType] = "application/x-www-form-urlencoded";
    wc.UploadStringCompleted += WinesUpdated;

    var wineInfo = string.Format("Name={0}&Category={1}&Year={2}&Price={3}",
                   HttpUtility.UrlEncode(_wine.Name),
                   HttpUtility.UrlEncode(_wine.Category),
                   _wine.Year,
                   _wine.Price);

    if (_wine.WineId == 0)
    {
      // POST api/Wine
      wc.UploadStringAsync(new Uri(WebApiUrl), "POST", wineInfo);
    }
    else
    {
      // PUT api/Wine/5
      var webApiUrl = string.Format("{0}/{1}", WebApiUrl, _wine.WineId);
      wineInfo = string.Format("WineId={0}&{1}", _wine.WineId, wineInfo);
      wc.UploadStringAsync(new Uri(webApiUrl), "PUT", wineInfo);
    }
  }

  private void DeleteButton_Click(object sender, RoutedEventArgs e)
  {
    var confirm =
```

```
      MessageBox.Show("Delete this wine?", "Confirm", MessageBoxButton.OKCancel);

    if (confirm != MessageBoxResult.OK)
    {
      return;
    }

    // DELETE api/Wine/5
    var wc = new WebClient();
    wc.Headers[HttpRequestHeader.ContentType] = "application/x-www-form-urlencoded";
    wc.UploadStringCompleted += WinesUpdated;

    var webApiUrl = string.Format("{0}/{1}", WebApiUrl, _wine.WineId);
    wc.UploadStringAsync(new Uri(webApiUrl), "DELETE", _wine.WineId.ToString());
  }

  private void WinesUpdated(object sender, UploadStringCompletedEventArgs e)
  {
    if (e.Error != null)
    {
      MessageBox.Show("Error: " + e.Error.Message);
      return;
    }

    LoadWines();
  }

  private void CancelButton_Click(object sender, RoutedEventArgs e)
  {
    this.LoadWines();
  }

 }
}
```

We'll explain all of this code in just a moment, right after you implement it in the project. To do so, follow these steps:

1. Right-click the *WineCloudPhone* project in Solution Explorer, and choose Add | Class.
2. Name the new class **Wine.cs**, and click Add.
3. Replace the template code with the code shown earlier in Listing 10-5 (or paste it in from the listing file downloaded from the book's companion website).
4. Right-click the *MainPage.xaml* file in Solution Explorer (already created in the *WineCloudPhone* project), and choose View Designer. This opens a split view of the main page, with a design view on the left and a XAML code editor on the right.
5. In the XAML code editor, replace the template code generated automatically by Visual Studio with the code shown earlier in Listing 10-6 (or paste it in from the listing file downloaded from the book's companion website).

6. Right-click the *MainPage.xaml* file in Solution Explorer, and choose View Code.
7. Replace the template code with the code shown earlier in Listing 10-7 (or paste it in from the listing file downloaded from the book's companion website).
8. Edit the URL in the *WebApiUrl* string constant at the top of Listing 10-7 with the name you used for the Microsoft Azure website, assuming the name *winecloudweb* was not available to you.
9. Click the FILE menu, and choose Save All, or press Ctrl+Shift+S.

First we'll explain the *Wine* model class (Listing 10-5). This class reflects the *Wine* entity in the EDM in the DAL. Web API services are very lightweight, and consequently, they do not advertise their schemas with metadata as WCF services can. Thus, there is no way to automatically generate client-side proxy classes that reflect the service-side entities, which means you manually need to re-create the desired entity classes (the *Wine* class, in this case) to represent a model in the phone app.

Now shift focus to the main page itself. The key points to note about the XAML markup in Listing 10-6 are the two *StackPanel* objects, named *WineListPanel* and *WineDetailPanel*. As mentioned, only one of these panels at a time will be made visible by the code-behind. In the markup, *WineListPanel* has a *ListBox* that displays all the wines, and embedded within the *ListBox* is a *DataTemplate* that defines how each wine in the list should be rendered. The template has three *TextBlock* elements, which render three parts of each wine. The *Text* property in each *TextBlock* is set to a *Binding* with a *Path* that points to a specific property of the *Wine* class: *Name*, *Year*, and *Category*. Also note that the Style of the first *TextBlock* is set to *PhoneTextExtraLargeStyle*, while the other two are set to *PhoneTextSubtleStyle*. This means that the wine name will appear nice and large in the list, with the year and category beneath in a smaller font size.

The list box also has a *SelectionChanged* event handler that fires in the C# code-behind whenever the user selects a wine from the list (that is, when the user taps one). When the code-behind responds, *WineListPanel* gets hidden and *WineDetailsPanel* gets made visible so that the user can edit the selected wine. There is also an Add button beneath the text box that the user can tap to add a new wine. This also toggles the panel, but it binds the UI to a new *Wine* object, rather than an existing *Wine* object from the list.

The second panel, *WineDetailsPanel*, contains four *TextBox* controls for editing the information of a new or existing wine. Again, the controls have a binding path to a specific *Wine* property, but this time, *Mode=TwoWay* is also specified. This small but critical detail is all that's needed to implement bi-directional binding—properties of the bound object appear in the text boxes, and changes made by the user in those text boxes are pushed back into the bound object. Beneath the text boxes is a Save button to push the changes through the Web API service, through the DAL, and back to the SQL Database. There is also a Cancel button, which returns to the wine list panel, discarding any changes made on the details panel. Finally, there is a Delete button, which is hidden when entering a new wine.

Now turn your attention to the code-behind shown in Listing 10-7. First, notice the *using* statement for *Newtonsoft.Json*. This imports the namespace for the Json.NET library so that it can be easily called to deserialize JSON responses from the Web API services. Next, notice the *WebApiUrl* string constant defined at the top of the class, which points to the Wine Web API controller at URL *http://winecloudweb.azurewebsites.net/api/Wine*. Remember to change this constant accordingly if you named the website differently because *winecloudweb* was not available.

Right beneath the constant, you see the *_wine* variable defined as a private (page-level) variable of type *Wine*. This variable will hold an instance of the new or existing *Wine* object being created or updated in *WineDetailsPanel*. The page has a *DataContext* property that represents the object currently bound to the XAML. When the list panel is being displayed, the *DataContext* is set to the array of wines returned by the Web API service (which displays all the wines in the list box), and when the details panel is displayed, the *DataContext* is set to the *_wine* variable (which bi-directionally data-binds one specific wine to the text boxes).

In the *PhoneApplicationPage_Loaded* event, you can see that *LoadWines* is called. The *LoadWines* method prepares a *WebClient* object to issue an HTTP request, and it sets the HTTP *Accept* header to *application/json*. This lets the server know that the client is able to receive a response in JSON format. Next, the code registers a handler for the *DownloadStringCompleted* event. This specifies *WinesLoaded* as the callback function to the *asynchronous* service call. What this means is that your code doesn't wait for a response after it calls the service. That would be a *synchronous* service call, which is never permitted in Silverlight, because synchronous calls block the UI while waiting for the service response. To keep the device responsive while interacting with services, only asynchronous service calls are allowed. So rather than waiting for a response, the *WinesLoaded* method is called automatically when the *DownloadStringCompleted* event fires, which means that the service is ready to return its response.

After registering on the *DownloadStringCompleted* event, the *DownloadStringAsync* method is called. This method takes a URL as a parameter, which is the URL to the Wine Web API services, and it issues an asynchronous GET request over HTTP. After issuing the asynchronous request, the method completes. As explained, the UI now remains responsive while the service processes the request, and the *WinesLoaded* method is called automatically when the service returns with its response.

The *WinesLoaded* method first examines the *Error* property of the *DownloadStringCompletedEventArgs* parameter passed into the callback. This checks to make sure that the service call succeeded without an error. An array of *Wine* objects is then created in the *wines* variable from the JSON response. This is accomplished by calling the *JsonConvert.DeserializeObject* method of the Json.NET library, passing in the *Result* property of the *DownloadStringCompletedEventArgs* parameter that contains the JSON-formatted string returned by the service.

At this point, *wines* is populated with the complete list of wine objects, deserialized from the JSON response returned by the service. The visibility properties are now set to show the list panel and hide the detail panel, and the *LayoutRoot.DataContext* property is set to *wines*, which binds the array to the list box.

When the user clicks the New button, the *NewWineButton_Click* event handler fires. The event handler code simply assigns *_wine* to a new *Wine* object instance, setting a few default properties to start the user off entering a new wine. After toggling the panels to display the data entry text box controls and hiding the Delete button, *LayoutRoot.DataContext* is set to *_wine*, which binds new wine object to the text box controls.

Next, the *WineListBox_SelectionChanged* event handler fires when the user taps on a wine in the list. This event actually fires several times, as selected items are either added or removed. The code is interested only in the event that fires when there is exactly one object in the *AddedItems* property of the *SelectionChangedEventArgs* variable passed in as *e*. It then extracts the tapped wine object into *_wine*, Finally, it toggles the panel and sets *LayoutRoot.DataContext* to *_wine*, just as it does for a new wine (though this time the Delete button is made visible).

When the user clicks the Save button, the *SaveButton_Click* event handler fires and it's time to push the changes back to the Web API service, which either creates or updates a wine in the database. The first part of the save logic works the same in either case. The code creates a new *WebClient* object and sets the HTTP *ContentType* header to *application/x-www-form-urlencoded*, which lets the service know that the client is sending URL-encoded strings in the HTTP header. Then it registers a handler for the *UploadStringCompleted* event. This specifies *WinesUpdated* as the callback function to the asynchronous service call. After registering on the *UploadStringCompleted* event, a URL-encoded key-value-pair string containing the wine's *Name*, *Category*, *Year*, and *Price* properties is built and stored in *wineInfo*. At this point, the save logic is handled differently for creating a new wine or updating an existing wine.

If the *WineId* property is zero, this is a new wine. In this case, the *UploadStringAsync* method is called. This method takes a URL as a parameter, which is the URL to the Wine Web API services. It also accepts an HTTP method parameter, which is set to POST. Thus, the code issues an asynchronous POST request over HTTP, which inserts the new wine. If *WineId* is not zero, this is an existing wine. In this case, *UploadStringAsync* is still called, but with a few differences. First, the URL for the Web API call is appended with */id* (where *id* is the value of *WineId*). Second, the *WineId* property is prepended in the URL-encoded key-value-pair string because it is part of an existing wine entity. And third, the HTTP method parameter is set to PUT. Thus, the code issues an asynchronous PUT request over HTTP, which updates the existing wine.

When the user clicks the Delete button, the *DeleteButton_Click* event handler fires, and the user is first prompted to confirm before deleting the wine. Then the code creates a new *WebClient* object, sets the HTTP *ContentType* header to *application/x-www-form-urlencoded*, registers a handler for the *UploadStringCompleted* event, and appends */id* to the URL for the Web API call—just the same as when updating an existing wine. This time, however, only the wine ID is passed in the HTTP header; there is no need to pass all the properties of an entity that is about to be deleted. The code then issues the asynchronous DELETE request over HTTP, which deletes the existing wine.

The *WinesUpdated* method is the callback function for all three asynchronous service calls: POST, PUT, and DELETE. As with *WinesLoaded*, this method first examines the *Error* property of the *UploadStringCompletedEventArgs* parameter passed into the callback to ensure that the service call succeeded without an error. If an error occurred, a message is displayed. Otherwise, *LoadWines* is called. This queries the service again to retrieve an updated wine list, and then toggles the display panels to view the list.

Testing the Windows Phone application

You can test the app now, using the phone emulator provided by the SDK. The phone emulator can only run on a physical machine; it will not run inside a virtual machine. Furthermore, your physical machine's BIOS must support the necessary hardware virtualization required by the emulator, and that support must be enabled in the BIOS. If Visual Studio is unable to run the emulator for any reason, it displays the message "Deployment failed because no Windows Phone 8 phone was detected. Make sure a phone is connected and powered on" when you attempt to run the Windows Phone project.

To test the Windows Phone application, follow these steps:

1. Right-click the *WineCloudPhone* project in Solution Explorer, and choose Set As Startup Project.
2. Press F5 to build and run the app in the phone emulator (which can take a long time to load). The wine list should appear as shown in Figure 10-42.

> **Tip** When you want to stop the app during a debugging session, don't close the emulator. Instead, just stop your code execution inside Visual Studio and keep the emulator running so that it can host your app the next time you press F5.

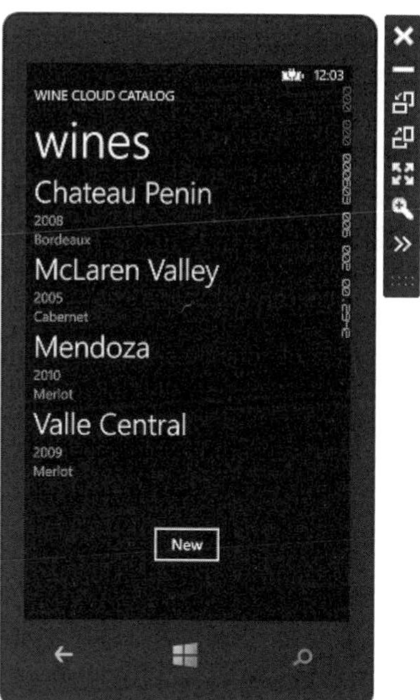

FIGURE 10-42 The wine list displayed in the Windows Phone emulator

3. Click on the third wine. The details page for Mendoza is displayed for editing.

4. Try editing the price. Click on the Price text box and change the value, as shown in Figure 10-43. (You need to click on the emulator's on-screen keyboard; the emulator will not respond to your machine's physical keyboard.)

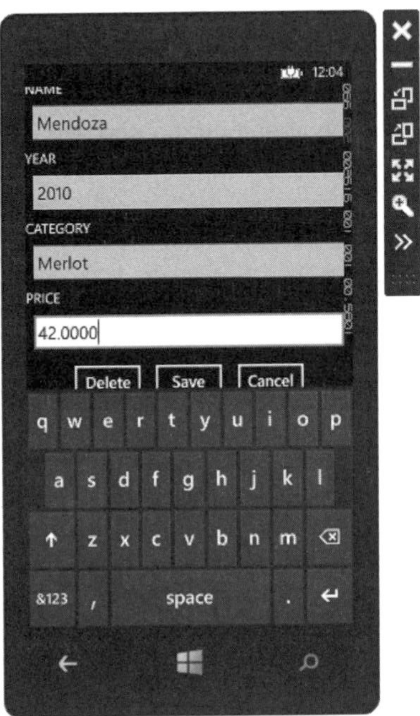

FIGURE 10-43 Editing a wine's price in the Windows Phone emulator

Spend some time now to experiment a bit more with the app. Go ahead and create some new wines, update a few of them, and delete one or two. Then congratulate yourself—you've built a complete layered cloud solution on Microsoft Azure SQL Database, end-to-end, cloud-to-phone!

Summary

This chapter covered a lot of ground. There are myriad ways to create cloud solutions, and many different tools and technologies are available for you to create them with. To be successful with any of them, you need to design a properly layered stack of components to deliver a reliable, maintainable, and scalable solution. In this chapter, you learned how to do just that using Microsoft Azure SQL Database and readily available Microsoft .NET technologies.

After importing a SQL Database into a Visual Studio SQL Server Database project, you extended the design by adding new columns, tables, and stored procedures. Then you published the new design back to SQL Database and shifted focus to the data access layer. You created an Entity Data Model (EDM) to use Entity Framework as the data access layer, and then built an ASP.NET MVC website over the EDM to support order entry. After testing the website locally, you deployed it to the cloud to run on Microsoft Azure. Then you added Web API REST services to the website, which supports CRUD operations against the *Wine* table. Finally, you built a Windows Phone 8 wine catalog app that consumes the Web API services, allowing users to view, create, update, and delete wines in the database.

When creating your own solutions, you have many more alternatives than those presented in this chapter. For example, you don't need to use Entity Framework; you can instead create your own data access layer using conventional ADO.NET. Instead of creating the website using ASP.NET MVC, you can choose to create it using ASP.NET web forms. And rather than using Web API, you can build the service layer using raw WCF, WCF Data Services, or WCF RIA Services. Regardless of which particular technologies you choose, however, applying the principles presented in this chapter will guide you in implementing a proper layered design across the various tiers of your cloud solution.

Index

A

abstraction, 3–4, 217, 313
access control, 12, 35–38, 106–111, 170
  least privilege principle, 108–109, 111
  with stored procedures, 307–312
action methods, 321, 326–327, 338
Active Directory, adding users, 170
ADO.NET, 217
  connection pooling, 234
  data access layer, building, 312–313
  database connections, managing, 234
  Dataset objects and data adapters, 313
  encapsulating, 239
  raw objects, 312–313
  sharding with, 254–259
  SqlConnection class *OpenWithRetry* extension method, 59
  transient fault handling, 237–238
  Web API controllers, building, 230–233
AdventureWorks database, installing, 151–154
agent keys, 204
Agent service, 59
agents, 174
aging policies, 56
allowed IP addresses, 12
  See also firewall rules; SQL Database Firewall
ALTER DATABASE statement, 44
applications
  auditing, 99
  building, 289–354
  in the cloud, 2
  connection faults, recovering from, 235–243
  data synchronization, 179
  geographic locations, 179, 243
  hackers, protecting from, 99
  health, monitoring, 261
  load balancing, 179–180
  physical distance from databases, 55, 179, 243
  regulatory requirements, complying with, 99
  repository pattern, 314
  scaling, designing for, 218
  tables, indirect access to, 307–312
  volume purchase plan, 55
ASP.NET MVC websites, 321–335
ASP.NET Web APIs *See* Web API controllers; Web API services; Web APIs
attack surface, reducing, 108. *See also* security
auditing, 59, 99
authentication
  with management certificates, 281, 283
  selecting type, 41
  SQL Database support for, 58
  of users, 105–111
  Windows Integrated authentication, 170
authorization of users, 105–111, 170
automated BACPAC export schedule, 120–121
automated data synchronization schedules, 200–202
Automated Export feature, 120–121
Azure *See* Microsoft Azure

B

backup storage, 51–53
backup-and-restore process, 59, 112–121
backups, 112–121
  automated, 59
  geo-replicated storage for, 55
  removal strategy, 55
  transactional consistency, 59
BACPAC files, 30
  for backups and restores, 112, 115–121
  creating, 34–35, 59
  data migration with, 70–80
  database objects for export, 75
  exporting, 34–35, 74–77, 115–117, 120–121

BACPAC files (*continued*)
importing to SQL Database instance, 77–80
transactional consistency of, 120–121
bandwidth-based fees, 9, 79
basic authentication, 170
bcp (SQL Server Bulk Copy), 80–86, 153
bi-directional binding, 350
bi-directional synchronization, 195–196
blob containers, 73–74
blob storage, 54, 60, 115, 244–245
block blobs, 115
Browser role, 170
Browser Service, 59
browsers
content negotiation, 230
MVC websites, running from, 335
reports, running from, 149–150, 168–169
Web APIs, testing, 228–230
Business Intelligence Developer Studio (BIDS), 151
Business Intelligence project templates, installing, 151, 154–156
Business (Standard) edition of SQL Database, 55, 58

C

Cache service, 244–245
caching, client-side, 244
catalog views, 280
Change Data Capture (CDC), 59
change scripts, 301, 303
check constraints, 310
circular references, 338–339
class library projects, 314–315, 323, 324
client agent service, 204
client bandwidth pricing, 51
client connections, allowing through firewall, 101–105
client protocols, SQL Database support for, 58
clients, pushing data changes to, 174
client-side storage and caching, 244
cloud computing, 1–4, 218
cloud databases. *See also* databases; SQL Database
location of, 215
synchronizing, 182–202
cloud reporting, 3, 123–171
Cloud Service Fundamentals in Windows Azure, 259
cloud solutions, 289–354
ASP.NET Web API services, creating, 336–341
data access layer, creating, 312–321
delivery of, 3
deploying to SQL Database, 301–304, 312
importing into SQL Database, 297–300
iterative development cycle, 305
layered architecture, 289–292
sample database, building, 292–293
sample solution stack, 289–291
scaling, 2–3
SQL Server Database project, creating, 295–296
stored procedures, creating, 307–312
table columns, adding, 300–301
tables, creating, 305–307
target platform, setting, 296–297
website, creating, 321–335
Windows Phone application, creating, 341–354
cloud storage
browsing, 78
Microsoft Azure Storage Account for, 35
cloud-based Microsoft Azure SQL Database. *See* SQL Database
CLR (Common Language Runtime), 60
clustered indexes, 61
code in the cloud, 2
codebases, 57, 63–64
collations, 31–34
columns, table
adding, 300–301
check constraints on, 310
null values, 300–301
command prompt, opening, 46, 83
Common Language Runtime (CLR), 60
compatibility issues, 88–94
compliance, 98–99
compression, 60
compute resources, 218, 234
load distribution across, 251–259
partitioning, 250–259
reserving, 245
conflict resolution in data synchronization procedures, 196–200, 214–215
Connect To Server dialog, 41–42
advanced version, 110–111
Connect to Server errors, 109–110
connected development, 294
connection pooling, 234
connection strings
@server requirement, 58
entity, locating, 324
passwords in, 316
quick-start link to, 38–39
viewing, 38–39
connections
dropped, 59
faults, recovering from, 234–236
limitations on, 58–59, 234
managing, 234–243

connections (*continued*)
monitoring with DMVs and DMFs, 277–280
multiple pending, 58
opening late, closing early, 234
pooling, 234
prevention of, 102 *See also* firewall rules
specifying database, 110–111
throttling, 235
Transient Fault Handling Application Block, 235–243
transient faults, 234–243 viewing, 278, 280
console applications, creating, 283–287
constraints, disabling during import operations, 85
Content Manager role, 170
content negotiation, 230
controllers, MVC, 321
action methods, 326–327
extending, 327
Home controller, 321, 325–326
scaffolding, 325–326
URLs, mapping to, 321
controllers, Web API, 223–228, 230–233, 336–339
copy database operation, 112–115
COUNT function, 141
CREATE DATABASE statement, 43, 57
CREATE DATABASE...AS COPY OF statement, 113–114
credentials, user, 99
CRUD actions, 336–337
custom authentication, 170
custom code in reports, 124
Custom Create database creation option, 31, 33–34
customers of cloud vendors, security responsibilities, 98–99
CustomerShard class, 254, 256
cyber attacks, preventing, 98

D

DACPAC (Data-tier Application Component Package) files, 30, 70, 80
DAL. *See* data access layer (DAL)
data
check constraints, 310
in cloud, 2
formatting in reports, 162–163
geo-replication, 71
incremental changes and updates, 63
referential integrity, 19
regulatory compliance, 99
scripting, 69
service layer over, 27
summarizing at database and report levels, 157
validation rules, 307–312
data access, 106–111, 170
encapsulating in stored procedures, 243–244, 307–312
with Entity Framework, 313
over HTTP, 336
performance, 217
securing, 98
data access layer (DAL)
ADO.NET, building with, 312–313
class library projects, creating, 314–315
creating, 290–291, 312–321
referencing, 323–324
repository pattern, 314
data aggregation with SQL Data Sync, 177
data compression, 60
data entry, 21–24
data importing *See* importing
data migration, 63–86, 88–94
data partitioning, 13, 58, 61, 250–259, 276
data redundancy, 60–61
data sources, report, 125, 135, 138
creating, 139–140, 158–159
data stores, maintaining, 63–64
data synchronization *See* SQL Data Sync; sync groups; synchronizing data
data validation, 307–312
database access, 12, 35–38, 106–111, 170, 307–312
database administration, 30
See also SQL Database management portal
database collations, 31–34
database connections *See* connections
Database Copy feature, 59, 112–113
database dynamic management views (DMVs), 275–278
database objects
developing, deploying, and managing, 70
mapping to .NET objects, 217
naming conventions, 60
scripting, 68
T-SQL scripts, generating for, 91–92, 94
database queries *See* queries
database-level permissions, 108–109
databases. *See also* on-premises SQL Server databases; SQL Database
changes, discovering and replicating, 173
changing between, 61
configuring, 44
connection strings *See* connection strings
copying, 112–113
creating, 13–15, 184
creating in Microsoft Azure portal, 31–35
creating in PowerShell, 48–49
creating in SSMS, 43

databases (*continued*)
- creating with Service Management API, 283–287
- current number, 265
- deleting, 40, 44, 50, 77
- edition, 33–34, 44, 55–56
- exporting, 115–117
- firewall rules *See* firewall rules
- fragmentation information, 276
- free space, 56, 270
- importing, 31, 34–35, 297–300
- incremental changes and updates, 63, 191
- index statistics, 276
- I/O, locking, latching, and access method activity, 276
- load distribution across, 251–259
- local, 64–66 *See also* on-premises SQL Server databases
- migrating to SQL Database, 63–94
- mirroring, 60–61
- monitoring, 263–280
- new query window, 43, 65, 106–107, 109
- offline management, 300
- operational metrics, 265–269
- page and row-count information, 276
- partitioning, 13, 250–259
- physical distance from applications, 243
- populating, 21–24
- querying, 24–26 *See also* queries
- reporting *See* reporting; reports
- saving data to, 22
- scripting, 68 *See also* Transact-SQL (T-SQL)
- service layer over, 307
- sharding, 13, 252–254
- size, 31, 33, 44, 55–58, 270, 276–278
- synchronizing, 173–174 *See also* SQL Data Sync; synchronizing data
- transactional consistency, 112
- updating, 194–195
- upgrading to SQL Database Premium, 249–250
- usage metrics, 265–269
- *varbinary(max)* or *image* file storage, 54
- waits statistics, 276

Dataset objects and data adapters, 313
datasets, data synchronization, 188–191, 215
datasets, report, 135, 138, 140–143
Data-tier Application Component Package (DACPAC) files, 30, 70, 80
Data-Tier Applications (DACs), 70, 74–77, 80
data-transfer pricing, 51
dbmanager security role, 107
deleting
- data in Windows Phone 8 apps, 352
- databases, 40, 44, 50, 77, 113
- firewall rules, 104
- tables, 81

Developer Command Prompt, 281
disaster recovery, 60–61, 97, 112–121
DMFs *See* dynamic management functions (DMFs)
DMVs *See* dynamic management views (DMVs)
DROP DATABASE statement, 44, 113
DROP TABLE statement, 81
dropped connections, 59
dynamic management functions (DMFs), 275–280
dynamic management views (DMVs), 275–280

E

EDM *See* Entity Data Model (EDM)
EDMX files, 223, 313
EF *See* Entity Framework (EF)
endpoints, VM, 131–132
entities, 318–320, 325
entity connection string, 324
Entity Data Model (EDM), 313–314
- class library projects, creating, 314–315
- conceptual schema, 313
- creating, 315–321
- data connection, 315
- data source, 316
- .edmx files, 313
- entity classes, 318
- mapping, 313, 320
- metadata, 313
- model contents, 315
- as model in MVC applications, 323–324
- navigation properties of entities, 318–319
- result bindings, 319
- storage schema, 313
- stored procedures, 317, 319–320
- tables, selecting, 317
- version setting, 317

Entity Data Model (EDM) designer, 223
Entity Framework (EF), 217
- Code First feature, 223–228, 313
- Connection Resiliency feature, 59
- conventions, 224
- data access layer, building, 312–321
- data context, 226–227
- database first approach, 313
- database initialization strategy, 224, 228
- database resource consumption, 234
- Entity Data Model, 313–314
- performance overhead, 217
- pluralization naming strategy, 224–225, 227
- POCO (Plain Old CLR Object) classes, 223

Entity Framework (*continued*)
RESTful Web APIs, building, 218–228
schemas, mapping between, 314
sharding, 259
Transient Fault Handling Application Block and, 239–243
Visual Studio scaffolding feature and, 321
Web API controllers, adding, 226–227
Web APIs, creating, 225–228
entity models, 223–224, 230
error code 40544, 276
errors, 109–110, 235, 276, 329–330
event tables, 280
exception handling, 329–331
ExecuteAction method, 239–243
execution dynamic management views (DMVs), 278–280
execution performance, monitoring, 277–280
execution speed, optimizing, 217
Export Database feature, 115–117
Export Data-Tier Application wizard, 74–77
exporting, 35, 83–84
Automated Export feature, 120–121
BACPAC files, 115–117
export files, 120–121
extended events, 60
extended stored procedures, 60
Extensible Application Markup Language (XAML) binding features, 345

F

F5 key, 43
fan-out queries, 256, 259
file streaming, 60
firewall rules, 9, 12, 35–38, 48, 102–105
See also SQL Database Firewall
for local network access, 35–36
quick-start link, 36
for remote IP address access, 35–36
report server access, 130–132
foreign-key table relationships, 65, 306, 318–319
forms-based authentication, 170
FROM clause, 140–141
Full-Text Searching (FTS), 60
fully qualified names, 134
functional partitions, 250–251

G

Generate And Publish Scripts wizard, 68–69
geographic region, 8–9
of applications, 179, 243
of cloud databases, 215
of Microsoft Azure Storage account, 71
pricing and, 51
synchronization and, 176–179
geo-replication, 52–53, 55, 71
GET requests, 326
GROUP BY clause, 140–141
GUI management tools, 261. *See also* Microsoft Azure management portal; SQL Database management portal; SQL Server Data Tools (SSDT); SQL Server Management Studio (SSMS)

H

hackers, protecting against, 99
hardware, hypervisor virtualization technology on, 2–3
high availability, 112
horizontal partitioning, 251–259
HTTP data access over, 336
HTTP requests and responses, 223, 230, 283–287, 326, 351–352
hub databases, 174, 186
Huey, George, 86
hypervisor virtualization technology, 2–3

I

IaaS (Infrastructure as a Service), 3–4
image file storage, 54
Import Database feature, 31, 77–80, 117–119
importing
BACPAC files, 117–119
databases, 34–35, 77–80
nonclustered indexes, triggers, constraints, 85
into SQL Database instance, 84–86
with SQL Server Integration Services, 63
incremental changes and updates, 63
index partitioning, 61
index statistics, 276
Infrastructure as a Service (IaaS), 3–4
instance names of local SQL Server database, 64
instance objects, 70
Internet Explorer, 150
See also browsers
Internet hosting, cloud computing service level, 1
IP addresses
allowed, 12, 35
current client IP address, 104
firewall rules for, 101–104
learning remote addresses, 37

J

JavaScript Object Notation (JSON), 336, 338–339
Json.NET, 343–344

L

language settings, customizing, 31
latency, 9, 215, 243–244
least privilege principle, 108–109, 111
legacy systems, data migration from, 63–94
local machines, 2, 12
  See also servers
local networks, enabling database access, 35–36
local SQL Server databases, 64–68, 83–84
local sync agent, 204–211
locks, monitoring, 280
logical administration, 57
login user names @*server* requirement, 58
loginmanager security role, 107
lookup data, client-side storage of, 244
Lucene text search engine library, 60

M

maintenance, 4, 63–64
malicious attack prevention, 98
management, 99, 261, 275–287
  GUI tools for, 261 *See also* Microsoft Azure management portal; SQL Database management portal; SQL Server Data Tools (SSDT); SQL Server Management Studio (SSMS)
management certificates, 281–283
manual syncs, 191–196
mapping
  objects, 217
  between schemas, 314
  stored procedures to entities, 319–320
  URLs to controllers and actions, 321
master database, 102, 106–110, 134–135, 280
matrixes, report, 157, 160–161
metadata, 244, 278
Microsoft account, 5–7, 46–47
Microsoft Azure, 1–4
  ASP.NET Web Application projects, deploying to, 331–335
  authentication for, 281, 283
  compute resources, scaling up, 218
  free trial subscription, 7–8
  management certificates, 281–283
  preview services, 120–121, 174, 246
  pricing, 7, 9, 50–54, 79
  Queue storage, 244–245
  scaling, 3 *See also* scalability
  security, 99
  SQL Reporting, 123–124
  staying current with, 57–58
  storage services for nonrelational data, 244–245
  subscribing to, 7–8
  Table storage, 244–245
  volume purchase plan, 55
Microsoft Azure Blob Storage, 35, 54, 60, 115, 244–245
Microsoft Azure Cache, 244–245
Microsoft Azure cloud, 2–4
  See also cloud computing; cloud solutions
Microsoft Azure Customer Advisory Team, 235, 259
Microsoft Azure datacenters, 2, 51, 55
Microsoft Azure Management Application Programming Interface (API), 261
Microsoft Azure management portal, 9, 31–40
  BROWSE CLOUD STORAGE dialog box, 78
  CONFIGURE link, 37
  connection strings, obtaining, 38–39
  copy database operation, monitoring, 114–115
  CREATE A SQL DATABASE SERVER link, 9–10
  CREATE SERVER dialog, 10–11
  Custom Create database option, 33–34
  database usage metrics, 265–266
  databases, creating, 31–35
  databases, deleting, 40, 77
  databases, importing, 77–80
  Export Database Settings dialog, 115–117
  firewall rules, managing, 35–38, 102
  IMPORT DATABASE dialog, 77–79
  local agent service, configuring, 207–208
  logging in, 9
  main portal page, 9
  MANAGE URL link, 15–16
  management certificates, 281–283
  Microsoft Azure Storage account, creating, 71–74
  monitoring with, 264–269
  publish profile for websites, 333–334
  Quick Create database option, 31–33
  quick-start links for databases, 36
  server usage overview, 264–265
  servers, creating, 9–11
  SQL Data Sync configuration, 174
  SQL Database management portal, accessing, 15, 192–193
  SQL Database Monitor page, 267–269
  SQL Database Premium, signing up for, 246–247
  SQL Database Premium quota, requesting, 248
  SQL Database Premium quota request status, 248–249

Microsoft Azure management portal (*continued*)
SQL Database servers, list of, 102–103
SSRS, configuring in VM, 128–130
storage access keys, generating, 71
SYNC link, 188
VM endpoints, creating, 131–132
VMs, creating, 126–128
websites, creating, 331–334
Microsoft Azure PowerShell cmdlets, installing, 44–45
Microsoft Azure Service Dashboard, 269–270
Microsoft Azure Service Management API, 71, 281–288
Microsoft Azure services *See* services
Microsoft Azure SQL Data Sync, 173–216
Microsoft Azure SQL Database *See* SQL Database
Microsoft Azure Storage, 35, 71–80
browsing, 78, 117–118
geo-replication, 52
pricing, 51–52
Microsoft Azure Traffic Manager, 179–180
Microsoft Azure Trust Center, 99
Microsoft Silverlight, 15–16, 82, 183, 341, 343, 351
Microsoft Visual Studio *See* Visual Studio
Microsoft.AzureCat.Patterns.Data.SqlAzureDalSharded library, 259
migrating data, 63–94
migration wizard, 86–94
mirroring, 60–61
models, entity, 223–224, 230
Model-View-Controller (MVC) applications, 222–223, 323–331
Model-View-Controller (MVC) framework, 291–292
Model-View-Controller (MVC) websites, 321–335
Model-View-ViewModel (MVVM) pattern, 344
monitoring, 261, 263–280
database operations, 265–266
database size, 276–278
database usage, 265
dynamic management views and functions, 275–280
metrics, displaying, 267–269
with Microsoft Azure management portal, 264–269
Microsoft Azure Service Dashboard, 269–270
query performance, 271–275
sample database, creating, 261–263
server usage, 264–265
services health, 269–270
with SQL Database management portal, 270–275
MSDN subscribers, Azure pricing for, 7
multipart names for database objects, 60
Multiple Active Result Sets (MARS), 58
multitenant services, 98
MVC. *See* Model-View-Controller (MVC) applications; Model-View-Controller (MVC) websites

N

naming conventions for database objects, 60
navigation properties of entities, 318–319
.NET Framework 3.5, 153
network bandwidth fees, 9, 51–53, 79
network latency, reducing, 243–244
network round trips, minimizing, 243–244
network traffic, reducing, 244
new query window, 43, 65, 106–107, 109
Newtonsoft.Json assembly, 336, 343–344
importing namespace for, 350–351
nonclustered indexes, 85
nondeterministic behavior, 310
nonrelational data, 244–245
NuGet Package Manager, 235–236
Json.NET, downloading and adding, 344
numeric data, formatting in reports, 162–163

O

Object Explorer, 40, 42
object relational mapping (ORM), 217, 312
See also Entity Framework (EF)
objects
developing, deploying, and managing, 70
mapping to .NET objects, 217
naming conventions, 60
packaging as DACPAC files, 70
scripting, 68
T-SQL scripts, generating for, 91–92, 94
offline projects, 294
online transactional processing (OLTP), 178–179
on-premises SQL Server databases, 64–66. *See also* databases
abstraction levels, 3
BACPAC files, creating, 34–35
instances, 1
latency, 243
migrating to SQL Database, 63–94
mirroring, 60–61
nonrelational and binary data in, 244
size, calculating, 51
sync agent, registering with, 209–211
sync group, adding to, 211–214
synchronizing, 174–176, 202–215 *See also* synchronizing data
on-premises SQL Server servers, 2
See also servers
ORM (object relational mapping), 217, 312

P

PaaS (Platform as a Service), 4, 218
partitioning data, 58, 61, 250–259
  page and row-count information, 276
  sharding, 13, 251–259
password policy, 107
passwords in connection strings, 316
performance
  in the cloud, 218
  of cloud reporting, 124
  of data access, 217
  database connections overhead, 234
  latency, reducing, 243–244
  optimizing and tuning, 217, 244–245
  of queries, 245, 271–275
permissions, 108–111, 170
physical administration, 57
physical data centers, 98, 99
physical storage with PaaS, 4
Plain Old CLR Object (POCO) classes, 223–224, 230
Platform as a Service (PaaS), 4, 218
port 80, 130–132
port 1433, 58
port allocation, 58
POST requests, 326, 352
PowerShell, 44–50
  administrator credentials, 48
  -*Collation* switch, 49
  configuring for Microsoft account, 46–47
  context associated with server and credentials, 48
  database collation, changing, 49
  database edition, changing, 49
  database size, changing, 49
  databases, creating, 48–49
  databases, deleting, 50
  databases, viewing, 49
  -*Edition* switch, 49
  firewall rules, creating, 48
  -*Force* switch, 50
  management, automating, 281
  master databases, 49
  -*MaxSizeGb* switch, 49
  server access, 47–48
  servers, creating, 47–48
PowerShell Integrated Scripting Environment (ISE), 46
PowerShell Microsoft Azure cmdlets, 44–45, 48, 49
Premium edition of SQL Database, 58, 245–250
preview release software, 120–121, 174, 246
pricing for Microsoft Azure
  bandwidth, 9, 51–53, 79
  Blob Storage, 54
  data transfer, 51
  file storage, 54
  geographic location and bandwidth pricing, 51
  online pricing calculator, 50
  pricing structures, 7
  storage, 50–51
  storage space, 51–52
  support plans, 53–54
primary keys, 67
primary transactional database, replicating, 178–179
privacy, 98–99
public cloud platforms *See* Microsoft Azure
public cloud vendors
  auditing services, 99
  compliance certifications, 99
  hackers, protecting against, 99
  malicious attack prevention, 98
  multitenancy management, 98
  security responsibilities, 98–99
publish process, 301–303, 312
.*publishsettings* file, 47
PUT requests, 352

Q

queries, 24–26
  editing, 273
  encapsulating, 27, 243–244
  error code 40544, 276
  execution plans, 273–275
  fan-out, 256, 259
  memory grants, 278
  optimizing, 245
  performance, 271–275
  query plan details, 272–273
  query plans, cached, 278
  query plans, showing, 278
  running, 193–194
  in stored procedures, 141, 243–244
query code, 140–141, 157
query filters, 25–26
Queue storage, 244–245
Quick Create database creation option, 31–33
quick-start links, 36, 38–39

R

RDL authoring tools, 125
.rdl files, 169
.rdp files, 128
read-only permissions, 108–111

records, aging policies, 56
Red-Gate Data Compare, 63
Red-Gate SQL Compare, 63
redundancy, data, 60–61
reference databases, 174, 184, 186–187
referential integrity of data, 19
regulatory requirements, complying with, 99
relational data, storage in SQL Database, 244–245
relational databases, 250
  See also databases; SQL Database
reliability, 217, 234–244
Remote Desktop sessions, 128
remote IP addresses, enabling database access, 37–38
replication, 61
Report Builder, 123, 125
  browser, running report from, 149–150, 168–169
  data sources for reports, 138–140
  datasets for reports, 138, 140–143
  date and time of report execution, 138
  Getting Started dialog, 137
  images, adding to reports, 139
  installing, 135–137
  launching, 137
  layout of report, 143–145
  matrix control, 138–139
  previewing reports, 135, 145–147
  Report Data pane, 138–139
  report parameters, defining, 139
  reports, creating, 137–150
  reports, saving and running locally, 145–147
  Row Groups and Column Groups panes, 139
  SSRS, deploying reports to, 147–149
  table control, 138–139
  user interface, 138
Report Definition Language (RDL), 123
Report Designer, formatting data, 162–163
Report Manager, 130, 149, 170
report server, 124, 130–132
Report Server Database Configuration Wizard, 129–130
Report Server Project Wizard, 158–162
Report Server projects, 150–169
reporting, 123–171
  Report Builder, 135–150
  requests, performance impact of, 179
  sample database, creating, 132–135
  security of reports, 170
  service URL, 149
  virtual directory, creating, 129
  Visual Studio Report Server projects, 150–169
  VM, creating, 125–132
  VM, shutting down, 171
Reporting Services *See* SQL Server Reporting Services (SSRS)
reports
  bar charts, 164–166
  creating with Report Builder, 137–150
  creating with Visual Studio, 156–162
  data source, 125, 135, 138–140, 158–159
  dataset, 125, 135, 138, 140–143
  date and time of execution, 138
  deploying to SSRS, 135, 147–149, 166–168
  drill-down capabilities, 163
  executing, 146
  formatting, 162–163
  layout, 125, 135, 143–145
  matrixes in, 157, 160
  previewing, 145–147, 163
  queries, defining, 159–160
  RDL format, 125
  running from browser, 149–150, 168–169
  running locally, 145–146
  saving, 145
  security, 170
  summarizing data in, 157
  title, 143
  user role assignment, 170
repository pattern, 314
requests. *See* HTTP requests and responses
  monitoring with DMVs and DMFs, 277–280
Resource Governor, 61
REST services, 336
RESTful Web APIs, 218–228
restore database operations, 117–119
RetryPolicy class *ExecuteAction* method, 239–243
round trips, minimizing, 243–244
routing, 179
  in MVC applications, 321

S

SaaS (Software as a Service), 4, 289
scalability, 2–4, 218, 245–250
  functional partitions, 250–251
  OLTP activity, separating from reporting activity, 184
  partitioning for, 58
  sharding, 251–259
  synchronizing between multiple locations, 178–179
SCC (source code control), 294–295
schemas, 156, 313
  changing before migration, 80
  compare operations, 301–303
  deploying to SQL Database, 91, 94
  mapping, 313–314

schemas (*continued*)
- migrating, 77–83
- referencing objects in, 60
- scripting, 69
- storage, 313

searching, 60
security, 97–121, 170, 216
- firewall, 101–105 *See also* SQL Database Firewall
- users, authenticating and authorizing, 99, 105–111

server certificates, 61
server logins, 105–107
server-level permissions, 107–108
server-level principals, 106–107
server-level security roles, 107–108
servers, 2, 8–12, 47–49, 183
- accessibility to cloud services, 10
- authentication method, 41
- firewall settings, 12, 35–38, 102, 103 *See also* firewall rules; SQL Database Firewall
- fully qualified names, 41
- geographic region, 8–9
- health, monitoring, 263–280
- instance names, 64
- physical access, securing, 98
- PowerShell access, 47–48
- usage, viewing, 264–265

Service Broker, 61
service levels, 3
Service Management API, 281–288
service outages, 269
services, 2–4
- Agent service, 59
- Allowed Services list, 105
- asynchronous service calls, 351
- auditing, 99
- Browser Service, 59
- Cache service, 244–245
- client agent service, 204
- data center regions, 243
- geographic region, 8–9
- health, monitoring, 261, 269–270
- local agent service, 207–208
- Microsoft Azure services, 105, 120–121, 174, 244–246
- multitenant, 98
- outages, 269
- reporting *See* SQL Server Reporting Services (SSRS)
- REST services, 336
- Service Broker, 61
- Service Management API, 281–288
- SQL Server Integration Services, 63
- Web API services, 336–341

sessions, monitoring with DMVs and DMFs, 277–280
Shard class, 254–256
sharding, 13, 251–259
ShardRoot class, 254
Software as a Service (SaaS), 4, 289
source code control (SCC), 294–295
spoke databases, 174
SQL Data Sync, 61, 173–216
- automated sync schedules, 200–202
- best practices, 215–216
- clients, 174
- conflict resolution, 196–200
- direction settings, 187
- exporting data from SQL Server to SQL Database, 175
- importing data from SQL Database to SQL Server, 175–176
- incremental change tracking, 191
- manual syncs, 191–196
- multiple cloud databases, synchronizing, 178–180
- multiple locations, sharing data between, 176–177
- one-way and two-way synchronization, 174
- performance, 215
- reference databases, 174
- sample database, creating, 180–182
- security measures, 216
- SQL Server on-premises database, creating, 202–203
- sync agents, 204–215
- sync groups, 174, 182–188
- sync rules, 188–191
- Traffic Manager and, 179–180

SQL Database, 1
- applications, co-locating with, 55
- Automated Export feature, 120–121
- backing up, 112–121
- Business edition, 55, 58
- communication port, 58
- comparison to SQL Server, 57–62
- connecting from SSMS, 41–42
- connection limitations, 58–59
- constraints of, 57
- cost-related items, 50–56
- database connections, managing, 234–243
- editions, switching between, 13
- exporting data *See* exporting
- firewall rules *See* firewall rules
- Generally Available features, 120
- high-availability features, 112
- importing, 297–300 *See also* importing
- Microsoft account, 5–7
- Microsoft Azure subscription, 7–8
- migrating databases to, 63–94

SQL Database (*continued*)
- monitoring health and usage, 263–280
- monthly charges, 56
- networking requirements, 101
- online pricing calculator, 50
- as PaaS solution, 4
- performance, 244–245 *See also* performance
- port number, 42
- Premium edition, 55, 58, 249–250
- Preview features, 120–121
- pricing, 50–56, 215
- SaaS solutions, 4
- scaling up, 245–250
- scripts compatible with, 69
- securing, 100–111 *See also* security
- signing up for, 5–8
- size limitations, 57–58
- sizes, switching between, 13
- SQL Service Database projects, deploying to, 301–304, 312
- synchronization *See* SQL Data Sync; synchronizing data
- unsupported features, 59–61
- upgrading to SQL Database Premium, 249–250
- Web edition, 31, 55, 58

SQL Database APIs, 281

SQL Database Firewall, 101–105, 184
- *See also* firewall rules

SQL Database instances, 13–30, 100–101
- BACPAC files, importing, 77–80
- importing data into, 84–86
- naming, 79
- server for hosting, 79

SQL Database management portal, 15–17
- accessing from Microsoft Azure portal, 192–193
- ad-hoc query window, 24–25
- connections and sessions, monitoring, 279–280
- data entry, 21–24
- database administration features, 30
- database size, checking, 277–278
- database summary page, 270–271
- dropping and re-creating databases, 82
- foreign-key designer, 20
- logging in, 16, 82
- monitoring performance and usage with, 270–275
- Query Performance page, 271–272
- Query Plan Details area, 272–273
- stored procedures, creating, 27–29
- Summary view, 17
- table designer, 18–20
- T-SQL scripts, executing, 70
- views, creating, 27

SQL Database Management REST API, 105

SQL Database Migration Wizard, 87–94
- *See also* migrating data

SQL Database servers
- *See also* servers
- AdventureWorks database, deploying to, 153
- Allow Windows Azure Services To Access The Server option, 11, 105
- connecting to using SQL Database Migration Wizard, 91–92
- databases, deleting from, 77
- *master* database, 106
- permissions, 107–109
- SQL Database Premium quota, adding, 248

SQL Database Service Dashboard, 270

SQL Data-Tier Applications, 70, 74–77, 80

SQL Server, 1
- *See also* on-premises SQL Server databases
- exporting data, 175
- Express edition, 58, 64
- Express With Advanced Services edition, 126
- hosting in Azure virtual machines, 3, 60–61
- importing data, 175–176
- vs. SQL Database, 3–4, 57–62
- synchronization service, 174 *See also* SQL Data Sync

SQL Server Authentication, 41, 105

SQL Server Bulk Copy (bcp), 80–86, 153

SQL Server Data Tools For Visual Studio 2012, 158

SQL Server Data Tools (SSDT), 41, 151
- BACPAC file import restrictions, 80
- bi-directional editing, 300–301
- Business Intelligence add-in for Visual Studio, 123
- Business Intelligence project templates, installing, 151, 154–156
- connected development, 294
- DACPAC files, defining and deploying, 30
- DACPAC files, importing into, 80
- database projects, testing, 295
- databases, creating, 180–182, 292–293
- disconnected development, 294
- table designer, 300–301
- T-SQL scripts, building and running, 64

SQL Server Database projects
- creating, 295–296
- database definition, 295
- *dbo* folder, 300
- deploying, 301–305, 312
- importing from SQL Database, 297–300
- offline changes, 305
- target platform, setting, 296–297

SQL Server instances, 65–66, 202–203

SQL Server Integration Services (SSIS), 63

SQL Server Management Objects (SMO), 40–41
SQL Server Management Studio (SSMS), 40–44
  advanced Connect to Server dialog, 110–111
  Connect To Server dialog, 41–42, 64–65
  Database Engine, connecting to, 110
  databases, configuring, 44
  databases, creating, 43
  databases, deleting, 44
  downloading, 40
  exporting Data-Tier Applications, 74–77
  fully qualified server names, 38, 41
  Generate And Publish Scripts wizard, 68
  graphical designers and dialogs support, 40–41
  launching, 41, 65, 134
  new query window, 43, 65
  Object Explorer, 40
  server logins, creating, 106–107
  sharded databases, creating, 252–254
  SQL Database, connecting to, 41–42
  T-SQL scripts, generating automatically, 68–70
  T-SQL scripts, running, 65
  T-SQL scripts, viewing, 69–70
SQL Server Object Explorer, 304
SQL Server Reporting Services (SSRS), 3, 123–124
  authentication of users and applications, 170
  Configuration Manager, 128–129
  configuring in virtual machine, 128–130
  database, creating, 129–130
  deploying reports to, 147–149
  formatting capabilities, 150
  free version, 126
  Report Manager, running reports from, 149–150
  Report Manager virtual directory, 129–130
  security in, 170
  Visual Studio as authoring tool, 151
  VM SSRS service URL, 166–167
  VM to host, creating, 125–132
.sqlexpress instance name, 64
SSDT *See* SQL Server Data Tools (SSDT)
SSMS *See* SQL Server Management Studio (SSMS)
SSRS *See* SQL Server Reporting Services (SSRS)
SSRS-in-a-VM solutions, 124
statements result set metadata, 278
storage, 50–51, 244
  See also Microsoft Azure Storage
stored procedures, 27–29, 60, 243–244, 307–312
  mapping to entities, 319–320
  performance statistics, 278
  queries in, 141
  system, 61
  testing, 29–30
strong password policy, 107
sync agents, 204–215
sync groups, 174, 182–189, 192
  conflict resolution behavior, 174, 196–200, 214–215
  on-premises SQL Server databases, adding, 211–214
  ready status, 187, 191
  scheduling syncs, 200–202, 215
  sync loops, 215
  sync rules, 188–191
sync loops, 215
sync rules, 188–191
synchronizing data, 215
  automated schedules, 200–202
  conflict resolution, 196–200
  costs, 179
  dataset, defining, 188–191
  direction settings, 187
  exporting data from SQL Server to SQL Database, 175
  importing data from SQL Database to SQL Server, 175–176
  manual, 191–196
  multiple locations, sharing data between, 176–177
  one-way and two-way, 174–177
  with SQL Data Sync, 61, 173 *See also* SQL Data Sync
  sync agents, creating, 204–215
  sync groups, creating, 182–188
  sync rules, creating, 188–191
  testing, 195–196
sys.database_connection_stats view, 80
sys.dm_database_copies view, 114
sys.event_log view, 280
system stored procedures, 61

T

table partitioning *See* partitioning data
Table storage, 244–245
tables, 17–19, 30, 305–307
  access control, 307–312
  aggregating rows, 141
  aliasing, 140–141
  change tracking, 191
  check constraints on, 310
  clustered indexes, 61
  columns, adding, 18, 300–301
  data, inserting, 21–24, 67–68
  deleting, 81–82
  foreign keys, 19, 22–23, 306
  ID primary key column, 18
  Is Identity? option, 18, 21
  joining, 24–26, 140–141
  migrating data into and out of, 83–86

tables (*continued*)
NULL values, 22
partitioning, 251–259
populating using T-SQL script, 67–68
primary keys, 21–22
relationships between, defining, 19–20
scripting, 68
service layer over, 307
updating, 304
validation rules, 307–312
table-valued parameters, batching, 244
tabular data stream (TDS), 57
Task Parallel Library, 256, 259
TCP port 80, 130–132
TCP port 1433, 58
tenants of cloud vendors, privacy from, 98
text search engine library, 60
throttling, 235
Traffic Manager, 179–180
transaction dynamic management views (DMVs), 280
transactional consistency, 59, 112, 120–121
Transact-SQL (T-SQL)
change scripts, 301, 303
FROM clause, 24, 26
CREATE DATABASE statement, 43
data migration with, 64–70
database engine type property, 69
for database queries, 24
databases, creating, 180–181, 219–221, 292
DROP TABLE statement, 81
editing, 300–301
EXEC statements, 29
executing, 43
foreign-key table relationships, 65
generating automatically, 68–70
IDENTITY_INSERT setting, 67
left outer joins, 24, 26, 28
local SQL Server database, creating, 65
populating local databases, 67–68
query filters, 25–26
Remove-AzureSqlDatabase cmdlet, 50
reporting, preparing databases for, 133
role assignment management, 107–108
server logins, creating, 107
sharded databases, 252
SQL Database support, 57
SQL Database use of, 60
types of data property, 69
user management, 107–108
WHERE clause, 25–26
transient connection faults, 234–235, 237–243
transient error conditions, 239–243
Transient Fault Handling Application Block, 59, 235–243
Transparent Data Encryption (TDE), 61
triggers, 85, 278, 310
tuning queries, 245
two-part names for database objects, 60
two-way synchronization, 176–177

U

unstructured data, 60, 244–245
UPDATE statement, 194–195
URLs
managing, 15–16
mapping to controllers and actions, 321
usage, monitoring, 263–280
USE statement, 61, 135
users
authenticating and authorizing, 105–111
Browser role, 170
Content Manager role, 170
creating, 108
routing to closest data center, 179–180
security credentials, 99

V

validation, data, 307–312
varbinary(max) file storage, 54
vendors, security responsibilities, 98–99
views, database, 27
views, dynamic management (DMVs), 275–280
views (in MVC applications), 321, 327–328
virtual machines (VMs), 60–61, 126–132
globally unique name, 147
with IaaS, 3
saving reports to, 148
shutting down, 128, 171
SSRS service URL, 166–167
virtual private networks (VPNs), 60–61
virtualization layer, 2–3
Visual Studio
Add Scaffold dialog, 325
ASP.NET Web Application project type, 222–223
bi-directional editing, 300–301
Business Intelligence Developer Studio version, 151
console applications, creating, 286–287
Data Tools Operations window, 303
database definitions, maintaining in, 295
databases, creating, 180–182
Dataset designer, 313
EDM designer, 223, 313, 318

Visual Studio (*continued*)
Entity Data Model, creating, 315–321
importing databases into database projects, 297–300
Mapping Details window, 320
NuGet package manager, 235–236
publishing databases, 301–303
references, adding, 323
scaffolding feature, 321, 325, 336–337
Solution Explorer, viewing, 222
solutions, building, 226, 228
solutions, creating, 221–222, 294–295
source code control, 294–295
SQL Server Database projects, creating, 295–296
SQL Server Object Explorer, 304
SSDT Business Intelligence add-in, 123
SSDT Business Intelligence project templates, installing, 151, 154–156
stored procedures, creating, 310–312
tables, creating, 30
target platform for database projects, setting, 296–297
Views folder, 327
Web API projects, creating, 222–223
Web API projects, deploying, 334–335, 340–341
Windows Phone apps, creating, 343
Windows Phone apps, testing, 353–354
Windows Phone SDK, 341–342
Visual Studio Report Server projects, 150–169
See also reporting; reports
AdventureWorks database, installing, 151–154
bar charts, adding to reports, 164–166
creating reports, 156–162
data sources, creating, 158–159
deploying, 150–169
designing, 150–169
formatting reports, 162–163
previewing reports, 163
project properties, 166–167
queries, defining, 159–160
Report Manager home page, 168
Report Server Project Wizard, 158–162
running reports from browser, 168–169
with SSDT Business Intelligence add-in, 125
SSDT Business Intelligence project templates, installing, 151, 154–156
VM SSRS service URL, 166–167

W

waits statistics, 276
Web API controllers, 223–230, 336–339
Web API services, 336–341
Web APIs
connection strings, setting, 227
content negotiation, 230
controllers, adding, 226–227, 230–233
creating, 222–223, 225–228, 321–323
data access layer, referencing, 323–324
deploying from Visual Studio, 334–335
deploying to Microsoft Azure, 331–335
entity connection string, 324
exception handling, 329–331
model class, adding, 225
referencing data access layer project, 323
referencing MVC and Web API assemblies, 322–323
RESTful Web APIs, building, 218–228
sample database, creating, 219–221
scaffolds, 226
services, defining in, 336
sharding with, 254–259
testing, 228–230, 233, 328–331
Transient Fault Handling Application Block, adding, 235–236
user interface, creating, 324–328
Web (Basic) edition of SQL Database, 31, 55, 58
web services, creating, 336–341
Web.config file, copying into entity connection string, 324
websites, 4, 321–335
whatismyipaddress.com, 37
Windows authentication, 58, 105
Windows Azure, 2
Windows Firewall With Advanced Security, 130
Windows Integrated authentication, 170
Windows Live ID, 5
Windows Phone 8 apps, 341–354
Windows Phone Databound App template, 344
Windows Phone SDK, installing, 341–342
Windows PowerShell *See* PowerShell

X

X.509 v3 certificates, creating, 281
XAML binding features, 345
XML, SQL Database support, 61
xml data type, 61

About the authors

Leonard G. Lobel is a Microsoft MVP in SQL Server and a Principal Consultant at Tallan, Inc., a Microsoft National Systems Integrator and Gold Competency Partner. With over 30 years of experience, Lenni is one of the industry's leading .NET and SQL Server experts, having consulted for Tallan's clients in a variety of domains, including publishing, financial services, retail, healthcare, and e-commerce. Lenni has served as chief architect and lead developer on large-scale projects, as well as advisor to many high-profile clients.

About Tallan

Tallan (*http://www.tallan.com*) is a national technology consulting firm that provides web development, business intelligence, customer relationship management, custom development, and integration services to customers in the financial services, healthcare, government, retail, education, and manufacturing industries.

Tallan is one of 40 Microsoft National Systems Integrators (NSI) in the United States, and a member of Microsoft's Business Intelligence Partner Advisory Council. For more than 25 years, Tallan's hands-on, collaborative approach has enabled its clients to obtain real cost and time savings, increase revenues, and generate competitive advantages.

Lenni is also chief technology officer (CTO) and cofounder of Sleek Technologies, Inc., a New York-based development shop with an early-adopter philosophy toward new technologies. He is a sought-after and highly rated speaker at industry conferences such as Visual Studio Live!, SQL PASS, SQL Bits, and local technology user group meetings. He is also lead author of *Programming Microsoft SQL Server 2012* (Microsoft Press, 2012). Lenni can be reached at *lenni.lobel@tallan.com* or *lenni.lobel@sleektech.com*.

Eric D. Boyd is the Founder and CEO of responsiveX (*www.responsiveX.com*), a Microsoft Azure MVP, and a regular speaker at national conferences, regional code camps and local user groups. He is so passionate about apps and cloud services that he founded responsiveX, a management and technology consultancy that helps customers create great web, mobile and client experiences, and these apps are often powered by cloud services. Eric launched his technology career almost two decades ago with a web-development startup and has served in multiple roles since, including developer, consultant, technology executive and business owner. You can find Eric blogging at *http://www.EricDBoyd.com* and on Twitter at *http://twitter.com/EricDBoyd*.

Free ebooks